The Craft of Oblivion

SUNY series in Chinese Philosophy and Culture

Roger T. Ames, editor

The Craft of Oblivion

Forgetting and Memory in Ancient China

Edited by
ALBERT GALVANY

Fish, c. 1400. China, Ming dynasty (1368–1644). Hanging scroll, ink and slight color on silk. The Cleveland Museum of Art, Gift of Herbert F. Leisy in memory of his wife, Helen Stamp Leisy. 1977.201

Published by State University of New York Press

© 2023 State University of New York

All rights reserved

Printed in the United States of America

No part of this book may be used or reproduced in any manner whatsoever without written permission. No part of this book may be stored in a retrieval system or transmitted in any form or by any means including electronic, electrostatic, magnetic tape, mechanical, photocopying, recording, or otherwise without the prior permission in writing of the publisher.

For information, contact State University of New York Press, Albany, NY
www.sunypress.edu

Library of Congress Cataloging-in-Publication Data

Name: Galvany, Albert, editor, author.
Title: The craft of oblivion : forgetting and memory in ancient China / edited by Albert Galvany.
Description: Albany : State University of New York Press, [2023] | Series: SUNY series in Chinese philosophy and culture | Includes bibliographical references and index.
Identifiers: LCCN 2022046515 | ISBN 9781438493756 (hardcover : alk. paper) | ISBN 9781438493770 (ebook) | ISBN 9781438493763 (pbk. : alk. paper)
Subjects: LCSH: China—Civilization—To 221 B.C.—Sources. | China—Civilization—221 B.C.-960 A.D.—Sources. | Chinese literature—To 221 B.C.—History and criticism. | Chinese literature—221 B.C.-960 A.D.—History and criticism. | Philosophy, Chinese—To 221 B.C. | Philosophy, Chinese—221 B.C.-960 A.D. | Memory.
Classification: LCC DS741.65 .C73 2023 | DDC 951/.01—dc23/eng/20221007
LC record available at https://lccn.loc.gov/2022046515

10 9 8 7 6 5 4 3 2 1

One who has perfected himself in the twin arts of remembering and forgetting is in a position to play at battledore and shuttlecock with the whole of existence.

—Søren Kierkegaard, *Either/Or*

Contents

List of Illustrations — xi

Acknowledgments — xiii

Introduction — 1
    Albert Galvany

PART I. HISTORIOGRAPHICAL AND POLITICAL NARRATIVES

Chapter 1
Cultural Amnesia and Commentarial Retrofitting:
Interpreting the *Spring and Autumn* — 25
    Newell Ann Van Auken

Chapter 2
Elision and Narration: Remembering and Forgetting in
Some Recently Unearthed Historiographical Manuscripts — 49
    Rens Krijgsman

Chapter 3
Shaping the Historian's Project: Language of Forgetting and
Obliteration in the *Shiji* — 71
    Esther Sunkyung Klein

Chapter 4
The Ice of Memory and the Fires of Forgetfulness: Traumatic
Recollections in the *Wu Yue chunqiu* — 97
    Olivia Milburn

PART II. PHILOSOPHICAL WRITINGS

Chapter 5
The *Daode jing*'s Forgotten Forebear: The Ancestral Cult   119
    K. E. Brashier

Chapter 6
So Comfortable You'll Forget You're Wearing Them: Attention
and Forgetting in the *Zhuangzi* and *Huainanzi*   153
    Franklin Perkins

Chapter 7
The Practice of Erasing Traces in the *Huainanzi*   181
    Tobias Benedikt Zürn

Chapter 8
The Oblivious against the Doctor: Pathologies of Remembering
and Virtues of Forgetting in the *Liezi*   215
    Albert Galvany

Chapter 9
Wang Bi and the Hermeneutics of Actualization   245
    Mercedes Valmisa

PART III. RITUAL AND LITERARY TEXTS

Chapter 10
Embodied Memory and Natural Forgetting in Early Chinese
Ritual Theory   271
    Paul Nicholas Vogt

Chapter 11
Exile and Return: Oblivion, Memory, and Nontragic Death
in Tomb-Quelling Texts from the Eastern Han Dynasty   297
    Xiang Li

Chapter 12
Lost in Where We Are: Tao Yuanming on the Joys of Forgetting
and the Worries of Being Forgotten   327
    Michael D. K. Ing

Contributors 349

Index 353

Illustrations

Figure 5.1	From the Yingchengzi mural. Eastern Han, Shagangtun (Liaoning).	120
Figure 5.2	From a tomb gate stone relief. Eastern Han, Suide (Shaanxi).	120
Figure 7.1	Unknown maker, China, *Ying Gong Ritual Vessel*, detail of inscription that includes some bird script.	188
Figure 7.2	Rubbing of the Ying Gong vessel's inscription.	188
Figure 7.3	Bird tracks in snow that resemble the character *ge* 个 and its bronze script (*jinwen* 金文) version.	188
Figure 11.1	The layout of the Litun tomb and the text on the tomb-quelling bottle.	311
Figure 11.2	The layout of tomb M3 of the Lingbao cemetery, Zhangwan.	312
Figure 11.3	The layout of the tomb of Fengjun Ruren.	313
Figure 11.4	The layout of the tomb in Baoji.	314

Acknowledgments

An edited volume is always the product of collective effort or, in other words, the result of a coordinated exercise in generosity. However, since it was mostly produced during a global health crisis, this book has required extraordinary commitment and selflessness. My first thanks as its editor go, therefore, to the contributors who, in such adverse circumstances in both personal and professional domains, showed unwavering enthusiasm and dedication to the project.

The idea for the book began to take shape in embryonic form some years after 2014, when I was invited to give a workshop in the Department of East Asian Studies at Princeton University as part of a reading group on Chinese philosophical texts for graduate students organized by Mercedes Valmisa and Sara Vantournhout. It is only fitting, then, that I should acknowledge my debt to this stimulating experience, which got me started on this project.

I would also like to express my gratitude to Roger T. Ames for his steadfast support, to James Peltz, Diane Ganeles, and other staff at SUNY Press for standing by me with their expertise and great patience throughout this process, and also to the anonymous reviewers for their detailed and very helpful critical reports. Many colleagues, although not directly involved, gave me their trust and valuable guidance, and I would especially like to mention Anthony Barbieri-Low, Romain Graziani, Jean Levi, Manel Ollé, Alicia Relinque, Juan Carlos Rodríguez Delgado, Armin Selbitschka, Song Gang, Roel Sterckx, Anne-Hélène Suárez, Julie Wark, and Oliver Weingarten.

Finally, I would like to acknowledge that this book has been supported by a research project grant (FFI2017.83593-P) cofunded by the Spanish Ministry of Education and Competitiveness (MINECO) and the European Fund for Regional Development (FEDER).

Introduction

Albert Galvany

In order to illustrate the basic aim of this edited volume about the relationship between forgetting and memory in ancient China, I would like to begin by drawing the reader's attention to the famous short story, "Funes the Memorious," by Jorge Luis Borges. The main character, Ireneo Funes, loses the ability to forget at the age of nineteen, after being thrown from a half-tamed horse and left paralyzed. The text, written as an obituary (a meaningful detail) by an anonymous narrator, describes the consequences of being cursed with infallible memory. At the beginning of the story, Funes is presented as a mnemonic prodigy who, after the accident, can recite by heart a book he borrowed only the previous day. As the story progresses, however, the problematic and even dramatic aspects of Funes's new condition are increasingly obvious. He remembers everything, but instead of making his world and his life bright and intense, this perfect memory breaks it down into its tiniest elements. Ireneo Funes dies only two years after his accident.

The cause of Funes's death is, in medical terms, congestion of the lungs, but the narrator—and the reader—inevitably supposes that his premature death is somehow connected with the burden of exceptional memory that has become impossible to bear. Toward the end of the obituary, the anonymous narrator adds these few lines: "I suspect, nevertheless, that he was not very capable of thought. To think is to forget a difference, to generalize, to abstract. In the overly replete world of Funes there were nothing but details, almost contiguous details."[1] Among other things, Borges's story highlights, with its dramatic plot, the important role played by forgetting in cognitive terms, how necessary its intercession is for perception and knowledge. As the story suggests, the advantages of forgetting are not only limited to this cognitive sphere, but they also affect existential matters and the way we lead our lives. Although it is clearly in the domain of fiction, Borges's story takes up Théodule-Armand Ribot's idea that "forgetfulness, except in certain cases, is not a disease of memory, but a condition of its health and life,"[2] or William James's famous observation that "in the practical use of our intellect, forgetting is as important a function as recollecting,"[3] thus elaborating on experiences noted in clinical psychology in the early years of the twentieth century and only confirmed in more recent research.[4]

Nobody wishes for a poor memory. The pangs of frustration we feel when we forget a colleague's name, an appointment, a friend's birthday or the precise location of an important quotation from an essential text motivate the desire to have all of our memories constantly available; too often forgetting is understood just as a scourge, a nuisance, a breakdown in an otherwise efficient mental capacity.[5] Yet, one only needs to skim the fictional case of Funes to appreciate the pain and complications associated with being unable to control which memories spring to mind, or with the loss of our capacity to forget. Forgetting is to lose our cherished past, to suffer confusion where there was understanding, or it is to neglect one's responsibilities to oneself or to others. It is something that one rarely does on purpose but is, rather, a human frailty to be avoided or overcome. However, forgetting is precisely what we want and need to do very often. Life is filled with unpleasant, even traumatic experiences that we would prefer to forget if we only could. If the existence of a duty to remember is controversial, the duty of forgetting seems a much more acceptable idea.[6] From this perspective, forgetting can be a positive force in human life, one that plays a decisive role in our existence.[7]

The reader's surprise at finding this implicit positive depiction of forgetting in Borges's story is partly due to the fact that our culture, like any other, tends to celebrate remembrance and forget about forgetting. Indeed, forgetting is often cast aside, naturally banished to occupy a marginal or inferior position, and simply thought of as being the negative converse of memory. From a conventional point of view that is tenaciously acceptable even today, memory has been presented as the radiant hero in the limelight while forgetting, defined as losing remembrance of something or ceasing to retain it in one's memory, has therefore been associated with the shady villain lurking behind the scenes.[8] By tradition, it is this focus of exclusionary opposition between the two phenomena that has prevailed until recent dates, in the academic world as well. Hence, the emphasis has been on its negative effects, its destructive powers, and the impossibility of constructing around it a technique or art equivalent to what memory inspires.[9] It is as if we somehow have nothing to say about forgetting, or if we can only refer to it in negative terms as a loss, something taken, an omission, lack, or distraction. This at least partially explains the extraordinary abundance of readily available scholarly works which, from several scientific disciplines, take as their object of study the various aspects of memory, whether it is from the individual or collective point of view, by contrast with the incredible scarcity of published monographs about forgetting.

Nevertheless, it must be admitted that, over the last two decades, the solidly distinctive quality of this exclusionary opposition when considering the relationship between remembering and forgetting has been diminishing in favor of a more comprehensive, less simple representation of the two processes. In this new perspective, remembering and forgetting tend to be understood as complementary forces rather than as antithetical processes that cancel each other out, and even as integral aspects through which cultural memory is formed and transformed.[10] Hence, in many of the disciplines coming together under the heading of the humanities, it has been understood that the study of forgetting and the study of memory cannot be separated in categorical and dichotomous ways.[11] Aleida Assmann, one of the pioneers in urging this change of paradigm, points out that, on all of its levels, memory should be defined as being an intricate interaction between remembering and forgetting, so that, "when thinking about memory, we must start with forgetting."[12] Accordingly, such different authors as the historian and philosopher Tzvetan Todorov and the anthropologist Marc Augé have recently drawn attention to the dangers inherent in certain rigid forms of the cult of memory and in unconditional and absolute praise of it, while also speaking out for the need always to include interaction with the positive forces of oblivion as they have much to contribute to an optimal management of memory.[13]

From this standpoint, we can claim that our sense of what memory is, then, seems to be defined by unstable oscillations between the latent and the explicit, the persistent and the momentary, the purposeful and the inadvertent, the remembered and the forgotten.[14] And although studies exclusively focused on memory continue to attract the attention of scholars, it is now clear that it is no longer possible to banish forgetting and that, accordingly, any rigorous research into the many aspects of memory must necessarily take into account the usually marginalized and forgotten dimension of oblivion. It is not surprising, then, that far from the exclusionary polarization that has prevailed until recently, Mary Carruthers, in the preface to the second edition of her celebrated study of Western medieval mnemonics, should state that it is necessary to explore "a kind of forgetting that itself results from an activity of memory,"[15] or that Anne Whitehead, even more explicitly, should conclude her guide to the field of memory studies with the statement that "forgetting, paradoxical as it may seem, constitutes a crucial if not an essential element in the future trajectory and direction of memory studies."[16] Forgetting, together with other forms of ignorance, loss, and deliberate or negligent suppression, which comprise a novel field of academic research called agnotology, is now increasingly validated as scholars are calling for a more complete, thorough, and accurate understanding of the cognitive, emotional, social, and political selection processes of past and present cultures.[17]

This less restrictive trend has also been reflected in several recent contributions in the study of ancient civilizations. The seminal works of the French scholar in ancient Greece, Nicole Loraux, in which she revived the crucial role played by the notion of forgetting just after the tyranny of the Thirty, in around 404 BCE at a particularly dramatic juncture in the political history of Athens, should be cited first of all.[18] Also important are the contributions of Charles W. Hedrick Jr. and of Harriet I. Flower who analyzed the subtle way in which memory and oblivion were interwoven in the political, penal, and social culture of the Roman Empire.[19] The clear significance of this new perspective is even reflected in publications that, once solely focused on aspects of memory, are now including reflections about oblivion, as if the idea of conceiving and examining memory as an autonomous phenomenon independent of forgetting is no longer so evident or natural. This is the case, for example, with the volume, edited by Luca Castagnoli and Paola Ceccarelli which, devoted to elucidating the concepts central to and underlying the theory and practice of memory in ancient Greece, which includes two chapters devoted to forgetting in a broad epigraph titled "Memory and Forgetting in the Classical Period";[20] and the volume devoted to the study of memory in Graeco-Roman literature, edited by

Katherine Mawford and Eleni Ntanou, which also includes a section titled "Oblivion," with three contributions dealing with the relationship between memory and forgetting.[21] The basic aim of our book is none other than to take up the changes we are now seeing in the study of memory and to move them into the domain of ancient China.

Naturally, memory is also perceived as an essential element playing a key role in many of the ritual, pedagogical, political, philosophical, and institutional expressions of classical Chinese civilization. In the intellectual landscape of ancient China, the virtues of memory are insistently emphasized from a standpoint which, in terms of both the individual and the collective, is at once political, social, and moral. There can be no doubt that memory is important for the life of individuals. It enables them to construct identities over time, despite the changes they will necessarily have to confront. But, moreover, self-cultivation, or the meticulous process of moral training by means of which an individual manages to become optimally integrated into the social and political structure in accordance, for example, with what is set out in the so-called Confucian school (*ru jia* 儒家), is inseparable from the constant exercise of memory, and recovering what was said and done in the past.[22] These patterns of individual reminiscences are in turn inserted into the broader narrative of the family. Organized to a great extent around the ancestor cult, the profusion of rites, offerings, and ceremonies, which have linked the world of the living with the realm of the dead since the earliest dynasties, gives particular prominence to genealogies, to history, and to stories about members of the lineages and ancestors.[23] This makes it possible to include the individual in a narrative of greater density and time span.

Given this background, it is hardly surprising that educational activity is also organized around the same desire to transmit acquired knowledge, to conserve the past, and to reactivate or recall it in order to apply it to the present.[24] Understood as the effective transmission of a cultural legacy endowed with political and moral significance, education revolves around memorizing texts and teachings that one must know how to apply properly. Memory plays an essential role, not only in this "mental" instruction but also in the achievement of a body molded by means of reiterated protocols and somatic movements codified in a series of rituals that organize political and social life. Hence, the ancestor cult, the virtue of filial respect, the techniques for self-cultivation, and the optimal development of interpersonal relations within a ritually codified hierarchical order require that nothing should be forgotten: the memory of one's progenitors, the master's teachings, instructions of superiors, codes of ceremonial behavior, the legacy of the sages of antiquity, relevant events of the past, and so on. It is a matter of recovering the lessons handed down by past sages,[25] of not forgetting the past so that it can become a model, a source of inspiration for the future.[26] This explains the fact that forgetting appears so frequently and in a good part of the classical literature with the exhortation of a negative nature and imperative value, as "do not forget" (*wu wang* 勿忘) and equivalents.[27]

Since memory has been assigned such a central role in Chinese civilization, it is mainly this that has attracted the attention of scholars in the last few decades and which, as a result, has also taken up a considerable part of their analytical efforts. Accordingly, there are several recent works that have offered a deepened understanding of the various aspects related to memory from the standpoint of the history of ideas. I would highlight as paradigmatic examples of this the two monographic studies, now classics in the field, by K. E. Brashier, *Ancestral Memory in Early China* and *Public Memory in Early China*.[28] Together with these seminal works, other monographic studies and collective volumes have appeared in the last few years examining several facets of memory from varying perspectives.[29] Circumscribed by the phenomenon of memory, conceived as an autonomous element, none of these important and rich contributions includes reflections on the relations that should be woven between remembering and forgetting. Of course, this does not mean that Western sinology is entirely bereft of relevant contributions on the relationship between oblivion and memory in ancient China, but it must be admitted that, by comparison, they are much less abundant. Moreover, with very few exceptions,[30] when seeking to shed light on this phenomenon, they tend to refer to the way it is presented in a single extraordinary textual source, the *Zhuangzi* 莊子.[31]

This edited volume aims to fill, at least partially, the main gaps detailed above by offering a selection of studies that not only consider that forgetting is an essential element for the further development of memory studies but also take as a general premise the idea that remembering and forgetting in ancient Chinese civilization should not be understood as isolated phenomena. Instead of conceiving of these two domains as belonging within a diametric and excluding opposition, our volume is founded on the idea that it is much more fruitful to analyze the sophisticated ways in which they interlink and overlap. This means, then, offering a perspective that allows the best possible illustration of the dynamics, tensions, and transitions between forgetting and remembering in a setting of cultural memory where centripetal forces of conservation met centrifugal forces of dispersion. Accordingly, the fundamental premise of this book is the need to lay aside this narrow notion of forgetting, which is understood as a purely negative, unidimensional process, in order to explore the wealth of alternative forms it can adopt in the cultural context of ancient China. Hence, following in the wake of seminal works by such scholars as Paul Connerton and Aleida Assman[32] who suggest several ways of classifying and accounting for the various facets of forgetting, the contributions making up this volume deal with such widely varying aspects of the phenomenon as erasure, cultural amnesia, selective forgetting, absentmindedness, concealment, obliteration, neglect, or pathologic and therapeutic oblivion.

Nevertheless, for all its pioneering and innovative nature, the aim of the volume is modest since it is limited to offering a sufficiently comprehensive sample of precursor works that integrate various aspects of forgetting into the study of memory. Hence, far from aspiring to present an all-encompassing survey that will cover every aspect of the issue, the purpose is to explore, from a variety of focuses covering an ample range of disciplines, perspectives, traditions, and periods, some of the ways in which the different ideas (and practices) of forgetting and remembering interact. Through the interdisciplinarity nature of this volume and the multiplicity of approaches of its essays we will try to shed new light on the features of the mechanisms of preservation and loss in ancient Chinese texts. The volume therefore brings together a wide range of contributions, methodologically structured around textual analysis and covering a good part of the predominant genres of the intellectual landscape of ancient China, which include historiographical writings, political discourses, philosophical essays, ritual treatises, religious documents, and literary pieces, both transmitted and excavated. We are of course aware that the ordering of this material into three sections (historiographical and political narratives, philosophical writings, and ritual treatises and literary texts) admits variations since, given the very condition of the texts being analyzed, which are irreducibly heterogenous in many cases, these taxonomies should not be understood rigidly. For example, a ritual treatise may contain passages that refer to a philosophical or literary dimension, just as a literary piece may draw on historical material and offer political lessons.

We present, then, a flexible ordering which, in keeping with an approximate chronological scheme for the chapters in each of the three parts, makes it possible to give the whole an organized structure. This is a set of texts whose coherence, as I have noted above, is shaped by the shared objective of shedding light on some of the many facets of forgetting and its links with memory. Moreover, their unity seems to be reinforced by a mesh of internal connections that bring the individual contributions together. Hence, as the reader will discover, although they can be read separately, the volume as a whole represents a fertile and congruent discussion among the twelve chapters that comprise it.

Part I: Historiographical and Political Narratives

No practice of memory is innocent or innocuous. All acts of remembering respond to a specific objective and, accordingly, it should not be assumed that someone decides to record facts simply for the sake of recording them. To the extent that every exercise of memory always involves a process of selection, whether deliberate or unintentional, from the moment a person (or a collective) ponders what to remember or what specific memories to preserve, decisions are also made about what must be forgotten, omitted, and silenced; memory is always an active process that involves selecting, reorganizing, and suppressing scraps of memories.[33] In fact, almost the only thing that the members of a society share is what they have forgotten, so that, as Joël Candau points out in this respect, society is less united by its memories than by its forgetting.[34] From this perspective, the dialectics of memory and forgetting take on different values in keeping with the various contexts wherein they apply but it is evident that, in any case, conservation and transmission of the past are always in line with religious, aesthetic, ethical, political, and rhetorical purposes that necessarily end up shaping the historic discourse while, at the same time, pointing to certain forms of forgetting or omission.[35] The chapters in part I are structured around several questions. How does forgetting play a role in the preservation, transmission, or restoration of historical memory? In such cases, should one speak of fertile ground for forgetting? If this is so, what kinds of forgetting can be beneficial or stimulating for those who actively participate in the preservation of memories? And what excessive aspects of forgetting and memory are recorded in documents with a historical vocation?

In chapter 1, "Cultural Amnesia and Commentarial Retrofitting: Interpreting the *Spring and Autumn*," Newell Ann Van Auken discusses the anxiety caused in later readers by the loss and forgetting of precise knowledge about the original sense of a good part of the *Spring and Autumn* 春秋—a register of individual events composed in the ancient state of Lu 魯 from 722 to 481 BCE and arranged chronologically—and also describes how two of the most important commentaries on this text, the *Gongyang* 公羊 and the *Guliang* 穀梁 traditions, set out to remedy the matter. It is the process of forgetting old ideas, that is, of "cultural amnesia" that makes commentaries necessary. Cultural amnesia transforms the past into a foreign country and, likewise, transforms texts written in the past into foreign writings. Just as we read texts in a foreign tongue through the interpretive medium of translation, we also read texts of a different time through the hermeneutical lens of a commentary. However, the *Spring and Autumn* reflects practices that were rooted in cultural norms of an earlier time, cultural norms that had apparently been largely forgotten by the time the *Gongyang* and the *Guliang* commentaries were composed. Although commentaries are often understood as simply explaining and elaborating on the original text, in fact, as Van Auken notes, they explain works whose meaning has been lost (or is in the process of being lost) and infuse old texts with new ideas. By presenting two case studies dealing with linguistic and interpretive changes, this chapter illustrates the ways whereby early commentaries offered new interpretations of an old text, which were only permitted after cultural amnesia had wiped the slate clean and thus opened up new ways of reading it.

In chapter 2, "Elision and Narration: Remembering and Forgetting in Some Recent Unearthed Historiographical Manuscripts," Rens Krijgsman addresses the question of remembrance and forgetting as it appears in two historiographical manuscripts that have recently surfaced: the *Rongchengshi* 容成氏, from the Shanghai Museum and the *Xinian* 繫年, from Tsinghua University. By offering a detailed comparative reading of these two looted bamboo-slip manuscripts, the chapter provides a nuanced description in which their differences in form and aim structure their approach to selection, amplification, and elision of memory and, consequently, frame their respective narratives. While previous scholarship has focused on how forces such as institutionalization, ritualization, and canonization have shaped cultural memory, in his contribution Krijgsman analyzes how specific target collections of historical narrative amalgamate local historiography. According to his reading of these new materials, both manuscripts provide stories and narrative in detail hitherto unseen in transmitted or unearthed preimperial historiographical documents while, at the same time, eliding information not immediately germane to their narrative. Krijgsman provides an analysis of how narrative triage influences the dynamic of remembering and forgetting and how these selections are themselves a function of the access texts had to particular memories and the contingencies inherent to textual transmission in early times.

In chapter 3, "Shaping the Historian's Project: Language of Forgetting and Obliteration in the *Shiji*," Esther Sunkyung Klein addresses the complex relationship woven between memory and forgetting in the work of Sima Qian by starting from a crucial question that structures and permeates her chapter: can forgetting perhaps have a positive function in a historiographical text like the *Shiji* 史記, which is to say a work that is devoted to the conservation and exaltation of memory? For Klein, the answer is affirmative, but it requires a more nuanced understanding of forgetting that involves distinguishing different levels of meaning within the historian's project. Her contribution is therefore organized into three sections that correspond to each of these levels of meaning around forgetting. First, she gives a detailed textual analysis of the term *wang* 忘, which tends to be translated as "forgetting," in order to demonstrate that its negative treatment in the *Shiji* is due to the fact that it does not so much suggest loss or obliteration as carelessness or negligence. The second section consists of a study of a series of terms that play a much more positive and relevant role in Sima Qian's project and that refer, precisely, to the inevitable nature of loss, a loss that pulsates powerfully in especially relevant parts of the text, such as the Qin bibliocaust, the ritual procedures fallen into oblivion, or the extinguished fame of certain remarkable individuals. Finally, Klein highlights the important role of active or deliberate forgetting, in the form of "silence," which also shapes Sima Qian's project, while referring to everything that is necessarily left out in the process of selection and transmission.

In chapter 4, "The Ice of Memory and the Fires of Forgetfulness: Traumatic Recollections in the *Wu Yue chunqiu*," Olivia Milburn discusses the interplay between memory and forgetting in the *Spring and Autumn Annals of Wu and Yue*, a Han dynasty (202 BC–220 CE) text structured around the prolonged and devastating political and military conflict between King Helü 吳王闔閭 (r. 514–496 BCE) and King Fuchai 吳王夫差 (r. 495–473 BCE) of Wu and their nemesis, King Goujian 越王勾踐 (r. 496–465 BCE) of Yue. In Milburn's account, during the desperate struggle for survival between the states of Wu and Yue, King Fuchai consistently sought not merely to forget the traumas of the past, but to kill and then obliterate the memory of anyone who reminded him of them. In Milburn's detailed analysis of the story, his character presents a sharp contrast to that of King Goujian of Yue, who seems determined to remember everything and everyone who has played a role in deciding his fate. King Fuchai's forgetfulness eventually leads to his ignominious demise and the collapse of his kingdom, while King Goujian's excellent memory proves to be very dangerous for friends and foes alike. As Milburn's careful reading of these anecdotes suggests, forgetting nothing can ultimately be as damaging as forgetting too much, so this text is highly ambivalent about the role of memory and oblivion.

Part II: Philosophical Writings

Remembering and forgetting are not only complementary processes in any given society, but they can also be instruments of subjugation or resistance to its underlying power institutions and structures. The mechanism of inclusion and exclusion of meaning tends to be controlled by the hegemonic ideology or the dominant social group, in such a way—as Michel Foucault surmised when he coined the term *contre-mémoire*—that, as in the case of knowledge, there is also a close relationship between memory and power.[36] In part II, we bring together contributions that are based on examination of rather peripheral philosophical texts that are a long way from the ideological emphasis, which, in the study of ancient China, tends to focus on the so-called Confucian school. These outlier texts share the characteristic of a desire to endow the different forms of forgetting with positive attributes and nuances, which very rarely occurs in other doctrinal corpuses in which reverence for memory prevails.

In chapter 5, "The *Daode jing*'s Forgotten Forebear: The Ancestral Cult," K. E. Brashier describes how the ancestral cult ritualizes forgetting. Recent ancestors who are individually remembered fade upward into the corporate lineage that then terminates at the lineage of the progenitor who most embodies De 德 and who acts as formless heaven's counterpart. On the other hand, the Dao 道 discourse philosophizes forgetting. It juxtaposes the named, fractured, ten thousand things in our conventional world with the singular De and, ultimately, with the nameless, blurry, unified Dao. In other words, both the ancestral cult and the Dao discourse trace out a spectrum that moves from individuation to unity, from tangible definition to loss of dualistic knowledge. However, as Brashier shows, these spectrums are not only parallel but they also explicitly overlap because the *Daode jing* 道德經 uses the ancestral cult to explain itself. After briefly outlining the relevant spectrums in both the ancestral cult and the Dao discourse, this chapter explicates a consistent number of passages in the *Daode jing* that directly rely on the ancestral cult, demonstrating that ritualized and philosophical forgetting both conclude in a shared oblivion. In the end, this chapter hypothesizes that the *Daode jing*'s basic argument is abstracted from the existing ancestral cult.

From early times, Chinese philosophers were convinced that self-cultivation techniques needed to address not only how a person makes deliberate judgments and chooses to act but also the patterns of attention, salience, and construal that determine how the world appears. Consequently, how the world appears conditions the overt values and choices we make, and even what we name as things and facts. In chapter 6, "So Comfortable You'll Forget You Have Them on: Attention and Forgetting in the *Zhuangzi* and *Huainanzi*," Franklin Perkins initially focuses on forgetting as obliviousness or failing to attend. In the first part of the chapter, he examines this sense of forgetting as an attention failure, placing it in the context of a broader concern with the optimal conditions for perceiving the world as it appears. On the basis of detailed analysis of some passages from the *Huainanzi* 淮南子 and contrasting them with partially supportive ideas from the *Xunzi* 荀子, Perkins outlines a theory of the conditions required to put into practice unbiased perception and comprehensive attention that would ideally exclude all forms of disturbance and neglect. In the second part of the piece, he shows how oblivion could be dangerous but also a desirable state to be cultivated and strengthened. This is precisely the case in the *Zhuangzi* where, as he demonstrates, the point is that oblivion serves several distinct functions that include advice for what he labels as selective attention and even for a kind of total forgetting. This more radical forgetting enables a stronger sense of impartiality when dealing with the present in its singularity and can liberate us from rigid fixations when experiencing life.

In chapter 7, "The Practice of Erasing Traces in the *Huainanzi*," Tobias Benedikt Zürn reconstructs the intellectual background of an important and ubiquitous expression in the early literature, that of being traceless (*wu ji* 無跡) and, more specifically, explores how it relates to both practices of embodiment and debates on remembrance, recording and erasure in the *Huainanzi*. In a first step, he provides a comprehensive philological analysis of the earliest connotations of the term *traces* beyond its literal meaning linked to the tracks of animals and other beings, to see the word as also referring to valuable receptacles that enshrine the actions and deeds of the past. From this basic understanding of traces as the actions and deeds of the past, Zürn extends his analysis to the realm of words, writings, and records that were thought to capture the knowledge, the forms of action, and discourses preserved in the traces of sages and rulers from bygone times. Finally, the chapter discusses how this accepted discourse about writings and records of past actions, words, and deeds expressing the wisdom of the past became contested in texts like the *Huainanzi*, which stresses the idea that perfect rulership and true sageliness are achieved by eradicating or hiding these traces. By introducing the idea of "tracelessness," texts like the *Huainanzi* justified not only their regime of body-politics but also powerfully rejected the culture of remembrance characteristic of the so-called Confucian school (*ru jia*) and other intellectual factions.

No doubt, many ancient Chinese political and philosophical writings gravitate around a pedagogical project that seeks to transform the individual into an accomplished subject by means of a firm commitment to memory. Nevertheless, even with this overwhelming presence of memory and its virtues, in some of the most important written works of ancient Masters literature (*zi shu* 子書) it is possible to find critiques and even sabotage of these prevalent ideas. In chapter 8, "The Oblivious against the Doctor: Pathologies of Remembering and Virtues of forgetting in the *Liezi*," Albert Galvany analyzes the sharp criticism of abuse of memory and the rehabilitation of oblivion that can be found in this often neglected, almost "forgotten" text. First, he discusses a set of anecdotes where forgetting occupies an essential place, showing that some stories in the *Liezi* 列子 fiercely attack the supposed virtues of memory and the associated notions that are upheld in some of the most influential philosophical doctrines of the times, while highlighting the negative consequences (political, epistemological, and ethical) deriving from the inability to forget. Then, with a comprehensive analysis of a vivid anecdote about a man who is suddenly stricken with amnesia, he shows how this text challenges ordinary perceptions of both memory and forgetting and holds out an alternative reading of the essential virtues that are concealed in oblivion.

If writings handed down from the past tend to be conceived, as suggested above, as traces that potentially harbor the capacity to express the sense of words proffered and deeds accomplished by the sages of antiquity, in chapter 9, "Wang Bi and the Hermeneutics of Actualization," Mercedes Valmisa reflects on the conditions and premises that allow the process of intermediation with the present to take place. Starting from her analysis of the concise and influential essay written by Wang Bi 王弼 (226–249) as part of his commentary on the Zhouyi 周易, "Clarifying Images" ("Ming xiang" 明象), Valmisa shows how Wang Bi presents a novel, fertile theory of interpretation, which she calls the Hermeneutics of Actualization. This is a theory about how to properly understand the meaning of a text that has been inherited from the authoritative voices of earlier sages. In order to interpret correctly the signs transmitted from the past, the reader must reject a relation of identity where the sign is equal to itself and welcome the gap onto which a new actualization of meaning can be grounded in the present. As Valmisa puts it, signs store and communicate the author's intentions but, in receiving them, the reader cannot stay at the superficial level of what the sign literally says but needs to search for the meaning in between the lines by paying attention to equivalences and structure. Reading in between the lines, which allows the reader to have access to the intention and thus to actualize the text, implies, as Valmisa demonstrates, a subtle dialectic and simultaneous relationship between getting and forgetting.

Part III: Ritual and Literary Texts

The third and final section comprises contributions that explore writings of ritual vocation (including not only documents that have been passed down but also recent unearthed material) and literary aspiration. The relationship between memory and forgetting unfolds into other polarities like omission and transmission, or loss and conservation, which ultimately refer to disappearance and survival. Hence, from this perspective, the crucial role played in ancient China by mourning ceremonies in the set of practices regulated by ritual brings to light an essential tension between the duty of honoring and preserving the memory of deceased loved ones and the need to ease pain by means of their disappearance in the gradual stages of forgetting. In keeping with this question and from a standpoint marked by a poetic sensibility, the limited and mortal nature that determines human existence is transformed into elaborate material for reflection about the possibility of tempering and even transcending, with procedures akin to forms of forgetting, the distress caused by acute awareness of this condition.

Within the disparate range of early Chinese writings on the theory of ritual there are ambiguous viewpoints on the nature of forgetting. The possibility of forgetting even such important figures as one's deceased parents appears as a fundamental threat against which ritual militates, although elsewhere it is acknowledged as a natural human tendency. Forgetting one's "root" (*ben* 本), alternately construed as one's basic nature or origins, poses a constant, existential danger, yet the ability to "forget" one's immediate circumstances may open the way to superior attainment. In chapter 10, "Embodied Memory and Natural Forgetting in Early Chinese Ritual Theory," Paul Nicholas Vogt shows that the dialogue of forgetting is bound up with conceptions of the body, in terms of both its sensual needs and sensory capacities and, through it, with what might be called the early Chinese "phenomenology of memory." His contribution takes as its launching point the collection known as the *Liji* 禮記, or *Records of the Rites*, exploring the ambiguity of its statements on forgetting as both an intrinsic process of the human organism and an obstacle to be combated through the structuring influence of ritual. Linking these formulations to pre-Qin and Han discourses on the self and the senses, it examines how early Chinese ritual theory explained the combined problem and opportunity of forgetting in both present and imagined past, sketching out the value of ritual as a response to the intrinsic vagaries of the human body.

Rather than texts including theoretical descriptions of ritual practices with prescriptive ends, the next chapter studies a type of entombed artifacts, the tomb-quelling texts, which were used with practical intent in funerary rites. In chapter 11, "Exile and Return: Oblivion, Memory, and Nontragic Death in Tomb-Quelling Texts from Eastern Han Dynasty," Xiang Li examines the conception of oblivion in tomb-quelling texts from the Eastern Han period and its relationship with a renewed understanding of death. Three layers of tomb-quelling texts verify that people considered oblivion as a process that involves both the erasure and revival of memories. The textual content of tomb-quelling texts presents oblivion as the expedient removal and the final retrieval of memory. The spatial dimension of tomb-quelling texts is seen in various strategies of placing these artifacts in a tomb with the aim of facilitating or reversing the process of oblivion. Moreover, tomb-quelling texts were employed as ritual tools in funerals that partly removed the dead from living people's memory while redefining the deceased as immortal entities. These artifacts clearly display the deceased as a group that is exiled from the earthly world but has the potential to return. By using them, survivors were not only exempted from painful memories of the deaths of their loved ones but are also enabled to call the dead to mind when necessary. The notion of nontragic death, implying reconciliation between the deceased and the living, is therefore made possible. The analysis of these materials explains why people in the Eastern Han were so expressive on the topic of dying, evanescing, and vanishing.

Finitude and mortality are also at the core of the last chapter in this volume. The fifth century poet and intellectual, Tao Yuanming 陶淵明 (365?–427), also known as Tao Qian 陶潛, was keenly aware of the constraints entailed in being an embodied creature with a finite life span. As Michael D. K. Ing shows in chapter 12, "Lost in Where We Are: Tao Yuanming on the Joys of Forgetting and the Worries of Being Forgotten," he found delight in activities that enabled him to temporarily forget these limitations. They included drinking ale in the company of like-minded people (some only found in the pages of books), which fostered a communion of sorts as the boundary between self and other became more porous. According to Ing, in these circumstances, ale served to loosen the boundaries between things—destabilizing the sense of a self that is rooted in a particular time and place. In contrast with others in his era, Tao Yuanming was skeptical about the possibility of immortality. However, ale seemed to allow him a glimpse into immortal life—a temporary shedding of time's restraints. The loss of an end point to his life was tied to the loss of a firm conception of his self, as his identity was at least partially predicated on awareness of an end. For him, this forgetting of Time's limitations induced a realization of a new self, a communal self that endured like the heavens and the earth. In this regard, ale is a sacred drink, immortalizing and sanctifying those who consume it, in such a way that the fetters of the self that often limit the individual from communing with other things separated by time and space are cut away. For Tao Yuanming, ale is, then, a kind of holy communion; a communion of forgetting limitations that may give us some relief from the tyranny of time.

Notes

1. "Funes the Memorious," translated into English by James E. Irby, in Jorge Luis Borges, *Labyrinths. Selected Stories and Other Writings* (New York: New Directions, 1964), 69–74, 75.
2. T.-A. Ribot, *Diseases of Memory: An Essay in the Positive Psychology* (New York: Appleton Century Crofts, 1882), 61.
3. W. James, *The Principles of Psychology*, vols. 1 and 2 (New York: Holt, [1890] 1980), 648.
4. The pioneering contributions of Alexander R. Luria in *The Mind of a Mnemonist* (Cambridge, MA: Harvard University Press, [1968] 1986) should be mentioned in this regard. Notable among many recent works is the study by Simon Norby, "Why Forget? On the Adaptative Value of Memory Loss," *Perspectives on Psychological Science* 10, no. 5 (2015): 551–78.
5. J. S. Nairne and J. N. J. Pandeirada, "Forgetting," in *Learning and Memory: A Comprehensive Reference*, ed. H. L. Roediger (Oxford: Elsevier, 2008), 179–94, 179.
6. See, for instance, David Rieff, *In Praise of Forgetting: Historical Memory and Its Ironies* (New Haven, CT: Yale University Press, 2016).
7. For an excellent compilation of positive reflections and assessments on the phenomenon of forgetting from the perspective of various experts in neurology and cognitive sciences, see Lauren Gravitz, "The Importance of Forgetting," *Nature* 571 (2019): 12–14.
8. Jens Broekmeier, "Remembering and Forgetting: Narratives as Cultural Memory," *Culture and Psychology* 8, no. 1 (2002): 15–43, 15.
9. This is precisely the position expressed by Umberto Eco in his much-cited article "An Ars Oblivionalis? Forget It!," *Publications of the Modern Language Association* 103, no. 3 (1988): 254–61.
10. See Sybille Krämer, "Das Vergessen nich vergessen! oder: Ist das Vergessen ein defizienter Modus von Erinnerung?," *Paragrama* 9, no. 2 (2000): 251–75. On the interplay between the art of memory and the art of forgetting, see also Louisa Passerini, "Memories between Silence and Oblivion," in *Contested Pasts: The Politics of Memory*, ed. Katharine Hodgkin and Susannah Radstone (London: Routledge, 2003), 250.
11. See Roberto Cubelli, "A New Taxonomy of Memory and Forgetting," in *Forgetting*, ed. Sergio Della Sala (New York: Psychology Press, 2010), 42.
12. A. Assmann, "Memory, Individual and Collective," in *The Oxford Handbook of Contextual Political Analysis*, ed. Robert E. Goodin and Charles Tilly (Oxford and New York: Oxford University Press, 2006), 220. See also "To Remember or to Forget: Which Way out of a Shared History of Violence?," in *Memory and Political Change*, ed. Aleida Assmann and Linda Shortt (New York: Palgrave Macmillan, 2012), 68.

13. See T. Todorov, *Les abus de la mémoire* (Paris: Arléa, 1995), 14; and M. Augé, *Les formes de l'oubli* (Paris: Rivages, 2001), 21.

14. Geoffrey Cubitt, *Memory and History* (Manchester: Manchester University Press, 2007), 77.

15. M. Carruthers, *The Book of Memory: A Study of Memory in Medieval Culture* (Cambridge: Cambridge University Press, [1998] 2008), 6. See also Patrick J. Geary, *Phantoms of Remembrance. Memory and Oblivion at the End of the First Millenium* (Princeton, NJ: Princeton University Press, 1994).

16. A. Whitehead, *Memory* (London: Routledge, 2009), 157. In the field of social pyschology, David Middleton and Steven D. Brown also stressed the necessity to adopt a new perspective that could lead us "to a view of remembering and forgetting as interdependent ways of actualising and virtualising experience rather than its presence or absence." See D. Middleton and S. D. Brown, ed., *The Social Psychology of Experience. Studies in Remembering and Forgetting* (London: Sage Publications, 2005), viii.

17. With regard to the aims and domains of agnotology, I refer the reader to R. N. Proctor and L. Schiebinger, eds., *Agnotology: The Making and Unmaking of Ignorance* (Palo Alto, CA: Stanford University Press, 2008) and, more recently, Renata Salecl, *A Passion for Ignorance. What We Choose Not to Know and Why* (Princeton, NJ: Princeton University Press, 2020).

18. N. Loraux, *La Cité divisée. L'oubli dans la mémoire d'Athènes* (Paris: Payot, 1997).

19. C. W. Hedrick Jr., *History and Silence. Purge and Rehabilitation of Memory in Late Antiquity* (Austin: University of Texas Press, 2000), esp. 89–130; H. I. Flower, *The Art of Forgetting: Disgrace and Oblivion in Roman Political Culture* (Chapel Hill: University of North Carolina Press, 2006).

20. L. Castagnoli and P. Ceccarelli, eds., *Greek Memories. Theories and Practices* (Cambridge: Cambridge University Press, 2019). The chapters specifically devoted to forgetting are those by Andrea Capra, "Lyric Oblivion: When Sappho Taught Socrates How to Forget," 179–94; and by Ynon Wygoda, "Socratic Forgetfulness and Platonic Irony," 195–215.

21. K. Mawford and E. Ntanou, eds., *Ancient Memory: Remembrance and Commemoration in Graeco-Roman Literature* (Berlin: Walter de Gruyter, 2021). In this case, the chapters devoted to forgetting are those by Hannah Burke-Tomlinson, "Ovid's Labyrinthine Ars: Pasiphae and the Dangers of Poetic Memory in the Metamorphoses," 219–46; A. D. Morrison, "Divine Memory, Mortal Forgetfulness and Human Misfortune," 247–66; and Carlos Hernández Garcés, "Forgetfulness as a Narrative Device in Herodotus' Histories," 267–91.

22. Mark E. Lewis, *Writing and Authority in Early China* (Albany: State University of New York Press, 1999), 99–146.

23. See, for instance, Roderick Campbell, "Memory, Power, and Death in Chinese History and Prehistory," in *The Archaeology of Ancestors: Death, Memory,*

and Veneration, ed. E. Hill and J. B. Hageman (Gainesville: University Press of Florida, 2016), 81–101. As Martin Kern has pointed out, the sophisticated material and discursive paraphernalia of the Western Zhou ancestral sacrifice served at once for communication with the spirits of former generations and representation of the past as foundational for the present; it constituted the "aesthetics of memory" that governed the ritual performance and religious expression of the Western Zhou ancestral sacrifice. See M. Kern, "Bronze Inscriptions, the *Shijing* and the *Shangshu*: The Evolution of the Ancestral Sacrifice during the Western Zhou," in *Early Chinese Religion. Part One: Shang through Han (1250 BC–220 AD)*, ed. John Lagerwey and Marc Kalinowski (Leiden: Brill, 2009), 143–200, esp. 197.

24. Among other contributions, see Andrea Schmölz, *Vom Lied in der Gemeinschaft zum Liedzitat im Text: Liedzitate in den Texten der Gelehrtentradition der späten Chou-Zeit* (Egelsbach: Hänsel-Hohenhausen, 1993); Mark E. Lewis, *Writing and Authority in Early China*, 54–63; Jean Levi, "Éducation et Mobilité à l'Époque des Royaumes Combattants," in *Éducation et Instruction en Chine: Aux Marges de l'Orthodoxie*, ed. Christine Nguyen Tri and Catherine Despeux (Paris: Peteers, 2004), 5–22; and Constance A. Cook, "Education and the Way of the Former Kings," in *Writing and Literacy in Early China*, ed. Li Feng and David P. Branner (Seattle: University of Washington Press, 2011), 302–36.

25. Wang Xianqian 王先謙, *Xunzi jijie* 荀子集解 (Beijing: Zhonghua shuju, 1988), 1.2 ("Quan xue" 勸學).

26. This is the sense of the refrain cited by Jia Yi 賈誼 (200–169 BCE), "Matters of the past must not be forgotten so that they can be teachers in matters of the future" (前事之不忘, 後事之師也). By means of this, at least in part, he sought to explain the premature collapse of the Qin dynasty. In his view, the dynasty's leaders had been unable to learn or to extract valuable lessons from the past of the Zhou dynasty. See Yan Zhenyi 閻振益 and Xia Zhong 鍾夏, *Xinshu jiaozhu* 新書校注 (Beijing: Zhonghua shuju, 2000), 3.12 ("Guo Qin xia" 過秦下).

27. See, for instance: Gao Heng 高亨, *Shijing jinzhu* 詩經今住 (Shanghai: Shanghai guji, 1980), 412 ("Sheng min zhi she" 生民之什) and 497 ("Min yu xiao zi" 閔予小); Sun Xingyan 孫星衍, *Shangshu jingu wen zhushu* 尚書今古文注疏 (Beijing: Zhonghua shuju, 2004), 344 ("Da gao" 大誥); Shanghai Shifan daxue guji zhengli zu 上海師範大學古籍整理組, *Guoyu* 國語 (Shanghai: Shanghai guji chubanshe, 1980), 8.295 ("Jin yu er" 晉語二); Yang Bojun 楊伯峻, *Chunqiu Zuozhuan zhu* 春秋左傳注 (Beijing: Zhonghua shuju, 1981), 588 (Wen 12), 658 (Xuan 2), and 845 (Cheng 9); Sun Xidan 孫希旦, *Liji jijie* 禮記集解 (Beijing: Zhonghua shuju, 1989), 10.657 ("Li qi" 禮器) and 24.1209 ("Ji yi" 祭義); Yang Bojun 楊伯峻, *Mengzi yizhu* 孟子譯注 (Beijing: Zhonghua shuju, 1960), 138 ("Teng wen gong xia" 滕文公下) and 206 ("Wan zhang shang" 萬章上); Wang Xianqian 王先謙, *Xunzi jijie* 荀子集解 (Beijing: Zhonghua shuju, 1988), 9.173 ("Wang zhi" 王制).

28. K. E. Brashier, *Ancestral Memory in Early China* (Cambridge, MA: Harvard University Asia Center, 2011); *Public Memory in Early China* (Cambridge, MA: Harvard Asia Center, 2014).

29. Among the recent contributions, see the monograph by Li Min, *Social Memory and State Formation in Early China* (Cambridge: Cambridge University Press, 2018), as well as these two edited volumes: F. Allard, Yan Sun and K. M. Linduff, eds., *Memory and Agency in Ancient China: Shaping the Life History of Objects* (Cambridge: Cambridge University Press, 2018); and W. Swartz and R. F. Campany, eds., *Memory in Medieval China: Texts, Ritual, and Community* (Leiden: Brill, 2018).

30. As far as I know, one of the few academic contributions that have set out to clarify the relationship between memory and oblivion in a work other than the *Zhuangzi*, in this case a study devoted to analyzing the social changes occurring from the Eastern Zhou to the Han periods with regard to the way in which the Western Zhou past was remembered, disremembered, and forgotten, is the paper by Wang Ming-ke (王明珂), "Western Zhou Remembering and Forgetting," *Journal of East Asian Archaeology* 1, no. 1 (1999): 231–50.

31. Claude Romano, "Un étrange oubli," *Extrême-Orient Extrême-Occident* 27 (2005): 161–67; Romain Graziani, "Optimal States and Self-Defeating Plans: The Problem of Intentionality in Early Chinese Self-Cultivation," *Philosophy East and West* 59, no. 4 (2009): 440–66; Livia Kohn, *Sitting in the Oblivion: The Heart of Daoist Meditation* (Honolulu: University of Hawai'i Press, 2010); Mark Berkson, "Death in the *Zhuangzi*: Mind, Nature, and the Art of Forgetting," in *Mortality in Traditional Chinese Thought*, ed. A. Olberding and P. J. Ivanhoe (Albany: State University of New York Press, 2011), 191–224; Chris Fraser, "Heart-Fasting, Forgetting, and Using the Heart Like a Mirror: Applied Emptiness in the *Zhuangzi*," in *Nothingness in Asian Philosophy*, ed. J. Liu and D. Berger (New York: Routledge, 2014), 197–212; Livia Kohn, "Forget or Not Forget? The Neurophysiology of *zuowang*," in *New Visions of the Zhuangzi*, ed. L. Kohn (St. Petersburg, FL: Three Pines, 2015), 161–79; Linna Liu and Shihao Chew, "Dynamic Model of Emotions: The Process of Forgetting in the *Zhuangzi*," *Dao: A Journal of Comparative Philosophy* 18, no. 1 (2019): 77–90; Chris Fraser, "The Ferryman: Forget the Deeps and Row!," in *Skill and Mastery. Philosophical Stories from the Zhuangzi*, ed. K. Lai and W. W. Chiu (London: Rowman and Littlefield, 2019), 163–81; Youru Wang, "Therapeutic Forgetting and Its Ethical Dimension in the Daoist *Zhuangzi*," *Journal of Chinese Philosophy* 48, no. 4 (2021): 1–16.

32. P. Connerton, "Seven Types of Forgetting," *Memory Studies* 1, no. 1 (2008): 59–71; A. Assmann, *Formen des Vergessens* (Göttingen: Wallstein Verlag, 2016).

33. James Fentress and Chris Wickham, *Social Memory* (Oxford: Blackwell, 1992), 40.

34. J. Candau, *Anthropologie de la mémoire* (Paris: Presses Universitaires de France, 1996).

35. David Schaberg, "Song and the Historical Imagination in Early China," *Harvard Journal of Asiatic Studies* 59, no. 2 (1999): 305–61, esp. 359–60.

36. M. Foucault, *Dits et Écrits, II, 1976–1988* (Paris: Gallimard, 2001), 85.

PART I
HISTORIOGRAPHICAL AND POLITICAL NARRATIVES

Chapter 1

Cultural Amnesia and Commentarial Retrofitting

Interpreting the *Spring and Autumn*

NEWELL ANN VAN AUKEN

It is the passage of time and the forgetting of past norms that make commentaries necessary. Cultural amnesia transforms the past into a foreign country and likewise transforms works composed in bygone eras into alien writings.[1] Just as we read texts composed in other tongues through the interpretive medium of translation, we likewise approach texts written in other historical eras through the hermeneutical lens of commentary. Although commentaries are often conceived of as simply explaining and elaborating on primary texts, telling us what earlier works originally meant, in actuality, one of their major functions is to elucidate works whose meaning has been lost and, in so doing, commentaries infuse old texts with new ideas.[2] A commentary thus adapts an earlier work to a later context, creating a new interpretation that retrofits it to contemporary cultural and linguistic norms, much as translation adapts a source text to a foreign language and culture.

When a work is translated from one language to another, it is inevitably transformed. This transformation—even distortion—is unavoidable because of discrepancies between the language and culture of the source text and those of the receiving context. Writing of the translation process, Lawrence Venuti observes: "The foreign text undergoes a radical transformation in which it comes to support a range of meanings and values that may have little or nothing to do with those it supported in the foreign culture."[3] When a text is transposed from one language and culture to another, it is brought across into a new linguistic and cultural context, populated by people who use different words, have different experiences, and espouse different values; a translation is a text rewritten in a new linguistic and cultural system for new readers, and it must be adapted to suit that system. Commentary differs from translation in that it does not demand semantic or other forms of equivalency—that is, unlike a translation, a commentary does not aim to include components corresponding to every element of the primary text—but it nonetheless entails interpretation, bringing meaning across from one context to another.[4] Rather than bridging two foreign languages, which may exist simultaneously in time, commentaries bring works from the foreign country of the past into the familiar world of the present.

Assumptions of continuity with the past may lead commentators and their readers to believe that a commentary simply offers an accurate explanation to an otherwise inherently puzzling or difficult text. The similarity of the commentarial process to translation may be invisible when an earlier work and a later commentary are (at least ostensibly) written in the same language and when both are part of a single literary and cultural tradition. This is certainly true in the case of members of the orthodox canon of early China together with their commentaries, all written in Classical Chinese and part of a shared tradition.[5] Yet primary text and commentarial interpretation may be separated by several centuries, allowing for considerable change in language use and cultural norms. These differences may not be obvious to us as we look back from the vantage point of millennia later, and readers may be left with the misapprehension that primary text and commentary reflect a single, static, and unvarying values system. Similarly, commentators themselves may also have been unconscious of discrepancies between the norms of their age and those that informed the primary or source text, and they thus may have assumed an unrealistic level of continuity with the past. The assumption of continuity arises when the way things were has been forgotten or is no longer fully understood, and the past is not perceived as a foreign country. This creates room for commentators to interpret texts in ways that are relevant to contemporary meanings and values and to generate explanations that are readily understandable to their contemporaries. As this process occurs, distortion is both inevitable and invisible.

This study examines these issues as they are illustrated by the *Spring and Autumn* (*Chunqiu* 春秋) and two of its earliest extant commentaries, the *Gongyang* 公羊 and *Guliang* 穀梁 traditions. The *Spring and Autumn* is a register of events that was composed in the ancient Chinese state of Lu 魯 from 722 to 481 BCE. It is not a narrative history, but a series of records of individual events arranged chronologically. These records adhered to formal rules, which restricted what types of events could be recorded, along with formal features such as how precisely a record was dated, what main verb was used, how individuals were identified, and, for events involving participants from multiple states, the order in which participants were listed.[6] Over time, the *Spring and Autumn* came to be revered as a "Confucian" classic.[7] According to the orthodox view, no longer widely accepted, Confucius composed or edited its records, and in doing so, used "subtle words" (*weiyan* 微言) to convey "praise and blame" (*baobian* 褒貶). The term "subtle words" refers to the presence of slight variations in phrasing or terminology in the otherwise highly regular records, and "praise and blame" refers to the evaluation of events or actors in the records, evaluations that these terminological variations were presumed to embody. Understanding the connection between the subtle words of the records and the judgments of Confucius on their contents was widely assumed to be difficult or impossible without the assistance of a commentary or teacher, and the *Spring and Autumn* is therefore typically read through the medium of commentaries.[8]

In fact, the formal rules that govern the *Spring and Autumn* records can be identified through analysis of the records themselves, and we may confidently assert that the *Spring and Autumn* was in origin the product of Lu recording practices and cultural norms and not the editorial work of Confucius. The Lu record-keepers left no explanation for the rules and recording conventions they followed in composing the records, nor did they annotate the occasional irregularities, and we are thus unable to determine with complete certainty why, for example, certain types of records were always dated precisely, or why states were listed in the order they were, let alone the reasons for individual irregularities. Nonetheless, it is clear that the rules and recording conventions employed by the record-keepers were inextricably linked to and informed by the religion, culture, and political hierarchy of Lu from the late eighth to early fifth century BCE, the eponymous Spring and Autumn period.

Tremendous changes took place in Chinese culture, religious practice, and sociopolitical structures from the Spring and Autumn period to the late Warring States period (fifth to third century BCE), the earliest date assigned to the *Gongyang* and *Guliang* commentaries.⁹ Although the regular patterns of the *Spring and Autumn* are conspicuous, and the presence of exceptions is undeniable, these patterns and exceptions reflect recording practices that were deeply rooted in cultural norms of an earlier time, cultural norms that apparently had been largely forgotten by the time *Gongyang* and *Guliang* were composed. The combination of remembrance that the patterns of the records were significant, together with "cultural amnesia" resulting in loss of the context that informed those patterns, created a vacuum, a gap that demanded new interpretations. The commentarial explanations for *Spring and Autumn* recording conventions along with deviations from them were an attempt to fill this gap.

Indeed, the *Spring and Autumn* is a perfect example of a text that seems to require a commentary. The orthodox narrative of *Spring and Autumn* composition ascribes it to Confucius, and furthermore claims that in composing or editing it, he used variations in terminology to encode his judgments of events in its records. Confucius's terminological choices were presumed to be hidden and esoteric, and they came to be the subject of dispute among later generations of his followers. The *Shiji* 史記 describes the subsequent transmission of the *Spring and Autumn*, leading up to the composition of one of its early commentaries, the *Zuozhuan* 左傳.

> Seventy disciples received via oral instruction its traditions and meanings,¹⁰ which construed it as having words and phrases that criticized and disparaged, that praised and avoided, and that were suppressed and diminished; this could not be made manifest in writing. The Lu nobleman Zuo Qiuming feared the disciples would all diverge and become extreme, that each would [explain the *Spring and Autumn*] according to his own intent, and that its truth would be lost. Therefore, taking Confucius's historical records as a basis, he discussed all its sayings and completed Mr. Zuo's *Spring and Autumn*.
> 七十子之徒口受其傳指，為有所刺譏褒諱挹損之文辭，不可以書見也。魯君子左丘明懼弟子人人異端，各安其意，失其真。故因孔子史記具論其語，成左氏春秋。(*Shiji* 史記 14.509–10)¹¹

This narrative tells us that subsequent to Confucius's editorial labor, the main points of the *Spring and Autumn* were orally transmitted to the disciples; presumably this refers to teachings that explained the hidden meanings that the records were thought to encode, as the records themselves were transmitted in writing. It asserts that much was not visible in the written records, and the *Shiji* seems to indicate that although the records themselves were written, their latent significance—that is, what they criticized and disparaged, praised and avoided, and suppressed and diminished—was not apparent, and it was out of fear that this would be lost that the *Zuozhuan* was composed.

We may set aside the questions of whether the *Zuozhuan* was in fact compiled by Zuo Qiuming, and what the purpose of its compilation may have been; here I will simply note that I do not deem the assertions in the *Shiji* as likely to be historically accurate. Nonetheless, the preceding passage reflects profound anxiety about the potential disappearance of knowledge and loss of correct understanding of the records. In other early discussions of the composition and transmission of the *Spring and Autumn* too, this anxiety is a pervasive theme.[12] Although words for "remember" and "forget" are nowhere to be found in early writings that trace the history of the *Spring and Autumn* and its commentaries, such narratives are clearly deeply concerned with loss of knowledge, that is, with forgetting, and they depict commentaries as an appropriate measure to counteract that process.

Paradoxically, by the time this anxiety had been articulated, the loss that was so deeply feared had already been realized, and the early significance of the *Spring and Autumn* records had already been forgotten. Although the records did reflect value judgments and priorities, these were the priorities of Lu during the Spring and Autumn period, and not those of Confucius or of commentators who were active later still. The commentators lived in a different world, and by their time the significance of *Spring and Autumn* recording conventions, originally rooted in Lu norms and practices of earlier times, had receded into oblivion. What remained was the memory that the regular patterns of the records along with the subtle variations that departed from them were somehow meaningful. Commentarial interpretations sought to explain the records, but in so doing refocused and transformed the interpretation of the *Spring and Autumn* to bring it into line with the thought and cultural practices of later times.

In the following discussion, I examine this process of transformation by means of two brief case studies, which illustrate ways in which early commentators to the *Spring and Autumn* reanalyzed its patterns and interpreted them through the lens of later times, thereby setting forth new interpretations of an old text. Each case study contrasts the interpretations associated with a single word with patterns of usage in the *Spring and Autumn* records themselves. Obviously, the cultural amnesia that affected early commentators also restricts our understanding of the *Spring and Autumn* records. My proposals regarding the "original sense" of the records are based on analysis of the language and recording system of the *Spring and Autumn*. Our understanding of this text and the context in which it was composed is indisputably incomplete, but at least for the two cases I have chosen, our knowledge is sufficient to illustrate the process of cultural amnesia and interpretive creation at work.

Linguistic Change: The Case of *ji* 及

Neither *Gongyang* nor *Guliang* was written down until centuries after the *Spring and Autumn*, and naturally, language had evolved in the intervening period. It stands to reason that linguistic change had given rise to differences in grammar and lexicon—some substantial—of which commentators were not necessarily aware; dialect variation may also have played a role.[13] When the earlier sense of a word had fallen into disuse, quite naturally, commentators tended to substitute its current and, to them, familiar meaning in their attempts to explain it.[14] But the newer meaning did not always make sense in the original context, and commentators often struggled to reconcile the newer sense of a word with its use in the older record, resulting in explanations that at times seem forced or illogical.

The process of change in meaning has often been noted with respect to key words that express cultural values, such as *ren* 仁 (often translated "humaneness" or "benevolence"), *yi* 義 (rendered with such widely varying terms as "propriety," "justice," and "principle"), *de* 德 ("power" or "virtue"), and so on. Words such as these are culturally bound and freighted with meaning, and the evolution in how they were used and understood is indicative of transformations in norms and values. Language change also applies to less obviously loaded terms, such as simple verbs and grammatical particles, but in these cases, analysis of change is typically restricted to the purview of historical linguists, and the ramifications for intellectual history and the commentarial interpretation of texts remain largely unexplored.

Below I examine how the word *ji* 及 was used in the *Spring and Autumn* together with the ways it was explained in *Gongyang* and *Guliang*. Contrasting the use of *ji* in the *Spring and Autumn* records and its commentaries illustrates the twin processes of cultural amnesia and creative retrofitting at work.[15] In the *Spring and Autumn*, *ji* typically functions as a simple conjunction meaning "and" or "together with," or in battle records, "versus." In the language of the commentaries, *ji* was a full verb, whose primary meaning was "reach, extend to, come up to," and its sense as a conjunction had fallen into disuse, and was perhaps no longer current widely understood. Thus commentators were confronted with the task of explaining instances of *ji* that simply did not parse in their own language; this required them to innovate and inspired interpretations of the *Spring and Autumn* that invoked contemporary norms and thereby generated new ways of understanding the significance of the records.

The *Spring and Autumn* records usually employ *ji* as a grammatical particle, "and" or "with"; in a single, exceptional record, it is a full verb meaning "to catch up to."[16] As a conjunction, *ji* appears in records in which a Lu leader and one (or, less commonly, two) leaders from other states take joint military action or make a covenant together, as here.

> Our Lord and a nobleman of Qi made covenant at Ji.
> 公及齊大夫盟于蔇。(CQ, Zhuang 9.1, 178)

In this and the many similar records, *ji* simply conjoins subjects. In a somewhat more complex pattern, it occurs between opposing coalitions in battle records, as in this record, where it occurs between a list of members of a multistate coalition led by the Jin ruler and the opposing side headed by an unnamed leader of Chu.

> Summer. The fourth month. *Jisi*. The Hou of Jin, Qi troops, Song troops, and Qin troops did battle with the man of Chu at Chengpu.
> 夏。四月。己巳。晉侯、齊師、宋師、秦師及楚人戰于城濮。
> (CQ, Xi 28.4, 448)

Thus in battle records such as the preceding, *ji* serves as a conjunction between two opposing sides, which may comprise a single state or a list of several states.

Less commonly, *ji* conjoins objects, as in these two records, to which we shall return below.

Summer. The fifth month. *Renchen*. The Pheasant Gate and the two lookout towers burned.
夏。五月。壬辰。雉門及兩觀災。(CQ, Ding 2.2, 1528)

Spring. The royal first month. *Wushen*. Du of Song murdered his ruler, Yuyi, and his nobleman, Kongfu.
春。王正月。戊申。宋督弒其君與夷及其大夫孔父。(CQ, Huan 2.1, 83)

The objects it conjoins may be inanimate, as in the buildings that burned, recorded in Ding 2, or may be human, as in the two murder victims of Huan 2.

At this point in the discussion, it is also necessary to note a feature that pertains to all lists in the *Spring and Autumn*, namely, that lists invariably observed hierarchical order, enumerating individuals in order of importance or rank. The Lu ruler was thus mentioned first in any list that included him, and rulers were named before noblemen. Presumably this also applied to buildings or physical objects, such that larger or more important buildings were listed first. This feature applies to all *Spring and Autumn* records with lists, regardless of whether they used the word *ji*, and it is therefore unrelated to the function or meaning of the word *ji*.

Linguistic analysis of *Spring and Autumn* records is unusually straightforward, in large part because of the homogeneous nature of the text and the simplicity of its records. The records are (at least grammatically) unproblematic: they employ lexicon in consistent ways and adhere to regular syntactic patterns. By contrast, the *Gongyang* and *Guliang* commentaries contain a diachronically heterogeneous mixture of features, making linguistic analysis considerably more complex. Because these commentaries were written well after the primary text, their lexical and grammatical usage reflects a different and later stage of the Chinese language. Yet when quoting phrases from the primary text, they may employ words or grammatical patterns in ways that are not representative of the commentators' contemporary usage. The distinction between earlier, "borrowed" linguistic features and those native to the commentators' own language is not marked in the commentary, nor is it necessarily obvious to readers.

If we bear this distinction in mind when examining commentarial passages with *ji*, we discover that its use in the commentaries differs significantly from its use in the records. Specifically, only when quoting the *Spring and Autumn* is *ji* used to mean "and" or "with"; this usage was simply not a feature of the language of *Gongyang* or *Guliang*. More interesting still, commentarial attempts to explain *Spring and Autumn* records with *ji* suggest that the earlier usage was no longer fully understood by the time the commentaries were written, and instead the commentators attempted explain its usage in terms that accorded with the more familiar linguistic rules of their own time.

In the language of the commentaries, *ji* is a full verb, "reach to, extend to," in either a temporal or spatial sense. Examples in *Gongyang* include phrases such as "had not yet come up to the proper time" (*bu ji shi* 不及時) and "did not extend to foreign [states]" (*bu ji wai* 不及外), and in *Guliang*, "did not arrive for the [military] event" (*bu ji shi* 不及事).[17] In both commentaries, the default conjunction was not *ji* but *yu* 與. To some extent, the commentators understood the equivalence between *ji* in the *Spring and Autumn* records and their own word *yu*. Thus *Gongyang* explicitly glosses *ji* in the *Spring and Autumn* as equivalent to *yu* in its own language, and both commentaries occasionally substitute *yu* for *ji* when paraphrasing the *Spring and Autumn*, as here, in reference to Zhuang 9.1, translated above.

> On account of what did the [Lu] lord make covenant with a nobleman?
> 公曷為與大夫盟? (*Gongyang*, Zhuang 9, 7.2b)

Such paraphrasing seems to confirm that both commentaries implicitly understood the basic equivalence of *ji* in the *Spring and Autumn* to *yu* in their own language, yet neither commentary is consistent in treating *ji* as a simple conjunction equivalent to *yu*. Instead, both by default understand it as a verb meaning "reach, extend to (in time or space)" and their comments seek to explain cases in which this default reading obviously does not apply. This can be illustrated most clearly by comments on records in which *ji* conjoins objects.

Gongyang remarks on the fire recorded in Ding 2.2 (translated above) read *ji* as a verb meaning "extend to, reach, arrive at [a location]." This is evident in the assumption, present in both *Gongyang* and *Guliang*, that *ji* by default should refer to the spread of the fire across space, starting in one building and reaching to another.[18] At the same time, the commentaries also agree that the fire began at the lookout towers, which are mentioned after the Pheasant Gate. Thus the facts seem to contradict the anticipated default reading of the record, which in the language of the commentaries should mean "reached the lookout towers." *Gongyang* offers the following explanation:

> Why is it that [the record] says "The Pheasant Gate reaching to (*ji*) the two lookout towers burned"?[19] It was because the two lookout towers were lesser. This being the case, then why did they not say, "The Pheasant Gate burned, and it reached the two lookout towers"? It was because the primary fire was in the two lookout towers. If the primary fire was in the two lookout towers, then why did they mention them afterward?[20] It was because they did not go from lesser reaching to greater.
> 其言「雉門及兩觀災」何? 兩觀微也。 然則曷為不言「雉門災, 及兩觀」? 主災者兩觀也。 時災者兩觀, 則曷為後言之? 不以微及大也。 (Gongyang, Ding 2, 25.4a)

Gongyang recognizes the *Spring and Autumn* convention of identifying the more important entity first; that is, records "did not go from lesser extending to (*ji*) greater." Thus the commentator still appears to understand *ji* as a verb meaning "extend to, reach, arrive at," but rather than interpreting this "reaching to" in a concrete spatial or temporal sense, he reads *ji* as referring to hierarchy, reaching from the more important entity (the Pheasant Gate) to the less important (the lookout towers). It is noteworthy too that *Gongyang* does not attempt to explain this passage with the conjunction *yu*, "and." Instead, the commentary invokes the regular *Spring and Autumn* convention of hierarchical listing order but construes it as a property of the word *ji* rather than an independent feature of all lists. In so doing, *Gongyang* maps its default reading of *ji* as a verb meaning "reach, extend to, come up to [in time or space]"—and also, apparently, in relative rank or importance—onto sentences in which *ji* was simply a conjunction.

The preceding example is a fairly straightforward one, and although we can identify an interpretive shift and reanalysis, according to which *ji* comes to be understood as a verb and hierarchical listing order is attributed to the presence of *ji*, the new interpretation does not require the primary text to support meanings, values, or priorities that it did not originally convey. The *Guliang* interpretation of *Spring and Autumn* record Huan 2.1 (translated above) is somewhat more complex and entails a more substantial interpretive shift. In this record too, *ji* conjoins objects, a ruler and a nobleman, both murder victims. *Guliang* observes that the order in which victims are listed in the record differs from the order in which they were killed and sees this as requiring explanation.

> Given that Kongfu died first, why is it that the record says "*ji*"? Recording the respected reaching to (*ji*) the base is the principle of the *Spring and Autumn*. Why is it that Kongfu died first? Du wanted to murder his ruler but feared not succeeding; thereupon he first killed Kongfu. It was because Kongfu was between them.
> How do we know that he first killed Kongfu? It is said, "When the son has already died, the father cannot bear to declare his name; when the vassal has already died, the lord cannot bear to declare his name." From this we know that the ruler must have followed him. Kong was his lineage. Fu was his style or posthumous name.
> 孔父先死, 其曰「及」何也? 書尊及卑,《春秋》之義也。孔父之先死何也? 督欲弒君而恐不立, 於是乎先殺孔父。孔父閒也。何以知其先殺孔父也? 曰:「子既死, 父不忍稱其名, 臣既死, 君不忍稱其名。」以是知君之累之也。孔, 氏, 父, 字謚也。(*Guliang*, Huan 2, 3.3a)[21]

The opening observation of this passage, that hierarchical listing is a basic principle of the *Spring and Autumn*, is certainly accurate, and if *Guliang* had simply understood *ji* to mean "and," with the "revered" person listed before the "base," no further explanation would have been necessary. Yet the remainder of the remark indicates that *Guliang* takes *ji* to be a verb meaning "reach, come up to," assuming that it normally reflected a temporal or spatial sequence. Thus, *Guliang* expects readers to understand the *Spring and Autumn* record, which mentions the ruler first, as implying a chronological chain of events whereby the assassin first murdered the ruler and then the nobleman. Yet somehow the commentator is also quite certain that this was not the actual sequence of events.[22] He thus goes to great lengths to reconcile this reading with the (to him, contradictory) wording of the record.

The *Guliang* commentary on this record begins, like the *Gongyang* remarks on the progression of the fire, by stating the principle that *ji* did not necessarily indicate a chronological progression but could also indicate reaching from higher to lower rank.[23] Explaining why Kongfu was killed first, it notes the logic of killing the nobleman—the ruler's protector—before the ruler himself. The next question is how we know that Kongfu actually was killed first; that is, what about the wording of the record would indicate this sequence. Here, *Guliang* explains that this is indicated by the form used to designate Kongfu, which does not include his name (*ming* 名), a point that the commentary links to a prohibition on the use of names during mourning, which in turn is explained as the result of an emotional response to bereavement. Presumably, if Kongfu had been killed after his ruler, there would be no need to avoid identifying him by name.

This explanation is, at best, tortuous and far-fetched. While *Spring and Autumn* designations for rulers do vary depending on whether a record concerns an action, a death, or a funeral, noblemen are always referred to by the same form, regardless of whether they are living or dead. Thus Kongfu would have been identified the same way, regardless of when he was killed. Furthermore, many noblemen in the *Spring and Autumn* are referred to with the suffix *-fǔ*, and this does not seem to be a posthumous name, nor is it connected to any sort of taboo or naming prohibition.[24] Yet the earlier meaning of *ji* as simply "and" had been forgotten and displaced by the sense of "reach to [in time]"—a sense that could not easily be reconciled with this record. This obvious incongruity opened up a new interpretive space, which *Guliang* filled with an innovative explanation.

Both *Spring and Autumn* records discussed in this section are completely unremarkable. They use regular, unmarked language and adhere to conventional listing order. *Gongyang* and *Guliang* strive to explain features of the *Spring and Autumn* that they must have found confusing, yet they are misled by the fact that the word *ji* in their language no longer functioned as it did in the *Spring and Autumn*. In interpreting Ding 2.2 concerning the spread of the fire, *Gongyang* reanalyzes *ji* as associated with hierarchical listing order; although the analysis of component parts differs from the original, no new values are imposed on the text. The *Guliang* explanation of Huan 2.1, by contrast, introduces explanations linking the record to naming conventions, mourning practices, and an emotional response to bereavement, shifting focus away from the earlier *Spring and Autumn* preoccupation with hierarchy; in so doing, it interprets the record as embodying values and meanings that may have been prevalent when the commentary was composed but that were not originally present in the text.

Interpretive Change: The Case of *ren* 人

The second case study explores discrepancies in the use of the word *ren* 人, "person," in *Spring and Autumn* records and explanations in the commentaries. In *Spring and Autumn* records, *ren* is employed to refer to individuals who are deliberately left unnamed. This much is agreed on by both commentaries and is consistent with *Spring and Autumn* usage. Where primary text and commentary diverge pertains to the reasons why some individuals are called *ren* instead of being named. The original ramifications of referring to someone as an unnamed *ren* seem to have been lost, and commentators thus filled this gap with new explanations that fit better with contemporary norms and expectations.

Analysis of *Spring and Autumn* records with *ren* demonstrates conclusively that whether an individual was designated *ren* in lists was determined by relative rank.[25] As explained in the preceding section, *Spring and Autumn* records that refer to multiple participants list them in hierarchical order, and if a record mentions the Lu ruler, he is always listed first. More generally, rulers are listed before heirs apparent and noblemen, and within each category (rulers, heirs, and noblemen), individuals are listed in order by state, with higher-ranking states appearing earlier in lists.[26] Individuals designated *ren* consistently appear at the end of lists, occurring after identified individuals. That is, they appear in the position of lowest rank, as illustrated by these two records. In the first example, the rulers (titled Hou and Bo) are listed before named nobility, and the unnamed leaders occur at the end; in the second, named nobility from higher-ranking states are given priority over unnamed individuals from lower-ranking states.

> *Guichou.* Our Lord met with the Hou of Jin, the Hou of Wei, the Bo of Zheng, the Bo of Cao, the Heir Apparent of Song, Cheng, Guo Zuo of Qi, and the man of Zhu to join together in covenant at Qi.
> 癸丑。公會晉侯、衛侯、鄭伯、曹伯、宋世子成、齊國佐、邾人同盟于戚。(CQ, Cheng 15.3, 871)

> Summer. Shu Yi met with Zhao Yang of Jin, Yue Daxin of Song, Beigong Xi of Wei, You Ji of Zheng, the man of Cao, the man of Zhu, the man of Teng, the man of Xue, and the man of Lesser Zhu at Huangfu.

夏。 叔詣會晉趙鞅、宋樂大心、衛北宮喜、鄭游吉、曹人、邾人、滕人、薛人、小邾人于黃父。 (CQ, Zhao 25.3, 1449)

Records like these two, in which individuals from higher-ranking states are identified by title or name and those from lower-ranking states are called *ren*, are typical. The connection between *ren* and low rank relative to others is demonstrated by the regular correlation between *ren* and lower-ranking states together with the relegation of *ren* to the end of ordered lists. It seems highly improbable that Lu record-keepers consistently knew only the identities of leaders from larger, higher-ranking states, but not those from lower-ranking states, and indeed, many of these unnamed *ren* are identified in other texts, including the *Zuozhuan*. This allows us to further conclude that the term *ren* was employed as a means of deliberately excluding the identity of certain individuals. Being identified and thus recognized in the *Spring and Autumn* was associated with prestige, and the word *ren* thus had the dual function of depriving lower-ranking individuals of recognition and of reserving recognition and prestige for those of higher rank, thereby emphasizing their place in the top echelons of the hierarchy.

The *Guliang* commentary shows little awareness of the link between *ren* and hierarchy; to a lesser extent, this is true of *Gongyang* as well. Instead, both commentaries assert that *ren* was used to convey criticism. The notion that the ostensibly neutral word *ren* conveyed criticism is not entirely unreasonable. It is not difficult to imagine how, over time, passively withholding acknowledgment on account of inferior rank could have been reinterpreted as active denial of recognition in order to signal inferiority, and how *ren* could ultimately have come to be understood as outright criticism.

Indeed, just such a transformation is evident in *Gongyang* commentarial remarks concerning *ren*. Instead of understanding *ren* as a means of withholding identification and acknowledgment, *Gongyang* focuses on the word *ren* itself as a derogatory label, asserting that individuals referred to as *ren* were "inferior ones" (*wei zhe* 微者), and that *ren* was employed in order to "criticize" (*bian* 貶).[27] By suggesting that in some records, *ren*, a designation of low rank, was used precisely in order to criticize, these claims obscure the distinction between "criticism" and "low rank." *Gongyang* thus interprets the word *ren* itself to have carried pejorative force. *Guliang* likewise understands the word *ren* as conveying a negative evaluation but, in contrast to *Gongyang*, at times it invokes moral misconduct as the reason for designating a person as *ren*. Thus the word *ren* underwent a transformation from a word used as a method of passively withholding identification to a designation with actively negative or critical intent.

This is illustrated by the *Guliang* remarks on the following record:

> Winter. Our Lord and the man of Qi hunted at Zhuo.[28]
> 冬。公及齊人狩于禚。 (CQ, Zhuang 4.7, 162)

The *Guliang* commentary identifies the unnamed individual as the Qi ruler. Curiously, it not only assumes that *ren* carries pejorative force but further asserts that by designating an individual who is listed together with the Lu ruler as *ren*, the record is implicitly critical of the Lu ruler.[29]

> "The man of Qi" refers to the Hou of Qi. Why did [the record] say *ren*? In debasing the counterpart of the [Lu] lord, they thereby debased the [Lu] lord. On account of what did they debase the [Lu] lord? Since he did not take revenge for his grudge, his hatred was not dispelled. The record derided him for not dispelling his hatred.
> 齊人者,齊侯也。其曰「人」,何也?卑公之敵,所以卑公也。何為卑公也?不復讎而怨不釋。刺釋怨也。 (*Guliang*, Zhuang 4, 5.7a–b)

When viewed in light of the regular conventions governing *Spring and Autumn* use of *ren*, at first glance, the claims set forth in *Guliang* may seem utterly nonsensical. As explained in the preceding section, regular patterns of usage in the *Spring and Autumn* demonstrate that the word *ren* was employed because of the hierarchically low position of the individual whose identity it concealed; apparently, its primary function was to withhold recognition from the person called *ren*. At the same time, use of *ren* also permitted the records to avoid explicitly listing lower-ranking individuals together with those of higher rank, perhaps out of respect for those of higher rank.[30] Thus, the designation *ren* certainly did not denigrate others in the same list who were identified, as the *Guliang* commentary suggests; to the contrary, it called attention to the fact that the identified persons (in contrast to the unnamed *ren*) were accorded recognition, thereby affirming their high position.

Just as astonishing is the assertion that the target of criticism is none other than the Lu ruler. The *Spring and Autumn* records are overwhelmingly devoted to displaying the high-ranking position of the Lu ruler and to concealing instances in which the Lu ruler or the Lu state was placed in a subordinate or inferior position.[31] That a record in the *Spring and Autumn* would aim to undercut the ruler's position at the pinnacle of the hierarchy is unlikely in the extreme. The commentary does not make its reasoning explicit, but we may speculate that underlying this surprising claim is the assumption that Lord Zhuang's 莊公 conduct warranted criticism. The commentator expected to read the record as derisive, but at the same time, he also realized that the Lu ruler himself could not be openly criticized, nor could Lu rulers be referred to as *ren*. He thus interpreted this record, in which the ruler was listed together with a person designated *ren*, as conveying oblique criticism of the Lu ruler. The connection between using *ren* to withhold recognition and thereby emphasizing the Lu ruler's high place in the hierarchy had been lost, which in turn permitted a reanalysis whereby the pejorative force of *ren* could be transferred to the Lu ruler.

It is worth asking why *Guliang* assumed that the Lu ruler deserved to be criticized. The commentary alludes to a feud between Lord Zhuang and the Qi ruler, but we must turn to the *Shiji* for a full account.[32] The ruler in question was Lord Xiang of Qi 齊襄公. Lord Xiang was considered an enemy, since he had been involved in an incestuous liaison with his own half-sister and Lord Zhuang's mother, Lady Jiang 姜, and he had conspired with her to murder her husband and Lord Zhuang's father, Lord Huan of Lu 魯桓公. *Guliang* evidently blamed Lord Zhuang for not taking revenge on his father's assassin, and thus asserted that he deserved derision (*ci* 刺). That this interpretation was flawed was not at all obvious to the *Guliang* commentators. Indeed, to them, what must have been most conspicuous was that *ren* had a negative connotation and that Lord Zhuang, by hunting together with his father's murderer, had engaged in shockingly immoral conduct. The imperative for a son to exact revenge for wrongs against his father was certainly a deeply held value by the time *Guliang* was written.[33] Yet it is far from clear that this view was current as early as the Spring and Autumn period; when the *Spring and Autumn* was composed, concealing the ruler's flaws in order to preserve the dignity of his lofty position appears to have been a higher priority. The priorities that led to the use of *ren*, namely, the profound reverence for rulers in contrast to those of lower rank together with the deep-set prohibition on acknowledging the Lu ruler's shortcomings, had been displaced by a different set of norms.

The *Guliang* claims about the implications of *ren* in Zhuang 4 certainly suggest that by the time the commentary was composed, the principles and conventions that originally governed the use of *ren* were no longer fully understood, but we should not regard these claims as complete nonsense. Rather, they emerged from a mixture of cultural amnesia and uneven remembrance. Cultural amnesia had wiped away the priorities underlying the recording practices associated with *ren* together with the prohibition on criticizing the Lu ruler; more generally, the system of values and hierarchy underlying the *Spring and Autumn* itself had been consigned to oblivion. At the same time, tenuous memory of the linkage between *ren* and inferior status—a linkage that, to some extent, was visible in the records—provided a direction for interpreting records using *ren*. This mixture of forgetting and remembrance permitted commentators to generate new interpretations of records that corresponded to and reinforced the values of their own time.

Conclusions

In the opening section of this paper, I cited Lawrence Venuti's comments on translation, which are worth revisiting now. Venuti observed that a translated text supports "meanings and values that may have little or nothing to do with those it supported in the foreign culture." He describes this process at greater length elsewhere.

> Any literary work is a complicated artifact that supports meanings, values, and functions specific to its originary language and culture. During the translation process, however, it is dismantled, disarranged, and finally displaced, so that the translated text, even while maintaining a semantic correspondence, comes to support meanings, values, and functions that are specific to the translating language and culture—and most likely new to the source text.[34]

The transformation Venuti describes is not deliberate on the part of the translator. These new "meanings, values, and functions" are inscribed onto a text simply by virtue of using a new language, whose words and phrases have different histories and bear different connotations from those of the "originary language."

Venuti's remarks concern translation, a process of linguistic "bringing across" in which the source language and translating language are foreign to one another. This study focuses on commentary, not translation, and one might argue that the comparison to translation is not apt, since the commentaries I examine remain within the same linguistic and cultural tradition and are separated instead by time. Indeed, the language of the *Spring and Autumn* records (composed from the eighth to fifth century BCE) and that of the *Gongyang* and *Guliang* commentaries (probably no earlier than the third century BCE) may be considered similar enough to obviate the need for a "translation." At the same time, changes to cultural norms and values had altered expectations of what the original text might mean and had generated room for misunderstanding, and this in turn required explanation; these explanations took the form of commentaries.

A commentary differs from a translation in that it seeks to unpack the meaning of the original text by defining, paraphrasing, explaining, and offering additional background information or historical detail, whereas a translation aims to present the primary text in a different language. In contrast to a translation, a commentary does not displace the original text but augments and supports it. Yet translations and commentaries both impose new values on a text. The very nature of the *Spring and Autumn*, a text that employed highly regular patterns and that deliberately used conspicuous deviations from those patterns to convey meanings and values, left it in particular need of commentarial support. At the same time, the absence of any explanations for the regular phrasing of the records, combined with the memory that they reflected value judgments, left the *Spring and Autumn* peculiarly susceptible to cultural amnesia and commentarial retrofitting.

The two cases I have explored in this study both involve words whose meaning or significance in the *Spring and Autumn* had been lost by the time the commentaries were written. Consequently, records with these words no longer made sense, or perhaps were perceived as defying contemporary norms, and thus required commentarial explanation. In the first case, we saw that the word *ji* was understood as a verb meaning "reaching to" in a temporal sense, and the *Guliang* commentary had to go to great lengths to justify its claim that, contrary to contemporary expectations, the nobleman Kongfu had died before his ruler. Yet the commentary did not give what to us might seem like the simplest and most obvious explanation, that in the language of the *Spring and Autumn* records, *ji* was a conjunction rather than a verb. Instead, the commentary invoked the grief of bereavement and prohibitions on posthumous use of names and in so doing, inscribed new values and norms onto the records. The prohibition cited by the commentary was not consistent with use of names in the *Spring and Autumn* records, but was new to the text, as was the claim that the prohibition itself, like the phrasing of the record, was governed by grief—finding it "unbearable to declare" the name of the deceased. Similarly, the word *ren* was employed by the records to withhold recognition from those of lower rank, whereas both *Gongyang* and *Guliang* reanalyzed it as pejorative, and *Guliang* took the further step of asserting that it was employed to convey oblique criticism of the Lu ruler. The very notion of criticizing the Lu ruler was alien to the *Spring and Autumn*, and although the conduct for which he was allegedly disparaged was utterly despicable according later norms, it may not have been as troubling in earlier times. Both of these brief case studies thus explore instances in which the values that originally informed certain records had been wiped away by the passage of time, and the commentaries endeavor to make sense of these records and to reconcile their wording with contemporary expectations.

L. P. Hartley was correct in describing the past as a foreign country: as he observed, "they do things differently there."[35] As the gulf between present and past widens, the way they did things in the "there" of the past fades, and the reasons that they did things that way are lost and fall into oblivion. It is this process that transforms the past into a "foreign country," a place whose culture and values have become alien to denizens of the present age and hence require explanation.

Notes

1. The famous observation "The past is a foreign country" is the opening line of L. P. Hartley's novel, *The Go-Between* (New York: Avon Books, 1971 [orig. pub. 1953]), 11. I owe the phrase "cultural amnesia" to Piotr Michalowski, "Commemoration, Writing, and Genre in Ancient Mesopotamia," in *The Limits of Historiography: Genre and Narrative in Ancient Historical Texts*, ed. Christina Shuttleworth Kraus (Leiden, Boston, Köln: Brill, 1999), 88.

2. See for example the remarks of Glenn Most, who writes that "one function of a commentary is to (re-)confirm, (re-)distribute, and (re-)impose within a society an authority whose meaning is no longer entirely self-evident. The authority in question would not need a commentary if it were completely

self-explanatory (for then its words would suffice for itself)"; Glenn W. Most, Preface, *Commentaries—Kommentare* (Göttingen: Vandenhoeck & Ruprecht, 1999), x.

3. Lawrence Venuti, "Translation, Interpretation, Canon Formation," in *Translation and the Classic: Identity as Change in the History of Culture*, ed. Alexandra Lianeri and Vanda Zajko (Oxford: Oxford University Press, 2008), 27–51, 30.

4. For a helpful discussion of various types of equivalency in translation, see Eugene Nida, "Principles of Correspondence," in *The Translation Studies Reader*, ed. Lawrence Venuti (New York and London: Routledge, 2000), 126–40.

5. J. Marshall Unger has insightfully noted the peculiar role of the Chinese writing system in masking the difference in earlier and later written works; see Unger, *Ideogram: Chinese Characters and the Myth of Disembodied Meaning* (Honolulu: University of Hawai'i Press, 2004), 6.

6. For discussion of recording conventions and patterns, see Newell Ann Van Auken, "Could 'Subtle Words' Have Conveyed 'Praise and Blame'? The Implications of Formal Regularity and Variation in *Spring and Autumn (Chūn Qiū)* Records," *Early China* 31 (2007, published 2010): 47–111; see too Van Auken, *Spring and Autumn Historiography: Form and Hierarchy in Ancient Chinese Annals* (New York: Columbia University Press, 2023).

7. I acknowledge the highly fraught nature of the word "Confucian," which I use simply to designate those texts that are traditionally claimed to have been composed or edited by Confucius or to have been used by him in instructing his followers.

8. That the *Spring and Autumn* was considered to demand commentarial support is evident from the difficulty of finding an edition of the text without a commentary. In modern times the *Spring and Autumn* is always printed together with at least one of three major commentarial traditions; it probably ceased to circulate as an independent text by the Song dynasty if not earlier. The two late imperial editions of the *Spring and Autumn* without commentary—one prepared by Mao Qiling 毛奇齡 (1623–1716) and the other by Duan Yucai 段玉裁 (1735–1815)—were extracted from editions with commentaries and do not represent continuous transmissions.

9. For an overview of the complex issue of *Gongyang* and *Guliang* dates, see Zhao Boxiong 趙伯雄, *Chunqiu xue shi* 春秋學史 (Jinan: Shandong jiaoyu, 2004), 54–58; see too Göran Malmqvist, "Studies on the *Gongyang* and *Guuliang* Commentaries, Part II," *Bulletin of the Museum of Far Eastern Antiquities* 43 (1975): 19–69, esp. 22.

10. An equally tenable translation would be "transmitted meanings."

11. Sima Qian 司馬遷 (ca. 145–ca. 86 BCE), *Shiji* (Beijing: Zhonghua shuju, [1959] 2002), 14.509–10.

12. See also *Hanshu*, "Yi wen zhi" 藝文志 (Treatise on Arts and Letters), 30.1701, 1715, and 1723.

13. The *Spring and Autumn* was a Lu text, but the "Yi wen zhi" states that Master Gongyang (公羊子) was from the state of Qi 齊; see *Hanshu* 30.1713; see also Zhao Boxiong, *Chunqiu xue shi*, 36.

14. Writing of translation, Eugene Eoyang remarks that "in understanding something new, isn't the first instinct to relate it to something old and familiar?"; Eoyang, "The Maladjusted Messenger: Rezeptionsästhetik in Translation," *Chinese Literature: Essays, Articles, Reviews* (CLEAR) 10, no. 1/2 (1988): 61–80, 73; and in discussing interpretation of another classic, the *Changes*, Geoffrey Redmond and Tze-ki Hon comment on "common patterns of misinterpretation that arise on first encounter with unfamiliar ideas," and note that "Initial efforts at comprehension often construe the new as variants of what is already known"; Geoffrey Redmond and Tze-ki Hon, *Teaching the I Ching (Book of Changes)* (Oxford: Oxford University Press, 2014), 197.

15. For a full discussion and analysis of all patterns using *ji* 及 in the *Spring and Autumn*, approached through the rubric of historical linguistics rather than commentary studies, see Newell Ann Van Auken, "*Spring and Autumn* Use of *Jí* 及 and Its Interpretation in the *Gōngyáng* and *Gǔliáng* Commentaries," in *Studies in Chinese and Sino-Tibetan Linguistics: Dialect, Phonology, Transcription and Text* 漢語與漢藏語研究：方言、音韻與文獻, ed. Richard VanNess Simmons and Newell Ann Van Auken (Taipei: Institute of Linguistics, Academia Sinica, 2014), 429–56.

16. For this unique record, see *CQ*, Xi 僖 26.3, 437. Here and throughout, references to individual *Spring and Autumn* records are keyed to Yang Bojun 楊伯峻, ed. and comm., *Chunqiu Zuo zhuan zhu* 春秋左傳注 (rpt. Taipei: Fuwen, [1981] 1991). They are marked *CQ* and designated by ruler, year, and entry number, using Yang Bojun's numbering scheme, followed by the corresponding page number.

17. *Chunqiu Gongyang zhuan He shi jiegu* 春秋公羊傳何氏解詁, He Xiu 何休 (129–82), comm., *Sibu beiyao* 四部備要 (SBBY) ed., (hereafter *Gongyang*), Wen 9, 13.13b; Zhao 22, 23.9a; and Xi 1, 10.1b–2a; and *cf.* Yin 1.1, 1.5b–6b. For comparison, see *Chunqiu Guliang zhuan Fan shi jijie* 春秋穀梁傳范氏集解, Fan Ning 范甯 (339–401), comm., SBBY ed., (hereafter *Guliang*), Yin 1, 1.3a–b. The word *ji* also occurs in the compound *leiji* 累及, meaning "implicate, involve," but does not have this sense when used alone.

18. *Guliang* likewise tries to justify the fact that the record does not reflect the chronological progression of the fire, proposing that the Pheasant Gate was mentioned first out of respect; see *Guliang*, Ding 2, 19.4a.

19. Here and elsewhere, I have translated quotations of *Spring and Autumn* records as the commentators seem to have understood them, and not as I believe they were originally intended to be read.

20. This translation follows Qing commentator Chen Li 陳立 (1809–1869), reading *shi* 時 as an error for *zhu* 主; see Chen Li, *Gongyang yishu* 公羊義疏, SBBY ed., 4:69.2b–3a.

21. For another translation, see Malmqvist, "Studies," part I, 96.

22. It is not clear why the commentators believed that the nobleman Kongfu was murdered first, just as it is uncertain why they believed that the fire progressed from the lookout towers to the Pheasant Gate. We may surmise that the commentators had access to other material that included accounts of these events, although they do not cite the authority of other sources. The murders of Song ruler Yuyi and nobleman Kongfu are recounted in the *Zuozhuan*; see Yang Bojun, *Chunqiu Zuo zhuan zhu*, Huan 2, 85; the fire at the Pheasant Gate and lookout towers is not.

23. For other remarks that read *ji* as indicating sequence from revered to base (尊及卑), see *Guliang*, Zhuang 12, 5.15b; Xi 10, 8.5b; Xi 30, 9.15a; and Ding 11, 19.13b.

24. The suffix *fu* 父 (read third tone and sometimes written 甫) is an honorific suffix added to a male name; it does not mean "father" (*fu*), written with the same character but read fourth tone in modern Mandarin. *Guliang* elsewhere glosses it as "A beautiful designation for a male" (男子之美稱也); Yin1, 1.2a. Zheng Xuan's 鄭玄 annotations on the phrase 某甫 are similar; see *Yi li zhushu* 儀禮注疏, SBBY ed., "Shi guan li" 士冠禮 3.5b.

25. For discussion, see Newell Ann Van Auken, "Who Is a *rén* 人? The Use of *rén* in *Spring and Autumn* Records and Its Interpretation in the *Zuǒ*, *Gōngyáng*, and *Gǔliáng* Commentaries," *Journal of the American Oriental Society* 131, no. 4 (December 2011): 555–90, esp. 559–66. Although *ren* has been incorrectly translated as plural by James Legge and others, early commentaries concur in understanding *ren* as referring to an individual, and this understanding is corroborated by the fact that in *Zuozhuan* narratives corresponding to *Spring and Autumn* records, the *ren* of the records are consistently identified as individuals, not groups.

26. For the sequence of states in the *Spring and Autumn*, see Van Auken, "Subtle Words," 89–90; see too chapter 4 of Van Auken, *Spring and Autumn Historiography*, especially 110–113.

27. Numerous *Gongyang* passages link *ren* to "*bian*"; examples include Zhuang 30, 9.3b–4a; Xi 27, 12.6a–b; Xi 28, 12.8a; Xi 28, 12.10a–12a; Xi 33, 12.16b–17b; Wen 7, 13.9b–10a; Wen 14, 14.6b–7a; Xuan 11, 16.3a–b; Xuan 15, 16.7b–9a; and Ding 1, 25.1b–2a. The term *ren* is identified with *wei zhe* in *Gongyang*, Yin 8, 3.9b; Zhuang 4, 6.7b–8a; Zhuang 6, 6.9a; Xi 28, 12.8a; Xi 33, 12.16b–17b; and Xiang 30, 21.10ab.

28. The *Zuo* version of the *Spring and Autumn* (cited here) has Zhuo 樣, while the *Guliang* version has Gao 郜; see *Guliang*, Zhuang 4, 5.7a–b.

29. Two other commentarial passages that claim that *ren* applies to someone other than the person so designated are *Guliang*, Zhuang 5, 5.7b–8a and Xi 27, 9.10a–b; the first of these (like the passage discussed here) also applies to the Lu ruler.

30. The *Zuozhuan* sets forth just such an interpretation of several records with *ren*; see *Zuo*, Wen 2, 526; Xiang 8, 956; and Xiang 26, 1115–16; for discussion see Newell Ann Van Auken, *The Commentarial Transformation of the Spring and Autumn* (Albany: State University of New York Press, 2016), 70–72.

31. This is indicated not only by the placement of Lu leaders at the beginning of lists, but further by the tendency to omit records of Lu's battlefield defeats, and to record murders of Lu rulers—certainly the ultimate subjugation and humiliation—as natural deaths.

32. *Shiji* 33.1530; see also *Gongyang*, Huan 1, 5.14a–15a.

33. *Liji jijie* 禮記集解, ed. and comm. Sun Xidan 孫希旦 (b. 1736) (Taipei: Wenshizhe, 1990), "Qu li (shang)" 曲禮上, 87; and "Tan gong (shang)" 檀弓上, 200.

34. Lawrence Venuti, "Hijacking Translation: How Comp Lit Continues to Suppress Translated Texts," *boundary 2* 43, no. 2 (2016), 182.

35. Hartley, *The Go-Between*, 11.

Chapter 2

Elision and Narration
Remembering and Forgetting in Some Recently Unearthed Historiographical Manuscripts

Rens Krijgsman

Before the finds (archaeological or otherwise) of historiographical manuscript-texts from the Warring States period, our study of the Chinese past was informed to a great extent by selections made in and leading up to the early empires. This selection of canonical and related materials was by no means absolute or necessarily enforced by institutions. The *Shiji* 史記, for example, often contains multiple renditions of events in the ancient past and many texts escaped the acts of censorship-cum-canon formation that characterized the early empires' attempt at controlling the narrative. Nonetheless, with recent discoveries, many texts have emerged that speak to pasts remembered differently. The selection processes of remembering and forgetting such narratives play out on different levels,

---

This article is a preliminary result of the project "Western Dissemination and Research of Chinese Unearthed Texts" 中國出土文獻的西方傳播與研究 (G1817) supported by the "Paleography and Chinese Civilization Inheritance and Development Program" 古文字與中華文明傳承發展工程. I would like to thank Albert Galvany, Newell Ann Van Auken, and the anonymous reviewers for their careful reading and helpful comments.

from individual authors, to textual communities, to institution and state-backed enterprises.

But how are memories turned into narrative? Remembering and forgetting represent two sides of a process of selection.[1] Memories of events relevant to the individual or group are preserved and amplified, and others are discarded, downplayed, or merely referred to. Relevance here is shorthand for meaning: selections and arrangements of events in time construct narratives that speak to (and inform) our identity, describe (and to an extent, prescribe) our place in the world, or allow us to explain the reasons why and how something happened.[2] This process of selection and meaning construction plays out in the neurology of individual memory, and governs the narratives that bind people together in larger groups and cultures.[3] In this process of remembering and forgetting, narrative structures time and integrates different forms of discourse, it informs (and is informed by) the way we construct the past. As Brockmeier summarizes: "our ability to localize ourselves in time and history—and this may be one of the basic functions of memory—seems to be grounded, both sociogenetically and ontogenetically, in narrative discourse. [. . .] Insofar as the emergence of cultural memory, that is, historical consciousness, is concerned, narrative is essential in connecting other forms of discourse and symbolic mediation, and integrating them into the symbolic space of a culture."[4] Aleida Assmann has argued that these selections influence the construction of canon and archive on an institutional level, wherein texts and the possibility of memory are either foregrounded or consigned to storage.[5] As I show in this paper, this was not always a smooth or programmatic process and not all memories are narrated equally. And while storytelling influences the selection of what to remember and what to forget, this selection is in itself burdened with the weight of tradition in the form of previous selections.

In this study, I focus on the very dynamic of selection as it shows in individual texts. By examining the narration of reference, amplification and elision, time, and focalization, I analyze the specific means through which narratives select, amplify, elide and organize memories in order to form meaningful selections to their recipients. In particular, I examine two looted manuscripts carrying narratives about the ancient and the near past, the Shanghai Museum's *Rongchenshi* 容成氏 and Qinghua University's **Xinian* 繫年.[6]

The *Rongchengshi*

The *Rongchengshi* is a philosophical-historiographical manuscript-text covering a time span from legend up to the historical founding kings Wen 文 (1099/56–1050) and Wu 武 (1049/45–1043) of the Western Zhou 周 (1045–771 BCE).[7] The manuscript in its current form is incomplete, several slips are broken and some are missing altogether. As a result, many different reconstructions have been advanced, and certain disputed sections aside, we now have a good grasp of the general structure and program of the text.[8] It is written in Warring States Chu 楚 script on 53 bamboo slips with the title written on the back of slip 53.[9]

The narrative can be divided into four distinctly structured epochs composed of seven self-contained units: (1) the pre-Yao monarchs; the cycle of the three sovereigns, (2) Yao 堯, (3) Shun 舜, and (4) Yu 禹; two dyads of good and bad rulers, (5) Kings Jie 桀 and Tang 湯, and (6) Zhou 紂 and Wen; and (7) King Wu's conquest of the Shang 商. Each of these sections can be structurally divided up to the sentence level, which will be discussed below. Key to the text's structure is that the divisions in the narrative are clearly indicated using temporal markers and formula introducing and concluding the respective period. The periods themselves are linked by connecting formula and even individual events within the text are tightly linked together using connectives. As a result, the narrative reads as a continuous whole, creating the rhetorical illusion that every event, from minor clash or innovation, to changes in rule and epoch are all intimately connected through a series of causal steps. But this interconnectedness belies the fact that vast tracts of time are passed over. Because much of the narrative is the stuff of legend, no absolute time frame can be provided. Heuristically speaking, the roughly 2,300 characters of the text can be said to span the equivalent of the period from the Neolithic to the Bronze Age.[10] It goes without saying that selections had to be made in order to fit such a vast time-span into a single coherent narrative.

The principal rationale behind this coherence comes from a philosophical program in the narrative aimed at promoting abdication while at the same time showing a decline in the virtue of governance over the ages. Where the legendary rulers could practice a type of laissez-faire governance with smooth rule transfers through abdication, later epochs see increasingly oppressive forms of government intervention and more violent forms of strife and war. To illustrate how the text realizes the selection and organization of material forming such a narrative, I will focus here on the legendary pre-Yao period in particular.

> [In days of yore, when Rongchengshi . . . Zun]lushi, Hexushi, Qiaojieshi, Cangjieshi, Xuanyuanshi, Shennongshi, Hang X shi, Lubishi ruled the realm, they each did not pass on their rule to their sons but gave it to the worthy. Their virtue was clear and meritorious, and they elevated care; their government was ordered yet they did not use rewards; they bestowed office but did not confer titles; they did not exert upon the people and tirelessly brought order to chaos. This is why they are called worthy. When Datingshi ruled the realm, he cared deeply and took little; he exerted himself to work for the people; and involved himself to exercise governance. Thereupon titles and emoluments where established for the first time. He abdicated the realm to Youyu Tong, Youyu Tong said: "Virtue has quickly deteriorated!" Thereupon, he did not reward or fine; he did not punish or kill; in the states there were no hungry people, and on the roads there were none who had died of unnatural causes. High and low, noble and base, everybody found what suited them. Those beyond the four seas visited, those within came to court. Bird and beast came in audience, and fish and turtle paid tribute. Youyu Tong corrected the government of the realm for nineteen years and ruled the realm, after thirty-seven years he died.
>
> [昔者容成氏 . . . 尊]盧氏、赫胥氏、喬結氏、倉頡氏、軒轅氏、神農氏、杭丨氏、墉運氏之有天下也, 皆不授其子而授賢。其德酋 (獸) 清, 而尚愛, (1) 其政治而不賞, 官而不爵, 無勉於民, 而治亂不倦, 故曰賢。及囗[大?]¹¹ (43) 囗 [盈 (庭)]氏之有天下, 厚愛而薄斂焉, 身力以勞百姓, (35B) 入奴 {安} (焉) ¹²以行政。於是乎始爵而行祿。以讓於有虞迵, 有虞迵曰: "德速衰 (32) 矣"。¹³ 於是乎不賞不罰, 不刑不殺, 邦無飢人, 道路無殤 (4) 死者。上下貴賤, 各得其宜。四海之外賓, 四海之內廷。¹⁴禽獸朝, 魚鼈獻, 有虞迵匡天下之政十又九年而王天下, 三十有七 (5) 年而歿¹⁵終。

Even in this short section, various techniques are used to narrate the passing of time and the relations between events. In its present state, the text opens with a list of legendary rulers, some of whom are known from received tradition, such as Xuanyuan 軒轅 and Shennong 神農; others are not previously known.[16] Because all members of the list are bestowed the same quality, the text is able to compress time and quickly incorporate a range of rulers to make a key point: this legendary period was conceived of as a utopia. The rulers did not have to make any effort, they did not need to labor or tax the people, and merit did not need to be stimulated by title or reward. In this idealized meritocracy, rule was passed on to the worthy and not by primogeniture—setting the standard and the philosophical agenda for the rest of the text. By comparison, when the *Shiji* 史記 narrates the same era, rulers are linked together in a complex lineage narrative aimed at providing a single heritage for the empire ruled by the Han, and any figures outside of this narrative receive less or no attention.[17]

Because the focus of the *Rongchengshi* is on the virtuous character of this utopic age and the subsequent decline in later ages, different figures are remembered. For example, two figures are narrated to contrast explicitly with the utopic period. Datingshi 大庭氏 is presented as the first ruler to break the pattern: he personally had to involve himself (i.e., meddle with the ideal state of affairs) in order to motivate the people. At this point, the text credits him with the invention of the system of rank and emoluments. By marking it as a historical first, the invention is singled out as a turning point in the narrative. The narrative immediately voices its disapproval through Youyu Tong 有虞迵, a scion of the Youyu clan (from which Shun is supposed to hail). This ruler, previously unknown from tradition, is the first to be given a voice in the text. Curtly he pronounces that virtue has degraded—the idea of decline runs throughout the text—after which his rule is presented as again reverting to older practice.

Of interest here is that the *Rongchengshi* includes exactly those figures that are (largely) forgotten in other narratives.[18] Rulers such as Youyu Tong are therefore not burdened by the weight of tradition and present a blank slate used to inscribe core qualities into the memory of the period as figureheads for the text's argumentative program. In the process, the speed of narration slows down. Youyu Tong's length of reign and life are specified and he is given a voice, focusing the narrative on the level of the individual ruler instead of the broad strokes describing a whole epoch. Throughout the *Rongchengshi*, such shifts in narrative pace and focus are used to control the selection of story matter. Where the list skips through large swathes of time (and potential memory), presenting instead a set of generic qualities, detailed descriptions of figures like Youyu Tong allow the narrative to introduce key qualities and set up turning points and causal links in the story. The narrative that follows presents the well-known cycle of the three emperors—Yao, Shun, and Yu. The specification of Youyu Tong's time of death allows the narrative to present a natural transition between the rulers by suggesting a seamless, causal, connection in time without actually making it explicit. Furthermore, by providing a rarely detailed instance of an origin story for the rule of Yao,[19] highlighting his slow emergence from a small fief to general recognition and final establishment as emperor by the people in the realm (the merit-based overtones of the story providing a functional equivalent to the abdication script presented earlier), the narrative further smooths over any potential hesitance in accepting this link.

> In days of yore Yao resided between Danfu and Diaoling, he gave generously and regularly offered in thanks to the spirits, he did not encourage yet the people labored, he did not punish or kill yet there were no thieves and villains, he was very lenient and yet the people adhered. Thereupon, those within a hundred miles (*li* 里) were under his lead, and the people of the realm came to him, they revered and established him as if he were the son of heaven. Thereupon, [it extended up to] everything within a thousand miles. Thereupon, he held the plaque and stood up straight, the four directions turned to him in harmony, and he was welcoming so that the people from the realm came to him. [. . .] thereupon the people of the realm considered Yao to be excellent at raising worthies, and in the end established him as their ruler.
> 昔堯處於丹府與藋陵之間，堯散施而時時賽，[20]不勸而民力，不刑殺而無盜賊，甚寬而民服。於是乎方(6)百里之中率，天下之人就，奉而立之，以爲天子。於是乎方圓千里，於是乎持板正立，四向委[21]和，懷以來天下之民。(7) [. . .] 於是乎天下之人，以 (11) 堯為善興賢, 而卒立之。(13)

This section, shortened here in the interest of space, provides one of the most detailed memories yet for the early years of Yao's reign. The narrative is segmented in gradual causal steps (using *yu shi hu* 於是乎 "thereupon") from his rule over a hundred and then a thousand miles, following his quest for worthies, up to his eventual establishment as son of heaven. Other narratives that provide an origin for Yao at all tend to single out that he was born to Diku 帝嚳, leaving detailed description for his time as son of heaven. The detailed description given to Yao in the *Rongchengshi* (the narrative goes on further to describe how he went looking for worthies before settling on Shun) stands in strong contrast to the rather parsimonious and ad hoc treatment given to the classical bad rulers in the narrative.

In treating the period between the legendary ruler and flood controller Yu up to the rise of the wicked Jie, for example, several devices are employed to quickly pass over absolute time (albeit legendary) in favor of narrative time. In the space of a few lines, the story presents Yu's failed abdication to Gaoyao 皋陶 and Yi 益, the usurpation by his son Qi 啓, up to the sudden rise of Jie sixteen generations later. These events all contain the seeds for action-packed stories filled with strife—as indeed explored in other texts,[22] but the *Rongchengshi* chooses to elide these aspects in order to quickly fast-forward to the appearance of the tyrant Jie.

> Yu had five sons, but did not make them his successors. He saw Gaoyao's worthiness and wanted him to become his successor. Gaoyao then abdicated five times to the worthies of the realm, after which he called in sick, no longer came out in public and died. Thereupon Yu abdicated to Yi, Qi thereupon attacked Yi and took [the realm] for himself. Qi ruled the realm and after sixteen generations Jie arose.
> 禹有子五人，不以其子為後，見 (33) 皋陶之賢也，而欲以為後。皋陶乃五讓以天下之賢者，遂稱疾不出而死。禹於是乎讓益，啓於是乎攻於益自取。(34) [啓]王天下十有六年<世>[23] 而桀作。(35a)

The first half of this short passage is formulaic. The same formula wherein the sons are passed over in favor of a worthy minister, who in turn tries to refuse before finally accepting the realm, is also used to describe the transfer between Yao and Shun, and between Shun and Yu. Here the abdication fails and the rule is usurped. The elision of anything that might have occurred in the sixteen generations from Qi to Jie again suggests a form of causality between the failed abdication and the later rise of the tyrant Jie. Such a reading is favored by the text's argument for decline over the ages, moving further away from the ideal of abdication and rule by virtue. The use of formulae is likewise a form of elision, similar to the time-skips, it allows the narrative to get rid of any detail that would draw the audience away from this main point. These selections in what to remember and what to forget are therefore programmatic and serve a narrative and philosophical point. This approach is by no means unique, and other texts amplify and elide different elements to make their respective points.[24]

In short, the *Rongchengshi* both elides and amplifies different memories in order to create a seemingly continuous and causal narration of events. Temporal markers are used cleverly to introduce first occurrences, which in turn are employed productively to steer the narrative toward other linked events. This control of pace, alternating between thicker and thinner description, allows the text to frame all its events as if they were leading up to a grand narrative of gradual decline from the ideal of abdication.

*Xinian

Where the *Rongchengshi* uses legendary and historical stories to advance a philosophical agenda, the *Xinian deals with historical events only, albeit with their own historiographical biases. As will become clear below, while the *Xinian uses many of the same tools of elision and expansion to form narrative cohesion in its individual sections, it lacks an overall programmatic hand in molding the larger narrative. As a result, elements that would otherwise have been suppressed in favor of a smoother, more coherent, or politically expedient narrative remain present in the text. The fact that the text "forgets" much less is telling. It shows that forgetting and elision are crucial in forming a programmatic account of the past.

Spanning 138 numbered bamboo slips divided in twenty-three marked sections, the manuscript is decidedly longer than the *Rongchengshi*. It covers events from the Zhou conquest of the Shang up to the wars between Jin 晉 and Chu 楚 during the Warring States period (ca. 1046–386 BCE). Much of the scholarship on the text has focused on how it differs from the received account and what genre of historical writing it represents. In Pines's analysis, the text presents an "informative history" read by "a relatively small group of high officials who needed to know the historical background for the current balance of power."[25] In particular, the text is preoccupied with the development of the relations and conflicts between Jin and Chu. One would assume then that the goal of the *Xinian would be to introduce and inform readers of those elements germane to that conflict at the expense of other actors and events. But that is not the case.

As Milburn and Pines have argued, the text likely drew from a number of different source texts, using Zhou, Jin, and Chu chronology and featuring historically different practices of grammatical particle usage between the early and later sections of the text.[26] Given this composite nature, the question of selection becomes all the more relevant. Why did the composers of the *Xinian choose this particular set of materials for inclusion?

Judging from the *Xinian as a whole, the emphasis of the text lies on the history of the relationship between Jin and Chu, and the inclusion of the first four sections detailing the demise of the Zhou are probably used as an introduction to the rise of the states that would be the main players of Spring and Autumn politics. In particular, as Li Ling has argued, the rise of states such as Qin 秦 and Zheng 鄭 are mentioned in this section because of their important roles in the course of Spring and Autumn politics, especially in the development of the relation and conflict between Jin and Chu.[27] As a result, one would expect the states that feature a prominent role in the narrative of the *Xinian to also be given prominence in the opening sections narrating the origins of the states. As will become clear below, while this is true to an extent, some states that have a prominent role in the narrative are hardly mentioned at all. Others, not featured prominently are instead given an origin story. I suggest this shows that the individual sections were not tailor-made for the *Xinian, and were probably selected in-whole from a corpus of preexisting materials.

The first section of the Xinian presents a narrative describing the origins of the crisis of the Zhou that would eventually lead to the rise of the individual states discussed in sections 2–4. In the second section, while there is plenty of room for narrating the details of individual events and people—the intrigue surrounding the famous femme fatale Bao Si 褎姒 comes to mind—the narrative elides such details for a more matter of fact and broad-stroke description of the major events leading up to the fall of the Zhou. In particular, it focuses on introducing the various states and rulers involved.

> King You of Zhou took a wife from Western Shen, and she gave birth to King Ping. The king also took a woman from

the people of Bao, this was Lady Bao Si, and she gave birth to Bopan. Lady Bao Si was favored by the king. His Majesty loved Bopan, and thus forced King Ping into exile: King Ping fled to Western Shen. King You raised an army and laid siege to King Ping at Western Shen, but the people of Shen were not afraid. The people of Zeng then joined with the Western Rong in order to attack King You; King You and Bopan were killed and the Zhou dynasty was destroyed. The lords of the various states and the elders then established King You's younger brother, Yuchen, in Guo, and he became King [Xie Hui]. He was established for twenty-one years, after which Chou, Marquis Wen of Jin, killed King Hui in Guo. Zhou was without a king for nine years, so the lords of the various states began not to pay court to Zhou. Marquis Wen of Jin met King Ping at Shao'e and had him take the throne in the capital. In the third year, he moved the capital east, taking up residence in Chengzhou. The people of Jin then began to open up land around the capital. Lord Wu of Zheng was the leader of the lords in the eastern regions. When Lord Wu passed away, Lord Zhuang was established; when Lord Zhuang passed away, Lord Zhao was established. His Grandee Gao Zhi Qumi killed Lord Zhao and established his younger brother Meishou. Lord Xiang of Qi met the other lords at Shouzhi, killing the unratified lord, Meishou, and rending Gao Zhi Qumi apart with chariots. He established Lord Li instead and the state of Zheng began from this point on to be well-governed. King Wen of Chu then opened up land at Hanyang.

周幽王取妻于西申,生平王。王又取褒人之女,是褒姒,生伯盤。褒姒嬖于王,王 (5) 與伯盤,逐平王,平王走西申。幽王起師圍平王于西申,申人弗畀。繒人乃降西戎以 (6) 攻幽王。幽王及伯盤乃滅,周乃亡。邦君諸正乃立幽王之弟余臣于虢,是攜惠王。(7) 立二十又一年,晉文侯仇乃殺惠王于虢。周亡王九年,邦君諸侯焉始不朝于周。 (8) 晉文侯乃逆平王于少鄂,立之于京師。三年乃東徙,止于成周。 晉人焉始啟 (9) 于京師。鄭武公亦正東方之諸侯。武公即世,莊公即位;莊公即世,昭公即位。 (10) 其大夫高之渠彌殺昭公而立其弟子眉壽。齊襄公會諸侯于首止,殺子 (11) 眉壽,車轢高之渠彌,改立厲公。鄭以始正。楚文王以啟于漢陽。」 (12) 28

This section, after narrating the fall of the Zhou, introduces the regional lords for the first time. After Marquis Wen of Jin 晉文侯 (780–746) killed King Hui of Xie 攜惠王 (?–760), and the lords stopped paying court to Zhou, the various foundational acts of the states are described, each marked with *shi* 始 ("for the first time"). The choice of singling out these events as firsts is crucial for the status of these sections as origin stories for the states prominent in the rest of the *Xinian*. The people of Jin are described as opening up land around the capital, a sign of the state's prowess. Next, Zheng is introduced, and after listing through a number of generations and killings, the rule of Lord Li of Zheng 鄭厲公 (700–697) is chosen by the narrative as the moment when Zheng was properly governed for the first time. In between, Lord Xiang of Qi 齊襄公 (697–686) is brought up as a ruler of influence. The section ends with a first mention of Chu opening up lands, without "for the first time" as a time marker; instead it is linked to the previous narrative using *yi* 以 "using/with this," possibly to suggest that Chu made use of the new power balance to expand its territory.

So far so good, all of these states will play a significant role in the remainder of the narrative and all are introduced in ways showing their influence on future political affairs. The third section provides an origin narrative focused solely on the Qin, who acting as a protective screen for the Zhou, eventually became an important state.

> When King Wu of Zhou defeated the Yin, he established the Three Guardians in Yin. When King Wu died, the Shang city rose in rebellion, killing the Three Guardians and establishing Geng, Viscount of Lu. King Cheng repeatedly attacked the Shang city, killing Geng, Viscount of Lu. Feilian fled east to the Shanggai clan, whereupon King Cheng attacked Shanggai and killed Feilian. He moved the people of Shanggai west to Zhuwu, in order that they might control the Nuzha Rong. These were the ancestors of the Qin. From one generation to the next they were the protectors of Zhou. When the Zhou royal house declined, King Ping moved east and took up residence in Chengzhou. At this point Qin Zhong moved east into the lands of Zhou, in order to guard the tombs of the Zhou [ruling house]. Qin then began to become an important [state].
> 周武王既克殷，乃設三監于殷。武王陟，商邑興反，殺三監而立彔子耿。成(13)王續伐商邑，殺彔子耿。飛廉東逃于商蓋氏，成王

伐商蓋，殺飛廉，西遷商（14）蓋之民于邾吾，以御奴(盧+又)之戎：是秦先人，世作周扞。周室既卑平王東遷，止于成（15）周。秦仲焉東居周地以守周之墳墓。秦以始大。⌐（16）

Here, the section skips back in time to the Zhou conquest of the Shang, in order to set up the origins of Qin. To be sure, Qin plays an important role in the *Xinian's narrative but why it merited a separate section is unclear. The idea of states forming a protective screen around the Zhou is of course relevant in understanding the history of the Zhou polity, its move to the east, and its gradual demise; perhaps it was included in the source text for this reason. This becomes clearer in the fourth section where Wei 衛 is introduced. In that section, the question of relevance becomes even more stringent, as Wei hardly features in the *Xinian narrative, other than being included among a range of other states in the famous narrative of Lord Wen of Jin's peregrinations.

> When King Cheng of Zhou and the Duke of Zhou moved the Yin people to Luoyi, they remembered the reasons why the Xia and the Shang dynasties had collapsed. Thus they established junior members of the ruling house [in fiefs] far and wide in order that they might act as a protective screen for Zhou. Thus they initially established Wei Shu Feng at Kangqiu, in order that he might rule over the remaining Yin people. The men of Wei from Kangqiu moved to Qiwei. In the seventeenth year of the reign of King Hui of Zhou, King Liuhu of the Red Di raised an army and attacked Wei. He inflicted a terrible defeat on the Wei army at Qiong, and Marquis You was killed by him. The Di thereupon occupied Wei, and the people of Wei moved east and crossed the Yellow River, travelling towards Cao. They established Shen, Lord Dai [of Wei] as their new ruler, and the Honourable Qifang fled to Qi. When Lord Dai passed away, Lord Huan of Qi summoned all the regional lords with a view to fortifying Chuqiu, [establishing] the Honourable Qifang there: he became Lord Wen. When Lord Wen passed away, Lord Cheng was established. The Di people again crossed the Yellow River and attacked Wei at Chuqiu, so the Wei people had to move from Chuqiu to Diqiu.

周成王，周公既遷殷民于洛邑，乃追念夏商之亡由，旁設出宗子，以作周厚 (17) 屏，乃先建衛叔封于康丘以侯殷之餘民。衛人自康丘遷于淇衛。周惠王立十 (18) 又七年赤翟王峁虎+口起師伐衛，大敗衛師於睘。幽侯滅焉，翟遂居衛。衛人乃東 (19) 涉河遷于曹焉立戴公申。公子啟方奔齊。戴公卒，齊桓公會諸侯以城楚丘，囗 [立] (20) 公子啟方焉是文公。文公即世，成公即位。翟人又涉河伐衛于楚丘，衛人自楚丘 (21) 遷于帝丘。⌐ (22)

Here again, the narrative skips back in time to provide an origin for Wei. To be sure, the story of Wei's movements—the Red Di 赤狄 hot on their heels—is an important memory not just for the people of Wei themselves but also for understanding the development of the Zhou state. Nevertheless, it does not have much to bring to the *Xinian*'s narrative. By comparison, the origins of Zheng's proper rule are tightly intertwined with Jin and will continue to appear numerous times in larger roles throughout the *Xinian*. Qi 齊 too is mentioned in roles of influence both in sections 2 and 4, but is not given a specific origin; all the while it takes on great significance in the latter sections. Song 宋, Wu 吳, and Yue 越 are all mentioned frequently throughout the *Xinian*, and especially Wu has pivotal roles in the narrative, but they are not mentioned in this first part at all.[29] In short, there is not a good match between the origin stories of the states and their eventual importance in the narrative. While one could argue that there simply was not a lot of material available detailing the early history of some of these states, this is belied by the range of story material present in other texts. Or one could argue that relevance to the narrative as a whole was not an important criterion for selection, but that still does not explain why Wei is given such focused treatment—the *Xinian* would have worked perfectly fine without this section.

Possibly, this section might be more about the juxtaposition between Wei as a stand-in for Huaxia as a whole and the Red Di as the cultural other.[30] To support this idea, the importance of the *rong* 戎 peoples (an exonym, just as "Red Di"), both in the other three sections of this part of the *Xinian* and their role in, for example, the Lord Wen of Jin narrative, could be adduced. Nevertheless, the fact that cultural others are predominantly present in the opening sections suggests that this might have been a concern of the source text rather than of the *Xinian* as a whole. Xie Weiyang has argued that the incorporation of this story might be because the example of Wei was understood as the prime case of the enfeoffment of an important state both in scope and complexity.³¹

Taken together, these observations reveal a more fundamental concern: forced by cultural outsiders to move their capital three times, the story of Wei stands *pars pro toto* for the larger narrative of the Zhou's demise—likewise forced to move their capital in response to outside aggression—and this is likely why the source text selected it. The *Xinian took from this text, perhaps rather indiscriminately, materials providing broad origins for the geopolitical situation in which its narrative played out. Judged from this perspective, the selection process of the *Xinian does not suggest the use of tailor-made sections, and it supports earlier arguments by Milburn and Pines that there likely was not significant rewriting of the source materials to suit the overall narrative.³² Put differently, where a text such as the *Rongchenshi* elides information irrelevant to its argument, to the point of "forgetting" information otherwise crucial to a completer understanding of the past, the *Xinian is much less programmatic in its selection. Because the text is cobbled together from a variety of sources and likely did not undergo much of the editing that would characterize a more purpose-crafted narrative, it tends to "remember" events not germane to the overall narrative. These events were remembered in writing as a byproduct of compilation, and a more programmatic approach would have been more selective. This alerts us once again that the program or philosophical point of a text is often revealed more in what is forgotten than in what is remembered.

Discussion

Based on these observations, it becomes clear that the *Xinian is very different from the *Rongchengshi* in how it incorporates memories of events into its narrative. The latter went to great pains to mold its narrative material into one organized scheme with clear narrative progression. It incorporates rare or even unique materials in order to set up its narrative program and elides other memories to smoothen the causal links required to have a tightly interwoven and structured story. On the sentence level, it reinforces this through a meticulous use of temporal connectives to suggest causal relations between events. In its narration, every event is relevant to both the main thrust of the story and to set up the next event. By comparison, the *Xinian employs similar techniques but only realizes such integration on the level of the section and not for the narrative as a whole. Drawing materials from a variety of sources from different periods, the *Xinian does not unify the different chronologies and perspectives into a purpose-built story. The narrative includes sections not immediately relevant to the development of the story as a whole and skips back and forth in time across sections.

These fundamental differences in turning memory into narrative stem in large part from the differences in genre of the two texts. The Rongchengshi aims to tell a story that makes a philosophical point about succession based on merit. It is therefore much more programmatic in how it forms memories of the past to its plot. But this should not be taken to mean that it did not have to deal with established tradition. As all texts dealing with the past, the Rongchengshi did not operate in a vacuum but resonated intertextually with other narratives of the Warring States. Cases in point are the legendary king list at its beginning or the ways it cites the humble beginnings of Yao and Shun, which in both form and content finds counterparts in early Chinese literature.[33] The narrative's argumentative power lies in how it weaves these memories—rare or well-known—together into a convincing story of gradual decline.

The *Xinian, for its part, also features many novel perspectives on the early Zhou,[34] and its use of preexisting historical materials should not be understood as if the text automatically followed a consensual account of the past. Each individual section of the *Xinian tells its own short story. That we can extrapolate from that a focus on Jin-Chu relations is a result of the large presence in the narrative of sections following the chronology and major events of Jin and Chu, respectively. But to say it is a purpose-crafted and plotted story would be inaccurate. While not suggesting that the material is the same form as the Bamboo Annals or the Chunqiu, the *Xinian calls to mind the difference between a proper historical narrative and the chronicle as proposed by Hayden White.[35] Where the former tells a coherent story (histoire) with beginning, middle, and end to serve a particular point, the latter stops *in media res*—there is no closure. Indeed, the final section of the *Xinian does not provide a resolution to the conflict between Jin and Chu. Like a chronicle, the narrative stops in the now of the scribe who does not have the virtue of hindsight to imbue meaning through closure on the events narrated. While the Rongchengshi appears to present a history in this narrative sense of the word, the end of the text is missing, making it unclear whether or not it provides a resolution to the central problem of declining virtue.

To narrate, then, is to shape memories into a story. The *Xinian's arbitrary selection, inherited from texts where the selection might have made more sense, is a direct result of its resistance to narrating a story. A story aims to generate meaning through closure, but such meaning only emerges from the selective elision and activation of memories, shifts in pace of narration, and the indication of clear turns in the plot. When the *Xinian employs such narrative devices, such as the indication of historical firsts examined above, they rarely have relevance beyond the individual subsection. Events are related with so few details that any discussion of what the text "forgets" becomes almost irrelevant, as there is so much more material that could have been included. This lack of programmatic meaning construction does not mean that we cannot deduce a potential role or use for the text's selection of events, but it does caution us not to compare it too readily to the much more complex narratives relating to the Springs and Autumns such as the *Zuozhuan*.

Conclusion

In this paper I have argued that the different ways in which the past is remembered in the *Rongchengshi* and the *Xinian is a function of the way the narrative selects and integrates memories. On the one hand, the form and purpose of the narrative determine which memories are selected and how they are integrated. On the other hand, the weight of tradition—the already remembered—influences and constrains the possibilities of narration. This dynamic plays out both in the cultural memory broadly conceived and more narrowly within individual texts. The more closely integrated the structures of cultural memory and the more densely populated with memories of specific events, the harder it becomes for a narrative to reconceive the relations between these events. The *Rongchengshi*'s narrative elides those memories obfuscating its own argumentative program, and it amplifies those figures and events preserved less clearly in the cultural memory of the Warring States, productively tying together otherwise disparate events into a tightly structured narrative. The *Xinian's selection of memories is twice-removed: it selected material from at least three different source texts, which themselves had their own criteria for selecting what and how to remember. This selection of ready-made materials is a question of access to specific sources, and following Pines, it is not unlikely that these consisted at least in part of scribal records. While this could possibly explain some of the reticence of the narrative to rework the materials, nonetheless, the *Zuozhuan* and *Guoyu*—in themselves at least partly based on such materials—have no qualms with presenting an integrated narrative, including imagined dialogue.[36]

It is important to acknowledge, therefore, that the differences in narration between the *Rongchengshi* and *Xinian is not because one deals largely with legend and the other with historical events—a distinction that may not have been made during the Warring States period, anyway. Likewise, it does not appear that some form of institutional attempt at creating a favorable history steered the selection and narration of the texts—the *Xinian, Pines notes, while eliding domestic troubles in favor of focusing on foreign relations, has no problems with admitting disastrous defeats by the Chu state.[37] Instead, I have argued that the demand for specific meaning in the narrative, aimed at making a philosophical point in the one, and an informative reference for the power balance in the other, steered both the selection and narration of memory.

The significance of this observation lies in the composite nature of so many narratives of the Warring States and later. In drawing on memories of the past as source material—whether anecdotal, archival, or some other form—historiographical narratives inherited the selection biases of their sources. As a result, some memories were increasingly forgotten—not because of the unimportance of the events itself, but because later narratives did not require them to make a meaningful story. Likewise, other memories gained in complexity—either because of plot requirements, or the need to provide precedent in the past for more recent events. This need also provided an important avenue to revive largely forgotten memories, and whether remembered faithfully or imaginatively, they were thus made accessible to other constructions of the past. The *Xinian brings in an important distinction, some memories of past events were included for more contingent reasons, and likewise, not every text was as cavalier in eliding memories not necessary for its overall narrative development. It is also clear that these selections often need not have been the result of institutionalized practices, activist editors, or conscious attempts at forming an archive. Rather, the driving power of the storyline and its narrative requirements should perhaps be seen as providing a stronger motor for the selection of memories, whether on the level of the text as a whole or for its component parts.

Notes

1. Jens Brockmeier, "Remembering and Forgetting: Narrative as Cultural Memory," *Culture & Psychology* 8, no. 1 (2002): 15–43, 22.

2. Jan Assmann, *Cultural Memory and Early Civilization: Writing, Remembrance, and Political Imagination* (Cambridge: Cambridge University Press, 2011).

3. Jerome Bruner, "The Narrative Construction of Reality," *Critical Inquiry* 18, no. 1 (1991): 1–21, 4.

4. Brockmeier, "Remembering and Forgetting: Narrative as Cultural Memory," 28.

5. Aleida Assmann, "Canon and Archive," in *Cultural Memory Studies: an International and Interdisciplinary Handbook*, ed. Astrid Erll and Ansgar Nünning (Berlin: de Gruyter, 2008), 105–16.

6. *Shanghai Bowuguan cang Zhanguo Chu zhushu* 2 上海博物館藏戰國楚竹書 (二), ed. Ma Chengyuan 馬承源 (Shanghai: Shanghai Guji chubanshe, 2002), 91–146 (images), 249–93 (transcription), and *Qinghua Daxue cang Zhanguo zhujian (2)* 清華大學藏戰國竹簡(貳), ed. Li Xueqin 李學勤 (Shanghai: Zhongxi shuju, 2011), vol. 1 (images), vol. 2 (transcription). An asterisk indicates a title bestowed by the editors rather than one provided by the manuscript. These two collections were donated to the institutions after having been bought on the Hong Kong antique market. Consensus has it that they were likely robbed from Warring States tombs in the Chu region (roughly covering modern-day Hubei province and parts of surrounding provinces). The manuscripts were carbon dated to the mid-third century BCE and were the subject of countless studies; they are generally considered authentic. For discussions on the issues of studying nonarchaeologically retrieved manuscripts, see Paul R. Goldin, "*Heng Xian* and the Problem of Studying Looted Artifacts," *Dao* 12 (2013): 153–60, and Christopher J. Foster, "Introduction to the Peking University Han Bamboo Strips: On the Authentication and Study of Purchased Manuscripts," *Early China* 40 (2017): 167–239.

I have previously expressed my views on this issue in Rens Krijgsman, "A Self-Reflexive Praxis: Changing Attitudes to Manuscript and Text in Early China," *Early China* 42 (2019), 77–78n8. This discussion is and should be ongoing, and I welcome efforts toward scientific verification and further contextualization of these artifacts, a process that I believe is not served by ignoring them or scholarship that relies on them as source materials. Being employed at an institution responsible for the protection and study of looted manuscripts and the restoration and study of previously largely unattended albeit archaeologically retrieved materials, I am in an ethically precarious position. While perfectly situated to fully appreciate the issues of funding allocation, availability of manpower and resources, let alone the cultural and political concerns surrounding these artifacts, any statement I might make on the (proper) use of these artifacts is immediately compromised by the fact that they directly and indirectly contribute to my livelihood.

7. Reign dates follow Edward L. Shaughnessy, "Calendar and Chronology" (table 1), in *The Cambridge History of Ancient China: from the Origins of Civilization to 221 BC*, ed. Michael Loewe and Edward L. Shaughnessy (Cambridge: Cambridge University Press, 1999), 25–29.

8. In this article I use the edition prepared by Sun Feiyan 孫飛燕, *Shangbojian* Rongchengshi *wenben zhengli ji yanjiu* 上博簡《容成氏》文本整理及研究 (Beijing: Zhongguo shehui kexue chubanshe, 2014), which incorporates all major studies up to early 2014, citing variant readings where I disagree. In preparing the current translation I have consulted Yuri Pines, "Political Mythology and Dynastic Legitimacy in the *Rong Cheng shi* Manuscript," *Bulletin of the School of Oriental and African Studies* 73, no. 3 (2010): 503–29, and Sarah Allan, "Abdication and Utopian Vision in the Bamboo Slip Manuscript, *Rongchengshi*," *Journal of Chinese Philosophy* suppl. to vol. 37 (2010): 67–84.

9. Its slips are roughly 44.5 centimeters in length and feature between 42 and 45 graphs each, leading to roughly 2,300 graphs for the whole manuscript.

10. The legendary rulers at the beginning of the text are often understood to represent tribal leaders from the Neolithic. While this represents an obviously flawed attempt to historicize myth and legend, it gives a good sense of the relative time scale conceived of by the narrative.

11. Zi Ju 子居 (pen name), "Shangbo er *Rongchengshi* zai bianlian" 上博二《容成氏》再編聯, Fudan daxue chutu wenxian yu guwenzi yanjiu zhongxin wang 復旦大學出土文獻與古文字研究中心網, June 7, 2008, http://www.gwz.fudan.edu.cn/SrcShow.Asp?Src_ID=452, notes that 43 and 35B likely formed one slip, connecting as follows: "及□(43) □氏," following Shan Yuchen 單育辰, *Xin chu Chujian* Rongchengshi *yanjiu* 新出楚簡《容成氏》研究 (Beijing: Zhonghua shuju, 2016), 31; the latter figure probably refers to Datingshi 大庭氏, another legendary monarch often featured in lists such as these.

12. Guo Yongbing 郭永秉, *Dixi xinyan* 帝系新研—楚地出土戰國文獻中的傳說時代古帝王系統研究 (Beijing: Beijing daxue chubanshe, 2008), 45n2 suggests that while the graph in question appears to be 奴, it is likely an error here for 安 (焉).

13. I follow Shan Yuchen, *Xin chu Chujian* Rongchengshi *yanjiu*, 12, who argues this was originally one slip, reading *yi* 矣 instead of *nei* 內.

14. Chen Jian 陳劍, "Shangbo Chujian *Rongchengshi* yu gushi chuanshuo" 上博楚簡《容成氏》與古史傳說, in Lishi yuyan yanjiusuo 歷史語言研究所, ed., *Zhongyang yanjiuyuan chengli 75 zhounian jinian lunwenji—Zhongguo nanfang wenming xueshu yantaohui* 中央研究院成立75週年今年論文集-中國南方文明學術研討會 (Taipei: Academia Sinica, 2003), (1–23), 17n5 reads as 廷 preserving the parallel.

15. Following Chen Jian 陳劍, "Shangbojian *Rongchengshi* de pinhe yu bianlian wenti xiaoyi" 上博簡《容成氏》的拼合與編聯問題小議, *Shangboguan*

cang Chu zhushu yanjiu xubian 上博館藏戰國楚竹書研究續編 (Shanghai: Shanghai shudian chubanshe, 2004), 327–34.

16. Attempts have been made to align all of the rulers with figures from received tradition, but most of these have been forced at best. See, especially, Liao Mingchun 廖明春, 2002, "Du Shangbojian Rongchengshi zhaji yi" 讀上博簡《容成氏》札記（一）, Jianbo.org, December 27, 2012, http://www.jianbo.org/Wssf/2002/liaominchun03.htm; and Huang Ren'er 黄人二, 2003, "Du Shangbo cangjian Rongchengshi shuhou" 讀上博藏簡容成氏書後, Jianbo.org 15/01/2003, http://www.jianbo.org/Wssf/2003/huanrener01.htm. For differences with a similar type of list in the *Zhuangzi* 莊子 chapter "Quqie" 胠篋, see Allan, "Abdication and Utopian Vision," 75.

17. Guo Yongbing, *Dixi xinyan*, 27–42.

18. For example, Datingshi is only mentioned in one other pre-Qin text, the *Zhuangzi* "Qu qie" chapter. See note 15, above. Youyu Tong, in turn, is not known from tradition but for his clan, the Yu, known from the legendary emperor Shun.

19. See Guo Yongbing, *Dixi xinyan*, 62–65 for other versions.

20. Following Liu Xinfang 劉信芳, "Shangbo cang zhushu shidu" 上博藏竹書試讀, *Xueshujie* 學術界 1 (2003): 94–97, 97.

21. Following He Linyi 何琳儀, "Di er pi Hujian xuanshi" 第二批滬簡選釋, *Shangboguan cang Chuzhushu yanjiu xubian* 上博館藏楚竹書研究續編, 451–52.

22. For an overview of these narratives and their structural patterns, see Sarah Allan, *The Heir and the Sage: Dynastic Legend in Early China* (San Francisco, CA: Chinese Materials Center, 1981).

23. Following Li Rui 李銳, "Du Shangboguan cang Chujian (er) zhaji" 讀上博館藏楚簡（二）剳記, *Shangboguan cang Chuzhushu yanjiu xubian* 上博館藏楚竹書研究續編, 528–29, who argues that *nian* 年 is a mistake for *shi* 世; according to *Shiji* there are indeed sixteen rulers between Qi and Jie.

24. For example, the *Shiji* "Xia Benji" 夏本紀, in addition to framing the transfer of rule from Yi to Qi as abdication, has something to say about most rulers in-between and mentions all by name; on the other hand, when providing the origins of Shun, even though all figures are named (because of the lineage focus of the narrative), any details on their character or reign are excluded (or their lack excused) by noting that they were all unremarkable figures: "Yu Shun was called Chonghua, whose father was called Gusou [. . .] there were seven generations from Changyi up to Chonghua. From Qiongchan up to Emperor Shun, they were all unremarkable men." 虞舜者，名曰重華。重華父曰瞽叟 [. . .] 昌意：以至舜七世矣。自從窮蟬以至帝舜，皆微為庶人。For a careful reflection on the processes of selection in the *Shiji*, see Klein's contribution in this volume.

25. Yuri Pines, "Zhou History and Historiography: Introducing the Bamboo Manuscript Xinian," *T'oung Pao* 100, no. 4–5 (2014): 287–324; the quote is from p. 321. See also his "History without Anecdotes: Between the *Zuozhuan*

and the *Xinian* manuscript," in *Between History and Philosophy: Anecdotes in Early China*, ed. Paul van Els and Sarah A. Queen (Albany: State University of New York Press, 2017), 263–99.

26. Olivia Milburn, "The *Xinian*: An Ancient Historical Text from the Qinghua University Collection of Bamboo Books," *Early China* 39 (2016): 53–109; Pines, "Zhou History and Historiography," 293–98.

27. Li Ling 李零, "Du jian biji: Qinghua Chujian *Xinian* di yi zhi di si zhang" 讀簡筆記：清華楚簡《繫年》第一至四章, in *Qinghuajian* Xinian *yu gushi xintan* 清華簡《繫年》與古史新探, ed. Li Shoukui 李守奎 (Shanghai: Zhongxi shuju, 2016), 48–54, 49.

28. Text edition and translation follows Milburn, "The *Xinian*: An Ancient Historical Text."

29. Wu is mentioned for the first time rather offhandedly later in the narrative (section 15) "The Wu people submitted to the authority of Chu" 吳人服於楚, despite the pivotal role it had in the conflict between Jin and Chu.

30. I owe this observation to class discussions with my student, Liu Zemin 劉澤民.

31. Xie Weiyang 謝維揚, "You Qinghua jian *Xinian* xiao yi Zhou chu zhuhou guo diwei de tedian" 由清華簡《繫年》小議周初諸侯國地位的特點, in *Qinghuajian* Xinian *yu gushi xintan*, 25–26.

32. Milburn, "The *Xinian*: An Ancient Historical Text," 108; Pines, "History without Anecdotes," 286.

33. For an overview and analysis see Rens Krijgsman, *Early Chinese Manuscript Collections: Sayings, Memory, Verse, and Knowledge* (Leiden: Brill, 2023), chapter 2.

34. See the discussion in Milburn, "The *Xinian*: An Ancient Historical Text," 67–71.

35. Hayden White, "The Value of Narrativity in the Representation of Reality," *Critical Inquiry* 7, no. 1 (1980): 5–27.

36. David Schaberg, *A Patterned Past: Form and Thought in Early Chinese Historiography* (Cambridge, MA: Harvard University Asia Center, 2001).

37. Pines, "History without Anecdotes," 285–86.

Chapter 3

Shaping the Historian's Project
Language of Forgetting and Obliteration in the *Shiji*

Esther Sunkyung Klein

The historian's calling would seem to entail a painstaking struggle against the relentless forces of forgetting, using recorded memory as a hedge against time's destruction. In the letter attributed to the great historian Sima Qian 司馬遷 (b. 145 BCE), he describes his historical masterwork, the *Shiji* 史記 (*Historian's Records*), as "gathering in a net the discarded old lore of the realm, investigating it in actions and events, and examining in it the patterns of success and failure, flourishing and ruin" (網羅天下放失舊聞, 考之行事, 稽其成敗興壞之理).[1] Earlier in the work, in an anthologized essay by Jia Yi 賈誼 (201–169 BCE), we also find a revealing proverb: "Earlier matters not forgotten are the teacher of later matters" (前事之不忘, 後事之師也).[2] Forgetting would seem to be the historian's nemesis.

In other strands of the early Chinese tradition, by contrast, forgetting seems to take on a more positive aspect. The *Zhuangzi* 莊子, "Qi wu lun" 齊物論 (Discussion on equalizing things) says, almost ecstatically: "We forget years, we forget rightness; we are shaken and roused by the boundaryless, and so: lodge it in the boundaryless!" (忘年忘義, 振於無竟, 故寓諸無竟).[3] The *Shiji* engages in a desperate quest exactly to preserve and "remember" both years and rightness. If, as the *Zhuangzi* suggests, forgetting is an entry point to "boundaryless," Sima Qian wants his boundaries intact and well-defined. He is even explicit about seeking "to investigate the border between heaven and human" (究天人之際).[4]

The thoroughness of the historian's opposition—to forgetting years and rightness—is in itself illustrative. A bare chronicle records years but gives no judgments about rightness. An ethical text records judgments but no years (and here, "years" may perhaps be understood, not just as mere chronology, but as a metonym for historical specificity). The *Shiji* aspired to record both, and really that is what historical study *is* in the premodern Chinese context: a way of preserving a dated account of events and imbuing it with "rightness," or moral significance.[5] Different histories simply combine these two aspects in different ways, or differ as to what constitutes "rightness" in their respective contexts.

Is there, then, any more positive role for "forgetting" in a Chinese historiographical text like the *Shiji*? I would propose that there is, but grasping it requires us to separate out different levels on which "forgetting"—or, more broadly construed, "oblivion"—may come into play within the historian's project. On the first, most obvious level, "forgetting" (*wang* 忘) is explicitly mentioned as a salient and undesirable possibility, with almost no positive uses of the term. But, I will argue, this term refers to forgetting primarily, or even exclusively, in the more limited sense of "neglecting" or "failing to call to mind." On the second level, I will consider forgetting that encompasses a larger scope: the consciousness of loss and obliteration (*mie* 滅 or *yinmie* 堙滅) that constitutes forgetting on a broad cultural level rather than on the part of a single individual. In the *Shiji*, this obliteration-as-forgetting plays a rhetorical and motivational role as an implicit impetus to creative reconstruction (or, indeed, construction). Finally, but most tentatively, I will briefly discuss "silent" forgetting and its essential underlying role in the activity we translate as "transmission" (*chuan* 傳 or *shu* 述).

Forgetting: Salient and Undesired

The first question to ask is does "forgetting" actually have a classical Chinese equivalent? And is the closest equivalent in fact *wang* 忘, as translators and bilingual dictionaries would have us believe? There are just under a hundred instances of *wang* 忘 in the *Shiji* (with some near-exact repetitions); many are from source material rather than having been composed by the historian. As one might expect, the vast majority of instances refer to an undesirable act. The speaker is almost always either promising not to *wang*, or enjoining someone else not to. Ultimately, many of the uses seem to recall the formulaic language of bronze inscriptions and the *Shi* 詩 (Odes) and *Shu* 書 (Documents).[6] They also seem fairly consistent with the way the term *wang* is used in the *Zuozhuan* 左傳 (Zuo traditions), an earlier historical text that was one of the *Shiji*'s sources.[7] It is no surprise that the most common objects of (non-)forgetting are in some sense moral or moralizing: the realm, the welfare of its people, one's duty to the ruler, one's ancestors and their intentions, and the worth or merit of splendid people. Rounding out this list are obligations of various kinds, mostly arising from past relationships, or sometimes events that demand vengeance.

None of this actually answers the question of whether *wang* means "to forget" in the *Shiji*, however. In the majority of cases, its meaning seems much closer to "neglect," "overlook," or "let slip": that is, it has less to do with *losing information one used to know*, and more to do with *failing to remain focused on the object in question*, or failing to make considerations of that object primary in determining one's course of behavior.[8] This kind of meaning remains within the scope of the English word *forget*: if you say to your beloved on the eve of separation, "Don't forget me," it is not out of concern that the beloved will be so absentminded as to forget, for example, your name.[9] Instead, your concern is that they might neglect to consider the significance of your relationship when deciding on a course of action.

Such is the case with the advice of his officials to a reluctant Emperor Wen 文 (Liu Heng 劉恆, b. 202 BCE, r. 180–157 BCE) in the first year of his reign: "To preemptively establish an heir-apparent is a way of giving due importance to the ancestral temple and altars of state—of not forgetting (i.e., neglecting) the realm" (有司曰:「豫建太子,所以重宗廟社稷, 不忘天下也」).[10] Here the object of *wang* is the entire realm, something whose bare existence no one would be likely to forget. Obviously, that is not the officials' intended meaning. Instead, taking due precaution regarding one's succession plan is a way of acting that is consistently informed by a *consciousness of what would be beneficial* for the entire realm, rather than for some smaller part of it (the emperor's own preferences or comfort, for example). In addition, *bu wang* 不忘 is placed in parallel with *zhong* 重, which I have translated as "to give due importance to." If the association carries any weight, one could conclude that *wang*'s opposite is not "remembering," but rather "valuing."

The peasant Chen She 陳涉 (d. 208 BCE), whose rebellion would go on to topple the mighty Qin 秦 empire, promised his companions of the plough, "When I become wealthy and honoured, I will not forget you" (苟富貴, 無相忘).[11] The manner of this not-forgetting is demonstrated later in the chapter: when Chen She becomes king, an acquaintance from his peasant days really does come to visit. Chen She happily entertains this humble guest, showing off his newly acquired wealth and status. When the old friend begins to grow overly familiar, however, the king has him summarily executed, betraying the promise of his early days.[12] Though this incident was not directly related to Chen's swift downfall, the historian may have included it in part to undermine Chen's moral authority and show he did not deserve to rule. Here and throughout the *Shiji*, forgetting (and its opposite) are more about the ability to honor moral obligation than about mere practical consequences.

Rhetorically, the mention of forgetting (as opposed to, say, the positive use of a term like "remember") brings to salience the possibility and even likelihood of forgetting. That is, it emphasizes not just the importance of that which must not be forgotten, but also the very real possibility of forgetting it. Doing one's duty and keeping one's promises is extremely difficult, as is maintaining a felt connection with one's ancestors in changing times, or with one's friends and allies in changing circumstances. Failing to do these things—forgetting, overlooking, neglecting—is generally much easier. People in the pages of the *Shiji* demonstrate that they are worthy of commemoration in part by emphasizing that they did do the hard thing, or by enjoining others to do likewise. Such is the moving scene of King Zhao of Chu's 楚昭王 (r. 515–489 BCE) death in the midst of a military operation. On his deathbed he calls together his younger brothers and senior officers and offers to yield the sovereignty to several brothers in turn, thereby passing over his own sons. Each brother refuses until the youngest brother, Zilü 子閭, sorely pressed and on the eve of battle, finally agrees. When the king has breathed his last, Zilü explains to his other brothers,

> It was when the king's illness was at a crisis that he passed over his own son in order to yield to us. The reason this humble servant agreed to his request was only in order to carry out his [original] intentions. Now that our reigning king is dead, how could this humble servant dare forget our reigning king's [original] intentions?!

王病甚，捨其子讓群臣，臣所以許王，以廣王意也。今君王卒，臣豈敢忘君王之意乎！ [13]

Zilü then proceeds, with his brothers' help, to settle the disposition of the troops and immediately establish King Zhao's son as ruler. In contrast to the many succession struggles that litter the pages of Chinese history, those most in the position to seize their own advantage here are instead inspired to overlook the king's desperate last-minute decision to abdicate and instead carry out what they understood as his original intention to have his son succeed him. Here the language gives us a literal opposite to *wang*, which is *guang* 廣 (broad, broaden): the younger brother would not dare forget what he knew the king had originally wanted and instead carries it out—or literally expands it, perhaps even "takes an expansive view of it." Since he remains mindful of the king's original intention, he takes a broad rather than narrowly literal interpretation of the king's wishes, and in so doing reveals his moral superiority.

Another speech, this time a warning by the Duke of Zhou 周公 (ca. eleventh century BCE), links forgetting (or neglect) to disaster through the use of homophones.

> Those who act as parents work long and hard on behalf of their patrimony; when descendants grow arrogant and forget [*wang*] this, they thereby ruin [*wang*] their families. Can anyone in the filial role afford to be neglectful about this?!
> 為人父母，為業至長久，子孫驕奢忘之，以亡其家，為人子可不慎乎！ [14]

This passage plays on the near-homophonous association between *wang* 忘 (forget, neglect) and *wang* 亡 (destroy). According to the *Shuowen jiezi* 說文解字 (*Explaining Graphs and Analyzing Characters*), this second *wang* had an older, original meaning of "to flee, to defect" (*tao* 逃)[15]; the meaning of "destroy" is extensional: what we run away from and neglect is often destroyed as a matter of course. Forgetting is a mental defection, and so here serves as the link between arrogance and destruction. The passage is explicit about forgetting's opposite, in this case *shen* 慎: to be cautious about, to be mindful or attentive to, to be earnest and sincere.

Forgetting is a kind of mental defection from that to which one should be attentive. Connected with that aspect of its meaning, we find one of the rare seemingly positive uses of the term in the *Shiji*: King

Mu of Zhou 周穆王 (tenth century BCE) goes on a hunting trip and is described as being "so [immersed in] joy that he forgets to return" (樂而忘歸).¹⁶ Does this episode mark a positive role for forgetting within the pages of the *Shiji*? As it turns out, it does not: in context, the king's joyful "forgetting" is also "neglect." We find out in the very next line that while the king is off enjoying himself, a rebellion breaks out and he is forced to race back and restore order. The story is familiar from *Mu Tianzi zhuan* 穆天子傳 (*Tradition of Mu, son of heaven*); as Pei Yin's 裴駰 (fifth century) *Shiji* commentary notes, the incident is also recorded in the *Zhushu jinian* 竹書紀年 (*Bamboo annals*).¹⁷ Interestingly, though, the *Shiji* version differs from the others in directly juxtaposing this moment of joyous abandon with the sinister consequence.

King Mu's forgetting his homeland leads him to neglect his responsibilities. On the other hand, in Sima Qian's portrait of Qu Yuan 屈原 (ca. 340–278 BCE), it is the *refusal* to forget his homeland that brings him to despair and eventually suicide.

> Though he had been sent into exile, [Qu Yuan] still looked to the Chu capital with anxious concern; his heart was still bound to King Huai, and he never forgot [*wang*] his longing to go back.
> 雖放流, 睠顧楚國, 系心懷王, 不忘欲反。¹⁸

Before Qu Yuan's death, a fisherman asks him why he has been reduced to such a state, also suggesting that he should instead compromise and change with the times. Qu Yuan clings steadfastly to his purity, asking, "How could I let shining whiteness be darkened by the mundane world's muddle and turmoil?" (安能以皓皓之白而蒙世俗之溫蠖乎?).¹⁹ Neither the historian nor the reader seems likely to take the fisherman's side in the debate. Qu Yuan's refusal to forget his emotional commitment to his homeland leads him to despair and death but also brings him cultural immortality as a celebrated patriot. The terms opposite to forgetting here are very clear, and obviously emotional: his anxious concern (*juan* 睠) and homeward gaze (*gu* 顧), the binding of his heart (*xi xin* 系心).

In addition to such "moral" or "moralizing" uses of the term *wang*, there are also uses that I would characterize as pragmatic, though there is not a sharp dividing line between the categories. Here, what must not to be forgotten tends to involve pain, humiliation, or the need for vengeance. Also in this category are cases where the object is a danger, generally the political or military threat posed by another state. In a few cases, the object of forgetting is a particular skill or method, which also seems more pragmatic than moral. These pragmatic nonforgettings are somewhat more antisocial, while the moral ones are prosocial: that is, the end results here tend to be destructive rather than preservative. Nonetheless, these refusals to forget are also narrated as heroic. A representative example is another famous Chu 楚 expatriate, Wu Zixu 伍子胥 (526–484 BCE), who when forced to flee his state "ran into difficulties on the banks of the Jiang and was reduced to begging for food on the road" (方子胥窘於江上, 道乞食).[20] Treated far more brutally than Qu Yuan by his ruler (who this case executes his father and brother), Wu Zixu is also unable to forget his homeland, but for the opposite reason—because his hatred is implacable. Despite the wretchedness and seeming hopelessness of Wu Zixu's circumstances, Sima Qian asks rhetorically, "how could his will for even the briefest moment forget [the Chu capital of] Ying" (志豈嘗須臾忘郢邪) and the revenge he craved there? (It could not.)[21] Here, forgetting's opposite is indicated only by the larger context of the story: after his traumatic departure from Chu, the brilliant and talented Wu Zixu enjoys good fortune and high office in the neighboring state of Wu 吳. Over and over, however, he jeopardizes his position in order to continue seeking revenge. When the king who wronged him unfortunately dies before Wu Zixu can kill him, Wu digs up the corpse and lashes it three hundred times.[22] It is another instance where forgetting—an easing of the intense tautness of focused attention—might seem salutary. But despite expressing anxiety over the extremes to which the "poison of resentment" (*yuan du* 怨毒) can lead, Sima Qian nonetheless describes Wu Zixu admiringly as "a man of fierce integrity" (*lie zhangfu* 烈丈夫) and praises him for "casting aside lesser principles to expunge a far greater wrong" (棄小義, 雪大恥).[23] In the historian's view, even Wu Zixu's insane fixation cannot be construed as something better laid to rest and forgotten.

There are only a few clearly positive uses of the term *wang* in the pages of the *Shiji*. The least ambiguous is a quotation from *Lunyu* 論語 (*Analects*), in which Confucius 孔子 (551–479 BCE) suggests that his disciple Zilu 子路 (Zhong You 仲由, 542–480 BCE) should describe him as one who "in pouring forth his passion forgets to eat; in joy forgets his cares" (發憤忘食, 樂以忘憂).[24] It is significant that the source for this passage is an entirely different genre of text and not native, so to speak, to the historiographical ecosystem. Ignoring that, however, the second phrase in the *Lunyu* quotation resembles the one in the King Mu story: both are about being immersed in joy. In the case of Confucius, however, one might assume that his joys are paradigmatically appropriate. To put it bluntly, he can get away with being immersed in joy since he is a sage. Furthermore, what he forgets while immersed in joy can be seen as an emotional state of anxiety rather than any duty or obligation that is being neglected.

The first phrase seems to belong to a different type, of which there are a few other instances in the *Shiji* as well: where the forgetting expresses a trade-off between two duties. In these cases, the lesser one is (properly) forgotten because the greater one is the focus. In "The Hereditary Household of Zhao" (*Zhao shijia* 趙世家), the prime minister Fei Yi 肥義 (d. 295) is said to be so concerned about the looming threat of a coup that he "forgets to sleep at night and forgets to eat when hungry" (夜而忘寐, 饑而忘食).[25] His anxiety for the realm *is* his duty and outweighs other duties such as attending to his own rest and nourishment. Describing the neglect of a lesser duty is a way of showing intensity of focus on the greater one, and so Fei Yi's attitude is portrayed approvingly.[26] Similarly, Confucius forgetting to eat in his passion (presumably for learning or for teaching) is not a negative characteristic because the higher duty (to others, to learning) rightly outweighs the lower one. Another example of forgetting as a trade-off can be found in the "Wei gongzi liezhuan" 魏公子列傳 (Arrayed Traditions of the Prince of Wei), where the arrogant prince is cleverly enjoined by one of his retainers,

> There are things that must not be forgotten and things that cannot *but* be forgotten. When someone else has done Your Highness a good turn, Your Highness must not forget it; but when Your Highness has done someone else a good turn, I beg Your Highness to forget it.
> 物有不可忘, 或有不可不忘。夫人有德於公子, 公子不可忘也; 公子有德於人, 願公子忘之也。[27]

Attention is always a game of trade-offs, and the early historiographic tradition is subtle enough to acknowledge that proper focus on one thing at times requires one to deliberately put another thing out of one's thoughts.[28] I will return to the "trade-off aspects" of forgetting in the last part of the paper.

Trade-offs offer the *Shiji*'s only examples of positive forgetting, and even such instances are sometimes undermined by the overall context. An example of this was the description of King Mu losing himself in joy and the negative consequences that are narratively made to follow from this inattention (i.e., the rebellion). An even more subtle subversion can be found in a description of Han Emperor Wu's (Liu Che 劉徹, b. 157 BCE, r. 141–187 BCE) fascination with the economic policies of Zhang Tang 張湯 (d. 116 BCE): "Every day at the dawn court, Tang would submit items of business and discuss state expenditures; the Son of Heaven [was so enthralled that he] would forget to eat until late in the day" (湯每朝奏事, 語國家用, 日晏, 天子忘食).[29] In form, this passage resembles descriptions of worthy advisers and appreciative rulers. Here, however, in the chapter on "Harsh Officials" (*kuli* 酷吏), the historian's initial comment makes it clear that he thinks policies like Zhang Tang's are terrible governance and harmful to the realm: "Mister Lao[30] stated that '... the more laws there are, the more thieves there will be.' The Honourable Senior Historian said, These words are so true!" (老氏稱:「……法令滋章, 盜賊多有。」太史公曰: 信哉是言也!).[31] Sima Qian also portrayed Zhang Tang himself as a rather poisonous character, e.g., "Tang was the kind of person who frequently lied to others" (湯為人多詐).[32] The emperor's respectful attention to such a man, to the point of forgetting his own physical needs, is almost an indictment against the emperor: to go along with such an adviser would be bad enough, but this emperor's forgetting bodily needs betrays an intense enthusiasm that is clearly misguided.

Overall, these representative examples have shown that *wang* 忘 is rarely a positive term in the *Shiji*. Its sphere is emotional and attentional rather than factual. It occurs in contexts of warning, admonition, or assurance (that the person will not forget)—in contexts where forgetting, in the sense of neglecting or overlooking or letting slip, is a salient and undesirable possibility. On the rare occasions when the term is positive, it is as part of a trade-off where something is properly forgotten out of concern for or attention to something more important.

All this confirms the initial supposition that Chinese historiography would not, at least explicitly, have much use for forgetting. It also, however, seems to bear out worries that *wang* might not be the type of forgetting most relevant to historiography. The forgetting we are looking for is a concept whose opposite is historical memory. Surprisingly few instances of *wang* involve anything specific to the enterprise of history writing. With a very few exceptions, what one "does not dare to forget" is duty or revenge. In just one instance, and that a quotation from another source, we *do* find the word *wang* used in direct relation to the lessons of the past. What follows is Jia Yi's beautiful description of the role of past lessons in present governance, also cited at the beginning of this chapter:

野諺曰，	An aphorism of the common people says,
前事之不忘，	"Past deeds not forgotten are
後事之師也。	the teacher of the future deeds."
是以君子為國，	This is why the noble man acting on behalf of the state
觀之上古，	observes [the lessons] of high antiquity,
驗之當世，	tests them in the present age,
參以人事，	compares them with human concerns,
察盛衰之理，	searches out the patterns of flourishing and decline,
審權勢之宜，	investigates the appropriateness of power and strategy,
去就有序，	is systematic in discarding and promoting,
變化有時，	is timely in altering and transforming,
故曠日長久而社稷安矣。[33]	and for this reason his term is long-lasting and the altars of state are secure.

This is a quotation, and indeed, a quotation within a quotation. Superficially it might remind a Western reader of Cicero's claim that "history is the teacher of life" (*historia [est] magistra vitae*),[34] or the popular aphorism, "Those who cannot remember the past are condemned to repeat it."[35] It is difficult to know how the seemingly analogous classical Chinese saying might have functioned in a popular context during the Han dynasty, but as situated in Jia Yi's essay, the forgetting (and the teaching) still remains more a matter of attention and analysis than of pure preservation. The worry is *not*, in this context, that we will no longer know about past events. Instead, the concern is that we might not pay them the correct kind of attention, or understand them in the right way. Hence Jia Yi's prescription involves observation, testing, comparison, and most of all investigation into specific types of patterns (*li* 理). The manner in which past events act as "the teacher of life" is not just by being known or preserved, but by being attended to and studied in the prescribed ways.

In addition to the aphorism quoted by Jia Yi, there are two other uses of the word *wang* that bear some relation to the historiographic enterprise. In a speech by the scholar-diplomat Li Yiji 酈食其 (268–204 BCE) to a would-be ally, he praises his employer, Liu Bang 劉邦 (later Han Emperor Gaozu 高祖, r. 202–195 BCE) for generously distributing the spoils of war. He also denigrates Liu Bang's rival Xiang Yu 項羽 (232–202 BCE) by saying about him that, "of people's achievements, not one does he remember; of people's crimes, not one does he forget" (於人之功無所記, 於人之罪無所忘).[36] Here the opposite of *wang* is *ji* 記, which as a verb could mean either "to remember" or "to record." Even here, though, Li Yiji's true implication is that Xiang Yu does not make the correct attentional trade-offs, placing too much weight on mistakes and too little on achievements. It is only secondarily a comment on the warlord's record-keeping practices.

A final instance can be found in the "Lishu" 曆書 (Treatise on the Calendar), which describes ancient calendrical officials, the quasi-mythical Chong 重 and Li 黎, from whom Sima Qian himself claims descent.[37] The employment of these officials by the legendary sage king Zhuanxu 顓頊 was described as "causing the return to ancient conventions" (使復舊常) that had previously brought about calendrical good order and well-being. Disorder among the lords of the land, however, again disrupted this state until "Yao returned to following[38] the descendants of Chong and Li, not forgetting the past, causing them to be in charge of it once again, and also establishing the office(s) of Xi (and) He" (堯復遂重黎之後, 不忘舊者, 使復典之, 而立羲和之官).[39] As a result of this good deed, legend has it, the realm is returned to a state of calendrical good order and enjoys a considerable diminution of disasters. Sima Qian himself was a calendrical official, and frequently underscores the connection between calendrics and history. Nonetheless, the context of this passage suggests that "the past," which Yao does not forget, is not meant to be the *content* of the official records, but rather the ancient institutional structure that provided for officials to do the recording. We are meant to understand that the feudal lords, even if they resisted the practice of having officials like Chong and Li, were at least aware of the existence of such officials; they simply were unwilling to pay due attention to their importance. This is the flaw that Yao rectified.

While all these uses of *wang* lie within the scope of the English word *forgetting*, they do not cover the full scope of the term. What they leave out is the notion of "obliteration" or true loss. This is by no means because the early historical tradition lacked such a concept. Just the opposite: consciousness of loss and the threat of loss loomed so large in ancient Chinese historical consciousness that it required a different set of metaphors and associations. When the *Shiji* itself—particularly in the historian's own comments—addresses true loss and forgetting in regard to historical records, it uses different language and does so with a different purpose.

Obliteration and Creative Construction

When we say something or someone is "gone but not forgotten," we mean that something meaningful remains. To preserve or create that "something meaningful" is an important aspect of Sima Qian's project. Because of this, it makes sense to look specifically at moments in the *Shiji*, where forgetting is not just a salient possibility but an incontrovertible fact. One event that comes immediately to mind, because of its importance in Chinese tradition, is the Qin bibliocaust. The term that the *Shiji* uses in describing that loss, and especially the loss of historical archives, is *mie* 滅 (obliterate). Before getting to that notorious event, it is worth considering other *Shiji* events that are described in similar language so as to get a better sense of the term.

The term *mie* is ubiquitous in the *Shiji* and spans a great number of meanings and uses. But one key subset involves the loss of meaningful historical information. Even more interesting, *mie* is frequently used this way in the context of the historian's own remarks, where it is also found in conjunction with another character, now written variously *yin* 堙 (to bury, to discard) or *yan* 湮 (to submerge, neglect).[40] In the *Shiji* "Feng shan shu" 封禪書 (Treatise on the *feng* and *shan* sacrifices), for example, we find that since these almost mythical royal sacrifices have not been performed for over one thousand years, "the ceremonial procedures have in that interval fallen into oblivion, and one can no longer obtain details or record the lore about them" (故其儀闕然堙滅，其詳不可得而記聞云).[41] From that point of apparent discouragement, the chapter goes on to gather up and recount all the information that *was* available concerning the history of these sacrifices, effective constructing, or reconstructing a tradition for them and presenting them as the ultimate seal on a ruler's legitimacy.[42] The historian's creativity in putting together this account is also a reflection of the creative energy of the seventy scholars (*ru* 儒)[43] who were summoned to reconstruct the rites, and that of the emperor himself who eventually performed them according to a design of his own.

> Among the scholars some argued that "in ancient times those who performed the *feng* and *shan* used padded cartwheels, being loth to do injury to the mountain's soil, stones, plants, and trees. Having swept the ground, they did the sacrifice with a mat made of rushes and peeled stalks; it is said that the ceremony was simple to perform." The First Emperor listened to their debates, in which each diverged from the others and all were difficult to put into practice. Thereupon he dismissed the scholars [and made his own version]. . . . The rituals were to some extent selected from the one used by the Chief Invocator to worship the High God at Yong. But the details were sealed and all hidden away, so that no one at the time could record what was done.
> 諸儒生或議曰:「古者封禪為蒲車, 惡傷山之土石草木; 埽地而祭, 席用葅稭, 言其易遵也。」始皇聞此議各乖異, 難施用, 由此絀儒生。……其禮頗采太祝之祀雍上帝所用, 而封藏皆祕之, 世不得而記也。[44]

The power of these "lost" sacrifices lies in their very lostness. As Mark Edward Lewis put it, despite the fact that even by the early medieval period scholars had concluded that these sacrifices were invented in the Qin, "from the perspective of the men of the Han the mystery of the sacrifices testified not their novelty but to their antiquity."[45] Sima Qian does not give the full range of the scholars' suggestions here (a mystery in itself), but the emperor's annoyance aside, the flourishing debate shows vividly how a consciousness of *something having been forgotten* can act as a spur to creative reconstruction. When the emperor dismisses the scholars and takes the process into his own hands, it is perhaps because he realizes that such creative reconstruction is not something he should delegate. The *Shiji* account gives strong narrative clues that this ritual was not successful, detailing the bad weather that the First Emperor encounters and the speedy collapse of the dynasty thereafter.

The Han part of the chapter then describes another collective effort to re-create the specifics of these rites. The passage, clearly a deliberate parallel to the Qin instance quoted above, again shows the failure of the scholars. One key aspect of their failure is their inability to engage in reimagining the rituals: "The various scholars, having already been unable to clearly analyse the events connected to the *feng* and *shan*, were furthermore shackled to the odes, documents, and other ancient texts, and as a result were unable to unleash [their creativity]" (群儒既已不能辨明封禪事, 又牽拘於詩書古文而不能騁).[46] Eventually, others step in and rituals referred to as "*feng*" and "*shan*" are indeed carried out. Although many have read into the historian's description of the process a sense of critical intent, the account does contain some narrative markers of success as well as a very specific description of what was done. And if we take these seriously, the narrative arc goes from a starting point of loss and arrives in the end at a minutely detailed description of success. The creative endeavor of constructing a ritual, and the historiographical activity that mirrors it, are only possible because the purported "original rites" had been forgotten. This is explicit in the *Shiji* account, which also criticizes the scholars for insisting on squabbling unproductively over the shreds of the past rather than seizing the opportunity to remake it.

Other instances of the term *mie* in this usage have a similar inspirational effect. In the "Bo Yi liezhuan" 伯夷列傳 (Arrayed traditions of Bo Yi), it is the recluses, the "men of cliffs and caves," whose collective fame has been "obliterated and extinguished while their praises have gone unsung" (類名堙滅而不稱). "It is tragic!" the historian comments, and goes on to immortalize them in one of the most famous and complex chapters in the whole *Shiji*. Looking at the rich literary tradition celebrating recluses,[47] one can hardly say that their praises go unsung *after* the *Shiji* immortalized them. But the sense of loss—of threatened oblivion—that pervades the *Shiji* account is an intrinsic part of its, and Bo Yi's, perpetual fame. Sima Qian is careful to emphasize that "although Bo Yi and Shu Qi were worthy, it was due to the Master that their reputations were burnished with glory" (伯夷、叔齊雖賢, 得夫子而名益彰).[48] Eighth century commentators rightly extended this key role of reconstruction and transmission to the *Shiji* account as well.[49]

In much the same way, the *Shiji* account of the *youxia* 遊俠 (unconstrained heroes) is also founded on a sense of loss. "The commoner heroes of pre-Qin times," writes the historian, "have vanished away, sunk into oblivion. How deeply I resent this! But according to what I have heard, at the beginning of the Han there was . . ." (自秦以前，匹夫之俠，湮滅不見，余甚恨之。以余所聞，漢興有……).⁵⁰ Again, the historian founds a tradition upon a sense of loss, and his own regret over that loss. In this case, he crafts an account of these men as heroes rather than ruffians, concluding as follows:

> Though they often struck out against the constraints of the culture in their times, their private sense of rightness was utterly pure and unselfish. In that there is much to praise. Their fame is not groundless, and those who gathered around them had reason to do so.
> 雖時扞當世之文罔，然其私義廉絜退讓，有足稱者。名不虛立，士不虛附。⁵¹

In this case too, perhaps even more than with Bo Yi, the tradition created in the *Shiji* struck a chord with later ages. Great novels such as *Outlaws of the Marsh* (*Shuihu zhuan* 水滸傳) are widely and even explicitly acknowledged to be following in this tradition.⁵²

Turning back now to the Qin bibliocaust, I would argue that, based on the processes observed above, the consciousness of tragic loss and desperate threat it engendered made it a net positive for the Confucian Classics. First, it allowed Confucian classicists and scholars of later times to present their forerunners as victims of a tyrant whose hostility toward tradition was ultimately the downfall of his dynasty. Second, it made space. It cleared the way for the reconstruction (or, indeed, construction) of Classics that better suited the time. The *Shiji* played a role in developing this type of response, so evident in almost every mention of the bibliocaust throughout the tradition. What is somewhat less discussed, however, is another victim of the bibliocaust: the archival records of the states.

> When Qin had fulfilled its intention [to conquer the other states], it burned the odes and documents of the realm. The archival records of the lords of the land were hit particularly hard. This is because they were deemed to contain pointed critiques and ridicule. Many [versions] of the odes and documents were stored in people's houses and so they have

resurfaced. But the archival records were stored only in the [archive] chamber of Zhou and so they were utterly obliterated (*mie*). What a pity! What a pity!

秦既得意, 燒天下詩書, 諸侯史記尤甚, 為其有所刺譏也。詩書所以復見者, 多藏人家, 而史記獨藏周室, 以故滅。惜哉, 惜哉! [53]

As with the other accounts of loss and reconstruction, this passage serves to justify a creative act, the compilation of the *Shiji* "Liu guo nian biao" 六國年表 (Table by years of the six states).[54]

Sima Qian's reconstructive project is not limited just to chronology, however. He also did his best to re-create the lost records state-by-state in the "basic annals" (*benji* 本紀) and "hereditary households" (*shijia* 世家) sections of the *Shiji*. A curious passage at the end of one of these chapters hints at the logic behind his overall plan: it seems that he was intent on tracing the posterity of the ancient sages and their most illustrious ministers.

舜之後, 周武王封之陳, 至楚惠王滅之, 有世家言。	As for the descendants of Shun: King Wu of Zhou enfeoffed them at Chen. Coming down to the point at which King Hui of Chu obliterated them, it is spoken of in a "hereditary household" [chapter].
禹之後, 周武王封之杞, 楚惠王滅之, 有世家言。	As for the descendants of Yu: King Wu of Zhou enfeoffed them at Qi. King Hui of Chu obliterated them. It is spoken of in a "hereditary household" [chapter].
契之後為殷, 殷有本紀言。	As for the descendants of Qi, they became the Yin. The Yin are spoken of in a "basic annals" [chapter].
殷破, 周封其後於宋, 齊湣王滅之, 有世家言。	After the Yin were conquered, Zhou enfeoffed their descendants in Song. King Min of Qi obliterated them. It is spoken of in a "hereditary household" [chapter].
后稷之後為周, 秦昭王滅之, 有本紀言。	As for the descendants of Hou Ji, they become the Zhou. King Zhao of Qin obliterated them. The Zhou are spoken of in a "basic annals" [chapter].
皋陶之後, 或封英、六, 楚穆王滅之, 無譜。	As for the descendants of Gaoyang, some were enfeoffed at Ying and some at Liu. King Mu of Chu obliterated them. There is no genealogy.

伯夷之後, 至周武王復封於齊, 曰太公望, 陳氏滅之, 有世家言。	As for the descendants of Bo Yí,[55] coming to [the time of] King Wu of Zhou they were enfeoffed once more in Qi. King Hui of Chu obliterated them. It is spoken of in a "hereditary household" [chapter].
伯翳之後, 至周平王時封為秦, 項羽滅之, 有本紀言。	As for the descendants of Bo Yì, coming to the time of King Ping of Zhou they were enfeoffed at Qin. Xiang Yu obliterated them. It is spoken of in a "basic annals" [chapter].[56]

It is worth noting that within the admittedly formulaic structure of these notes, the destruction of the sagely scions is closely linked with the construction of the *Shiji* chapters.[57] The fact that they are gone from the world leaves all the more room for the *Shiji* to remake them in a way that is useful to its own particular project. Grant Hardy argued that the *Shiji* is a microcosm, a miniature "world of bamboo."[58] While this idea may not be wholly convincing in all the cases where Hardy tries to apply it, I think that in this instance it does work: the *Shiji* is trying to re-create what has been lost and forgotten, both in textual terms and perhaps even in the real world as well.

Transmission and "Silent" Forgetting

Up to this point, the focus has been on the *language* of forgetting: places in the *Shiji* that are marked by the possibility or reality of forgetting while actually engaging with its opposite, whether mindfulness or creative reconstruction. But in the pages of a history there must also be real forgetting, "silent" forgetting that is not marked in the text by an attempt at recovery. That is to say, it is worth considering the things that are actually, and probably deliberately, left out.

Recent work on the Han period has made a fascinating attempt to "see around" the *Shiji* account—to identify its distortions and omissions—and is able to give us some sense of what was silently forgotten. To cite just two brief examples, Liang Cai, building on scholarship that casts doubt on narratives about the "victory of Han Confucianism," argues that the *Shiji*'s presentation of scholars in the "Rulin liezhuan" 儒林列傳 (Arrayed traditions of the forest of scholars) chapter created a collective identity that had not previously existed.[59] And Jonathan Markley's study of Han-Xiongnu relations compares the *Shiji* accounts with less well-known sources and shows what Sima Qian must have suppressed in order to create (for example) his long-accepted portrait of Emperor Wen as an ideal ruler.[60]

Here I am concerned less with the *content* of what was silently forgotten in this way. Instead, I want to consider the process itself and what it means in the context of the historiographic enterprise as a whole. Nietzsche, in *On the Advantage and Disadvantage of History for Life*, claimed that an excess of history was a destructive force that "injures every living thing and finally destroys it, be it a man, a people or a culture."[61] He added that "Cheerfulness, clear conscience, the carefree deed, faith in the future, all this . . . depends on there being a line which distinguishes what is clear and in full view from the dark and unilluminable; it depends on being able to forget at the right time as well as to remember at the right time."[62]

Nietzsche identified forgetting—the ahistorical experience of life—with the happiness of an animal "enthralled by the moment, neither melancholy nor bored," as the above-quoted *Lunyu* phrase would have it, "in joy forgetting cares" (樂以忘憂). Or in the *Zhuangzi*'s terms, "forgetting years, forgetting rightness." Nietzsche was probably wrong about animals,[63] but I think he was right that joyful vitality has difficulty coexisting with too much consciousness of the past.

Of course, the *Shiji* was not so much concerned with joy as with duty, resentment, and the creation of narratives. Still, Nietzsche's insight remains relevant. Like the magician's theatrical flourishes, Sima Qian inserts his laments about the obliteration of precious sources, while at the same time effacing, by sleight-of-hand, all that which he did not find "useful for life." We only find this "manipulation of interest"[64] objectionable—and studies like Markley's and Cai's startling—because we have inherited a notion of history quite similar to the one Nietzsche was inveighing against: history as a science of exactness and completeness, "knowledge, taken in excess without hunger."[65] Sima Qian, whose sense of history was quite different,[66] did gather up what was in danger of being lost but at the same time also made sure that some of it stayed lost. Both the Ren An letter and the Jia Yi quotation mention patterns (*li* 理): we are given to understand that Sima Qian's goal was "to examine the patterns of success and failure, arising and destruction" (稽其成敗興壞之理);[67] the phrase was perhaps inspired by Jia Yi's "searching out the patterns of flourishing and decline" (察盛衰之理).[68] A pattern emerges (only) through attentional trade-offs: the sharpened consciousness of some details and the darkening of others. The ability to perceive a pattern requires an aspect of ruthlessness: of paring away, forgetting (neglecting), or even destroying some of the details.

This brings me to my last keyword, *shu* 述 (*to transmit*). The famous *Lunyu* passage "transmitting and not creating, being trustworthy and loving antiquity" (述而不作, 信而好古)[69] is sometimes presented as a rejection of innovation.[70] We often talk about *shu* as if it were mere copying (or faithful reproduction)—and as if only *zuo* 作 (initiation, creation) were an act of creativity (or fabrication). Apparently echoing the *Lunyu* saying, the *Shiji*'s dialogue with Hu Sui has the Sima Qian persona disavowing Hu Sui's comparison with the "sagely" historical creation *Chunqiu* 春秋 (*Spring and Autumn Annals*) by explaining his work in terms of transmission, preservation, *mere tidying up*.

且余嘗掌其官,	. . . Moreover, having once held responsibility for [my
廢明聖盛德	fathers'] official duties, if I now
不載,	*cast aside* the enlightened sages' flourishing virtue
滅功臣世家賢	so it be *not recorded*,
大夫之業	*obliterate* the legacy of meritorious ministers, hereditary households, and worthy officers
不述,	so it be *not transmitted*,
墮先人所言,	*let fall* what my ancestor spoke of:
罪莫大焉。	no crime would be greater than this.
余所謂	What I call
述故事,	*transmitting* past events,
整齊其世傳,	*putting in order* their generations and traditions,
非所謂作也。	is not what is called "*creating*" [fabricating].[71]

Yet the *Shiji* itself shows us that *shu* itself is not a transparent process of reproduction. It is also a creative act of selection, reconstruction, and even destruction. The *Shiji* preserves an account of Confucius's creation of the *Shi* 詩 (Odes) canon that amply demonstrates this: "Of old, there were more than three thousand odes; when Confucius came along, he eliminated those that were redundant and selected those that had could be of service to rites and rightness" (古者詩三千餘篇, 及至孔子, 去其重, 取可施於禮義), a mere 305.[72] One need not accept the literal truth of the account to take the larger point, that many no-longer-extant texts were not accidentally or tragically destroyed, but rather deliberately left by the wayside. Sima Qian (who may have seen himself as a second Confucius)⁷³ followed the same approach. He is justly celebrated for including sources that others did not,⁷⁴ but this is just to say that his selection criteria differed from those of others—not that he included everything available to him. He begins the (in)famous "Bo Yi" chapter, for example, by piously observing that one can "still investigate the trustworthiness" of scholars' writings, however voluminous, "by reference to the Six Arts" (猶考信於六藝).⁷⁵ Those that do not make the cut are presumed to be left by the wayside. He ends the same chapter with a lament on how many lives must vanish without a trace, unless they encounter influential transmitters—"the swift steed" (驥), "the gentlemen of blue cloud" (青雲之士)—who can meaningfully carry their names forward to later generations.⁷⁶ Without explicitly saying so, he must be placing his own work in the category of swift steeds and blue-cloud gentleman. That also means that in the same textual moment as he laments processes of forgetting and destruction, Sima Qian is also serving as their agent: transmission is an act that takes up some things and, inevitably, leaves others behind.

Successful history-making is a process that can only occur through forgetting, through neglecting, and ultimately through destroying everything that the historian does not consider useful for life. This is the only way of preserving and perceiving useful patterns in the thick texture of reality. Much of the Chinese tradition shows how easy it is to forget this lesson, preserving *everything* and thereby creating stultifying, unreadable, indigestible history. When Sima Qian grieves his losses, his lamentations mark the horizon lines within which his history can thrive, the spaces that have been opened (however painfully) for the creative process of reconstruction.

Notes

1. Ban Gu 班固, *Hanshu* 漢書 (Beijing: Zhonghua shuju, 1962), 62.2735 ("Letter in Reply to Ren An" 報任安書).
2. Sima Qian 司馬遷, *Shiji* 史記 (Beijing: Zhonghua shuju, 1959), 6.278.
3. Wang Shumin 王叔岷, *Zhuangzi jiaoquan* 莊子校詮 (Taipei: Zhong yang yen jiu, 1994), 2.91. The subject of all verbs is unspecified in the original, so it could be first person, third person, or even imperative.
4. *Hanshu*, 62.2735. "Border" and "boundaryless" are not exact antonyms, but compared to the constellation of things *wu jing* 無竟 can mean in a Zhuangzian context—without limit (*wu jing* 無境), without end (*wu qiong* 無

窮), without furthest bound (*wu ji* 無極), and so on (glosses supplied in *Zhuangzi jiaoquan*, 2.93)—the *Shiji*'s use of *ji* 際 as a metaphorical place of interaction between two realms forms a plausible strong contrast.

5. For a use of yi 義 in just such a context, consider the conventional description of Confucius's work on the *Chun qiu* 春秋 (*Spring and Autumn Annals*) as "subtle words with profound moral meaning" 微言大義. The saying derives from a letter by Liu Xin 劉歆 (*Hanshu*, 36.1968), closely echoed in the *Hanshu*, 30.1701 ("Yi wen zhi").

6. In the *Shi Zai Ding* 師釐鼎 inscription, "the Son of Heaven does not forget the fine virtue of Gong Shangfu" (天子亦弗忘公上父懿德): Qiu Dexiu 邱德修, *Shang Zhou jinwen jicheng shiwen gao* 商周金文集成釋文稿 (Taipei: Wunan tushu chuban gongsi, 1986), #1437. This is comparable to how, in the *Shiji*, a ruler asks rhetorically "how [he] could dare to forget for even one day the merit of the general" (豈敢一日而忘將軍之功哉; *Shiji* 80.2430). The *Yu ding* 禹鼎 inscription praises Lord Wu 武公 for not forgetting their shared ancestors (肆武公亦弗叚望 (忘) 朕 (朕) 聖且 (祖) 考; *Shang Zhou jinwen jicheng* #1438). In the *Shijing* "Min yu xiao zi" 閔予小子, we find "Oh august kings, your successors think of you and do not neglect you" 於乎皇王、繼序思不忘: Mao #286; *Mao shi Zhengyi* 毛詩正義, in Ruan Yuan 阮元, *Shisan jing zhu shu* 十三經注疏 (Beijing: Zhonghua shuju, 1989), 19c.598. In the *Shiji*, we find the statement that "the ruler has not forgotten [the former rulers] Dukes Li, Xuan, Huan, and Wu, and in sorrow could not bear to cut off their sacrificial altars" (君不忘厲、宣、桓、武公, 哀不忍絕其社稷; *Shiji* 40.1768). Finally, in the *Shangshu* we find the line, "I admire your virtue; I pronounce you earnest and will not forget it" (予嘉乃德, 曰篤不忘): *Shangshu zhengyi* 尚書正義, in Ruan Yuan, *Shisan jing zhu shu*, 13.200. A speech in the *Shiji* also refers to the ruler's "cleaving to loyal ministers and not forgetting old friends" (親忠臣不忘舊故; *Shiji* 79.2422). Although none of these comparisons are close enough to count as verbal parallels, the sense in which the term is being used and the rhetorical function it plays are both quite similar.

7. A casual survey of the *Zuozhuan* shows an overwhelming majority of negative instances, with the few (ambiguous) exceptions involving things like a state forgetting its former loss after restitution had been made (*Zuozhuan* "Min" 2.9; Stephen W. Durrant, Li Wai-yee, & David Schaberg, *Zuo Tradition* [Seattle: University of Washington Press, 2016], II. 246–47), or the populace not yet having forgotten (i.e., gotten over) recent disasters ("Xi" 24.2; *Zuo Tradition*, II. 382–83).

8. See Franklin Perkins "So Comfortable You'll Forget You're Wearing Them: Attention and Forgetting in the *Zhuangzi*" in this volume for further discussion of this aspect of *wang*.

9. This unlikely possibility is, however, explored to great comic effect in the P. G. Wodehouse story, "The Rummy Affair of Old Biffy," in P. G. Wodehouse, *Carry On, Jeeves!* (New York: A. L. Burt, 1928), 159–93.

10. *Shiji*, 10.526.

11. *Shiji*, 48.1949. Technically, the line could also be translated, "Should we become wealthy and honoured, let us not forget one another."

12. *Shiji*, 48.1960.

13. *Shiji*, 40.1718. See also the version in *Zuozhuan* "Ai" 6.4 (*Zuo Tradition*, III. 1866–1867), where the younger brother is referred to as Gongzi Qi 公子啟.

14. *Shiji*, 33.1520. According to Yuri Pines, who gives translations of both, this is a later retelling of a passage in the *Shangshu* "Wu yi": Y. Pines, "A Toiling Monarch? The Wu yi 無逸 Chapter Revisited," in *Origins of Chinese Political Philosophy: Studies in the Composition and Thought of the Shangshu*, ed. Martin Kern and Dirk Meyer (Leiden: Brill, 2017), 362n9. The *Shangshu* version does not refer to forgetting (*wang* 忘) but in the corresponding position in the passage contains a reference to the descendants' lack of awareness or understanding (*bu zhi* 不知).

15. Xu Shen 許慎, *Shuowen jiezi Shuowen jiezi xin ding* 說文解字新訂 (Beijing: Zhonghua shuju, 2002), 12.844.

16. *Shiji*, 5.175. Another version of the same story, with very similar wording, can be found on *Shiji*, 43.1779.

17. Pei Yin cites Guo Pu 郭璞 (276–324), who gives the line as an explicit quotation (*Shiji*, 5.176n13).

18. *Shiji*, 84.2485.

19. *Shiji*, 84.2486.

20. *Shiji*, 66.2183. See also Olivia Milburn's analysis ("The Ice of Memory and the Fires of Forgetfulness," this volume) of how due attention to vengeance is thematized in the conflict between Wu and Yue, that is, the larger story cycle in which the Wu Zixu narrative is embedded.

21. *Shiji*, 66.2183.

22. *Shiji*, 66.2176.

23. *Shiji*, 66.2183.

24. *Shiji*, 47.1928; *Lunyu* 7/19 (*Shisan jing zhu shu*, 2483). For a slightly different analysis of this passage, see Albert Galvany, "The Oblivious against the Doctor: Pathologies of Remembering and Virtues of Forgetting in the *Liezi*," in this volume.

25. *Shiji*, 43.1814.

26. It is important to note that Fei Yi's anxiety is provoked by his ruler's failure to properly attend to an imminent threat, so while his forgetting to sleep and eat speaks well of his character, the need for it points to an overall negative situation. Interestingly, Jonathan Markley argues that this entire episode has been editorially manipulated by Sima Qian to subtly convey a message of contemporary relevance: J. Markley, *Peace and Peril: Sima Qian's Portrayal of Han-Xiongnu Relations* (Turnhout, Belgium: Brepols, 2016), 4–7.

27. *Shiji*, 77.2382. See also the parallel in *Zhan guo ce* 戰國策 (*Stratagems of the warring states*): Liu Xiang 劉向, *Zhan guo ce* 戰國策 (Shanghai: Shanghai

guji chubanshe, 1978), 25.912 ("The Lord of Xinling kills Jin Bi" *Xinling jun sha Jin Bi* 信陵君殺晉鄙).

28. For further discussion of the relationship between attention and memory, see Galvany (this volume).

29. *Shiji*, 122.3140.

30. The unusual appellation *Lao shi* 老氏 refers to Laozi 老子, as shown by the fact that the quoted line appears with only minor differences in the *Dao de jing* 道德經 (*Classic of the Way and virtue*). See Zhu Qianzhi 朱謙之, *Laozi jiaoshi* 老子校釋 (Beijing: Zhonghua shuju, 2000).

31. *Shiji*, 122.3131.

32. *Shiji*, 122.3138.

33. *Shiji*, 6.278.

34. Despite the verbal similarity, in context the meaning feels very different: "History, truly the witness of time, the light of truth, the life of memory, the teacher of life, the messenger of antiquity" (*Historia vero testis temporum, lux veritatis, vita memoriae, magistra vitae, nuntia vetustatis*; *De Oratore* II.36, [1862]; trans. adapted from J. S. Watson, *Cicero. On oratory and orators* [New York: Harper and Brothers, 1860], 92).

35. Variously attributed in a number of different versions; the above-quoted version comes from George Santayana, but the sentiment is widespread: G. Santayana, *The Life of Reason: Reason in Common Sense*, vol. 1 (New York: Scribner, 1905), 284.

36. *Shiji*, 97.2695.

37. *Shiji*, 130.3285–86.

38. A parallel version in the *Guoyu* has "Yao returned to nourishing the descendants of Chong and Li" (堯復育重黎之後), which may perhaps serve as a guide in how to interpret the slightly odd use of *sui* 遂 here, if indeed *sui* is not a corruption: Shanghai Shifan daxue guji zhengli zu 上海師範大學古籍整理組, *Guoyu* 國語 (Shanghai: Shanghai guji chubanshe, 1980), 8.563 ("Chu yu xia" 楚語下).

39. *Shiji*, 26.1257. Sources disagree as to whether Xi and He refer to two distinct clans or to a single figure, Xihe. In the *Shan hai jing* 山海經 and *Chuci* 楚辭, Xihe is a female deity associated with the management of the sun (Yuan Ke 袁珂, *Shan hai jing jiaozhu* 山海經校注 [Shanghai: Shanghai guji chubanshe, 1983], 15.381; Hong Xinzu 洪興祖, *Chuci buzhu* 楚辭補注 [Beijing: Zhonghua shuju, 2000], 1.27, 3.93). Interpreting the name as referring to two clans may result from the well-known commentarial tendency towardeuhemerism.

40. For *yin* 堙, *Shuowen jiezi* has 堊 (13.907); see also *yan* 湮 (12.741). The difference between the two must originally have involved the manner of disposal (by burying in the ground or sinking into the water). The two characters were homophonous in the Han however (the *fanqie* gloss is 於真 for both), so one should probably not make too much of the difference.

41. *Shiji*, 28.1355.

42. The fact that they were so rarely performed was meant to be indicative in itself, showing how few rulers could rise to what was set up as an extremely high standard. Most of the stories recounted by Sima Qian involve virtuous ministers attempting to dissuade regional lords from attempting them. *Shiji* 28.1355–65.

43. There is considerable debate surrounding the translation of *ru*, which is often appropriately rendered "Confucians" or "classicists." For a discussion and review of debates, see Esther S. Klein, *Reading Sima Qian from Han to Song: The Father of History in Pre-modern China* (Leiden: Brill, 2019), 17–20. In this context I have opted for "scholars" because their potential affiliation with Confucius is not immediately relevant.

44. *Shiji*, 28.1367.

45. Mark Edward Lewis, "The *feng* and *shan* sacrifices of Emperor Wu of the Han," in *State and Court Ritual in China*, ed. J. P. McDermott (Cambridge: Cambridge University Press, 1999), 50–80, 53.

46. *Shiji*, 28.1397. *Cheng* 騁 is somewhat freely rendered in my translation. Literally it means "to gallop" but is used in the *Zhuangzi* to describe the unconstrained behavior of a person possessing royal charisma (*wang de* 王德; *Zhuangzi jiaoquan* 12.421), and in the *Xunzi* to describe a situation where talented people are able to "fully unleash their abilities" 騁其能 (Wang Xianqian 王先謙, *Xunzi jijie* 荀子集解 [Beijing: Zhonghua shuju, 1988], 12.238).

47. See, for example, Alan J. Berkowitz, *Patterns of Disengagement: The Practice and Portrayal of Reclusion in Early Medieval China* (Stanford, CA: Stanford University Press, 2000) for a detailed study on how reclusion is portrayed in early medieval Chinese culture.

48. *Shiji*, 61.2127.

49. See Klein, *Reading Sima Qian from Han to Song*, 197–202.

50. *Shiji*, 124.3183.

51. *Shiji*, 124.3183.

52. For example, see David L. Rolston, *How to Read the Chinese Novel* (Princeton, NJ: Princeton University Press, 2014), 131.

53. *Shiji*, 15.686.

54. According to its preface, the table relies heavily on the only surviving state record (the highly deficient records of Qin) and possibly supplements it with other surviving texts: "Despite [the loss of the state archives], the flexible tactics of the warring states can also to some extent be selectively used" 然戰國之權變亦有可頗采者 (*Shiji* 15.686). Are the "flexible tactics" referring to texts describing such tactics, such as those now preserved under the title *Zhan guo ce* 戰國策, or are they real-world strategies? Is the selection process an editorial one, or does Sima Qian mean to say that such strategies are worth attending to because they are useful in the real world? He could easily have made this explicit

in either direction and the fact that he does not suggests that the ambiguity might be deliberate, or that both alternatives were intended.

55. This does not refer to the Bo Yi, who starved to death on Mount Shouyang, but rather to the more ancient Bo Yi, who "assisted Yao in with the ceremonial rites" 佐堯典禮 (*Shiji*, 42.1757).

56. *Shiji*, 36.1585.

57. It is unclear why Sima Qian placed such importance on the feudal states, but some passages within the *Shiji* appear to offer clues. For example, the preface to the "Gaozu gong chen hou zhe nianbiao" 高祖功臣侯者年表 (Table by years of Gaozu's meritorious ministers and lords) extols the regional rulers of antiquity as "keeping their fiefs whole for the purpose of guarding and protecting the Son of Heaven" (自全以蕃衛天子): *Shiji*, 18.877.

58. Grant Hardy, *Worlds of Bronze and Bamboo: Sima Qian's Conquest of History* (New York: Columbia University Press, 1999).

59. Liang Cai, *Witchcraft and the Rise of the First Confucian Empire* (Albany: State University of New York Press, 2014), 45–76.

60. J. Markley, *Peace and Peril: Sima Qian's Portrayal of Han-Xiongnu Relations*, 79–139.

61. Friedrich Nietzsche, *On the Advantage and Disadvantage of History for Life* (P. Preuss, trans.) (New York: Hackett, 1980), 10.

62. Nietzsche, *On the Advantage and Disadvantage of History*, 10.

63. See V. L. Templer and R. R. Hampton, "Episodic Memory in Nonhuman Animals," *Current Biology* 23, no. 17 (2013): 801–06, https://doi.org/10.1016/j.cub.2013.07.016; and N. S. Clayton and A. Dickinson, "Episodic-like Memory during Cache Recovery by Scrub Jays," *Nature* 395 (1998): 272–74, https://doi.org/10.1038/26216.

64. To borrow a phrase from the literature of prestidigitation. See Henry Hay, *The Amateur Magician's Handbook* (New York: Crowell, 1950), 2.

65. Nietzsche, *On the Advantage and Disadvantage of History*, 24.

66. If we were to adopt Nietzsche's taxonomy (*On the Advantage and Disadvantage of History for Life*, 14), Sima Qian's approach to history could be seen, by turns, as monumental, antiquarian, and critical.

67. *Hanshu*, 62.2735.

68. *Shiji*, 6.278.

69. *Lunyu* 7/1 (*Shisan jing zhu shu*, 2481).

70. For example, in the Mohist critiques analyzed in Michael Puett, *The Ambivalence of Creation: Debates Concerning Innovation and Artifice in Early China* (Stanford, CA: Stanford University Press, 2002), 40–56.

71. *Shiji*, 130.3300. My translation adds emphasis to highlight the language of loss and obliteration that is being employed, as well as its compensatory opposite in the language of preservation and transmission.

72. *Shiji*, 47.1936.

73. See Stephen W. Durrant *The Cloudy Mirror: Tension and Conflict in the Writings of Sima Qian* (Albany: State University of New York Press, 1995), 10–27, which also contains an analysis of the Hu Sui dialogue.

74. For example, Li Wai-yee, "The Idea of Authority in the Shih chi (Records of the Historian)," *Harvard Journal of Asiatic Studies* 54, no. 2 (1994): 345–405, 377–78.

75. *Shiji*, 61.2121.

76. *Shiji*, 61.2127.

Chapter 4

The Ice of Memory and the Fires of Forgetfulness

Traumatic Recollections in the *Wu Yue chunqiu*

OLIVIA MILBURN

They have learned nothing, and forgotten nothing.

—Charles-Maurice de Talleyrand, on the return of the Bourbon royal family from exile

The conflict between the ancient kingdoms of Wu and Yue, which culminated in the destruction of Wu in 473 BCE, forms the basis of one of the great sagas of early Chinese literature. Accounts of their constant confrontations are scattered through many pre-unification and early imperial texts, and more such records have been recovered in modern times through archaeology, attesting to the great popularity of tales of this kind before the unification of China and into the early imperial era.[1] In antiquity, there does not appear to have ever been one single epic recounting this struggle; however, during the course of the Eastern Han dynasty, some five hundred years after the final conquest of Wu by Yue, the transmitted textual tradition was knitted together to form a sustained narrative: the *Wu Yue chunqiu* 吳越春秋 (Spring and Autumn Annals of the Kingdoms of Wu and Yue) by Zhao Ye 趙曄

(fl. 60–80 CE).² The *Wu Yue chunqiu* is thought to have been written sometime between 50 and 70 CE, given that it made use of the *Yuejue shu* (which records no date after 52 CE) as a source, and is itself quoted, though not by name, in the *Lunheng* 論衡 (Doctrines Weighed), which was compiled between 70 and 80 CE.³ This fictional account made use of a vast range of sources about the conflict between Wu and Yue, but rearranged and reinterpreted them for dramatic effect creating a highly complex interlocking narrative.⁴ This chapter will focus on the way that remembrance is discussed in the *Wu Yue chunqiu*, in particular in the characterization of the last monarch of Wu, King Fuchai 吳王夫差 (r. 495–473 BCE), and his nemesis, King Goujian of Yue 越王勾踐 (r. 496–465 BCE).

The story told in the *Wu Yue chunqiu* remains well known in China to the present day. The two kingdoms of Wu and Yue were locked in conflict from the beginning of their recorded history, and eventually matters reached a crisis point. Taking advantage of the declaration of national mourning following the death of King Yunchang of Yue 越王允常 (d. 497 BCE), King Helü of Wu 吳王闔閭 (r. 514–496 BCE) invaded his southern neighbor, hoping for an easy victory. This proved to be a disastrous decision. Meeting the Yue forces in battle at Zuili 檇李, the Wu army suffered an ignominious defeat, and the king sustained such severe injuries that he was dead within days. Three years later his successor, King Fuchai, invaded Yue, and after a series of bloody battles captured his enemy's capital city. King Goujian of Yue, pinned down at Mount Kuaiji 會稽山, negotiated a surrender that led to him being held as a prisoner of war in Wu for a number of years. After this appalling calamity, King Goujian spent more than twenty years rebuilding his kingdom, and in 473 BCE it was his turn to take revenge. After a series of brutal campaigns, the kingdom of Wu was destroyed, and King Fuchai was forced to commit suicide. These dramatic events are arranged and systematized in the *Wu Yue chunqiu*, to create a contrasting pairing between King Fuchai and King Goujian. The former is portrayed as endlessly forgiving and forgetting, blind to the dangers that beset his kingdom and deaf to any remonstrance. King Goujian, on the other hand, is as a man tormented by his memories of past humiliation and defeat, endlessly alert to any opportunity for vengeance, constantly worried that he might overlook some hidden threat. Both are shown as dangerous, vindictive men, murdering anyone they feel to be a challenge to their authority. For the author of the *Wu Yue chunqiu*, a monarch who remembers everything is a truly terrifying figure, but then so is a monarch who forgets too much.

Narrative Structures in the *Wu Yue chunqiu*

The *Wu Yue chunqiu* is the earliest surviving work of Chinese fiction which deserves to be considered as a novel. However, this text was traditionally classified as a work of history, and appeared as such in early library catalogs, categorized as a miscellaneous work (*zashi* 雜史).[5] It is only in modern times that it has become common to describe it as a fictional text (*xiaoshuo* 小説), comparable to other earlier writings such as the *Mu Tianzi zhuan* 穆天子傳 (Tradition of Mu, Son of Heaven), or the *Yan Danzi* 燕丹子 (Prince Dan of Yan).[6] The *Wu Yue chunqiu* differs from these other texts in its much greater length, more complex plotting, and great narrative skill in building psychologically plausible characters. Indeed, those modern scholars who categorize it as fiction have frequently chosen to describe it as the earliest *yanyi* 演義 (historical romance).[7] Zhao Ye demonstrated great technical skill in constructing his tale, bringing together elements taken from a wide variety of disparate sources to create a seamless narrative: a powerful tale of relentless brutality in the quest for revenge. It is well known that there is a significant increase in the level of violence recorded in the *Wu Yue chunqiu* compared with previous accounts; for example, older texts do not always say that Prince Qingji of Wu 吳王子慶忌 was assassinated by order of King Helü of Wu.[8] Likewise, although many earlier works mention that King Goujian suffered many humiliations when a prisoner of war in Wu, they do not claim that he was forced to taste King Fuchai's diarrhea in order to convince him of his subjection.[9] The profoundly traumatizing experiences attributed to the characters in this novel serve to highlight the importance of memory as a theme underpinning both plot and the development of the main protagonists.

The surviving transmitted text of the *Wu Yue chunqiu*, which has unfortunately suffered some textual loss, consists of ten chapters in total.[10] The first half of the book, the five "inner" (*nei* 內) chapters, deal with events from the perspective of the kingdom of Wu, while the five "outer" (*wai* 外) present the story from the perspective of Yue. This division of the text, which appears to give preeminence to Wu over Yue, has long caused bafflement since the *Wu Yue chunqiu* seems quite even-handed in its treatment of events.[11] The impression of balance achieved within the narrative is a particular accomplishment given the uneven temporal coverage of events.[12] Leaving on one side the opening chapters of each half of the book which deal with legendary heroes in remote antiquity, the fact remains that the Wu part of the novel covers one 112 years, from 585 to 473 BCE, and the Yue part covers 22 years, from 492 to 469 BCE. This means that the first half of the book describes the rise of the kingdom of Wu to a position of great power within the Chinese world, at the same time as which the seeds of its eventual destruction were sown; and then the second half of the novel, in its four chapters on the life of King Goujian of Yue, covers exactly the same period as the one chapter on King Fuchai of Wu which concludes the first half of the book. This structuring, with a brief description of events from the perspective of one side fitting in with a much more detailed account focusing on the other side of the conflict, no doubt posed great challenges for the author. At the same time, the narrative is characterized by a strong interest in creating complimentary and antagonistic pairings: sometimes two characters are presented in opposition (such as the warring monarchs, Fuchai and Goujian), or as matching (such as the former's loyal servants, Wu Zixu 伍子胥 and Gongsun Sheng 公孫聖).[13] These pairings wend their way through the novel, appearing now on the Wu side and now on that of Yue. They serve to highlight the author's understanding of the Wu-Yue conflicts as a whole, where the original sources of contention had long been forgotten and were indeed irrelevant: all that was left by the time the final battles were being fought was the bitter memory of recent painful humiliations and an unquenchable thirst for vengeance.

King Fuchai of Wu

The image of King Fuchai of Wu found in the *Wu Yue chunqiu*—a man forever forgiving and forgetting—is not unique to this text. Numerous previous portrayals recorded his willful blindness to the dangers posed by the ongoing existence of the kingdom of Yue. This aspect of the characterization of the last king of Wu hinges on one particularly dramatic incident; after King Helü was fatally injured, lying on his deathbed he demanded that his successor avenge him: "You must never forget Yue" (*bi wu wang Yue* 必毋忘越).[14] This mandate to avenge the death of his father was supposedly integrated into the last king of Wu's daily routine. According to the *Zuozhuan*, King Fuchai arranged that he should be constantly reminded of the terrible circumstances in which King Helü had died.

> [King] Fuchai employed a man to stand in the courtyard and every time he went in or out, [the man] always asked him: "Fuchai! Have you forgotten that the king of Yue killed your father?" Then he would reply: "No! How could I dare to forget!"[15]
> 夫差使人立於庭, 苟出入, 必謂己曰: 「夫差! 而忘越王之殺而父乎?」則對曰: 「唯! 不敢忘!」

For some reason, the *Wu Yue chunqiu* does not record the death of King Helü of Wu, since the "Helü neizhuan" 闔閭內傳 (Inner Tradition of King Helü) documents nothing after the year 504 BCE, and the "Fuchai neizhuan" 夫差內傳 (Inner Tradition of King Fuchai) does not pick up the story until 485 BCE. It is likely that this omission is the result of textual loss, and the *Wu Yue chunqiu* did originally include a passage in which King Fuchai was instructed in his duty to remember the damage inflicted on him and his kingdom by King Goujian of Yue. Throughout the novel, there are repeated reminders that the king ought to be calling this to mind, that he should be determined on vengeance, and that he has a specific duty to kill King Goujian to avenge his father's untimely death. References to this duty abound, particularly in the confrontations between King Fuchai and his senior minister Wu Zixu, who was absolutely determined to force the monarch to confront unpalatable truths, and remember things that he would much rather forget, and who ultimately paid for this with his life.

Given that the king of Wu had a moral obligation to kill the king of Yue, it is of course extremely unexpected that he did not do so, and it is from this decision that so many of his subsequent problems stemmed. Written some five hundred years after the event, at a time when numerous tales about the conflict between Wu and Yue were in circulation and the outcome would have been known to everyone, Zhao Ye was free to present this as a manifestation of the will of Heaven: Heaven gave Yue to Wu, and because they did not accept this gift, Yue was able to destroy Wu.[16] At a more mundane level, the decision not to execute the king of Yue is portrayed in the *Wu Yue chunqiu* as the result of King Fuchai's stupid stubbornness and corruption on the part of one of his senior advisers, Chancellor Bo Pi 伯嚭. To a later audience it was unthinkable that such an outcome could be possible without bribery, but it is likely that the rights and wrongs were considerably less clear at the time and some early accounts of these events ascribe benign motives to Bo Pi.[17] The relationship between the king of Wu and the king of Yue is at the heart of the *Wu Yue chunqiu* narrative: when King Goujian was held as an enslaved prisoner-of-war in Wu, the two interacted frequently, but with markedly different outcomes. King Fuchai came to love and trust the king of Yue, as a result of which he arranged his release from captivity; King Goujian came to truly hate the king of Wu for the abuse and humiliations he suffered. The discourse found here in the *Wu Yue chunqiu* is related to a wider theme found elsewhere in literature about the conflict between the kingdoms of Wu and Yue, concerning the mindless destructiveness of those in power; after having ruined things for others, they forget all about it, and are amazed that anyone else should remember the sufferings they have inflicted. This is encapsulated in a proverb recorded in the *Yuejue shu*: "Rats may forget the wall, but the wall does not forget the rats" (*Fu shu wang bi, bi buwang shu* 夫鼠忘壁, 壁不忘鼠).[18] King Fuchai was happy to quickly forget just how badly he hurt King Goujian, and he was baffled and upset to find the latter implacably bent on revenge.

One of the striking aspects of the characterization of King Fuchai of Wu in the *Wu Yue chunqiu* is that having decided to forgive the king of Yue for his role in the death of his father, he reacted very badly to any suggestion that his action might be questioned or considered unwise. The violence with which he greeted any opposition on this point is described in great detail, and it is clear that the king of Wu was not to be appeased by merely eliminating the source of criticism, he was determined to obliterate every trace of them from the face of the earth. This can be seen particularly in the treatment meted out to two men: Gongsun Sheng and Wu Zixu. The former was a scholar residing in the kingdom of Wu who made an unfavorable interpretation of a prophetic dream for King Fuchai, suggesting that he was in imminent danger from the forces of the king of Yue. This prognostication drew forth a remarkably aggressive response.

> When the king of Wu heard what he had to say, he was absolutely furious. "I am the Son of Heaven!" he shouted.

"The representative of the gods!" He had the strong knight, Shi Fan, beat [Gongsun Sheng] to death with an iron cudgel. Sheng raised his head towards the sky. "Alas!" he said. "Heaven knows that I am innocent of any crime! My loyalty is being treated as an offence; I die even though I have done nothing wrong! You are killing me because my straightforward advice is disregarded in favor of echoing [the king] in blind obedience! Throw my body deep in the mountains, that later generations may hear my voice." Afterwards, the king of Wu ordered his gatekeepers to dump his body at Mount Zheng. "Dholes and wolves will eat your flesh; wildfires will burn your bones, and when the east wind rises, it will scatter your remains far and wide. Once your flesh and bones have rotted away, how will you ever be heard?"[19]

吳王聞之，索然作怒，乃曰：「吾天之所生，神之所使！」顧力士石番，以鐵鎚擊殺之。 聖乃仰頭向天而言曰：「吁嗟！天知吾之冤乎！忠而獲罪，身死無辜以葬。 我以為直者，不如相隨為柱。提我至深山，後世相屬為聲響。」於是吳三乃使門人提之蒸丘。
「豺狼食汝肉，野火燒汝骨，東風數至，飛揚汝骸骨。 肉糜爛，何能為聲響哉？」

The demand that the bodies of his critics be destroyed until absolutely nothing remained is echoed in King Fuchai's execution of Wu Zixu. The *Wu Yue chunqiu* portrays the forced suicide of Wu Zixu as a truly egregious injustice on the part of the king of Wu, given that this text particularly stresses his role in putting King Fuchai on the throne in the teeth of considerable opposition.[20] When ordered to kill himself, Wu Zixu screamed a litany of complaints up into the skies, noting his many years of distinguished service in the government of the kingdom of Wu, his loyalty to two generations of kings, and his numerous successes in battle. The theme of ingratitude is hammered home in the terrible conclusion to his rant: "Now you have forgotten all that I achieved in stabilizing the country and instead you order me to die: is this not wicked?!" (今乃忘我定國之恩，反賜我死，豈不謬哉?!).[21] King Fuchai's reaction to hearing of Wu Zixu's accusations shows a strong parallel with his response to Gongsun Sheng's last words. King Fuchai again demanded that the body be reduced into atoms, this time by cutting off his head and then throwing the remainder of the corpse into the nearest waterway.

> The sun and moon will burn your flesh, the winds will dry your eyes, wildfires will burn your bones, and fish and turtles will eat your body. Once your bones have turned to ash, what will you see?[22]
>
> 日月炙汝肉，飄風飄汝眼，炎光燒汝骨，魚鱉食汝肉。 汝骨變形灰，有何所見？

It is characteristic of the portrayal of the last king of Wu in the *Wu Yue chunqiu* that he is utterly ruthless in dealing with anyone that he dislikes, but the objects of his affection, most notably King Goujian, can apparently do no wrong.[23] Anyone with the temerity to openly question his policy of appeasement toward Yue therefore faced an exceptionally gruesome and violent death. However, the injustice that claimed the lives of both Gongsun Sheng and Wu Zixu is referenced at the time of King Fuchai's own death by suicide. When the last king of Wu finally faced up to the mistakes he has made, the memory of these two men became a source of great torment to him. It is for this reason that he requested a most unusual style of burial, in which he would not have to confront any of those—living or dead—whom he betrayed. Just before falling on his sword, King Fuchai declared,

> I am too ashamed to live, but I am humiliated by dying [like this]. If the dead have awareness, I will be ashamed to appear before our former rulers in the Underworld; I will not be able to bear seeing my loyal ministers Wu Zixu and Gongsun Sheng. Even if the dead have no awareness, I have betrayed those who will survive me. Once I am dead, you must cover my eyes with my belt. I am afraid that even that may not be enough, so I want you to fold a piece of silk in three [and tie that in place], so that [my face] is completely covered. That way I will not see the living, and the dead will not see me. What more can I do?"[24]
>
> 吾生既慚，死亦愧矣。 使死者有知，吾羞前君地下，不忍睹忠臣伍子胥及公孫聖。 使其無知，吾負於生。 死必連縶組以罩吾目，恐其不蔽，願復重羅繡三幅，以為掩明。 生不昭我，死勿見我形。 吾何可哉？

The death of the last king of Wu would complete King Goujian's vengeance. In real life, it appears that some minor members of the Wu ruling house did escape and find sanctuary elsewhere: their names are known from bronze vessel inscriptions excavated in modern times.[25] However, in the terms of the *Wu Yue chunqiu*, such individual survivors are irrelevant. The kingdom of Wu was destroyed, and this destruction was brought about by King Goujian of Yue to expunge the memory of the insults heaped on him before, during, and after his surrender at Mount Kuaiji. King Fuchai had forgotten the need to avenge his own father's death with the blood of his enemies, and for this he paid a terrible price.

King Goujian of Yue

Following the invasion of the kingdom of Yue in 494 BCE, King Goujian of Yue was forced to surrender to King Fuchai, and he spent a number of years as a prisoner of war in Wu before he was finally allowed to return home. The sufferings he endured during this period are mentioned in many ancient texts, but the fullest description is given in the *Wu Yue chunqiu*, which makes repeated reference to all kinds of torments that are not mentioned in any earlier records.[26] These then contextualize and form the background to the king's unusually strong determination to take revenge on Wu and his willingness to wait and work many years to rebuild the government of his kingdom prior to launching the campaigns that would eventually destroy his enemy. In this context, yet again, the monarchs of Wu and Yue are presented in the *Wu Yue chunqiu* as a contrasting pair. While King Fuchai killed others because they reminded him of things he would rather forget, King Goujian tortured himself lest he might ever fail to call to mind some aspect of the horrific treatment inflicted on him.

> The king of Yue always remembered his commitment to take revenge upon Wu, and this was not a new pledge. He worked himself hard and racked his brains, day and night. When his eyes began to close, he would prick them with thorns; when his feet got cold, he would plunge them in water.[27] In the winter, he would hold a lump of ice to his chest, while summer would find him sitting by the fire. He suffered that he might temper his ambition: he hung a gall in the doorway that he might taste it when coming in or going out, so that

[the taste of bitterness] would be forever in his mouth.²⁸ In the middle of the night he would weep, and having wept, he would wail again.²⁹

越王念復吳讎, 非一旦也。苦身勞心, 夜以接日。目臥則攻之以蓼, 足寒則漬之以水。冬常抱冰, 夏還握火。愁心苦志, 懸膽於戶, 出入嘗之, 不絕於口。中夜潛泣, 泣而復嘯。

Both the king of Wu and the king of Yue ensured that they would be constantly reminded of the need to take revenge: King Fuchai received a verbal admonition, while King Goujian tasted the bitterness of defeat every time he licked the gall hanging by his door.³⁰ However, the former would find remembering his wrongs too difficult a task, while the latter would overreact every time a memory of the past was called to mind. In a conversation with his ministers following his return to his capital, King Goujian gave a remarkably vivid description of the way the trauma of his experiences afflicted him, as if it were a bodily mutilation or injury. The events that had damaged him so much were not restricted to his time in imprisonment, but also included the earlier invasion of Yue and the terrible battles fought at this time, which ended with the siege at Mount Kuaiji, when he and a handful of staunch defenders were reduced to terrible straits before finally being forced to surrender.³¹ As he made clear on this occasion, his desire for vengeance was upheld by the memory of the person he used to be.

> In the past, the ancestral shrines of the kingdom of Yue were abandoned, and I was taken prisoner. Our shame is known throughout the world, and my humiliation has been recounted to all the other lords. My feelings towards Wu can be compared to those of a cripple who has not forgotten that he used to be able to walk, or a blind person who has not forgotten that he used to be able to see.³²
>
> 昔者越國遁棄宗廟, 身為窮虜。恥聞天下, 辱流諸侯, 今寡人念吳, 猶躄者不忘走, 盲者不忘視。

The way that the king of Yue here describes traumatic memory being inscribed on the body as a constant reminder of the past mirrors an earlier treatment of this theme in the *Wu Yue chunqiu*. Famously, in order to convince King Fuchai of his loyalty and devotion, King Goujian tasted his urine and feces when the monarch of Wu became unwell. Afterward, the king of Yue was convinced that his breath had been permanently tainted by this experience, and so his ministers and servants chewed fishwort (*cencao* 岑草) to make their own breath smell bad.³³ This incident should probably be understood in the context of contemporary Eastern Han dynasty practices where the emperor required government officials to chew breath-freshening spices like cloves when attending court.³⁴ The standard expectation that a government minister would wish to smell pleasant was here turned on its head by the practices at the Yue court, which demanded that they stink. However, this incident again attests to the way that the *Wu Yue chunqiu* stresses the theme of King Goujian internalizing the memory of his traumatic experiences and reacting to them as if he had indeed suffered some kind of lasting wound or scarring to his body.

The conquest of Wu was an enormous achievement for the kingdom of Yue, but the magnitude of that achievement is undoubtedly distorted in early Chinese texts. It seems from contemporary historical records that the Central States were terrified of the might of the Wu army, but knew almost nothing about the military capabilities of Yue.³⁵ As a result, they do not provide a balanced perspective on the relative strengths of the two states, and to the present day the struggles between Wu and Yue are commonly portrayed as a kind of David and Goliath battle. Modern scholars have attempted to extrapolate army size and population statistics in general from the rare figures preserved in ancient texts, but with limited success.³⁶ However, it is clear that many observers at the time regarded Yue's victory as a truly stunning achievement. The conquest of Wu and the death of King Fuchai could no doubt have made a satisfactory conclusion for the *Wu Yue chunqiu*, but instead, the novel goes on to trace the fate of its characters up to the death of King Goujian in 465 BCE. This allows the author to return again and again to the importance of memory in the characterization of King Goujian. The king of Yue was consistently portrayed as someone deeply troubled by the possibility that he might have forgotten something important, while at the same time obsessively worrying over anything that he happens to call to mind. These traits can be seen first in his treatment of his minister Fan Li 范蠡, and then in the execution of Grandee Zhong 大夫種. According to all accounts, Fan Li resigned his position in the government of Yue after the conquest and disappeared: his ultimate fate is unknown. Numerous romantic legends sprang up about him, but these do not form part of this narrative.³⁷ Instead the *Wu Yue chunqiu* concentrates on the fact that after his departure, King Goujian had his finest artisans make a (presumably life-sized) metal sculpture in Fan Li's image, which he placed beside his throne so that it could be present when he made administrative decisions.[38] In this instance, the king had no wish to forget the loyal minister he had lost.

After the conquest of Wu and throughout the remainder of his reign, King Goujian repeatedly recollected the ministers he relied on to achieve victory, much as King Fuchai was determined to forget those who brought him to power. However, the monarch's treatment of the absent Fan Li can be contrasted with that meted out to Grandee Zhong, who continued in his service as prime minister of Yue. Remembering that he had presented a number of stratagems to destroy the kingdom of Wu, of which only three had proved necessary in practice, King Goujian began to dwell on the dangers that someone so intelligent might pose to the long-term security and stability of his kingdom. The memory of Grandee Zhong's past successes were too much for the king of Yue, who demanded that he commit suicide. These events prove the justice of Grandee Zhong's contention that King Goujian had a very limited capacity for understanding the character of those around them, and an unfortunate habit of fastening on certain events in the past as a source of present concern, when a more balanced overview of their interactions would have demonstrated that there was actually nothing to worry about. However, in this instance, there was nothing he could do to save himself. The king of Yue told Grandee Zhong to his face that he could only feel safe and secure providing that the latter was dead.

> "Your secret planning abilities and knowledge of the military arts has served to overthrow our enemies and capture their kingdom. Out of the nine stratagems that you put forward, three were enough to destroy the powerful state of Wu: the remaining six you still have [in reserve]. I would like you to take those remaining techniques to the underworld and plot against the people of Wu there, on behalf of our former kings."[39]
> 「子有陰謀兵法，傾敵取國九術之策，今用三已破彊吳，其六尚在子。 所願幸以餘術，為孤前王於地下謀吳之前人。」

If remembering past wrongs was crucial for maintaining morale during the many decades that it took to rebuild the infrastructure of the kingdom of Yue, righting the record was also said to have played a significant role in King Goujian's determination to conquer Wu. Although historical texts do not mention this aspect of his personality, the fictional king of Yue intended that he would always be recorded in a positive light, as someone who patiently endured great suffering and brutal mistreatment in order to achieve his ultimate goal. The *Wu Yue chunqiu* makes it clear that the king of Yue wanted to be remembered for his ultimate victory, with every humiliation having been wiped out by his subsequent triumphs, his annihilation of the kingdom of Wu, and the ignominious death of King Fuchai of Wu. This can be seen in the events recorded in the "Goujian fa Wu waizhuan" 勾踐伐吳外傳 (Outer Tradition of King Goujian's Attack on Wu) chapter: when feasting with his ministers after the conquest of Wu, one of the music masters performing at the banquet expressed his delight that King Goujian would be commemorated as a great monarch, who had not merely restored the reputation lost in his surrender at Mount Kuaiji but also gone on to become the most powerful ruler of his time. The anonymous music master complimented the king on his success in terms that might have seemed hyperbolic to an Eastern Han dynasty readership, but which, paradoxically, the popularity of the *Wu Yue chunqiu* would play a large part in making true.

> "Your majesty's respect for virtue has resulted in the transformation of your country into a place where justice reigns: you have executed the wicked, you have avenged the crimes committed against you and expunged the humiliations you have suffered, striking awe into the other lords and achieving the status of a Hegemon-King.[40] Your victories will be recorded in paintings; your successes carved into metal and stone. Paeans to you will be played on strings and pipes; and your name will be recorded on bamboo and silk."[41]
>
> 「君王崇德，誨化有道之國：誅無義之人，復讎還恥，威加諸侯，受霸王之功。 功可象於圖畫，德可刻於金石，聲可託於絃管，名可留於竹帛。」

King Goujian of Yue achieved his revenge, and he made his name famous throughout history, but this brought him no peace. Just as King Fuchai suffered endless reminders that his policy of forgetfulness was dangerous, King Goujian tormented himself lest he should have failed to remember some threat or danger. The traumas inflicted by the fighting between Wu and Yue marked both men right up until their deaths.

Conclusion

There are many writings in pre-unification and early-imperial-era China that deal with the subject of memory, but in few of them is the topic as pivotal as in the *Wu Yue chunqiu*. The reason for this is that the plot of this novel hinges on the theme of remembrance: in both Wu and Yue, people were profoundly scarred by the memory of the conquest of Yue in 494 BCE. At the heart of this narrative is the conflict over how these events would be commemorated. King Fuchai of Wu wished his generosity in allowing King Goujian of Yue to surrender to be remembered, as well as his magnanimity in releasing him from captivity and returning him to power in a much-reduced kingdom. This was the perspective of the victors. However, a quite different point of view was held by those they defeated, in which the king of Yue and the people he ruled were treated with unspeakable brutality, and with infinite patience and cunning they rebuilt their kingdom to the point where they could take their revenge. These events, and the competing views of history that they represent, form the basis of this narrative, and therefore it is not surprising that the novel returns again and again to the theme of memory, and how different participants can remember exactly the same historical event in opposing ways. Over and over again, those who have suffered defeat express a feeling of mutilation; it is as though the psychological damage inflicted on them could only be expressed in terms of physical loss. They remember the past as a time of wholeness, when in fact the past was as conflict ridden as the present, and their fears for the future are informed by the deep scars left by earlier wounds. Ultimately, however, the *Wu Yue chunqiu* is a plea for understanding and a warning—the marginalized and oppressed may one day require a reckoning, and history may not stand on the side of those who inflicted such terrible suffering on them.

Notes

1. Important accounts of this conflict can be found in the *Zuozhuan* 左傳 (Zuo's Tradition), *Guoyu* 國語 (Tales of the States), *Shiji* 史記 (Records of the Grand Historian), and *Yuejue shu* 越絕書 (Lost Histories of Yue). Recently discovered and excavated texts about the wars between Wu and Yue include the *Gailu* 蓋廬 (King Helü), *Yuegong qishi* 越公其事 (Records of the Lord of Yue), and *Xinian* 繫年 (Annalistic History). So far none of the newly recovered material

bears any close relation to the *Wu Yue chunqiu*, and therefore cannot clarify the vexed issue of how much of this text was actually the invention of the author.

2. A very short biography of Zhao Ye is given in Fan Ye 范曄 comp., *Hou Hanshu* 後漢書 (Beijing: Zhonghua shuju, 1973), 79B.2575.

3. For the dating of the *Yuejue shu*; see Li Bujia 李步嘉, *Yuejue shu yanjiu* 越絕書研究 (Shanghai: Shanghai guji chubanshe, 2003), 226–310; and Olivia Milburn, *The Glory of Yue: An Annotated Translation of the Yuejue shu* (Leiden: Brill, 2010), 37–64. The date of compilation of the *Lunheng* is discussed in Timoteus Pokora and Michael Loewe, "Lun heng," in *Early Chinese Texts: A Bibliographical Guide*, ed. Michael Loewe (Berkeley: Society for the Study of Early China and the Institute for East Asian Studies, University of California, 1993), 309–12; Shao Yiping 邵毅平, *Lunheng yanjiu* 論衡研究 (Shanghai: Fudan daxue chubanshe, 2009); and Zhong Zhaopeng 鐘肇鵬, *Wang Chong nianpu* 王充年譜 (Ji'nan: Qi-Lu shushe, 1983). Cao Lindi 曹林娣, "Guanyu *Wu Yue chunqiu* de zuozhe ji chengshu niandai" 關於吳越春秋的作者及成書年代, *Xibei daxue xuebao (Zhexue shehui kexue ban)* 西北大學學報 (哲學社會科學版) 4 (1982): 68–73, 89, working with the same materials, suggests the most likely date of composition for the *Wu Yue chunqiu* would be the period 58–75 CE.

4. The author of the *Wu Yue chunqiu* appears to have been familiar with every known transmitted text that records the wars between Wu and Yue, and this raises questions about how a poor scholar living in a remote area could have had access to such a wide range of historical, philosophical, and literary documents. Liang Zonghua 梁宗華, "Lun *Wu Yue chunqiu* de zuozhe he chengshu niandai" 論吳越春秋的作者和成書年代, *Suzhou daxue xuebao (Zhexue shehui kexue ban)* 蘇州大學學報 (哲學社會科學版) 3 (1993) 93–97, suggests that Zhao Ye may have visited Chang'an in 54 CE, when his teacher was summoned to serve on the staff of Liu Cang, King of Dongping 東平王劉蒼 (fl. 39–83 CE), since the necessary materials would only have been available in a capital city. However, this suggestion remains entirely speculative.

5. See for example Wei Zheng 魏徵, *Suishu* 隋書 (Beijing: Zhonghua shuju, 1973), 33.960; Liu Xu 劉昫, *Jiu Tangshu* 舊唐書 (Beijing: Zhonghua shuju, 1975), 26.1993; and Ouyang Xiu 歐陽修, *Xin Tangshu* 新唐書 (Beijing: Zhonghua shuju, 1975), 58.1463. The popularity of the *Wu Yue chunqiu* was such that a number of related texts recounting the same events were produced, though none of these survive; see Chen Qiaoyi 陳橋驛, "*Wu Yue chunqiu* ji qi jizai de Wu Yue shiliao" 吳越春秋及其記載的吳越史料, *Hangzhou daxue xuebao* 杭州大學學報 1 (1984): 91–97; and Zhou Shengchun 周生春, "Jinben *Wu Yue chunqiu* banben yuanyuan kao" 今本吳越春秋版本淵源考, *Wenxian* 文獻 2 (1996): 215–26.

6. Wang Hengzhan 王恒展, *Zhongguo xiaoshuo fazhanshi gailun* 中國小說發展史概論 (Ji'nan: Shandong jiaoyu chubanshe, 1999), 140–41; and Yang

Yi 楊義, *Zhongguo gudian xiaoshuoshi lun* 中國古典小說史論 (Beijing: Zhongguo shehui kexue chubanshe, 1995), 84–89. In late imperial sources, the *Wu Yue chunqiu* was still classified as history but the fictional elements were increasingly stressed; see, for example, Ji Yun 紀昀 et al. comp., *Siku quanshu zongmu tiyao* 四庫全書總目提要 (Shijiazhuang: Hebei renmin chubanshe, 2000), 1779, which describes it as "practically a novel or traditional tale" (*jin xiaoshuojia yan* 近小說家言).

7. Cao Lindi 曹林娣, "Shilun *Wu Yue chunqiu* de ticai" 試論吳越春秋的體裁, *Suzhou daxue xuebao (Zhexue shehui kexue ban)* 蘇州大學學報 (哲學社會科學版) 1 (1984): 86–89; and Huang Rensheng 黃仁生, "Lun *Wu Yue chunqiu* shi woguo xiancun zuizao de wenyan changpian lishi xiaoshuo" 論吳越春秋是我國最早的文言長篇歷史小說, *Hunan shifan daxue shehui kexue xuebao* 湖南師範大學學報 3 (1994): 81–85.

8. Different accounts of the fate of Prince Qingji are given in *Zuozhuan*, 1715–16 (Ai 20); *Lüshi chunqiu xin jiaoshi* 呂氏春秋新校釋, ed. Chen Qiyou 陳奇猷 (Shanghai: Shanghai guji chubanshe, 2002), 594–95 ("Zhonglian" 忠廉); and *Jinlouzi shuzheng jiaozhu* 金樓子疏證校注, ed. Chen Zhiping 陳志平, Xiong Qingyuan 熊清元 (Shanghai: Shanghai guji chubanshe, 2014), 1091 ("Zaji" 雜記).

9. This incident appears in the "Goujian ruchen waizhuan" 勾踐入臣外傳 ("Outer Tradition of King Goujian Becoming a Vassal") chapter; see *Wu Yue chunqiu jijiao huikao* 吳越春秋輯校匯考, ed. Zhou Shengchun 周生春 (Shanghai: Shanghai guji chubanshe, 1997), 125–26.

10. Problems with the transmitted text are well known, and various different theories have been proposed as to what is missing; see, for example, Qian Fu 錢福, "Chongkan *Wu Yue chunqiu* xu" 重刊吳越春秋序, in *Wudu wencui xuji* 吳都文粹續集, ed. Qian Gu 錢穀 (Siku quanshu edn.), 1.55a; Feng Kunwu 豐坤武, "*Wu Yue chunqiu* 'dai fei quan shu' bianshi" 吳越春秋 "殆非全書" 辨識, *Lishixue* 歷史學 131, no. 3 (2000): 82–84; and Liang Zonghua 梁宗華, "Xianxing shi juan ben *Wu Yue chunqiu* kaoshi" 現行十卷本吳越春秋考識, *Dongyue luncong* 東嶽論叢 1 (1988): 54–57. Quotations from the *Wu Yue chunqiu* that are not found in the present text are preserved in various anthologies and *leishu* 類書; see, for example, Ouyang Xun 歐陽詢 comp., *Yiwen leiju* 藝文類聚 (Shanghai: Shanghai guji chubanshe, 2007), 8.141; and 96.1672.

11. Xu Diancai 許殿才, "*Wu Yue chunqiu* shuolüe" 吳越春秋說略, *Shixue shi yanjiu* 史學史研究 1 (2007): 18–23; and Jin Qizhen 金其楨, "Shijie *Wu Yue chunqiu* de bukexiao zhi mi" 試解吳越春秋的不可曉之謎, *Shixue yuekan* 史學月刊 6 (2000): 42–47.

12. The same technical difficulty can be seen in historical texts such as the "Hereditary Houses" (*Shijia* 世家) chapters of the *Shiji*, which divide the narrative on geographical lines; see Zhang Yi 張義, *Zhongguo xushi xue* 中國敘事學 (Beijing: Renmin chubanshe, 2004), 129.

13. The importance of these matching pairings in constructing the narrative is discussed in Chen Huixing 陳慧星, "*Wu Yue chunqiu* de moulüe sixiang" 吳越春秋的謀略思想, in *Wu wenhua ziyuan yanjiu yu fazhan* 吳文化資源研究與發展, vol. 2, ed. Gao Xiechu 高燮初 (Suzhou: Suzhou daxue chubanshe, 1995), 63–75.

14. Sima Qian 司馬遷 et al. comp., *Shiji* 史記 (Beijing: Zhonghua shuju, 1959), 41.1740.

15. *Chunqi Zuozhuan zhu* 春秋左傳注, ed. Yang Bojun 楊伯峻 (Beijing: Zhonghua shuju, 1981), 1596 (Ding 14). See also *Shiji*, 66.2178; and *Shuoyuan jiaozheng* 說苑校證, ed. Xiang Zonglu 向宗魯 (Beijing: Zhonghua shuju, 2000), 228 ("Zhengjian" 正諫). This story is also referred to in Albert Galvany's chapter in this volume, "The Oblivious against the Doctor: Pathologies of Remembering and Virtues of Forgetting in the *Liezi*."

16. This point is reiterated at various junctures in the narrative; see *Wu Yue chunqiu*, 95 ("Fuchai neizhuan"); and 170 ("Goujian fa Wu waizhuan" 勾踐伐吳外傳).

17. See, for example, Yuan Kang 袁康, Wu Ping 吳平, comp., *Yuejue shu* 越絕書 (Shanghai: Shanghai guji chubanshe, 1985), 27 ("Qingdi neizhuan" 請糴內傳).

18. *Yuejue shu*, 27 ("Qingdi neizhuan").

19. *Wu Yue chunqiu*, 80 ("Fuchai neizhuan"). This account is derived from the *Yuejue shu*, p. 75 ("Ji Wuwang zhan meng" 記吳王占夢). It would remain popular into the medieval period, with versions also preserved in Yan Zhitui 顏之推, *Huanyuan ji* 還冤記, in *Jiu xiaoshuo* 舊小説, ed. Wu Zengqi 吳曾棋 (Shanghai: Shangwu yinshuguan, 1965), 141–42; and Daoshi 道世, *Fayuan zhulin* 法苑珠林 (Shanghai: Shanghai guji chubanshe, 1991), 490.

20. *Wu Yue chunqiu*, 66 ("Helü neizhuan"). Other accounts of King Fuchai's succession following the premature death of King Helü's original heir, Crown Prince Zhonglei 太子終纍, do not suggest that Wu Zixu played any role in these events at all; see, for example, *Shiji*, 31.1467–68; and 66.2177–78.

21. *Wu Yue chunqiu*, 85 ("Fuchai neizhuan"). As described in Esther Klein's chapter in this volume, portrayals of Wu Zixu focus strongly on his determined remembrance of painful facts, which plays into his incandescent rage at King Fuchai's forgetfulness.

22. *Wu Yue chunqiu*, 85–86 ("Fuchai neizhuan"). Zhang Jue 張覺, *Wu Yue chunqiu jiaozhu* 吳越春秋校注 (Changsha: Yuelu shushe, 2006), 134n8, suggests this speech is an interpolation resulting from a misplaced strip, leading to an almost identical line being written into the story both of the death of Gongsun Sheng, and of Wu Zixu. This theory ignores the strong connection maintained throughout the *Wu Yue chunqiu* between these two characters.

23. Murderous ill-temper seems to have been a characteristic of the historical King Fuchai; for example, the *Zuozhuan*, 1677 (Ai 13) records that when

attending an interstate meeting at Huangchi 黃池 in 482 BCE, the king was informed that his armies had just been defeated in battle. King Fuchai was so furious that he killed seven men who had the misfortune to be present when he was told of this loss.

24. *Wu Yue chunqiu*, 96 ("Fuchai neizhuan").

25. Three bronze dings made for Royal Grandson Wuren 無壬 (also given as Wutu 無土) were discovered in a cache of Eastern Zhou bronzes found at Gaowang si 高王寺, Fengxiang County 鳳翔縣, Shaanxi Province, in 1977. These bronzes are dated to after the fall of the kingdom of Wu, and are thought to have been commissioned by a surviving junior member of the royal house; see Dong Chuping 董楚平, *Wu Yue Xu Shu jinwen jishi* 吳越徐舒金文集釋 (Hangzhou: Zhejiang guji chubanshe, 1992), 79; and Jenny F. So, *Eastern Zhou Ritual Bronzes from the Arthur M. Sackler Collections* (New York: Arthur M. Sackler Foundation, 1995), 160.

26. References to the king of Yue being paraded through the streets of the Wu capital in the victory celebrations can be found in *Han Feizi jishi* 韓非子集釋, ed. Chen Qiyou 陳奇猷 (Beijing: Zhonghua shuju, 1958), 403 ("Yulao" 喻老); and *Huainanzi jishi* 淮南子集釋, ed. He Ning 何寧 (Beijing: Zhonghua shuju, 2006), 858 ("Daoying xun" 道應訓). General descriptions of the humiliating service King Goujian and his wife were forced to give to King Fuchai (the queen of Yue acted as his concubine for the duration of her husband's imprisonment) are preserved in *Mozi xiangu* 墨子閒詁, ed. Sun Yirang 孫詒讓 (Beijing: Zhonghua shuju, 2001), 2 ("Qinshi" 親士); *Shiji*, 31.1469; and *Huainanzi*, 1308 ("Renjian xun" 人閒訓).

27. In the *Huainanzi*, 1300 ("Renjian xun"), it states that on one occasion King Goujian "grabbed hold of [the sword] Longyuan and stabbed his thigh until the blood flowed down to his feet to punish himself" (援龍淵而切其股, 血流至足, 以自罰也). There seem to have been many stories preserved in ancient texts in which the king of Yue inflicted painful damage to himself to atone for his past mistakes.

28. The story that King Goujian had tasted gall to remind him of his defeat was widely used in Chinese propaganda during the twentieth century to promote nationalist aims; see Paul L. Cohen, *Speaking to History: The Story of King Goujian in Twentieth-Century China* (Berkeley: University of California Press, 2009).

29. *Wu Yue chunqiu*, 125 ("Goujian guiguo waizhuan" 勾踐歸國外傳).

30. This parallelism is rendered even more explicit in the *Shiji*, 41.1742, where every time he tastes the gall, King Goujian asks himself: "Have you forgotten the shame of Kuaiji?" (女忘會稽之恥邪).

31. Cannibalism is recorded in the *Xinshu jiaozhu* 新書校注, ed. Yan Zhenyi 閻振益, Zhong Xia 鐘夏 (Beijing: Zhonghua shuju, 2000), 269 ("Erbi" 耳痺). A number of accounts of the siege of Mount Kuaiji state that King Goujian

became suicidal under the strain of these events; see *Guoyu* 國語, ed. Shanghai shifan daxue guji zhenglizu 上海師範大學古籍整理組 (Shanghai: Shanghai guji chubanshe, 1978), 632 ("Yueyu shang" 越語上); and *Huainanzi*, 858 ("Daoying xun").

32. *Wu Yue chunqiu*, 138–39 ("Goujian guiguo waizhuan").

33. *Wu Yue chunqiu*, 125 ("Goujian ruchen waizhuan"). Fishwort (Houttuynia cordata) is identified according to Gao Mingqian 高明乾, Lu Longdou 盧龍鬥 et al., *Zhiwu gu Hanming tukao* 植物古漢名圖考 (Zhengzhou: Daxiang chubanshe, 2006), 334. This plant is noted for its strong, and to many people unpleasant, "fishy" smell, earning it another common name: *yuxingcao* 魚腥草 (fish-stink plant).

34. This is recorded in the *Hanguan yi* 漢官儀, in *Hanguan liuzhong* 漢官六種, ed. Sun Xingyan 孫星衍 (Beijing: Zhonghua shuju, 1990), 2, 137–38.

35. A number of early texts stress that Yue was considered a poor and backward country at this time; see, for example, *Xunzi jijie* 荀子集解, ed. Wang Xianqian 王先謙 (Beijing: Zhonghua shuju, 2008), 205 ("Wangba" 王霸); and *Han Shi waizhuan jishi* 韓詩外傳集釋, ed. Xu Weiyu 許維遹 (Beijing: Zhonghua shuju, 2005), 271 (8.1).

36. Shi Fang 施放, "Yueguo you meiyou keneng zai Langya jiandu?" 越國有沒有可能在琅琊建都, in *Haixia liang'an Yue wenhua yanjiu* 海峽兩岸越文化研究, ed. Fei Junqing 費君清, Wang Jianhua 王建華 (Beijing: Renmin chubanshe, 2005), 463–77; and Chen Guocan 陳國燦, Xi Jianhua 奚建華, *Zhejiang gudai chengzhen shi* 浙江古代城鎮史 (Hefei: Anhui daxue chubanshe, 2003), 36. This issue requires revisiting with the discovery of the *Yuegong qishi* manuscript, which speaks of significant migration to Yue during the reign of King Goujian.

37. See for example *Shiji*, 129.3256–57; and *Liexian zhuan jiaojian* 列仙傳校箋, ed. Wang Shumin 王叔岷 (Beijing: Zhonghua shuju, 2007), 58 ("Fan Li"). These legends would reach their apogee in the Ming dynasty, in the Kunqu play by Liang Chenyu 梁辰魚 (1520–1592), *Huansha ji* 浣紗記 (The Story of the Girl Who Washed Silk).

38. *Wu Yue chunqiu*, 172 ("Goujian fa Wu waizhuan"). This story is derived from the *Guoyu*, 659 ("Yueyu xia" 越語下).

39. *Wu Yue chunqiu*, 176 ("Goujian fa Wu waizhuan").

40. A number of ancient texts record that King Goujian was regarded as the last Hegemon (*ba* 霸) of the Spring and Autumn Period; see, for example, *Xunzi*, 205 ("Wangba"); and *Shiji*, 41.1746.

41. *Wu Yue chunqiu*, 171 ("Goujian fa Wu waizhuan").

PART II
PHILOSOPHICAL WRITINGS

Chapter 5

The *Daode jing*'s Forgotten Forebear
The Ancestral Cult

K. E. Brashier

In 1931, two archaeologists digging near Yingchengzi 營城子 in present-day Liaoning uncovered an elaborate Eastern Han brick tomb and were deeply impressed by its high-vaulted main chamber. "When one enters the dark ante-room and looks up at the interior of the vault, one can not help being surprised with the beautifully lined and coloured courses of bricks, which are revealed gradually in the candle light." But what surprised them more was how this large chamber completely enclosed a smaller one that in turn covered the coffin platform, and on the white stucco wall inside this smaller chamber was an elaborate fresco (fig. 5.1). Its lower figures were humans kneeling and bowing in homage before a table with a vessel presumably for ale; the upper figures consisted of a robed-and-hatted man with a sword, his wife or attendant at his side, facing a smaller figure in fuller robes, apparently emerging from the *qi* with a bird, a winged immortal and a dragon also roaming through the upper portion of this fresco. As to the emerging figure's identity, Seiichi Midzuno wrote in the report that "the old man is the shadow or spirit of the dead buried in this tomb."[1] This human figure—possibly the ancestor—materializing from the chaotic *qi* resembles a motif sometimes

Figure 5.1. From the Yingchengzi mural. Eastern Han, Shagangtun (Liaoning). From *Archaeologia Orientalis* 4 (1934), Tokyo. Fair use.

found in stone reliefs of contemporaneous Shaanxi tomb gates (fig. 5.2) featuring an old man leaning on a staff emerging from swirling *qi* in which various birds, dragons, and other beasts are also visible.[2]

Figure 5.2. From a tomb gate stone relief. Eastern Han, Suide (Shaanxi). *Zhongguo huaxiangshi quanji bianji weiyuanhui* 中國畫像石全集編輯委員會 5 (Jinan: Shandong meishu chubanshe, 2000), 102. Fair use.

This portrayal of otherworldly dynamic disorder has textual precedents. Prior to the Eastern Han, poetic traditions such as the "Yuanyou" 遠遊 or "Far Roaming" had already sketched out existence's confused periphery of shifting vapors, strange beasts, and winged immortals, ending with heaven and earth losing their definition and the protagonist losing his senses: "I gaze into the now-black/now-white, but there is no seeing; I listen to the agitated delirium, but there is no hearing" (視儵忽而無見兮; 聽惝怳而無聞).³ At the end of the "Darenfu" 大人賦 or "Poetic Exposition of the Great Man" by Sima Xiangru 司馬相如 (ca. 179–117), heaven and earth again disappear, and again the protagonist loses his own ability to perceive them: "I gaze into the blurry dimness, but there is no seeing; I listen to the agitated delirium, but there is no hearing" (視眩眠而無見兮; 聽惝怳而無聞).⁴ In later Han poetry, this chaotic, unfixed blurriness also seems to be the destination of the dead, where their former frames of reference break down. For example, Cai Yong 蔡邕 (133–92) described the whirling-and-drifting existence of a recently deceased Lady Ma 馬.

魂氣飄颻	The *qi* of her ethereal essence whirls and drifts;
焉所安神	Where can we settle her spirit?
兄弟何依	On whom can her sons now depend?
姊妹何親	To whom can her daughters draw near?⁵

The "ethereal essence" or *hun*-soul was a person's intangible vitality or dynamism, usually referenced only when it was in fact absent, such as in discussions about mental distress, the corpse, or the tomb.⁶ This description of the dead's state of flux is not unique to Cai Yong, as demonstrated by a father's lament for his dead son.

生時不識父	During his life, he never knew his father;
死後知我誰	Now that he is dead, will he understand who I am?
孤魂遊窮暮	His solitary ethereal essence travels the far reaches of night—
飄颻安所依	Whirling and drifting, on whom can he now depend?⁷

The Yingchengzi mural seems to depict someone materializing from that unfixed peripheral realm, and while we cannot verify with complete certainty Midzuno's interpretation of him being the ancestral spirit coming forward to attend the sacrifice, the likelihood does indeed resonate with these early poetic portrayals.

In space, the edges are darkened and blurred; in time, the increasingly forgotten dead are whirling and drifting. Such is how the conscious mind's own limits are given (ironically) concrete representation in the arts, the certain imagery of uncertainty. That is, the constraints of cognitive capacity get directly translated into the objects of that cognition; the blurring of details in the remembering mind becomes the actual blurring of the remembered people. Yet this inevitable blurring of memory also gets translated into a different kind of ontology, namely, a philosophical discourse centered on the Dao that is "blurry and indistinct" (*weihuang weihu* 惟恍惟惚)[8] and defies dualistic knowledge. This Dao is most famously known to us via the *Daode jing*.

In modern studies on memory, recollection regularly gets subdivided into categories such as semantic memory (e.g., what the *Daode jing* is), procedural memory (e.g., how to read the *Daode jing* in Chinese or English), and episodic memory (e.g., of when I myself had first read the *Daode jing* in school). If remembering can be thusly divided, perhaps forgetting should also have its own categories, a threefold division useful for the following hypothesis. First, there was *cognitive forgetting* or the familiar process of the brain simply losing details of the past. This kind of natural forgetting justified the veneration of early texts, including the so-called Confucian classics because these memorized works were what survived from sagely rulers when all else had indeed been forgotten. The Daoists in turn dismissed the same texts as mere "dregs" because they could not make up for all that was no longer remembered. Second, there was *ritualized forgetting*. In the ancestral cult, slowly fading memory was translated into a step-by-step reduction of sacrifices, as an analog process (i.e., with continuous, imperceptible gradations of change) was converted into a digital one (i.e., with discrete, perceptible gradations of change). But ritualized forgetting is more than overlaying a descriptive, tidy template onto a natural, gradual process; ritualized forgetting is also prescriptive, dictating of what will be remembered by habituating its participants to forget. Once great grandfather has been bumped from the regular sacrificial offerings because ritual deems him too distant, he is in fact no longer remembered as often as or in the same way he once was. That is, ritual is both a passive "model of" forgetting as well as an active "model for" forgetting.[9] Finally, there was *philosophical forgetting*. Here I refer to the ontology of the *Daode jing* and other texts that juxtapose, on one side, a highly demarcated here-and-now of the discretely perceived ten thousand things with, on the other side, the undefined and nameless Dao in which all such dualisms disappear. In philosophical forgetting, discursive knowledge dissolves. All three types of forgetting share a trajectory. In cognitive forgetting, we naturally tend toward blurriness over time; in ritualized forgetting, we recognize that blurriness as inevitable but also occasion it by giving structure to forgetting; in philosophical forgetting, we prioritize the Dao's blurriness, urging ourselves to return to it. The blur always wins.

The following hypothesis simply assumes cognitive forgetting as a biological given and instead focuses on ritualized and philosophical forgetting, the former via the ancestral cult in section I and the latter via the *Daode jing*'s discourse on the Dao in section II. These two paradigms are not only parallel but are also explicitly overlapped, and the focus of this argument is a half dozen *Daode jing* passages that directly reference the ancestral cult in section III. Because the two paradigms are indeed parallel and because one borrows language from the other, the concluding hypothesis is that the *Daode jing*'s basic blueprint for existence derives from the already-existing ancestral cult.

I. Ritualized Forgetting and the Ancestral Cult

Like others before him, the Classicist scholar Yang Xiong 揚雄 (53 BCE–18 CE) justified the origin of ancestral cult rituals as a way of giving form to the increasingly formless.

> The ghosts and spirits exist in a disarrayed wilderness, and they cannot be imagined in terms of locality or season, meaning that sacrifices to them lacked clear standards. Thus the sages reified the ghosts and spirits via the sacrificial guidelines.
> 鬼神耗荒, 想之無方, 無終無夏, 祭之無度。故聖人著之以祀典。[10]

The sages streamlined rituals that "reified" (*zhu* 著) the unframed spirits, bringing them back into focus and giving them definition. The *Classic of Filial Piety* or *Xiaojing* 孝經 uses the same term: "If the son of heaven shows respect to the lineage shrine, the ghosts and spirits become reified" (宗廟致敬, 鬼神著矣).[11] Because they were invisible to us and increasingly removed from us—dissipating into that uncultivated wilderness as we forgot them—the sages needed to devise a remembrance system that embodied a kind of "structured amnesia,"[12] an analog-to-digital conversion that bestowed order on forgetting. Hence ancestral tablets possessed a fixed shelf life, individually honored for a certain number of generations while they could still be remembered but physically removed to the corporate altar when eventually forgotten.

The following summary schematizes this fade, beginning with the rememberers themselves who were tidily assembled in ranked order before the tablets. It will next sketch out the line of subsequent ancestors—first those who were still individually remembered and second those who had faded into the lineage's corporate memory. Finally it will address the distant progenitor at the top of the lineage who was often paired with formless heaven.[13]

A. THE ORDERLY SACRIFICING DESCENDANTS

An Eastern Han farming-estate almanac known as the *Simin yueling* 四民月令 or *Monthly Instructions for People of Every Class* portrays the orderly rememberers as follows:

> When the day of the sacrifice arrives, they bring forward the ale to draw down the spirits. When that is done, the worthy and humble of the household, no matter how young or old, then sit before the ancestors in ranked order. The sons, their wives, the grandsons and the great grandsons each offer up spiced ale to the family head, toasting him with wishes of longevity in a joyous manner.
> 及祀日，進酒降神。畢，乃家室尊卑，無小無大，以次列坐於先祖之前；子、婦、孫、曾、各上椒酒於其家長，稱觴奉壽，欣欣如也。[14]

The "Zhongyong" 中庸 or "Focusing on Practice" in the *Liji* or *Ritual Records* echoes these ordinances, detailing how the living arranged themselves by generation and by family rank both to honor the dead and to venerate seniority among the living.[15] Again the emphasis is order, the living all clearly arranged relative to one another in their individuated places.

That desire for order extended to the space of the shrine as well. For example, the *Shijing* 詩經 or *Classic of Poetry* famously praised the tidiness at the Zhou ancestral shrine, as follows:

於穆清廟	O! The stately immaculate shrine—
肅雝顯相	Its distinguished attendants are respectful and harmonized.
濟濟多士	The many solemn officials
秉文之德	Uphold the potency (De) of King Wen
對越在天	Lest it dissipate in the heavens.[16]

A lack of tidiness might disrupt the intentions of the sacrificer, as suggested in the *Jiao shi yilin* 焦氏易林 or *Forest of Changes of Mr. Jiao*.

東門之壇	The altar at the east gate—
茹蘆在阪	Its banks are overgrown with madder.
禮義不行	The rituals and ceremonies are not carried out,
與我心反	Turning my mind upside down.[17]

In sum, the orderly sacrificial site was a small, temporary bubble of altar space and ritual time in contrast to the general "disarrayed wilderness" that lay beyond, to that chaotic darkness where the dissipating spirits might whirl and drift. As one Western Han court adviser explained, "everything in the rituals involving interaction with the spirits had to be immaculate and peaceful" (交神之禮無不清靜), and according to the *Huainanzi*, the sacrificial hall must be "sufficiently peaceful and immaculate to present offerings to the gods on high and to treat the ghosts and spirits with their proper rituals" (靜潔足以享上帝, 禮鬼神).[18] Order and demarcation were the watchwords for the here-and-now rememberers.

B. The Ancestors from Near to Far

That order and demarcation extended to the sacrifice recipients as well, at least to the most recent ancestors whose physical details and personal identities could still be remembered and visualized with clarity. For example, the presacrifice abstention was a tool to fix those details in the mind: "Think upon your ancestors' dwelling, think upon their amusing talk, think upon their intentions and ideas, think upon their entertainments and think upon their desires" (思其居處, 思其笑語, 思其志意, 思其所樂, 思其所嗜). According to the *Ritual Records*, all this thinking enabled the sacrificers to actually see each individuated ancestor at the sacrifice.[19]

As a group, the most recent generations were arranged into alternating generations flanking the principal tablet because that strict ordering of forebears "is how the sequence of fathers and sons, close and distant, old and young, near and far relations is demarcated without chaos" (所以別父子、遠近、長幼、親疏之序而無亂也).[20] At least ten early texts discuss precisely how many generations of recent ancestors the descendants were to commemoratively individuate, usually four for the son of heaven and only one or two for the lowest officials, commoners said to sacrifice to their ancestors using no dedicated altar.[21] In sum, ritual remembrance for recent ancestors was to be characterized by clearly individuating them in the memory and precisely sequencing them at the shrine.

Imperial ancestors *after* four generations no longer warranted such individuated remembrance because "their nearness has faded away" (*qinjin* 親盡).[22] But what happened to the ancestors who had faded from memory? Ritually speaking, they merged into the lineage's corporate identity. Explicitly drawing on ritual compendia at his disposal, Chancellor Kuang Heng 匡衡 (d. ca. 30 BCE) summarized, as follows:

> The ruler who had first received the mandate is personally connected to heaven, and so for ten thousand generations, his shrine is not decommissioned. As for all those who later continue the imperial undertaking, they are promoted through the five-shrine system. At the top, they are arrayed alongside the grand ancestor, only partaking in triennial sacrifices. This general principle resonates with heaven, and thus their prosperity and fortune last forever.
> 受命之君躬接于天，萬世不墮。繼烈以下，五廟而遷，上陳太祖，間歲而袷，其道應天，故福祿永終。[23]

Only the first recipient of heaven's mandate merited perpetual remembrance, and his shrine "at the top" of the five-shrine system also became the gathering point for ancestors promoted beyond the other four that were dedicated to the most immediate ancestors. No longer individually remembered, these faded ancestors received significantly fewer sacrifices, some ritual compendia specifying that they were also kept together in a *tiao* 祧 or "vault" of their own. This ritualized forgetting was in synch with the natural trajectory of the aforementioned cognitive forgetting: "This general principle resonates with heaven."[24]

Here and in other texts, the word "promoted" (*qian* 遷) to describe movement through the immediate shrines and then beyond is intentional. Ancestors faded, but they faded *upward*, a father's father always more important than a father in a culture that vaunted filial piety and age veneration. For example, while the more distant ancestors only received sacrifices every few years, that rarity in fact made those sacrifices all the more special. Or as court adviser Liu Xin 劉歆 (46 BCE–23 CE) explained, "The more distant means the more revered, and so the triennial sacrifice becomes the most significant" (彌遠則彌尊, 故禘為重矣).[25] This rationalization had been sanctioned by none other than Confucius himself who "respected the ghosts and spirits and distanced them" (敬鬼神而遠之).[26] He honored them *by* distancing them. In like manner, the *Ritual Records* contend, "The father is revered but not intimate" (父尊而不親), just as "the ghosts are revered but not intimate" (鬼尊而不親).[27] This sentiment is repeated in the "Five Forms of Conduct" ("Wuxing" 五行) excavated at Guodian that states, "Without distance, there is no respect; without respect, there is no solemnity; without solemnity, there is no reverence; without reverence, there is no honor; without honor, ritual is lost" (不遠不敬, 不敬不嚴, 不嚴不尊, 不尊不恭, 不恭亡禮).[28]

In sum, the highest ancestors were not only more remote but also more revered for being so. They found their worldly counterpart in the king or emperor who lived in his faraway capital hidden behind high walls, any direct contact with him "damaging his spiritual agency" (害於神),[29] in contrast to the ever-lower layers of his bureaucracy who were better known, more accessible, but less powerful. In other words, rarity increased value; distance was directly proportional to respect for both fading ancestors and faraway rulers.

C. THE ALWAYS-REMEMBERED PROGENITOR

In Kuang Heng's description above, the first recipient of heaven's mandate was functionally equivalent to the clan progenitor, the first and most distant ancestor who outranked all other forebears. Summarizing earlier ritual compendia, the Eastern Han's *Baihutong* 白虎通 or *White Tiger Hall Discussion* records, "The descendants who venerate the progenitor ancestor constitute the 'greater lineage group,' and this progenitor ancestor is venerated for a hundred generations" (宗其為始祖後者為大宗, 此百世之所宗也).[30] It then details the trunk lineage and the varying degrees of collateral lineages as the family spreads outward, and these distinctions between trunk and collateral lineages were to be strictly observed. The *Ritual Records* and other texts warn, "A son who is not the heir cannot make the sacrifices, and if he does, he must report it to the trunk lineage heir" (支子不祭, 祭必告于宗子).[31] With regard to the ancestors,

Wang Chong 王充 (27–ca. 100) wrote, "A late father will not eat the sacrifices from any son other than the eldest" (父不食於枝庶).³² Hence we end up with an image of a family tree, a multibranched clan in the present merging into fewer and fewer branches the further back it traces its past, eventually merging into a single trunk that disappears into the ground. This structure of the many merging into one, coupled with the idea of distinct individuations fading into the blurry wilderness, will be significant to the argument below.

The most famous lineage progenitors of the dynastic houses had emerged directly from heaven via miraculous events—their mothers stepping into giant footprints, swallowing bird eggs, or having dragons fly over them. These women gave birth to the lineage founders, thereby sidestepping the awkward question of foremost allegiance to the clan founder versus to his father, his father's father, and so forth. Such acts of heaven gave the famous lineages a clean start at the beginning and hence a better-defined in-group at the end. In turn, these progenitors were heaven's *pei* 配—that is, heaven's "counterpart," "coadjutor," or "complement," a role praised by the *Classic of Poetry*, *Classic of Changes* and elsewhere. According to the *Ritual Records of Dai the Elder*, descendants honored the progenitor's role as heaven's counterpart because it was "how one taught the people to recompense De and not forget their origins" (所以教民報德不忘本也)³³—"De" being the primal potency of the Dao when within humans (see below)—whereas the *White Tiger Hall Discussion* explains that heaven's counterpart served as an intermediary between the sacrificing lineage and heaven. "Thus we promote the progenitor ancestor, making him heaven's counterpart in terms of a guest-host relationship, which is the will of heaven" (故推其始祖, 配以賓主, 順天意也).³⁴ That is, the progenitor as "guest" was received by heaven as "host," the progenitor serving as a kind of transformer or transition point between the tangible human lineage and intangible heaven.

In summary, if we schematically imagine the basic ancestral cult as evidenced within numerous early texts, the following becomes apparent: First, the living descendants down below displayed order and gradation when they engaged in ritual remembrance of their ancestors. Second, the immediate ancestors who could still be remembered remained individuated in their enjoyment of the sacrifices, but the more distant ancestors who had faded from memory merged into a corporate body led by the single lineage progenitor. Finally, that lineage progenitor—the highest power in the human lineage and the embodiment of De—served as counterpart to the forces of formless heaven. From numerous, individuated, well-organized descendants below to a formless, singular heaven above, this ritual structure digitized the process of fading memory, becoming a map for venturing into the "disarrayed wilderness."

II. Philosophical Forgetting and the *Daode jing*

Making a seemingly abrupt shift, this argument now turns to a different map of that cosmos, although as will be seen, the basic topology is in fact the same.[35]

The backbone of the *Daode jing* is understanding how every A in conventional reality generates its not-A. Especially in language (i.e., in the naming of things), but generally in any form of conceptualization, every "thing-ed" thing implicitly generates its own not-thing, its own negative frame. For examples:

1. *The implicit* oppositional *negative frame*: The idea of beauty implicitly generates the idea of ugly, good generates bad, difficult generates easy, long generates short, high generates low, before generates after, and so forth.

2. *The implicit* spatial *negative frame*: A wheel only works if there is a not-wheel—that is, a hub where the axle will fit—at its center; a cup only holds water if there is a not-cup in the middle of it; walls make a room, but a not-wall (aka a door) is necessary if it is to be used; and so forth.

3. *The implicit* temporal *negative frame*: The idea of gathering inward can only be defined by first extending outward; the idea of weakening can only be defined by first strengthening; the idea of rejecting can only be defined by first accepting; and so forth.

4. *The implicit* categorical *negative frame*: Blue is defined by not-red, not-yellow, not-white, not-black; sweet is defined by not-salty, not-sour, not-bitter, not-pungent; and so forth.

These four frames can be deduced from the lists of examples given in chapters 2, 11, 36, and 12 of the *Daode jing*, respectively, and the simple fact that this text discretely clusters particular types of A/not-A examples implies that the *Daode jing* authors recognized these several distinct kinds of dualisms.

The Dao, simply put, is that which necessarily binds A to its not-A; it is a distinction-free state in which A and not-A are united within a common category. That is, it is what necessarily unites beauty to ugly, removing their apparent separateness because they are mutually dependent and mutually defining of one another. As their unifier without distinctions, the Dao itself is hence empty, formless, unfixed, indistinct, blurry, obscured, dark, bland, and nameless. (Each of these modifiers for the Dao is taken from the cited passages below.) In sum, the closer any thing gets to the Dao itself, the more that thing loses its separation from its not-that-thing and the more it manifests a primal "potency" or De within itself. As chapter 14 explains, when we near the Dao, we might use words such as *dimness*, *faintness*, and *slightness* to describe our attempts to see, hear, and feel it, respectively, but even those descriptors are still names: "Because it's so nebulous, those ways of sensing the Dao *can't* be named when they return to this state of not being things" (繩繩不可名, 復歸於無物). Or summarizing how the Dao was epitomized in antiquity, chapter 65 ends, "When the darkened De becomes deep and distant and when it becomes opposed to being thing-ed, only then do we reach Great Conformity" (玄德深矣, 遠矣, 與物反矣, 然後乃至大順).

At this point, an example might be useful to demonstrate how A/not-A dualisms manifest in conventional reality, here drawing on chapter 18.

> If the great Dao is set aside, then there are benevolence and proper relationships.
> If wisdom and intelligence emerge, then there is great artifice.
> If the relationships between father and son, elder and younger brother as well as husband and wife lose their harmony, then there are filial piety and affection.
> If the ruling houses fall into confusion and chaos, then there are loyal officials.
> 大道廢, 有仁義; 智慧出, 有大偽; 六親不和, 有孝慈; 國家昏亂, 有忠臣。[36]

Most interpretations assume this to be a diatribe against Confucianism, the watchwords of which were indeed "benevolence and proper relationships." They maintain that Daoists are here charging Confucians and their so-called benevolence as being hypocritical, artificial, false, classicist, unnatural, confusing, and annoying.[37] Their assumption is that because benevolence happened when the Dao fell, we must figure out a way of making benevolence look bad.

But this approach does not work even within the confines of the *Daode jing* itself. First, other chapters speak positively of benevolence.[38] Second, chapter 38 observes that "When the Dao was lost, there was the De; when the De was lost, there was benevolence; when benevolence was lost, there were proper relationships; when proper relationships were lost, there was ritual" (失道而後德, 失德而後仁, 失仁而後義, 失義而後禮).[39] If the standard interpretation of chapter 18 holds, then here in chapter 38 the De must likewise be hypocritical, artificial, and false because it arose when the Dao fell, but that would clearly be contrary to the rest of this *Classic of the Dao and the De*. Something else is going on.

If instead the idea of A/not-A—of implicit negative frames—is applied to chapter 18, then when benevolence arose, *not-benevolence also arose*, and so the Dao's homogenous state had indeed become lost. As the chapter then says, we recognize filial piety only when families are in chaos; we identify loyal officials only when states are in disorder.[40] In sum, any quality or thing is only identifiable by the coexistence of its contrasting not-that-quality or not-that-thing, but in conventional reality, that quality or thing instead gets elevated and treated as if it exists on its own. Such is true *even when naming the Dao itself* as the opening lines of the *Daode jing* explain. (The next section will explicate those lines.) Here chapter 18 is not singling out Confucian benevolence for attack but is instead making a statement about all dualisms.[41]

The thrust of the *Daode jing* is to then apply this idea of rising above A/not-A dualisms to rulership. When in chapter 53 the court is elevated through fine dress, good food and wealth, the surrounding overtaxed countryside becomes overgrown with weeds, the granaries emptied. In other words, when the ruler builds up the A, the not-A proportionally grows, too. Instead, the best rulers *do not* display themselves—that is, they do not make an A of themselves (chapters 59, 72)—and their subjects barely know such rulers are even there (chapter 17).[42] By not embracing dualistic knowledge themselves, those rulers also muddle the dualistic tendencies of their subjects (chapters 3, 49, 65), keeping them likewise ignorant and undesiring of dualistic objects. (From the first chapter of the received *Daode jing* onward, dualism goes hand-in-hand with a desire for things, with wanting an A as opposed to a not-A, meaning that this ontological argument in turn becomes an ethical argument.) As a ruler's survival guide for the Warring States period, the *Daode jing*'s message is: "Be savvy of the full consequences of your actions—that is, know how every A coexists with its not-A—and keep your head down so you do not become an A."

In summary, if we were to schematically imagine the *Daode jing*'s argument: First, at the bottom of the spectrum, people live in a conventional world of the ten thousand things where each dualistic A is distinct, its not-A usually ignored. Second, the sages pursue the attainment of De by realizing how A and not-A in fact define one another, gradually moving up from, for example, ritual to proper relationships to benevolence to De and then to Dao. Finally, that Dao up top—often associated with heaven—is a dark homogeneity where definition gets lost, where all A's and not-A's are blurred.

This threefold schematic is now familiar, replicating point-for-point the basic paradigm of the already-existing ancestral cult described above. Left here, this parallel would simply be a vague-but-interesting correlation, not a case of causation. However, the *Daode jing* itself repeatedly draws on ancestral-cult imagery to make its argument.

III. Establishing the *Daode jing*'s Paternity

Situating the *Daode jing* within the context of early rituals and practices can explain many of its enigmatic allusions. For example, chapter 20 compares the ideal individual with "an infant who has not yet smiled" (*ying'er weihai* 嬰兒之未孩),[43] and contemporaries of this text would have here recognized the naming ritual in which a father takes up his three-month-old infant, "induces it to smile and names it" (*ke er mingzhi* 咳而名之).[44] In other words, one's existence *before* the smile would literally have been a state of namelessness, a state beyond all A/not-A distinctions that is most desired in the Dao. Historical context is thus necessary for interpretive commentary.[45]

The foremost cultural phenomenon informing the *Daode jing*'s structuring paradigm comes not from the beginning of life but the end: the ancestral cult. In summary, we not only observe a resemblance in their underlying argument—that is, a spectrum from conventional individuation to ultimate homogeneity—we also can suggestively establish paternity through the ancestral cult's language that survives within the *Daode jing*. This line of reasoning will conclude with a half dozen examples in which the *Daode jing* directly draws on its forebear.

THE DEAD AS REMEMBERED SPIRITS: *DAODE JING* 33

The *Daode jing*'s brief chapter 33 consists of four couplets, the first three of which are relatively straightforward.

> Understanding others constitutes knowledge, but understanding the self constitutes enlightenment. Overcoming others is power, but overcoming the self is vigor. Understanding sufficiency is wealth; vigorous practice is possessing intent.
> 知人者知也，自知明也。朕人者有力也，自朕者強也。知足者富也。強行者有志也。[46]

The first two couplets prioritize dissolving the self over conquering others—wholly appropriate in a text that vaunts *wuwei* 無為 or "not acting upon" others—and the third couplet commends that self's sufficiency and hard work.

Yet the fourth and final couplet—the result of this well-focused lifetime—had perplexed us since at least the second century CE, with the Wang Bi commentary. Prior to the Mawangdui excavation, the phrase *si er buwang* 死而不亡 generated considerable confusion because of the difficulty in identifying the intended difference between *si* 死 and *wang* 亡, both potentially meaning "to die" and hence leading to poetic-but-vague interpretations of "dying without perishing."[47] Fortunately the Mawangdui versions—if they reflect the original intent—remove that confusion, replacing *wang* 亡 with *wang* 忘, "to forget."[48] Hence the fourth couplet reads,

> Those who do not lose their position endure; those who die but are not forgotten are longevous.
> 不失其所者久也，死而不忘者壽也。[49]

Unlike its English usage, the idea of "longevity" (*shou* 壽) in early Chinese can apply to one's total existence and included the afterlife before entirely fading away, *shou* being a common modifier for ancestral halls and tombs. Hence this final line clearly resonates with the ancestral cult's basic idea of remembrance equating with postmortem existence. The *unforgotten* dead persist. By extension, the preceding line perhaps alludes to ancestors not losing their tablet positions within the shrine as described above, although that conclusion is more speculative. Yet as will be seen, other *Daode jing* passages explicitly refer to the continuity of sacrifices to a worthy ancestor, the living preserving his name.

The Potential for Spirits to Fade Away: *Daode jing* 39

If ancestral existence is dependent on being remembered by the living, then spirits can potentially fade away when forgotten. While chapter 39 does not reference memory dependence, it does acknowledge how spirits, ancestral and otherwise, can indeed dissipate.

> These attained unity in the past: heaven attained unity and thereby became pure; earth attained unity and thereby became settled; the spirits attained unity and thereby became numinous. . . . If heaven were without it, its pure nature might break up; if earth were without it, its settled nature might collapse; if the spirits were without it, their numinous nature might fade away.
> 昔之得一者: 天得一以清; 地得一以寧; 神得一以靈 . . . 。天無以清, 將恐裂; 地無以寧, 將恐發; 神無以靈, 將恐歇。[50]

What is this "unity"? The same chapter explains that it is the evening-out of A and not-A from the perspective of the Dao, "the valued being reliant upon the mean as its root, and the high being reliant upon the low as its base" (貴以賤為本, 高以下為基).[51]

While this chapter does not explain how such unity is to be understood in terms of the spirits, it does assign them the ideal of being *ling* 靈, variously rendered as "efficacious," "numinous," or "having a numinous power." Other early texts and inscriptions indicate a spirit's numinous power could vary in intensity, such as in the phrase "their numinous power is especially spiritual" (其靈尤神) or "this spirit is very numinous" (神多靈). They also allude to that numinous power's potential to wane, particularly in the common phrase *hun er youling* 魂而有靈, alternatively *hun ru youling* 魂如有靈: "if the ethereal essence is [still] numinous," may it benefit us.[52] Here in the *Daode jing*, that numinous potency "fades away" (*xie* 歇) when the spirit's ideal unity is lost.

Moving Upward from Living Sages to Spirits to Ghosts: Chapter 60

Chapter 60 indirectly reinforces this idea that spirits have a finite amount of power when it comes to affecting the living.

> Governing a great state is like poaching a small fish.
> When the Dao oversees the world, then the ghosts lack spiritual agency. It is not just that the ghosts lack spiritual agency, the spirits are not troubled over the people. It is not just that the spirits are not troubled over the people, the sages are also not troubled over the people.
> And if the spirits and sages also don't trouble one another, then their De will return to and join with the Dao. 治大國若烹小鮮。以道蒞天下, 其鬼不神; 非其鬼不神, 其神不傷人; 非其神不傷人, 聖人亦不傷人。夫兩不相傷, 故德交歸焉。[53]

Reiterated in several other chapters, the overall message here is vaunting a hands-off approach. Neither the cooks, the ghosts, the spirits, nor the sages heavily intervene with their charges, all again favoring *wuwei* or "not acting upon" others. If the spirits and sages don't act upon the people and if they don't act upon one another, then their undiminished potency duly returns to the Dao. But why not the ghosts, too? Perhaps because "ghosts" (*gui* 鬼) have *already* "returned" (*gui* 歸), the two words being a common paronomastic gloss for one another. That is, because these two words sounded alike, they were often associated in meaning, and chapter 60 may be building off this particular association, which was well-established in early texts.

Within the ancestral cult, early ritual compendia also separate the ghosts from other ancestral spirits because the former had slipped beyond ritualized remembrance, their tablets to be removed from the individuated sacrificial altars. For example, the *Jifa* 祭法 or "System of Sacrifice" in the *Ritual Records* sets out the prescribed number of remembered ancestral spirits by virtue of rank, ending its description of each rank by noting that spirits who had slipped beyond the prescribed number were deemed "ghosts." It describes the case of the lowest ranks as follows:

> An office head is allowed one shrine, and that shrine is for his father. His grandfather has no shrine but he still receives sacrifices. When ancestors have slipped beyond the level

> of grandfather, they are deemed ghosts. Lower officials and commoners have no shrines, and when they die, they are deemed ghosts.
> 官師一廟︓曰考廟。王考無廟而祭之。去王考為鬼。庶士、庶人無廟, 死曰鬼。[54]

If this distinction is being observed in chapter 60, then this passage is simply moving down from distant ancestors (the ghosts), to near ancestors (the spirits), to the living (the sage rulers) in arguing for its hands-off approach. Starting with the ghosts who "lack spiritual agency" (*bushen* 不神), it begins this list with a group of entities who were indeed already recognized as no longer interacting with the living.

The Unforgotten Progenitor at the Top of the Lineage: Chapter 21

But when the *Daode jing* alludes to ancestral spirits, it is chiefly to the most distant of ancestors, the always-to-be-remembered lineage progenitor who, unlike the aforementioned ghosts, is in fact the best remembered and most powerful of ancestors because, having spawned it, he represents the corporate lineage as a whole. For example, chapter 21 offers a longer direct reference to the mechanics of the ancestral cult, equating the De with that progenitor. Briefly, let us unpack the idea of De before turning to this chapter.

What is De? Often rendered as "potency," "power" or "virtue" (the last in the older English meaning of "effective force" or "capacity to act," not to be confused with virtue as "moral excellence"), De is simply the Dao when instantiated within things, particularly within humans. The *Guanzi* offers a useful understanding of it relative to the Dao.

> The Dao of heaven is empty and without form. Because it is empty, it cannot be bent; because it is without form, it is unfixed. Being unfixed, it flows everywhere among the ten thousand things and never changes. The De is dwelling within the Dao, and those things "attain" (*de*) the De to live. . . . Not acting upon things (*wuwei*) is called the Dao; dwelling within the Dao is called the De. Hence the Dao cannot be separated from the De, and so we do not separate them when we discuss them. We only separate them in discussion to

highlight the fact that the De is our dwelling within the Dao. 天之道, 虛其無形。虛則不屈, 無形則無所位赶, 無所位赶, 故遍流萬物而不變。德者道之舍, 物得以生。 . . . 以無為之謂道, 舍之之謂德。故道之與德無閒。故言之者不別也。閒之理者, 謂其所以舍也。⁵⁵

This relationship between formless Dao and instantiated De within it is useful in understanding chapter 21, the entirety of which is as follows:

> When the great De manifested, it descended from the Dao alone. It was the Dao reified as a thing. Such blurriness, such indistinctness! Indistinct and blurry but with a form therein; blurry and indistinct but with a thing therein. Obscured and dark but with a seed therein; a seed perfectly real and with a point of dependency therein.
> From antiquity to the present, we have never discarded the name of that one who had first manifested the De, and it was duly passed down through our ancestors. And how do I know about the success our ancestors? Through *itself*.
> 孔德之容, 惟道是從。道之為物, 惟恍惟惚。惚兮恍兮, 其中有象; 恍兮惚兮, 其中有物。窈兮冥兮, 其中有精; 其精甚真, 其中有信。自古及今, 其名不去, 以閱衆甫。吾何以知衆甫之狀哉？以此。⁵⁶

The first part of this passage describes the appearance of the De within the Dao, from a blur, to a form, to a thing, to a seed with the potential for temporal prolongation or reproduction, and finally to a point of dependency as anchor for the subsequent lineage. The second part fixes that De in subsequent historical time, the first name established and then passed down from father to father through the generations. The forefathers are in fact connected *through* that name, and "through itself" at the passage's end refers to it being self-evident by the lineage's own existence in the present. Significantly, this connection between De and lineage sacrifice recurs at the beginning of chapter 54: "Firmly grounded, [the De] is never taken away; firmly embraced, it is never released; and because of it, future generations have never abandoned their sacrifices" (善建者不拔, 善抱者不脫, 子孫以祭祀不輟).⁵⁷

Contemporaneous readers of chapter 21 would have readily recognized this description as the emergence of the lineage progenitor from heaven whose name, preserved on a tablet, was indeed to be remembered forever in the sacrifices. In the ancestral cult, that progenitor was frequently and explicitly identified as the original manifestation of De in the lineage, as already seen in the *Classic of Poetry* and the *Ritual Records of Dai the Elder* cited above. For further examples, first the *Guliang Commentary to the Spring and Autumn Annals* records: "Thus as for those rich in De, their heritage is brilliant, but as for those poor in De, their heritage is meager. Therefore, the origin of initial De is honored, and he who is the first to be enfeoffed must be treated as first ancestor" (故德厚者流光, 德薄者流卑, 是以貴始德之本也, 始封必為祖).[58] Here the De is specifically associated with the first ancestor, the progenitor. For a second example, the *Zuo Commentary to the Spring and Autumn Annals* cites a Zhou historian explaining why the sage-ruler Shun still merited sacrifices as follows: "I have heard that flourishing De must have a hundred generations of sacrifices; the number of generations for Yu [= Shun] has not yet reached this" (臣聞盛德必百世祀; 虞之世數未也).[59] For a third example, some Han emperors were said to have warranted perpetual sacrifices rather than sacrifices terminating after four generations, and that was because they were said to have uniquely manifested this De, even though they themselves were not technically progenitors.[60] This last example is an exception that proves the rule. It was argued that these emperors were to be treated as exceptions because they, too, possessed progenitor-*like* De.

In sum, an early reader of the *Daode jing*, being familiar with the ancestral cult, would have seen the formless Dao as akin to heaven and the instantiated De as akin to that progenitor emerging from heaven, that De extending its line of influence down into the present, meriting perpetual sacrifices as noted in both chapters 21 and 54. The De is first "thing"; it is the seed and first point of lineage dependence or "trust"; it is the ancestral progenitor who bears the first "name." Elsewhere in the *Daode jing*, the De is often listed second in sequences such as in the aforementioned chapter 38, the Dao giving way to the De, in turn giving way to benevolence, then to proper relationships and then to rituals. The De is first "successor," first son in this conceptual lineage.

As an aside, chapter 21 here describes the "indistinct and blurry" Dao "with a form (*xiang*) therein." Similarly depicting the Dao as "ancestor of the ten thousand things" (*wanwu zhi zong* 萬物之宗), chapter 4 ends by saying that, while we do not know whose son the barely perceptible Dao is, it "precedes the gods taking form (*xiang*)" (*xiang di zhi xian* 象帝之先). Again there is a sense of sequence and of lineage, the subsequent gods being like the lineage progenitors—the two often functionally synonymous with one another—as they emerge from the Dao.

Boring Stew and the Bland Dao: Chapter 35

Chapter 35 also begins by urging the reader to "grasp the great form" (*zhi daxiang* 執大象), but it ends with the following images of the indistinct and the blurry:

> Music and tasty treats may make the passing guest halt, but what comes forth from the Dao's mouth is bland in its tastelessness. If you look for it, you will not be able to see it; if you listen for it, you will not be able to hear it; and if you employ it, you will not be able to use it up.
> 樂與餌, 過客止。道之出口, 淡乎其無味, 視之不足見, 聽之不足聞, 用之不足既。⁶¹

While not explicitly describing an ancestral sacrifice, there is much suggestive language here. For example, the spirits are sometimes referenced as "guests" (*ke* 客) to be lured in by the ancestral sacrifice's music, food and drink. As seen above in the *Monthly Instructions for People of Every Class*, the sacrificers "brought forward the ale to draw down the spirits." Furthermore, the inability to see and hear them is common imagery for the ancestral spirits. For example, "Focusing on Practice" attributes to Confucius the following:

> The De of the spirits and ghosts—does it not flourish? I may look for them but will not see them; I may listen for them but will not hear them. Yet they embody everything, leaving nothing behind. Because of them, the world's people carry out abstentions and purifications as well as don the proper dress in order to undertake their sacrificial offerings. The spirits and ghosts come flowing and flowing, as if they were there overhead, as if they were there to the left, to the right. The *Classic of poetry* says:
>
> Whether the spirits have arrived
> cannot be ascertained,
> and so could we ever let ourselves become indifferent?
> The manifestation of the subtle is like that! The irrepressibility
>   of sincerity is like that!
> 鬼神之為德, 其盛矣乎! 視之而弗見, 聽之而弗聞, 體物而不可遺。使天下之人, 齊明盛服, 以承祭祀, 洋洋乎如在其上, 如在其

左右。《詩》曰:「神之格思,不可度思,矧可射思。」夫微之顯,誠之不可揜如此夫! [62]

Early readers of the *Daode jing* would have likely recognized an overlap in the language describing the imperceptible Dao and the spirits who, manifesting De, are also beyond clear demarcation of eye and ear.

Yet chapter 35 draws on the ancestral cult in another way. According to Giles Boileau, its contrast of tasty treats and bland flavors might allude to ancestral rituals that distinguished between the offerings earmarked for recent ancestors and remote forebears, respectively. Those for recent ancestors were complex, distinctive, and sophisticated; those for the remote forebears were simple, unseasoned, and one-note. In early prescriptive texts, the latter was epitomized by the "great stew" (*dageng* 大羹)—meat simply boiled in water—its blandness perhaps closer to the homogeneity of the Dao itself, in which, to borrow language from above, the distinctiveness of any particular A has faded away. Boileau concludes, "In the *Daode jing*, passages mentioning taste and music could be interpreted as the philosophical metaphorization and modification of ritual elaborations on the value of the great stew / numerous tasty dishes system."[63] Prescribing how this stew should be kept separate from the rest of the food, excavated texts further confirm the stew's usage in ancestral sacrifices.[64]

The Dao and the De: Chapter 1

This system of simplicity/unity/boring stew, on one end, and complexity/deconstruction/tasty dishes, on the other, perhaps reaches its most famous philosophical expression in the opening lines of the *Daode jing*.

> As for the Dao, it is permissible to think of it as a "Dao," but that's not the continuous Dao.
> And as for naming, it is permissible to name, but that's not continuous naming.
> Namelessness is the first ancestor of the ten thousand things,[65]
> Whereas names are the mother of the ten thousand things.
> 道可道,非常道。名可名,非常名。無名萬物之始;有名萬物之母。[66]

By way of brief explanation, the first two lines are looking at the same problem from opposite sides. As already observed, the Dao is reaching toward *continuous unity*, which is a murky, undefined, nameless state;

naming is conversely reaching toward *continuous fracturing*, where every A is in its separate box. But in any discourse on the Dao, simply regarding the Dao itself as a thing, as a "Dao" (and hence defined by its not-that-Dao), flies in the face of any continuous or uninterrupted unity above A/not-A dualism.[67] Conversely, total fracturing is just as unreachable in such a discourse because, as also already observed, every A needs its not-A—beauty needs its ugly, high needs its low, and so forth—and so all the boxed A's cannot simply fly apart from one another in a bid for absolute deconstruction.[68] Hence the *Daode jing* begins with a caveat: by its very nature, it must work within this spectrum between ultimate unity and ultimate fracturing, between the absolutes of continuous Dao-ing and continuous naming. Furthermore, as chapter 1 will go on to say, Dao-ing and naming in fact define one another as well; they constitute a giant A/not-A. That is, unity can only be understood via fracturing and vice versa, and so the chapter concludes that this dualism, too, must ultimately be transcended.[69]

This Dao-ing/naming spectrum now helps us better understand the second couplet, in which the reader may have here noticed a divergence from standard translations. "Namelessness is the *first ancestor of* the ten thousand things." Usually *shi* 始 is rendered as "the beginning of" the ten thousand things. Yet *shi* is also the standard term for "lineage progenitor" in the ancestral cult, and here much better fits the parallel character of "mother" (*mu* 母) in the next line of the couplet. Furthermore, the distant, most-honored progenitor and the intimate, least-honored mother accurately mark out the two ends of the lineage spectrum, parallel to the spectrum of Dao-ing and naming in the first couplet. In chapter 21, we saw the name had first appeared with the emergence of De—the "successor" of Dao—and that single name of the lineage progenitor was the only one to be passed down through the generations from that time. Closer to mother and lost among the branches of this now-immense family tree, we *Daode jing* readers of conventional reality are located at the bottom of this language spectrum that is now awash with names, blindly dependent on boxed and defined objects, fixated by the A and forgetting of its not-A.[70] While we intimately know mother, we must return our reverential allegiance to that distant progenitor.

Conclusion

It is too easy to treat philosophies as sui generis—as unique unto themselves and divorced from mundane contexts. When we do connect idea systems to worldly matters, we tend to assume a one-way flow, the former trickling down to impact the latter. Someone has a good idea, and it catches on. Yet we rarely pause to consider how an idea system can itself be the unique product of its culture, crystallizing what's already embedded in its own circumstances. The *Lü shi chunqiu* 呂氏春秋 or *Spring and Autumn Annals of Mr. Lü* contends that we ought to consider this directionality as well.

> Someone gazing eastward will not see the western wall, and someone looking off toward the south will not notice the north. *Ideas depend on their location.*
> 東面望者不見西牆，南鄉視者不睹北方，意有所在也。[71]

Or as the Daoist Zhuangzi argued, any new thought—including thoughts about the Dao—is derived from all the already-existing thoughts around it.[72]

The "Dao" may have emerged out of that darkened, ineffable and continuous state that knows no dualistic Dao or not-Dao, but the *Classic of the Dao and the De* itself did not emerge ex nihilo. Its basic paradigm of discrete, mundane individuation shifting toward an ultimate ideal of blurry unity arose from habituated ritual practices of a lineage-based culture, and it retains the explicit language of that ancestral cult, from fading spirits and the potentially forgotten dead, to justified sacrifices and De-embodying progenitors.[73] Because the ancestral cult's "ritualized forgetting" undergirds Daoism's "philosophical forgetting," the ancestral cult is the *Daode jing*'s forgotten forebear.[74]

Notes

1. Osamu Mori and Hiroshi Naito, "Ying-ch'eng-tzu: The Han Brick-tomb with Fresco-Paintings, etc., near Chian-mu-ch'eng-J, South Manchuria," *Archaeologia Orientalis* 4 (1934), 5–7, of its English abstract by Kosaku Hamada. Midzuno's interpretation is convincing because the coffin platform itself jutted out from the lower-left-hand corner of this mural (i.e., where the empty space is), meaning the ancestor was portrayed as streaming outward from above the actual coffin whereas the descendants were setting out their sacrifices in front of it.

Li Xiang's contribution to this volume also describes "partitioned" tombs in which the corpse is placed in a central chamber nested within a larger one. (Li Xiang interprets this as an imprisoning cell to lock the dead in, although it's unclear how that interpretation would work here, particularly given the contents of this fresco.)

2. After Zhongguo huaxiangshi quanji bianji weiyuanhui 中國畫像石全集編輯委員會, *Zhongguo huaxiangshi quanji bianji* 中國畫像石全集 5 (Jinan: Shandong meishu chubanshe, 2000), 102 (pl. 137), the scratches and artifacts from the rubbing process removed.

3. *Chuci buzhu* 楚辭補注, annotated by Hong Xingzu 洪興祖 (Beijing: Zhonghua shuju, 2000), 174–75 ("Yuanyou" 遠遊).

4. *Shiji*, 117.3062. (All references to the standard histories are to the Zhonghua shuju editions.) The *Huainanzi* and *Liezi* include similar descriptions of the periphery.

5. *Cai zhonglang ji* 蔡中郎集, Sibu beiyao 四部備要 edition (Shanghai: Zhonghua shuju, 1936), 6.6b ("Situ Yuan gong furen Ma shi beiming" 司徒袁公夫人馬氏碑銘).

6. Brashier, "Han Thanatology and the Division of 'Souls.'" *Early China* 21 (1996), 125–58.

7. *Xian Qin Han Wei Jin Nanbeichao shi* 先秦漢魏晉南北朝詩, annotated by Lu Qinli 逯欽立 (Beijing: Zhonghua shuju, 1984), 12.342 ("Gushi" 古詩). This poem is attributed to Li Ling 李陵 (fl. end of second century BCE), but such attributions were already in doubt by the Jin dynasty. Few scholars now believe these poems were written by him, and they are more likely the product of the Eastern Han or perhaps later.

8. *Boshu Laozi jiaozhu* 帛書老子校注, annotated by Gao Ming 高明 (Beijing: Zhonghua shuju, 1996), 328 (chapter 21). Unless otherwise noted, all quotations from the *Daode jing* refer to the standard Wang Bi version (which this Mawangdui edition also includes).

9. Seventy years ago, the anthropologist Clifford Geertz famously argued that religious idea systems were simultaneously a "model of" and a "model for" existence, both describing the structure of cosmos (as well as our place in it) and prescribing it (detailing what we should do to properly conform to it). See Geertz, "Religion as a Cultural System," in *The Interpretations of Culture* (New York: Basic Books, 1973), 93–94. Ancestors naturally fade from memory and from existence; the ancestral cult guides that fade through prescribed sacrificial reductions across the generations. See also Paul Nicholas Vogt's discussion on ritual in this book.

10. *Taixuan jizhu* 太玄集注, annotated by Sima Guang 司馬光 (Beijing: Zhonghua shuju, 2005), 209 ("Xuanyi" 玄摛). For similar statements, see *Xunzi jijie* 荀子集解, annotated by Wang Xianqian 王先謙 (Beijing: Zhonghua shyjhu, 1988), 378 ("Lilun" 禮論); *Liji jijie* 禮記集解, annotated by Sun Xidan 孫希旦 (Beijing: Zhonghua shuju, 1989), 1220 ("Jiyi" 祭義).

11. *Xiaojing yizhu* 孝經譯注, annotated by Wang Shoukuan 汪受寬 (Shanghai: Shanghai guji, 1998), 77–81 ("Yinggan" 應感).

12. I used this term *structured amnesia* throughout *Ancestral Memory in Early China*, thinking I had coined it myself, unaware that the anthropologist J. A. Barnes had already written about "structural amnesia" in the 1940s.

13. This abstracted schematic comes from evidence assembled in Brashier, *Ancestral Memory in Early China* (Cambridge, MA: Harvard University Asia Center, 2011) and Brashier, *Public Memory in Early China* (Cambridge, MA: Harvard University Asia Center, 2014). This schematic is at best a generalization, but the coherence of the surviving evidence suggests that it was the standard against which practice and variation was measured.

14. *Simin yueling jiaozhu* 四民月令校注, annotated by Shi Shenghan 石聲漢 (Beijing: Zhonghua shuju, 1965), 1 ("Zhengyue" 正月). Replicated in several early texts, the *Yueling* 月令 or *Monthly Instructions* is for the ruler, keeping him in synch with the cosmos. The *Monthly Instructions for People of Every Class* is for people below the ruler, describing the operations of a farming estate.

15. *Liji zhengyi* 禮記正義, annotated by Kong Yingda 孔穎達, Shisanjing zhushu 十三經注疏 edition (Yangzhou: Jiangsu Guangling guji, 1995), 1629 ("Zhongyong" 中庸).

16. *Mao Shi zhengyi* 毛詩正義, Shisanjing zhushu edition, 583 ("Qingmiao" 清廟). These lines begin a famous poem in a Confucian classic that was regularly committed to memory. Hence this basic tension between artificially preserving an ancestor's De or "primal potency" (to be detailed below) via ritualized remembrance, on the one hand, and the cosmic periphery where that De would naturally dissipate, on the other, was well established.

As the ritual compendia make clear, King Wen was not in fact his lineage's first ancestor, but he had acquired the Zhou territory on which his descendants depended for their livelihood. Land acquisition was a criterion for being a first ancestor, and because King Wen had acquired the entire state, he functionally became a first ancestor, to be perpetually worshiped alongside the lineage's actual progenitor, Houji.

17. *Jiao shi yilin* 焦氏易林, *Congshu jicheng* 叢書集成 edition, vols. 703–5 (Shanghai: Shangwu yinshu, 1935–37), 103 ("Bi: ding" 賁: 鼎).

18. *Hanshu*, 73.3120 and *Huainan honglie jijie* 淮南鴻烈集解, annotated by Liu Wendian 劉文典 (Taipei: Wenshizhe, 1992), 265 ("Benjing" 本經), respectively.

19. *Liji jijie*, 1208–29 ("Jiyi"). Vogt's contribution to this book also details the *Liji*'s descriptions of remembrance. This ritual compendium was highly focused on the most immediate of ancestors—that is, one's parents who can still be visualized by the eyes, heard by the ears, and fully remembered by the mind, as Vogt describes. The rituals relegate memories of the ancestors to "a controlled space in the psyche," expressed at fixed places and fixed times.

20. *Liji jijie*, 1245 ("Jitong" 祭統). Vogt's contribution in this book describes how the "Jitong" is much concerned with the relative degrees of reverence to be paid to the ritual participants.

21. For a chart of the ten, see Brashier, *Ancestral Memory in Early China*, 63.

22. *Hanshu*, 73.3116. This number of remembered ancestors in the imperial line tallies with modern research, cognitive forgetting in nonliterate societies becoming absolute after four or five generations or about a century. See Roy A. Rappaport, *Ritual and Religion in the Making of humanity* (Cambridge: Cambridge University Press, 1999), 258.

23. *Hanshu*, 73.3122.

24. As referenced in note 9 above, Geertz argued that religious idea systems are both a model for and a model of existence. Kuang Heng is here summarizing a *model for* decommissioning shrines over time because it is a *model of* what is natural, what is "heaven."

25. *Hanshu*, 73.3129. Early texts debated the timing of the *xia* 祫 and *di* 禘, specifically whether they were held every three or five years. For a chart on the decreasing frequency of sacrifices to the dead, see Brashier, *Ancestral Memory in Early China*, 58–59.

26. *Lunyu jishi* 論語集釋, annotated by Cheng Shude 程樹德 (Beijing: Zhonghua shuju 1996), 406 ("Yong ye" 雍也). This is an example in which knowledge of the ancestral cult helps us reevaluate our interpretation of early texts. Most modern interpretations maintain that Confucius here disregarded the spirits as not relevant to his program, but as suggested here, his "distancing" them was in fact an act of respect, not dismissal.

27. *Liji jijie*, 1309–10 ("Biao ji" 表記).

28. Jingmen shi bowuguan 荊門市博物館, *Guodian Chu mu zhujian* 郭店楚墓竹簡 (Beijing: Wenwu, 1998), 150.

29. *Shiji*, 6.257. For more examples of this parallel between spiritual and worldly political distance, see Brashier, *Public memory in early China*, 204.

30. *Baihutong shuzheng* 白虎通疏證, annotated by Wu Zeyu 吳則虞 (Beijing: Zhonghua shuju, 1994), 394–95 ("Zongzu" 宗祖).

31. *Liji jijie*, 153 ("Quli" 曲禮).

32. *Lunheng jiaoshi* 論衡校釋, annotated by Huang Hui 黃暉 (Beijing: Zhonghua shuju, 1995), 668 ("Mingyu" 明雩).

33. *Da Dai liji jiegu* 大戴禮記解詁, annotated by Wang Pinzhen 王聘珍 (Beijing: Zhonghua shuju, 1989), 231 ("Chaoshi" 朝事).

34. *Baihutong shuzheng*, 561 ("Quewen" 闕文).

35. What follows is merely how I myself read and teach the *Daode jing*, and I admit that my argument may be unique. (I hope not.) I do not treat the *Daode jing* as poetically intuitive, as collected aphorisms, as a diatribe against Confucianism, or as a mystical exercise to soften up the mind through a constant repetition of contradictions. I instead see a consistent, logical argument about language and other forms of discursivity throughout, an argument then applied to rulership. Yet theme and space here require only a cursory summation, for which I apologize, and I own my many mistakes in interpretation.

36. *Boshu Laozi jiaozhu*, 310–11 (ch. 18).

37. These are all descriptors drawn from both popular and academic Western translations and commentaries.

38. See chs. 8 and 38.

39. *Boshu Laozi jiaozhu*, 5 (ch. 38).

40. Early commentaries were closer to this understanding of chapter 18 than are modern interpretations. The Xiang'er commentary explains, "In high antiquity, when the Dao was employed, all people were humane and responsible. All were of the same type so that the benevolent and dutiful were not distinguished from others. Today the Dao is not employed and people are all flawed. When occasionally there is a single person who is dutiful, that person is praised by all in contradistinction to others." See Stephen R. Bokenkamp, *Early Daoist Scriptures* (Berkeley: University of California Press, 1997), 104. In turn, the Heshang gong commentary here likens the Dao to the sun and benevolence to a star. We only notice the light of the stars after the sun sets, just as we only notice benevolence after it's no longer universally absolute.

This argument may be closer to the *Daode jing*'s intended meaning, but there remains a problem with it. One could equally make the *opposite* argument, that the Dao state was uniformly *not*-benevolent, the aberration of benevolence's arising then letting us define it. That is, the Xiang'er and Heshang gong commentaries are still caught up in valuing the content of benevolence—and trying to promote that benevolence as a desired ideal compatible with the Dao—rather than focusing on the relationship between all dualisms and the Dao. Because the *Daode jing* itself focuses on the nature of implicit negative frames, most of which are value-free (long/short, cup/not-cup, gathering-inward/extending-outward, ruler/ruled, etc.), and because it even argues against dualistically conceiving "the Dao" itself, I suspect it is not making any argument about values (i.e., benevolence equals good), only about logic (i.e., "benevolence" implies "not-benevolence," with no judgment of it being good or bad). See also the next note.

41. By extension, when it is observed in chapter 5 that heaven "is not benevolent" (*buren* 不仁), it is not arguing that heaven is wrathful and cruel (as translations usually render it) but only that heaven, being the closest natural analog to the Dao, does not operate in such dualistic terms. None of this is to say the *Daode jing* writers were not intentionally being provocative, and they may have disliked how the Confucian tradition assumed fixed terms and embraced dualisms. Yet the *Daode jing* was neither promoting nor attacking "benevolence" (or "proper relationships," or "ritual," etc.) per se.

42. For more on Daoist rulers remaining peripheral and hidden, erasing all traces of themselves, see Tobias Zürn's discussion of *Huainanzi* 14 in this volume.

43. *Boshu Laozi jiaozhu*, 319 (chapter 20).

44. *Liji jijie*, 764 ("Neize" 內則); *Baihutong shuzheng*, 406 ("Xingming" 姓名).

45. Knowing how names work also helps us interpret chapter 25. "I do not know its personal name, but its courtesy name is 'the Dao.' If I were forced to recognize it via a personal name, it would be 'Great'" (吾不知其名, 字之曰道, 強為之名曰大). At three months, the infant is given its personal name, and it would be disrespectful for the speaker in chapter 25 to use this humble appellation from childhood when addressing that person as an adult and would only do so when "forced." Rather, I should only use its courtesy name, its adult name ritually bestowed after puberty. In philosophical terms, any name prior to the courtesy name "Dao"—including "Great"—would still be dualistic and would move us further and further away from the actual Dao (as chapter 25 then continues to describe), and so again we can only use such expedient labels when "forced."

46. *Boshu Laozi jiaozhu*, 403–5 (ch. 33). Note how "knowledge" in the first line is here defined as explicitly dualistic, as understanding others or understanding via otherness. Throughout the *Daode jing*, "knowledge" refers to dualistic or A/not-A knowledge, which is why it is denounced.

47. For a discussion of different translations prior to Mawangdui, see Eduard Erkes, "死而不亡," *Asia Major: New series* 3 (1952/1953), 156–61. Erkes (158) concludes that the phrase "seems to point to Taoist practices which tried to secure a kind of perpetual life after death by preserving the body and thereby enabling it to retain the enlivening soul and its power." Homer Dubs (same cite, 160) disagrees with Erkes and contends that it "is plainly used to denote the immortality of fame and of influence."

48. In other texts, *wang* 亡 and *wang* 忘 are also paronomastically linked; they sound alike and so were argued to be connected in meaning. For example, see Esther Sunkyung Klein's contribution in this book about the *Shiji*. The Duke of Zhou there states that descendants who "forget" (*wang* 忘) their parents' hard work will cause their lineages "to perish" (*wang* 亡).

Klein and several other contributors to this book also note that, in early texts, the phrase *buwang* 不忘 is regularly used as an exhortation to not neglect something rather than to not cognitively forget something. (English does the same: "Don't forget to eat your vegetables.") Here "dead but not neglected" is possible—and may be closer to how Dubs (see preceding note) had rendered it—although we might then be tempted to treat *shou* 壽 as more metaphorical (a longevity of reputation or legacy) than literal (a longevity of personal existence). Given the *Daode jing*'s other references to spirits potentially fading away, to preserving the name of the first ancestor via ancestral sacrifices and so forth (see below), I take it more literally in this context. That is, they are dead, but as they are not neglected in ritualized remembrance, they achieve their longevity of personal existence. (For a longer discussion on how the living's ritualized remembrance prolonged the dead's existence, see Brashier, *Ancestral Memory in Early China*, 207–19.)

49. *Boshu Laozi jiaozhu*, 403–5 (ch. 33).
50. *Boshu Laozi jiaozhu*, 9–11 (ch. 39).
51. *Boshu Laozi jiaozhu*, 14 (ch. 39).
52. For particular references and a longer discussion of *hun er youling* and its variances, see Brashier, *Ancestral Memory in Early China*, 340–42, 437–38. For an extended example, see Brashier, *Public Memory in Early China*, 317–18.
53. *Boshu Laozi jiaozhu*, 118–21 (ch. 60).
54. *Liji jijie*, 1201 ("Jifa" 祭法). Perhaps the idea of "hungry ghosts" dates to this distinction of removing older spirits from their regular sacrificial offerings.
55. *Guanzi jiaozhu* 管子校注, annotated by Li Xiangfeng 黎翔鳳 (Beijing: Zhonghua shuju, 2004), 770 ("Xinshu shang" 心術上).
56. *Boshu Laozi jiaozhu*, 327–34 (ch. 21). Clarifying *fu* 甫 as *fu* 父, the Mawangdui version reads *yi yue zhongfu* 以閱衆甫 as *yi shun zhongfu* 以順衆父, making it "causing the obedience of the multitude of fathers."
57. The rest of chapter 54 explicitly references the De five times, making it clear that the De is the implied subject in this chapter's first sentence.
58. *Chunqiu Guliang jingzhuan buzhu* 春秋穀梁經傳補注, annotated by Zhong Wenzheng 鍾文烝 (Beijing: Zhonghua shuju, 1996), 299 (Xi 僖 15).
59. *Chunqiu Zuozhuan zhu* 春秋左傳注, annotated by Yang Bojun 楊伯峻 (Beijing: Zhonghua shuju, 1981), 1305 (Zhao 昭 8).
60. Brashier, *Ancestral Memory in Early China*, 111.
61. *Boshu Laozi jiaozhu*, 414–15 (ch. 35).
62. *Liji zhengyi*, 1628–1629, the *Shijing* quotation from *Mao Shi zhengyi*, 555 ("Yi" 抑). "Focusing on Practice" only addresses attempts to see and hear the spirits, whereas here the Wang Bi version of the *Daode jing* addresses seeing, hearing *and using* the Dao. A better parallel, the Guodian version of the *Daode jing* does not include "using" and instead simply concludes that, while the Dao cannot be seen or heard, "it still cannot be exhausted" (而不可既也). See Robert G. Henricks, *Lao Tzu's Tao Te Ching: A Translation of the Startling New Documents Found at Guodian* (New York: Columbia University Press, 2000), 115, 184. (Unfortunately, the Guodian version does not include any of the other five passages discussed here.)
63. Gilles Boileau, "The Sage Unbound: Ritual Metaphors in the *Daode jing*," *Daoism: Religion, History and Society* 5 (2013): 33. See also Boileau, "Some Ritual Elaborations on Cooking and Sacrifice in Late Zhou and Western Han Texts," *Early China* 23–24 (1998–99): 89–123; Brashier, *Ancestral Memory in Early China*, 317–18 (where I also apply the same argument to what we know of ancestral music).

64. See both frugality-justifying resurrection stories discussed by Huang Jie 黃傑 in "Fangmatan Qin jian 'Dan' pian yu Beida Qin du 'Taiyuan yousizhe' yanjiu" (放馬灘秦簡《丹》篇與北大秦牘《泰原有死者》研究) (http://www.bsm.org.cn/show_article.php?id=2085, accessed March 9, 2020).

65. Like other translators, here I follow early commentaries as well as the Mawangdui versions, replacing *tiandi* 天地 with *wanwu* 萬物 to better maintain the parallel structure. See *Boshu Laozi jiaozhu*, 222 (ch. 1).

66. *Boshu Laozi jiaozhu*, 221–23 (ch. 1).

67. Contrary to most translations that resort to a second (and much rarer) meaning for Dao (i.e., "to speak"), I simply take the second "Dao" in the opening line as a putative verb, as "to regard as Dao." The parallel line beginning the *De jing* (i.e., ch. 38) uses the same kind of logic and syntax: "The highest De is not regarded as 'De' and so De exists" (上德不德, 是以有德). Chapter 38 goes on to describe the De as humans *doing* the Dao, in the same manner that De is defined above.

68. This dichotomy occurs elsewhere in the Daoist tradition. For example, the *Liezi* describes a mythical land in the distant southwest that is free of all dualisms, where night and day, cold and heat, "lack differentiation" (*wangbian* 亡辨) and everything is hazy and dreamlike. This land is beyond A/not-A. Opposite to it in the distant northeast, another mythical land experiences only day, only heat, and is characterized by hardness, strength, oppression, and infertility. This land is purely A without not-A. In between, the Middle Kingdoms are characterized by equilibrium and stability in terms of *yinyang*, daylight, temperature, and so forth. This land is balanced A/not-A. See *Liezi jishi* 列子集釋, annotated by Yang Bojun 楊伯峻 (Beijing: Zhonghua shuju, 1985), 104–5 ("Zhou Mu wang" 周穆王). This spectrum in the *Liezi*'s mythical realm is the same as the more abstract "Dao-ing versus naming" in the *Daode jing*'s opening chapter.

69. I here refer to "blackening even the blackness" (玄之又玄). In sum, A/not-A thinking is itself an A.

70. Contemporaneous cosmogonies that reify the Dao as a first point in time would also locate us at the increasingly fractured end of history and hence closest to our "mother," naming.

Such cosmogonies aside, Paul Ricoeur defined a similar language spectrum, the unifying end being the polysemic language of poetry, religion, and symbolic discourse, whereas the fractured end is the monosemic language of science and taxonomy—that is, one word, one meaning. At the former end, meaning comes from words having multiple possibilities, chordlike as they resonate with one another, but Ricoeur observed that our everyday discourse is closer to the latter end, tending toward scientific deconstruction. Hence in terms of the *Daode jing*, that deconstructive "naming" end of the language spectrum would indeed be our closer relative, our "mother." See Ricoeur, "Poetry and Possibility," in *A Ricoeur Reader: Reflection and Imagination* (Toronto, ON: University of Toronto Press, 1991), 449.

Although not citing Ricoeur, Rappaport outlines a similar language spectrum but would shift the poetic/religious/symbolic discourse into the spectrum's middle, making room for an even more unity-espousing discourse, namely, the "high-order meanings" of ineffable mysticisms in which individual meanings get annihilated. He would probably have included the Dao among his high-order meanings. See Rappaport, *Ritual and Religion in the Making of Humanity*, 70–74.

71. *Lü shi chunqiu jishi* 呂氏春秋集釋, annotated by Xu Weiyu 許維遹 (Beijing: Beijing shi Zhongguo shudian, 1985), 13.11a ("Quyou" 去尤) (emphasis mine).

72. "Ideas are dependent on their locations." My own ideas about the *Daode jing* may be different from the norm, simply because they are dependent on my location, namely, my studies of the early Chinese ancestral cult.

With that in mind, here it is appropriate to extend my appreciation to Albert Galvany for his dogged persistence in pushing me to contribute to his book. In one of my repeated professions of having nothing worth saying (which may still be the case), I mentioned a passing thought about how the ancestral cult perhaps hovered behind the *Daode jing*. He pressed me for details, and this chapter is the result.

73. Other Daoist texts are, of course, likewise indebted to the basic paradigm of the ancestral cult. For example, the *Zhuangzi* praises someone whose mind is empty, twisting, and devoid of any who or what—that person's mind being "akin to not yet having begun to emerge from the Ancestor" (若未始出其宗); the *Huainanzi* thrice uses the same phrase for someone who has achieved the calm, dazed harmony of "grand pervasiveness" (*datong* 大通). *Zong* 宗 regularly refers to the clan foundation, and *shi* 始 here may allude to being "the first ancestor" or "progenitor." Regardless of the specific translation, the phrase clearly idealizes the beginning of the ancestral lineage and associates it with the Dao's nondiscursive all-pervasiveness. See *Zhuangzi jishi* 莊子集釋, annotated by Guo Qingfan 郭慶藩 (Beijing: Zhonghua shuju, 1997), 304 ("Ying diwang" 應帝王); *Huainan honglie jijie*, 193 ("Lanming" 覽冥), 201 ("Lanming"), 238 ("Jingshen" 精神).

74. Daoism isn't the only idea system that owes a debt to the ancestral cult. While some have argued otherwise, Confucianism isn't a religion in itself, but the ancestral cult is clearly its religious backbone. Its key ideas such as filial piety, proper relationships, and a veneration of antiquity are all given tangible expression in the ancestral cult's sacrificial rituals.

Furthermore, the structure embedded in early Chinese cosmogony (from primeval unity to *yinyang*, to the four seasons, to the five phases, and so forth, eventually to the ten thousand things) mirrors the structure of lineages (from progenitor to trunk lineage, to collateral lineages, and so forth, eventually resulting in the masses of the present). And like Daoist texts, early cosmogonic descriptions regularly retain explicit language and imagery drawn from the ancestral cult. For early Chinese writers, the ancestral cult is foremost among the "metaphors we live by."

Chapter 6

So Comfortable You'll Forget You Have Them On
Attention and Forgetting in the *Zhuangzi* and *Huainanzi*

FRANKLIN PERKINS

忘足, 履之適也。(When shoes are comfortable, the feet are forgotten.)[1]
—Guo Qingfan 郭慶藩, *Zhuangzi jishi* 莊子集釋

Reebok Skyscrape: So comfortable you'll forget you have them on.
—Reebok Skyscrape Forever television advertisement, 2014

Not Remembering and Not Attending

The English word *forget* and the classical Chinese term *wang* 忘 carry the same ambiguity: they are privative terms that can be opposed to remembering but also opposed to noticing or paying attention. "Oblivion" has the same ambiguity. Its earliest meaning is to fail to remember, but its dominant meaning has come to be a state of unawareness; for example, we might describe someone as "oblivious" to the world around them. As these terms suggest, memory and attention overlap in various ways. If we do not attend to something, we are unlikely to remember it in the future. In the other direction, at least some forms of attending require the ability to hold on to the immediate past. Under the category of "retention," John Locke places both memory and "contemplation," which functions "by keeping the idea which is brought into it, for some time actually in view."[2] Finally, to fail to remember is to fail to have in mind, so remembering could just be one specific form of a lack of awareness. The etymologies of the key terms support this view. *Oblivion* comes from Latin, where the root seems to be smoothing over or rubbing out. The word *forget* comes out of Germanic languages, where "for" is a privative term, making the original meaning to "un-get" or "fail to get." The Chinese character for *wang* combines the heart (*xin* 心), which usually marks characters associated with mental processes, and the character meaning to lack, lose, or destroy (*wang* 亡), suggesting a core meaning of absence from mind. In their origins, none of these terms have any specific temporal dimension linking them to memory.

The justification for distinguishing the two meanings of "forget" in English is the distinction between the positive terms to which forgetting is opposed: the meaning of "remember" is distinct from that of "attend to" or "notice." The distinction is primarily temporal, in that remembering refers to something from the past while attending refers to something present, but there is another significant difference in the common usage of the words. The object of not remembering is usually some bit of knowledge, some fact or truth. Not noticing or attending, however, is about how the world itself appears. It operates at a phenomenological level that precedes conscious judgments and the designating of facts. This phenomenological level of forgetting appears in the quotations that start this chapter, which bring to mind Heidegger's discussion of equipment (*das Zeug*). In concernful absorption with the world, we "forget" the things we use. Such things become conspicuous only when they do not function properly.[3]

In classical Chinese, the terms most frequently contrasted with *wang* involve awareness or perception.[4] The most obvious example is the contrast between *wang* and *jian* 見, seeing, a character that can also mean to appear or make manifest (pronounced as *xian*). To give just one example, the *Huainanzi* says the following:

> The noble see errors and forget the threat of punishment, so they can remonstrate. They see the worthy and forget being lowered in rank, so they can yield to others. They see where

there is need and forget becoming poor, so they can give generously to others.
君子見過忘罰, 故能諫; 見賢忘賤, 故能讓; 見不足忘貧, 故能施。[5]

The point is not about explicit values or judgments, but rather how the world appears to those who are properly cultivated, the noble (*junzi* 君子). They see where they can be of help and are oblivious to the sacrifices helping might entail. Other terms have a broader range of meanings. To *wang* is to not *si* 思, a term loosely translated as "to think" but with a particular sense of attending to or attending to in a certain way. To *wang* is to not *zhi* 知, to not know. *Zhi* can mean knowing-that and can mean knowing-how, but its most fundamental meaning is to perceive, recognize, or be aware of. The eyes and ears themselves are said to *zhi*, and Xunzi claims that *zhi* is a capacity shared by human beings and other animals.[6] Other terms focus more on affective engagement. *Wang* is contrasted with terms such as valuing (*gui* 貴), praising (*yu* 譽), blaming (*fei* 非), cherishing (*huai* 懷), nourishing (*yang* 養), and competing for (*zheng* 爭). It is sometimes opposed to *zhi* 志, being intent on a goal. Taken together, these terms reflect the fact that what we attend to or see is inseparable from our purposes and concerns, and vice versa. To forget (*wang*) something is to not see it and to not care about it. It is not surprising, then, that *wang* is sometimes paired with *man* 慢 or *xie* 泄, both of which mean to neglect. Unlike the English word *forget*, there is little clear evidence that *wang* had a distinct meaning of failing to remember.[7] *Wang* is just failing to attend or keep in mind, whether the object of neglect is something present, past, or future.[8] So the common phrase "sons and grandsons *buwang*" (子孫不忘) is naturally translated as "sons and grandsons will not forget [them]," but it could just as well be translated as "sons and grandsons will not fail to think of them."

In this chapter I will focus on forgetting as obliviousness or failing to attend. While that use of the term appears across many texts, I will concentrate on those that show a particular concern with managing attention. Chinese philosophers in the mid- to late Warring State period were convinced that self-cultivation needed to address not just how a person makes deliberate judgments and chooses to act, but also the patterns of attention, salience, and construal that determine how the world appears; that is, what is and is not forgotten. How the world appears then conditions the overt values and choices we make, as well as what we name as things and facts. The *Zhuangzi* is probably the earliest text to theorize the fact that different people experience the same things in different ways and that the way one experiences the world can be cultivated. While forgetting in the *Zhuangzi* has been widely discussed, I hope to shed new light on it by approaching it from within a broader discourse of attention.[9] That context will help illuminate the significance of forgetting in the *Zhuangzi* and the distinctiveness of its various functions. Thus, I will work backward in time, starting with the more explicit association of forgetting with a theory of attention from the early Han dynasty text the *Huainanzi*. I will then briefly consider how the *Huainanzi*'s views of unbiased perception (perception without forgetting) appear earlier in the *Xunzi*'s account of avoiding perceptual blind spots. With this context established, I will return to the *Zhuangzi* to see how it both sets a foundation for these views and offers a distinctive approach. While forgetting is usually presented as a danger, the *Zhuangzi* emphasizes the value of cultivating oblivion.

Attention and Forgetting in the *Huainanzi*

The *Huainanzi* is the earliest Chinese text to give a systematic account of attention. The key term for attention is *shen* 神, which has a range of meanings that make it difficult to define or translate.[10] The most concrete meaning refers to spirits or deities, as in the common phrase *guishen* 鬼神, ghosts and spirits. As an adjective or adverb, *shen* describes effects so efficacious as to appear almost inexplicable, somewhat like we would now describe something as magical. The more puzzling use of *shen* refers to a kind of power or force in the world, most likely conceived as a form of refined *qi* 氣, vital energy. In a recently excavated cosmogonic text, *shen* and *ming* 明 (luminosity or insight) arise early in the process of the differentiation of the world, generated after the pairing of heaven and earth (*tiandi* 天地) but before the pairing of *yin* 陰 and *yang* 陽.[11] *Shen* also exists as a force within people. It can come and go and can be more or less clear or turbid. In the *Huainanzi*, *shen* is a cognitive power associated with attention, quite close to what we would now label consciousness or awareness.[12]

The most systematic account of *shen* in the *Huainanzi* extends across the last parts of chapter 1, "Originating in the Way" (*Yuandao* 原道). It describes three key elements of a human being.

> Now, physical form is the abode of life; vital energy is the filling out of life; *shen* is the regulator of life. If one of them loses its place, then the three are harmed.
> 夫形者生之舍也；氣者生之充也；神者生之制也，一失位則三者傷矣。[13]

The text next describes how living things naturally do what they need to survive. Spiders and bugs avoid harm and pursue what they need, guided by the likes and aversions arising from their natural dispositions (*xing* 性). Humans act in a similar way, but they are described as being infused with vital energy and guided by *shen* (氣為之充而神為之使).[13] It would not be unusual to see natural dispositions (*xing*) as a configuration of vital energy, but the role of *shen* is new and distinguishes human beings from other animals. In justifying this claim, *shen* is explicitly linked to attention.

> As for people's intention, when it is occupied with something and *shen* is bound up with it, then when they walk, they stumble over sticks and hollows or bump their heads on branches and trees without being aware of it.[14] If you wave to them they cannot see; if you call to them they cannot hear. The ears and eyes have not left them but they cannot respond—why? *Shen* has lost its guard. Thus, when occupied by the small, one forgets the big. When occupied by the center, one forgets the outside. When occupied by the high, one forgets the low. When occupied by the left, one forgets the right. When there is no place it does not fill, there is no place it does not occupy. For this reason, one who values emptiness takes the tip of an autumn hair as their abode.
> 凡人之志各有所在，而神有所系者，其行也，足蹪趎坳，頭抵植木，而不自知也。招之而不能見也，呼之而不能聞也，耳目非去之也，然而不能應者，何也？神失其守也。故在於小則忘於大，在於中則忘於外，在於上則忘於下，在於左則忘於右。無所不充則無所不在。是故貴虛者，以毫末為宅也。[15]

Forgetting arises from the improper functioning of *shen*, which either loses what it is supposed to guard or loses what is supposed to guard it.[16] In any case, the result is partial oblivion: our focus on one thing causes us to forget everything else.

The relationship between *shen* and the responsiveness of our natural dispositions is explained in a passage that appears earlier in the same chapter.

> Human beings are born and are still: this is the natural dispositions. They are stimulated and then move: this is the harm of the dispositions. Things arrive and *shen* responds: this is the movement of recognition [*zhi* 知]. Recognition and things connect and then loves and hates are born from it. When loving and hating take fixed forms [*chengxing* 成形], then knowing is lured by what is outside and cannot return to the self. Then the natural coherence [*tianli* 天理] is destroyed. 人生而靜，天之性也。感而後動，性之害也。物至而神應，知之動也。知與物接而好憎生焉，好憎成形，而知誘於外，不能反己，而天理滅矣。[17]

Unlike other animals, things do not automatically provoke reactions in human beings.[18] Our *shen* must respond, and this response is the movement of awareness or recognition. Desires and aversions arise only after recognition or attention. Thus, something can be present before us, but if we are focused on something else so that our *shen* does not respond, we will not see it and will not react to it. That is forgetting

Like emotions, knowledge also depends on awareness. A passage in the second chapter, "Activating the Genuine" (*Chuzhen* 俶真), begins by once again describing natural human capacities. It then asks why, if we all have the same natural dispositions and affects, some people gain spirit-like insight (*shenming* 神明) while others are deluded and crazed.

> That by which they are regulated differs. Thus, *shen* is the source of knowing. If the source is clear, then there is insight [*ming* 明]. Knowing is the storehouse of the heart.[19] If knowing is impartial, then the heart is balanced. No one mirrors themselves in flowing river water; they mirror themselves in water that has stopped, because it is still. No one peers at their form in raw iron; they peer at their form in a bright [*ming*] mirror, because it is even.
> 其所為制者異也。是故神者智之淵也，淵清則明矣；智者心之府也，智公則心平矣。人莫鑒於流沫而鑒於止水者，以其靜也；莫窺形於生鐵，而窺於明鏡者，以睹其易也。[20]

Once again, *shen* is the first and most fundamental step. If that is clear, then knowing will be insightful or illuminating, and then the knowledge accumulated in the heart will be balanced. The metaphors of still water, and smoothed iron represent the first stage of cognition, which is awareness itself.

While attention mediates the relationship of the heart and dispositions to the world, it is not unambiguously in control. Physical form and *shen* can lose their relative positions. That happens when the loves and hates that arise spontaneously take on a fixed form, in which case attention is directed by desires and emotions rather than the reverse.[21] Most of the negative examples of forgetting in the *Huainanzi* result from excessive desires or emotions, as in the following two anecdotes:

> There was a person from Chu who boarded a boat that then encountered a windstorm. When the waves arrived, he threw himself into the water. It was not that he did not covet life or fear death but that sometimes in fearing death, one, on the contrary, forgets life. Thus, human cravings and desires are also like this. There was a person from Qi who stole gold. Just when the market was crowded, he arrived, took it, and ran off. When detained, he was asked the reason: "You stole gold in the middle of the market—why?" He responded: "I did not see the people; I just saw the gold." When our intention has what it desires, then we forget what we are doing.
> 楚人有乘船而遇大風者,波至而自投于水。非不貪生而畏死也,惑於恐死而反忘生也。故人之嗜欲亦猶此也。齊人有盜金者,當市繁之時,至掇而走。勒問其故,曰:「而盜金於市中,何也?」對曰:「吾不見人,徒見金耳。」志所欲,則忘其為矣。[22]

Another anecdote tells of Duke Sheng of Bo, who was so absorbed in plotting rebellion that he picked up a riding crop and leaned his chin against it, piercing his chin and never noticing the blood. Someone comments, "If you forget your chin, what won't you forget!" (頤之忘,將何不忘哉!).[23]

The forgetting caused by emotions and desires leads into a vicious circle. Desires and emotions direct our attention precisely to things that trigger those emotions and desires, while we forget those things that might moderate them. Shortly after the story about the thief, the chapter says,

> A fearful person in the night sees a marker post and takes it to be a ghost; sees a reclining rock and takes it to be a tiger. Fear seizes their vital energy.
> 怯者，夜見立表，以為鬼也；見寢石，以為虎也；懼掩其氣也。[24]

A fearful person sees the world as more frightening, making them even more fearful. In cases like this, the issue is not simply attending or not but rather attending in a certain way, something close to aspect perception.[25]

Awareness without Forgetting

The *Huainanzi* includes some references to the value of forgetting or obliviousness (sometimes borrowed directly from the *Zhuangzi*), but those are generally distinct from the discussions of *shen* and attention. In all of the passages from the previous section, forgetting is bad. The ideal is not necessarily to know all things but to know whatever is present in an unbiased way. The passage above mentioning the ability of water and smooth iron to mirror things continues as follows:

> When the heart arrives somewhere, *shen* swiftly occupies it. By returning it to emptiness, this melts away and is extinguished. This is the wandering of a sage.
> 心有所至而神喟然在之，反之於虛則消鑠滅息，此聖人之游也。[26]

Sages attend to various things, but they do not become fixated on them. Thus, they can turn their attention wherever it is needed.

If our patterns of attention are skewed, if we regularly forget certain things, then our affective life will be unbalanced and all of our knowledge and our philosophies will end up one-sided, narrow, and distorted. This point is made explicitly in chapter 10, "Profound Precepts" (*moucheng* 繆稱), which says that before taking up any task, one must first balance their intentions (*pingyi* 平意) and purify their spirit (*qingshen* 清神).[27] The situation is compared to pressing a seal into clay: if the seal is pressed straight, the impression will be straight; if the seal is pressed crooked, the impression will be crooked. Emotions are again used as an illustration: one bearing a burden (*zai* 載) of sadness will cry upon hearing a happy song, just as one bearing joy will laugh at someone crying. For this reason, one should strive to be empty. The passage concludes with another comparison to water.

Wisdom that is confused cannot be used for governing; water that is agitated cannot be used as a level.
智昏不可以為政，波水不可以為平。[28]

The discourse of the *Huainanzi* draws heavily from the *Zhuangzi*, but its focus on unbiased perception as underlying the ability to correctly evaluate things is closer to ideas that appear in "Jie bi" (解蔽) chapter of the *Xunzi*.[29] Like the *Huainanzi*, the "Jie bi" chapter distinguishes between how the world appears and the judgments that form on this basis. While most of the *Xunzi* focuses on the latter, the "Jie bi" chapter concentrates on the more fundamental level of perception. Rather than warning against forgetting, the key term in this *Xunzi* chapter is *bi* 蔽. The chapter begins: "In general, the trouble for human beings is that we *bi* to one corner but remain in the dark about the greater coherence" (凡人之患，蔽於一曲而闇於大理).[30] The literal meaning of *bi* is for one thing to block, cloak, or conceal another.[31] The *Xunzi* uses the term to describe the way our focus on one thing causes us to forget everything else. The opening line is followed by an account of how diverse ways develop: people fixate on one corner and miss everything else. That initial bias is then strengthened because people see only what supports their own view, forgetting the alternatives. Xunzi explicitly explains this in terms of attention and awareness, using examples similar to those appearing in the *Huainanzi*.

> If the heart is not engaged in it, then white and black can be in front but the eyes do not see them, thunderous drums can be in front but the ears do not hear them. How much more if the heart is engaged!
> 心不使焉，則白黑在前而目不見，雷鼓在側而耳不聞，況於使者乎！[32]

The problem is rooted in the structure of cognition.

> In general, the myriad things are differentiated and so some always block [*bi*] others. This is the common trouble for methods of the heart.
> 凡萬物異則莫不相為蔽，此心術之公患也。[33]

Cognition requires differentiation, which leads us to attend to one thing and forget the other. That is the central challenge for cultivating the heart.

For Xunzi, almost anything can become a *bi*. The opening passage is followed by a list based on dichotomies: desires can become *bi* and aversions can become *bi*, the past can become a *bi* or the present can become a *bi*. Different kinds of people will tend toward different *bi*: rulers are enticed by the people who attract them, while minister are blinded by their desire for more power. Philosophers also have their *bi*.

> Mozi was blinkered [*bi*] by use and did not recognize [*zhi*] cultured refinement. Songzi was blinkered by desire and did not recognize achievement. Shenzi [Shen Dao] was blinkered by law and did not recognize worthies. Shenzi [Shen Buhai] was blinkered by positional power and did not recognize wisdom. Huizi was blinkered by wording and did not recognize actualities. Zhuangzi was blinkered by heaven and did not recognize the human.
> 墨子蔽於用而不知文，宋子蔽於欲而不知得，慎子蔽於法而不知賢，申子蔽於埶而不知知，惠子蔽於辭而不知實，莊子蔽於天而不知人。[34]

Rather than use the term *wang*, forget, the passage uses a common synonym, *buzhi* 不知, to not know, recognize, or perceive. For each philosopher, their attention to one point made them oblivious to everything else. As a result, their entire way is exhausted by a one-sided focus on a single method or goal. The problem is not just for those creating their own way but applies just as well to selecting which philosopher to follow. Xunzi asks the following question:

> By what do people know the way? The heart. By what does the heart know? Emptiness, unity, and stillness.
> 人何以知道？曰：心。心何以知？曰：虛壹而靜。[35]

We can only know the way through the heart, so we can only choose well if the heart is free of biases or *bi*. Xunzi sets up three virtues of the heart: emptiness, unity, and stillness. To give one example, he says the following of emptiness (*xu* 虛):

> People are born and have knowing, and with knowing then they have intentions. Having intentions is storing, but even so

there is what is called emptiness. Not letting what is already stored harm what is about to be received is called emptiness.
人生而有知, 知而有志。志也者, 臧也, 然而有所謂虛, 不以所已藏害所將受謂之虛。[36]

Human beings cannot be free of intentions and commitments. Being alive involves recognizing and perceiving, and that process of knowing involves having intentions or motivations. Emptiness just means not letting those accumulated intentions harm our ability to perceive what is happening now. We can take this as an alternative to complete forgetting: we cannot avoid accumulating memories (storing in the heart), but we should bracket those in a way that avoids distorting perception.

These passages already show that, like the *Huainanzi*, the *Xunzi* is committed to an ideal of unbiased perception, where nothing is forgotten.

> Emptiness, unity, and stillness are called great clarity and insight. Of the myriad things: none take form without being seen, none are seen and not sorted, none are sorted and lose their place.
> 虛壹而靜, 謂之大清明。萬物莫形而不見, 莫見而不論, 莫論而失位。[37]

Before we can begin sorting and situating things, those things first must appear (*jian/xian* 見) to us. Xunzi also compares the heart to the mirroring capacity of still water, saying:

> Thus, the human heart can be compared to a pan of water. If it is set straight and is not moved, then the dirt and sediments sink to the bottom and clarity and brightness are on top. Then it is adequate for seeing one's whiskers and eyebrows and examining the patterns of the skin. If a faint wind passes over it, the dirt and sediments move below and the clarity and brightness are disrupted on top. Then one cannot use it even to get the correct general form.
> 故人心譬如槃水, 正錯而勿動, 則湛濁在下而清明在上, 則足以見鬚眉而察理矣。微風過之, 湛濁動乎下, 清明亂於上, 則不可以得大形之正也。[38]

The *Huainanzi* and the *Xunzi* share the goal of unbiased attention without forgetting, but they differ in what they think this can achieve. For Xunzi, the ideal is to be unbiased and comprehensive. He uses the term *jianzhi* 兼知, where *jian* means all-inclusive or all-incorporating,[39] the same term used by the Mohists for inclusive care (*jian ai* 兼愛). The "Jie bi" chapter, though, explicitly points out the impossibility of knowing everything, so comprehensiveness can only come within a limit: we should only strive to know those things relevant for a good human life.[40] Within that limit, Xunzi can view the way of Confucius (Kongzi) as perfect. Confucius had no *bi* and took comprehensive account of everything needed for human life. The *Huainanzi* takes a different direction. The sage does not have an all-encompassing philosophy, but rather the ability to choose whichever partial philosophy fits the circumstances. The *Huainanzi* compares philosophies to tools useful for different purposes. An unbiased person thus can respond to any circumstance that happens to appear.

Selective Oblivion in the *Zhuangzi*

With this context in place, we can now turn to the various roles for forgetting in the *Zhuangzi*. We have seen that both the *Xunzi* and the *Huainanzi* present judgments and emotions as dependent on the more fundamental way in which the world appears, on perception and forgetting. That assumes the world appears differently to different people, a point that the *Zhuangzi* is the first text to highlight.[41] One strategy the *Zhuangzi* uses to make this point is to juxtapose the experiences of different kinds of animals. One passage contrasts forms of temporality: the mushroom doesn't know day and night but a creature called "Dark Numinosity" experienced five-hundred-year cycles as its spring and fall.[42] Another contrasts experiences of food, shelter, and erotic beauty.[43] The *Zhuangzi* also emphasizes how differences in perceptions underlie differences in desires and judgments. People's desire to imitate Peng Zu depends on the temporal framework they inhabit. From the perspective of the cicada, one would be delighted to have lived a few days. From the perspective of Dark Numinosity, even Peng Zu died pitifully young. This point is applied explicitly to judgment in a passage describing a heart that has been "completed" (*cheng* 成).

> If we follow a completed heart and make it our authority, who alone is without an authority? How would it be only those

who know the alternations and whose hearts make choices of themselves that have them? The foolish would also have them. Not yet completed in the heart but having judgments of right and wrong—this is like leaving for Yue today and arriving there yesterday.
夫隨其成心而師之，誰獨且無師乎？奚必知代而心自取者有之？愚者與有焉。未成乎心而有是非，是今日適越而昔至也。[44]

The term *cheng* implies completion but also closure and limitation, as the *Huainanzi* passage on dispositions warns of the dangers of loves and hates taking fixed (*cheng*) shape or form (*xing* 形). The key point is that judgments of right and wrong (*shifei* 是非) only arise after the formation of some fixed perspective. That means that judgments must always be approached through a more fundamental concern with awareness or perspective itself.

The *Xunzi* and *Huainanzi* recognize this same point and respond by promoting an ideal of unbiased perception in which nothing is left in oblivion. There are traces of this idea in the *Zhuangzi*, as well. One well-known anecdote about Zhuangzi himself warns against the dangers of forgetting. It begins when Zhuangzi sees a strange bird fly past and pursues it into a protected forest, with his crossbow in hand. It continues as follows:

> He saw a cicada just attaining a beautiful shady spot but forgetting its self. A praying mantis raised its pincers and pounced on it, seeing gain but forgetting its physical form. The strange bird followed along to benefit from this, seeing benefit but forgetting its genuineness. Zhuang Zhou with pity said: "Ah! Things certainly entangle each other, different kinds inviting each other in."
> 睹一蟬，方得美蔭而忘其身；螳蜋執翳而搏之，見得而忘其形；異鵲從而利之，見利而忘其真。莊周怵然曰：「噫！物固相累，二類相召也。」[45]

Zhuangzi flees, barely escaping the game warden after him for poaching. He remains in his home for three days before venturing out again. When asked for an explanation, Zhuangzi says,

> I was guarding my physical form [*xing* 形] while forgetting my self [*shen* 身]; I was looking at turbid water and confused

it for a deep clear pool. Moreover, I have heard the master say: "In entering other customs, follow those customs." Today I was wandering in Daoling park while forgetting my self. A strange bird brushed my forehead and wandered among the chestnut trees while forgetting its genuineness. The warden of the chestnut trees took me as someone to punish. This is why I have not come into the courtyard.
吾守形而忘身，觀於濁水而迷於清淵。且吾聞諸夫子曰：「入其俗，從其俗。」今吾遊於雕陵而忘吾身，異鵲感吾顙，遊於栗林而忘真，栗林虞人以吾為戮，吾所以不庭也。[46]

This kind of experience is just what the *Huainanzi* warns against. Xunzi would say that Zhuangzi was blinkered (*bi*) by the bird and did not see his own danger.

In spite of passages like this, the *Zhuangzi* more often recommends forgetting. The cultivation of oblivion serves a few distinct functions in the text. The one that most directly contrasts the discourses we have seen so far can be called selective forgetting. Consider the following discussion of language:

> Fish traps are that by which one has fish; you get the fish and then forget the traps. Snares are that by which one has rabbits; you get the rabbits and then forget the snares. Words are that by which one has intentions; you get the intentions and then forget the words. How can I get a person who forgets words, so that I can have a word with him?
> 荃者所以在魚，得魚而忘荃；蹄者所以在兔，得兔而忘蹄；言者所以在意，得意而忘言。吾安得忘言之人而與之言哉？[47]

The phrasing here (*de* 得 x *wang* 忘 y) fits the kinds of language used in the *Huainanzi* and in the previous *Zhuangzi* passage, where attention to one side goes along with forgetting the other side, but here Zhuangzi recommends forgetting rather than warning against it. Like the fish traps and snares, the words are present but should not be noticed as present.[48] The ideal is *not* to see everything as it is. One passage says of government service,

> When a person is a minister or son, there surely is what cannot be avoided. Follow the actuality of affairs and forget yourself.

> Then, how could you have the leisure to reach delighting in life and hating death!
> 為人臣子者，固有所不得已。行事之情而忘其身，何暇至於悅生而惡死！ [49]

The truth is that you might die in such situations, and you surely cannot do what you really want to do. Since that cannot be avoided, it best to forget about it and focus on what can be done.

The ideal in these contexts is not total forgetting. We attend to one thing and forget others.[50] A passage in chapter 5 begins by describing two unusally shaped people who led kings to readjust their standards for what counted as normal. It then explains forgetting.

> Thus, when virtuosity [*de* 德] has what is strong, the form has what is forgotten. People do not forget what they should forget and forget what they should not forget—this is called really forgetting.
> 故德有所長而形有所忘，人不忘其所忘而忘其所不忘，此謂誠忘。[51]

There are things one should forget and things one should not forget. Attend to a person's *de* but be oblivious to the peculiarities of physical form. The line ends with an ironic reversal—the really bad kind of forgetting is forgetting to forget!

These examples show that, in contrast to the *Xunzi* and *Huainanzi*, the *Zhuangzi* (at least in some parts) is not recommending an ideal of unbiased perception. Rather than having things appear as they really are, have them appear in ways that will make them less distressing and more enjoyable. This position is common in the "Inner Chapters." Consider, for example, the two dialogues between Zhuangzi and Huizi at the end of the first chapter. In each, Huizi gives an example of something that he finds to be useless—a giant gourd and a big gnarled tree. In both, Zhuangzi replies by suggesting a use that is more a form of play. You could cut the gourd in half and float around on lake or river in it. You could lounge in the shade of the tree and relax. Surely the point here is not that Zhuangzi has more clearly seen the gourd and tree as they truly are. He is simply able to see them in more ways. That is better because it leads to enjoyment rather than frustration. The various claims in the *Zhuangzi* that life is worse than death should be read in the same way.

If they spoke the truth, sages would commit suicide. The point is that if you are facing death, it is better to have it appear as a relief than as terrifying. It would not be out of character for the *Zhuangzi* to say: life and death are both real, but when alive one should forget death and facing death one should forget life.

Invoking the discourse of forgetting, in this context, points to a cultivation of attention that goes deeper than deliberate judgments and evaluations. That appears in the contentment of Lian Shu, a sagely figure who lost a foot.

> Looking from the differences, your liver and gall bladder are like the states of Chu and Yue. Looking from their sameness, the ten thousand things are all one. Someone like this even does not recognize [*zhi* 知] what is appropriate for his ears or eyes. He has his heart wander playfully in the harmony of virtuosity. As for things, he looks at what makes them one and does not see what is lost. He looks at the loss of his foot as dirt left behind.
> 自其異者視之，肝膽楚越也；自其同者視之，萬物皆一也。夫若然者，且不知耳目之所宜，而遊心乎德之和；物視其所一而不見其所喪，視喪其足猶遺土也。[52]

While this passage uses not recognizing (*buzhi* 不知) and not seeing (*bujian* 不見) rather than forgetting (*wang*), the point is the same. Lian Shu is not upset by the loss of his foot because he literally does not see it, as he is looking at (*shi* 視) what is there and common rather than what is missing or lost. The same point appears in chapter 6.

> Not forgetting what began him and not seeking what ends him; being pleased when receiving it and forgetting when returning it—this is called not using the heart to harm the way and not using the human to assist heaven. This is called a genuine person.
> 不忘其所始，不求其所終；受而喜之，忘而復之，是之謂不以心捐道，不以人助天。是之謂真人。[53]

Genuine people are pleased when things go their way, but when loss arrives, they forget about it and let it go. The issue is not judging whether or not something is valuable, but rather attending to some things while forgetting others. Cultivating attention does not aim at accuracy but at wandering freely in the world without being troubled. That requires forgetting.

Skillfulness and Oblivion in the *Zhuangzi*

Along with selective forgetting, the *Zhuangzi* includes a more radical ideal of total oblivion. In a discussion with Confucius, Yan Hui says he is making progress. When Confucius asks what he means, Yan Hui describes a progression of forgetting. First, he forgets benevolence and rightness. Confucius says that is good, but not enough. Then he forgets ritual and music, but that is still not enough. Finally, Yan Hui says that he just sits and forgets (*zuowang* 坐忘). Confucius is intrigued and asks for an explanation. Yan Hui responds as follows:

> Dropping limbs and torso, dismissing acuity in hearing and sight, distancing physical form and leaving knowing, uniting with the great communing—this is called sitting and forgetting.
> 墮肢體, 黜聰明, 離形去知, 同於大通, 此謂坐忘。

Confucius replies,

> To be united is to have no preferences; to transform is to have no constancy. You are indeed a worthy! May I please follow you as your disciple.
> 同則無好也, 化則無常也。而果其賢乎! 丘也請從而後也。[54]

Much has been made of this passage, but the text gives us little to go on in interpreting it. It is common to take at least the first two stages of Yan Hui's forgetting in the sense of no longer remembering, but that is unlikely. As we have seen, *wang* commonly means not attending rather than not remembering, and that is the only plausible way to understand the final stage of sitting and forgetting.[55] As discussed earlier, not remembering and not attending are closely related: one can only attend to things such as benevolence and propriety because they have been learned and retained. Nonetheless, the point is not about eliminating benevolence, rightness, propriety, and music, but rather not attending to them in practice. That makes the passage much less of a direct rejection of the Confucian way. Yan Hui might indeed use ritual and music, but he can't be thinking about them.[56]

It is difficult to know what the final state of sitting and forgetting is supposed to be. Confucius tells us two things: one will have no preferences and one will have nothing fixed or constant. Similar associations appear around other passages that recommend forgetting. A passage from chapter 2 on harmonizing differences says to forget years and forget rightness in order to lodge in the boundaryless (*wujing* 無竟).[57] A statement among three friends connects living in mutual forgetting with having no limit (*wuji* 無極).[58] Another line attributed to Confucius says,

> They borrow from the differences in things but reside in the same unified body. They forget their livers and gall bladders and give up their eyes and ears, reversing and returning, ending and beginning, not knowing limits or bounds. In oblivion [*mangran* 芒然], they roam beyond the dust and dirt, wandering freely in the enterprise of not doing.
> 假於異物，託於同體；忘其肝膽，遺其耳目；反覆終始，不知端倪；芒然彷徨乎塵垢之外，逍遙乎無為之業。[59]

As in Confucius's reply to Yan Hui, forgetting is associated with both what unifies things and with the singularity of any given moment. It leads to the ability to go along with the world as it is.

In spite of the wording of some of these passages, it is implausible to take the Zhuangzi as advocating complete lack of awareness.[60] Most of the passages imply the contrary: a fine-tuned ability to respond to changes and adapt to whatever happens. Total oblivion is simultaneously perfect attunement.[61] One of the most important roles for forgetting in the *Zhuangzi* is in relation to skillful action, particularly in chapter 19, "Fathoming Life" ("Dasheng" 達生).[62] One passage repeats the lines from chapter 6 about forgetting bodily organs and wandering outside the dust but adds this conclusion: "This is called acting but not relying, leading but not controlling" (是謂為而不恃，長而不宰).[63] These words are Master Bian's advice to Sun Xiu, a consistent loser, meant to explain how to act effectively in the world. In the same chapter, a skillful ferry driver explains his ability to steer through raging rapids by saying that, as an excellent swimmer, he can forget about the water.[64] A skillful carver of wooden bell-stands explains that before selecting wood to carve, he fasts for seven days, eliminating cares for material rewards or the opinions of others and even forgetting the existence of his own body.[65] The story of Chui the artisan provides the passage from which the opening quotation of this paper was taken.

> When shoes are comfortable, the feet are forgotten. When a belt is comfortable, the waist is forgotten. When the heart is comfortable, right and wrong are forgotten. When affairs are comfortable, one does not change on the inside or labor on the outside. When one begins in comfort and is never not comfortable, that is the comfort of forgetting comfort.
> 忘足, 履之適也; 忘要, 帶之適也; 知忘是非, 心之適也; 不內變, 不外從, 事會之適也。始乎適而未嘗不適者, 忘適之適也。[66]

Forgetting in these contexts is almost the opposite of obliviousness. It enables dealing with the present in its singularity. After thoroughly forgetting, the woodcarver says he enters the forest and observes (*guan* 觀) natural dispositions (*tianxing* 天性).[67] He can then match his own naturalness to that of his environment (*yi tian he tian* 以天合天).[68] While not explicitly using the term *forget*, Cook Ding follows a similar process in which he no longer sees whole oxen. That negative process of reducing a certain kind of awareness allows him to engage what is really there: "I rely on the natural contours [*tianli* 天理], strike into the large gaps, let myself be guided by the large hollows, and adapt to what is firmly so" (依乎天理, 批大郤, 導大窾, 因其固然).[69]

As this link between skill and forgetting suggests, the contrast between these parts of the *Zhuangzi* and what we have seen from the *Huainanzi* and *Xunzi* is not one of direct opposition. The *Zhuangzi* still advocates an ideal of unbiased perception, even invoking the mirror.

> Do not act as a corpse for reputation. Do not act as a repository for schemes. Do not act as responsible for affairs. Do not act as a master of knowing. Fully embody the limitless and wander in the traceless. Fully use what is received from heaven but without appearing to gain. Just be empty. The utmost human being uses the heart like a mirror, not rejecting and not welcoming, responding but not storing. Thus, they can overcome things without harm.

> 無為名尸，無為謀府；無為事任，無為知主。體盡無窮，而游無朕；
> 盡其所受乎天，而無見得，亦虛而已。至人之用心若鏡，不將不迎，
> 應而不藏，故能勝物而不傷。[70]

The passage does not use the term *wang*, but storing (*cang* 藏) connects to retaining. The point is that we should respond but not cling, forgetting things as they pass.

On one level, we might say that the *Zhuangzi* merely employs a different rhetorical strategy. In a situation where our attention to *x* causes us to neglect *y*, the *Huainanzi* warns not to forget *y* while the *Zhuangzi* tells us to forget *x*. The difference, though, goes deeper than just rhetoric. What we can attend to is always limited, foregrounding some things and backgrounding others. The best we can do is move back and forth between objects, avoiding becoming too fixated on any one thing. Even if we could pay attention to both the left and the right, what about everything in between? As the *Zhuangzi* says: "Thus divisions have what is undivided; distinctions have what is undistinguished" (故分也者, 有不分也; 辯也者, 有不辯也).[71] Rather than moving from object to object or keeping the most relevant object in mind, as in the *Huainanzi*, the *Zhuangzi* suggests a diffuse awareness with no object at all.[72] In his account of Yan Hui's forgetting, Romain Graziani describes this as: "a radical oblivion, a form of intransitive oblivion, characterized by not being attached to any object in particular."[73] The problem of forgetting is best addressed with more forgetting rather than a futile attempt to control our attention. The result can be seen as a more radical form of impartiality.

> For ancient people, their knowing/perception [*zhi* 知] had what reached the utmost. Where did it reach? There were those who took it that things had never begun to exist. The utmost! All the way! Nothing more to add! Those next took there to be things but they had not begun to have borders. Those next took there to be borders among them but as not yet beginning to have right and wrong. The showing of right and wrong is that by which the way becomes defective. That by which the way becomes defective is that by which care is completed [*cheng*].
> 古之人，其知有所至矣。惡乎至？有以為未始有物者，至矣，盡矣，不可以加矣。其次以為有物矣，而未始有封也。其次以為有

封焉，而未始有是非也。是非之彰也，道之所以虧也。道之所以虧，愛之所以成。[74]

This passage describes the process of losing the original potentiality, interconnection, and singularity of things through the formation of a completed perspective. *Cheng* is connected to harm, divisions, and the labels of right and wrong. The kind of care that would be "completed," or we might better translate *cheng* here as "fixated," would stand opposed to a radicalized inclusivity that accepted everything and everyone as they are. Xunzi's claim that differentiation is an inevitable aspect of human cognition may be intended to argue against taking this kind of perception as an ideal.

It is tempting to dismiss Zhuangzi's account of total oblivion as superhuman, or at least a form of mysticism, but we all have experiences of the kind of attention involved when fully absorbed in skillful activities. We can imagine telling someone we are coaching: forget about your hands and focus on the ball! But we can also imagine telling someone: forget about your hands *and* forget about the ball! The former is beginner's advice; the latter advice for becoming an expert. Even so, it may seem implausible as advice for how to live our lives in general. Perhaps the highest ideal is a life like that of the ancient people who did not recognize objects at all, but that is hard to imagine. Here we should consider the *Zhuangzi* as a whole. Sitting and forgetting is not the only ideal. As we have seen in the story about Zhuangzi himself, it includes beginner's advice as well: don't get so absorbed in your pursuits that you forget the danger around you. It also includes advice for selective attention: focus on what you have and forget what is missing; focus on what all things have in common and forget about personal loss and gain. Whether or not these different uses of forgetting reflect different authors and sources, they come together to produce a comprehensive philosophy of cultivating oblivion.[75]

Notes

1. Guo Qingfan 郭慶藩, *Zhuangzi jishi* 莊子集釋 (Beijing: Zhonghua shuju, 1978), 19.662. Translations are my own but I have benefited and occasionally borrowed from Brook Ziporyn, *Zhuangzi: The Essential Writings, with Selections from Traditional Commentaries* (Indianapolis, IN: Hackett, 2009).

2. John Locke, *An Essay Concerning Human Understanding*. Edited by Peter H. Nidditch (Oxford: Oxford University Press, 1975), book II, chapter 10, 149–55.

3. In Heidegger's terms, the ready-to-hand loses its readiness-to-hand and becomes present-to-hand in a certain way (Martin Heidegger, *Being and Time*, translated by John Macquarrie and Edward Robinson [New York: Harper and Row, 1962], section 15, 102–4). Using the term *forget* might imply not forgetting as the default condition, but Heidegger would argue for the opposite view. Things exist primarily as ready-to-hand (as forgotten, we might say) and only sometimes become conspicuous, obtrusive, or obstinate.

4. For a detailed account of the uses of *wang* and its primary association with keeping in mind or valuing, see Esther Sunkyung Klein, "Shaping the Historian's Project: The Language of Forgetting and Obliteration in the *Shiji*," in this volume. In the context of ritual, Paul Nicholas Vogt also takes forgetting primarily as lack of awareness ("Embodied Memory and Natural Forgetting in Early Chinese Ritual Theory," in this volume).

5. He Ning 何寧, *Huainanzi jishi* 淮南子集釋 (Beijing: Zhonghua shuju, 1998), 10.709. Translations are my own but I have benefited from consulting John S. Major, Sarah A. Queen, Andrew Seth-Meyer, and Harold D. Roth (trans.), *The Huainanzi: A Guide to the Theory and Practice of Government in Early Han China* (New York: Columbia University Press, 2010).

6. Wang Xianqian 王先謙, *Xunzi jijie* 荀子集解 (Beijing: Zhonghua shuju, 1988), 9.164.

7. The *Classic of Songs* has a line that says, "when the center of the heart stores it, how could it day to day be forgotten?" (中心藏之、何日忘之) (*Shijing*, Mao 228). The *Shiji* contrasts *wang* with *ji* 紀, recording, by criticizing a bad leader who: "does not record peoples' accomplishments and does not forget their transgressions" (於人之功無所記, 於人之罪無所) (*Shiji* 97). Even in these cases, the point may be that what is stored in the heart or written down is easily brought into our attention. For more evidence on this point, see Klein (this volume).

8. This is supported by the occasional use of the phrase 忘舊, where the object of *wang* is specifically said to be the past (*jiu*). The *jiu* would be redundant if *wang* itself means failing to remember.

9. For some recent examples, see, Romain Graziani, "Optimal States and Self-Defeated Plans: The Problem of Intentionality in Early Chinese Self-Cultivation," *Philosophy East and West* 59, no. 4 (2009): 440–66; Mark Berkson, "Death in the *Zhuangzi*: Mind, Nature, and the Art of Forgetting," in *Mortality in Traditional Chinese Thought*, ed. Amy Olberding and Philip J. Ivanhoe (Albany: State University of New York Press, 2011), 191–224; Chris Fraser, "Heart-Fasting, Forgetting, and Using the Heart Like a Mirror: Applied Emptiness in the *Zhuangzi*," in *Nothingness in Asian Philosophy*, ed. JeeLoo Liu

and Douglas Berger (London: Routledge, 2014), 197–212 and "The Ferryman: Forget the Deeps and Row!," in *Skill and Mastery: Philosophical Stories from the Zhuangzi*, ed. Karyn Lai and Wai Wai Chiu (London: Rowman and Littlefield, 2019), 163–81; Linna Liu and Sihao Chew, "Dynamic Model of Emotions: The Process of Forgetting in the *Zhuangzi*," *Dao: A Journal of Comparative Philosophy* 18, no. 1 (2019): 77–90.

10. For discussions of *shen*, see, Harold D. Roth, "The Early Taoist Concept of *Shen*: A Ghost in the Machine?," in *Sagehood and Systematizing Thought in Warring States and Han China*, ed. Kidder Smith (Brunswick, ME: Asian Studies Program, Bowdoin College, 1990), 11–32; Michael J. Puett, *To Become a God: Cosmology, Sacrifice, and Self-Divinization in Early China* (Cambridge, MA: Harvard University Press, 2002), 21–23, 109–10, 123–33; C. Fraser, "Heart-Fasting, Forgetting, and Using the Heart Like a Mirror," 170–74; Wai Wai Chiu, "Zhuangzi's Idea of 'Spirit': Acting and 'Thinging Things' without Self-Assertion," *Asian Philosophy* 26, no. 1 (2016): 38–51. Most discussions of *shen* draw either from the "Nei ye" chapter of the *Guanzi* or from the *Zhuangzi*, but one needs to be cautious in applying accounts of *shen* in one text (or part of a text) to others.

11. *Taiyi sheng shui* 太一生水, strips 1–2. For the Chinese text and a translation, see Scott Cook, *The Bamboo Texts of Guodian*, 2 vols. (Ithaca, NY: Cornell East Asian Series, 2012). For discussions of the pairing of *shen* and *ming*, see Sandor P. Szabó, "The Term *shenming*: Its Meaning in the Ancient Chinese Thought and in a Recently Discovered Manuscript," *Acta Orientalia* 56, no. 2–4 (2003): 251–74 and Sharon Small, "A Daoist Exploration of *shenming*," *Journal of Daoist Studies* 11 (2018): 1–20.

12. Roth claims that the *Huainanzi* uses *shen* in a new way, applying it to normal cognitive activities. He says that perception is created by the responses of *shen* to external things and mentions that this is associated with attention ("The Early Taoist Concept of *Shen*: A Ghost in the Machine?," 20–21). Jung and Moon do not mention attention but say that *jingshen* 精神 is the "foundation of perception" and that dissipation of *jingshen* disrupts correct perception (Woojin Jung and Suk-yoon Moon, "A Study of the Heart of the *Huainanzi*: With the Contradictory Evaluations of Emotions as Clues," *Dao: A Journal of Comparative Philosophy* 17, no. 2 [2018]: 153–67, 164).

13. *Huainanzi jishi*, 1.85.

14. Harold D. Roth here takes *zhi* 志 as awareness, translating the start of this line "In general, when there is something that occupies people's awareness and their spirit is tied up in it" (Major et al., *The Huainanzi: A Guide to the Theory and Practice of Government in Early Han China*, 1.20). I suspect that *zhi*, which I have translated as intention, is orientation toward a goal and that *shen* (spirit) corresponds more to awareness.

15. *Huainanzi jishi*, 1.85.

16. The text is ambiguous on this point. I think the most likely reading is that the heart loses its guard over *shen*. In contrast, Roth supplies concentration as the object of *shen*'s guardianship, translating it as "Their spirit has lost what it is guarding [its concentration]" (Major et al., *The Huainanzi: A Guide to the Theory and Practice of Government in Early Han China*, 1.20).

17. *Huainanzi jishi*, 1.24.

18. My reading contrasts that of Puett, who takes the line on *shen* as describing the responsiveness of natural dispositions rather than as a distinct step within a progression. See Puett, *To Become a God*, 266–67.

19. Once again, I take the distinctions here somewhat differently from Roth, who translates *zhi* 智 as "consciousness" and *xin* 心 as mind (Major et al., *The Huainanzi: A Guide to the Theory and Practice of Government in Early Han China*, 2.11). I take *shen* itself as awareness or attention and then take *zhi* as the accumulation of what is known or recognized, leaving it closer to its common meaning of wisdom. *Xin* then is the physical organ in which both attention and knowledge are based.

20. *Huainanzi jishi*, 2.143–45.

21. *Huainanzi jishi*, 1.24. Griet Vankeerberghen discusses the way that emotions distort perception in the *Huainanzi*, giving a general account in terms of movement of *qi* 氣 (G. Vankeerberghen, "Emotion and the Actions of the Sage: Recommendations for an Orderly Heart in the Huainanzi," *Philosophy East and West* 45, no. 4 (1995): 527–44, 536–36).

22. *Huainanzi jishi*, 13.978.

23. *Huainanzi jishi*, 12.893. This anecdote and the previous one about the thief appear in slightly different forms in the *Liezi* and are discussed in Albert Galvany, "The Oblivious against the Doctor: Pathologies of Remembering and Virtues of Forgetting in the *Liezi*" (this volume). Galvany interprets both stories with more emphasis on the role of memory.

24. *Huainanzi jishi*, 13.980.

25. Galvany (this volume) discusses a similar example from the *Liezi*, in which belief that a neighbor has stolen an axe makes all of the neighbor's actions appear suspicious.

26. *Huainanzi jishi*, 2.147.

27. *Huainanzi jishi*, 11.776–77.

28. *Huainanzi jishi*, 11.777.

29. I do not know if the authors of the *Huainanzi* were aware of this particular chapter of the *Xunzi*, but there is evidence for at least an indirect textual link. Both chapters start from an example of how a fearful person will perceive things in the world as more frightening and then digress into a criticism of those who claim to see ghosts. That similarity is difficult to explain other by some textual connection. At the same time, the *Xunzi* uses a discourse that

makes little use of the term forgetting (*wang*) and attributes attention directly to the heart rather than *shen*.

30. *Xunzi jijie*, 21.386. Translations are my own but I have benefited from consulting Eric L. Hutton, *Xunzi: The Complete Text* (Princeton, NJ: Princeton University Press, 2016).

31. Grammatically, the object of *bi* is the thing that does the blocking, so *bi* has been translated as "obsessions" (Burton Watson, *The Basic Writings of Mo Tzu, Hsün Tzu, and Han Fei Tzu* [New York: Columbia University Press, 1967]), "fixations" (Hutton, *Xunzi: The Complete Text*), or "beguilements" (Kurtis Hagen, *Xunzi: A Philosophical Reconstruction* [Chicago, IL: Open Court, 2007]). These leave out the sense of blocking something else. Chris Fraser suggests "blinkering" in the sense of blinkering a horse (C. Fraser, "Knowledge and Error in Early Chinese Thought," *Dao: A Journal of Comparative Philosophy* 10 [2011]: 127–48, 138).

32. *Xunzi jijie*, 21.387.
33. *Xunzi jijie*, 21.388.
34. *Xunzi jijie*, 21.392–93.
35. *Xunzi jijie*, 21.395.
36. *Xunzi jijie*, 21.395.
37. *Xunzi jijie*, 21.397.
38. *Xunzi jijie*, 21.401.
39. *Xunzi jijie*, 21.396.

40. For a more elaborate discussion of this point, see Franklin Perkins, *Heaven and Earth Are not Humane: The Problem of Evil in Classical Chinese Philosophy* (Bloomington: Indiana University Press, 2014), 208–12.

41. My impression is that the *Zhuangzi* contains the earliest appearance of these views, but my account here does not depend on that chronology. The author of the "Jie bi" chapter knew of Zhuangzi and characterizes his philosophy as emphasizing heaven rather than the human and advocating going along with things, but we cannot be certain of the relationship between Xunzi's Zhuangzi and the text we now know as the *Zhuangzi*. The influence of the *Zhuangzi* on the *Huainanzi* is clear, but we do not know just how our *Zhuangzi* relates to the materials used by the *Huainanzi* authors.

42. *Zhuangzi jishi*, 1.11.
43. *Zhuangzi jishi*, 2.93.
44. *Zhuangzi jishi*, 2.56.
45. *Zhuangzi jishi*, 20.695.
46. *Zhuangzi jishi*, 20.696.
47. *Zhuangzi jishi*, 26.944.

48. For a discussion of various interpretations of this story, see Mercedes Valmissa, "Wang Bi and the Hermeneutics of Actualization" (this volume).

49. *Zhuangzi jishi*, 4.155.

50. This form can be compared to what Klein calls forgetting as expressing a trade-off between duties (Klein, this volume).

51. *Zhuangzi jishi*, 5.216–17.

52. *Zhuangzi jishi*, 5.190–91.

53. *Zhuangzi jishi*, 6.229.

54. *Zhuangzi jishi*, 6.284–85.

55. Although Livia Kohn gives an account of the *Zhuangzi* as a criticism of memory, she concludes by saying: "The word *wang* is thus best not read in its transmitted meaning of 'forget,' but in its literal graph as 'perish' (*wang* 亡) plus 'mind' (*xin* 心)" (L. Kohn, "Forget or Not Forget? The Neurophysiology of *zuowang*," in *New Visions of the Zhuangzi*, ed. L. Kohn [St. Petersburg, FL: Three Pines Press], 161–79, 176).

56. This interpretation of the passage can be compared to Valmisa's interpretation of the role of forgetting in relation to words, where the forgetting words does not entail completing losing them, but rather a certain relationship to them (Valmisa, this volume).

57. *Zhuangzi jishi*, 2.108.

58. *Zhuangzi jishi*, 6.264.

59. *Zhuangzi jishi*, 6.268.

60. For a careful articulation of this point, see C. Fraser "The Ferryman: Forget the Deeps and Row!"

61. As Heidegger says, "'Practical' behaviour is not 'atheoretical' in the sense of 'sightlessness.' [. . .] For the fact that observation is a kind of concern is just as primordial as that fact that action has *its own* kind of sight" (M. Heidegger, *Being and Time*, section 15, 99).

62. Accounts of skill in the *Zhuangzi* frequently include some discussion of forgetting. For recent examples, see Dušan Vavra, "Skillful Practice in the *Zhuangzi*: Putting the Narratives into Context," *Asian Studies* 5, no. 1 (2017): 195–219; C. Fraser, "The Ferryman: Forget the Deeps and Row!"; F. Perkins, "Skill and Nourishing Life," in *Skill and Mastery: Philosophical Stories from the Zhuangzi*, 15–32; and Steve Coutinho, "Skill and Embodied Engagement: *Zhuangzi* and *Liezi*," in *Skill and Mastery: Philosophical Stories from the Zhuangzi*, 85–99.

63. *Zhuangzi jishi*, 19.663.

64. *Zhuangzi jishi*, 19.642.

65. *Zhuangzi jishi*, 19.658–59.

66. *Zhuangzi jishi*, 19.662.

67. *Zhuangzi jishi*, 19.658–59.

68. *Zhuangzi jishi*, 19.659.

69. *Zhuangzi jishi*, 3.119.

70. *Zhuangzi jishi*, 7.307.

71. *Zhuangzi jishi*, 2.83.

72. This difference might be connected to a different conception of the agency attributed to *shen*. Whereas *shen* in the *Huainanzi* is the agent that attends and forgets, Berger, Fraser, and Chiu all see *shen* in the *Zhuangzi* as a form of agency that is enabled once the heart has engaged in forgetting (Douglas L. Berger, *Encounters of Mind: Luminosity and Personhood in Indian and Chinese Thought* [Albany: State University of New York Press, 2016], 52–54; Chris Fraser, "Heart-Fasting, Forgetting, and Using the Heart Like a Mirror: Applied Emptiness in the *Zhuangzi*"; and Wai Wai Chiu, "Zhuangzi's Idea of 'Spirit': Acting and 'Thinging Things' without Self-Assertion"). That is plausible, but I have some doubts that the *Zhuangzi* has a coherent discourse of *shen* or even uses *shen* as a technical term. For a different discussion of *shen* in the *Zhuangzi* focused instead on the *shenren* 神人, spirit-person, see Michael Puett, *To Become a God*, 123–33.

73. R. Graziani, "Optimal States and Self-Defeated Plans: The Problem of Intentionality in Early Chinese Self-Cultivation," 450.

74. *Zhuangzi jishi*, 2.74.

75. I am grateful to Esther Sunkyung Klein and Albert Galvany for their careful comments on earlier drafts of this paper.

Chapter 7

The Practice of Erasing Traces in the *Huainanzi*

Tobias Benedikt Zürn

The *Huainanzi* is an extraordinary scripture from the Western Han dynasty (206 BCE–9 CE) that is known for its constructed and comprehensive form.[1] This text, which Liu An 劉安 (c. 179–122 BCE), the king of Huainan 淮南 (modern-day Anhui 安徽 province), presumably commissioned to be submitted to young Emperor Wu 漢武帝 (born Liu Che 劉徹; 156–87 BCE; r. 141–87 BCE),[2] contains a plethora of discourses on the nature of the sage (*shengren* 聖人) who functions as a paradigmatic illustration of the ideal ruler in the *Huainanzi*.[3] For example, chapter 14, "Explaining Words" ("Quanyan" 詮言), which illustrates "basic truths about the ideal ruler and his governance," begins with a brief cosmogenesis in which Liu An and his erudite courtiers nested an elaborate discussion of the sage and her or his relationship with the celestial deity Grand One (Taiyi 太一).[4] After illustrating how all beings acquire a physical form (*xing* 形) during the world's birthing, Liu An's text states that the True Person (*zhenren* 真人), another synonym for the ideal ruler in the *Huainanzi*,[5] is different since she or he "ha[s] not yet begun to differentiate from the Grand One" (未始分於太一).[6] Contrary to the Myriad Beings (*wan wu* 萬物) that are "positively" defined by having (*you* 有) "distinctive qualities" (*ge yi* 各異), "distinguishing categories" (*leibie* 類

別), "separating groupings" (*qunfen* 群分), and physical forms, *Huainanzi* 14.2 depicts the sage by employing a sequence of negations:[7]

> The sage does not for the sake of a name/fame become a corpse; does not for the sake of stratagems store things up; does not for the sake of affairs take on responsibility; does not for the sake of wisdom become a ruler. She or he dwells in the formless, moves in the traceless, and wanders in the beginningless. She or he does not initiate things for the sake of good fortune, nor does she or he begin things to deal with misfortune. She or he remains in emptiness and nonbeing and moves when she or he cannot do otherwise.
> 聖人不為名尸，不為謀府，不為事任，不為智主。藏無形，行無跡，遊無朕。不為福先，不為禍始。保於虛無，動於不得已。[8]

According to *Huainanzi* 14.2's illustration, the sage is first and foremost defined by a series of actions she or he does not do (*bu* 不) and therefore "remains in emptiness and nonbeing" (*bao yu xuwu* 保於虛無), a region beyond the limits of the phenomenal world. Typical for proto-Daoist literature, the True Person dwells in (*cang* 藏 or *ju* 居), as well as moves (*xing* 行) and roams (*you* 遊) throughout a realm that is defined by being beyond time and space, as conveyed by the expressions formless (*wu xing* 無形), traceless (*wu ji* 無跡), and without a beginning (*wu zhen* 無朕).[9]

Since these terms and contrastive illustrations are ubiquitous in proto-Daoist writings on the True Person and the Dao, we tend to read them simply as metaphors for the realm "beyond dust and dirt" (*chen'gou zhi wai* 塵垢之外 or *chen'ai zhi wai* 塵埃之外).[10] In so doing, we turn a blind eye to the fact that these images arose in a specific discursive environment. In this chapter, I will reconstruct the intellectual background to one of these expressions, the term "tracelessness" (*wu ji*), and explore how it relates to both practices of embodiment (*ti* 體) mentioned in the *Huainanzi* and contemporaneous debates on remembrance (*ji* 記), record taking (*ji* 紀 or 記), and erasure (*mie* 滅 or *jue* 絕).[11]

First, I will showcase that the term "trace" (*ji* 跡/迹 or 蹟) took on several connotations beyond its literal meaning as the track of an animal or any other being (*wu* 物) in early China. In fact, *ji* were considered to be valuable containers that enshrine the actions (*xing* 行) and deeds (*shi* 事) of the past. Any being was thought to leave their traces in the dust and dirt (*chen'gou* 塵垢 or *chen'ai* 塵埃) of the phenomenal world, and these very traces could then be visited, engaged in, and sometimes even reanimated to create a connection with the past.[12]

In a second step, I demonstrate that this basic understanding of traces as the actions and deeds of beings was extended to the realm of words (*yan* 言), writings (*wen* 文), and written records (*ji* 記). Based on the myth that Cang Jie 倉頡,[13] a legendary official of the Yellow Emperor (Huangdi 黃帝), derived Chinese characters from bird tracks (*niaoji* 鳥跡),[14] writings and records of the past—like the aforementioned actions—were thought to capture the knowledge and ways (*dao* 道) of actions and words (particularly in the realms of governance and ritual) that had been preserved in the "traces of the sage kings" (*shengwang zhi ji* 聖王之跡).[15]

This discourse on traces as writings and records of actions, deeds, and words of the past that contain sage wisdom became contested in the third and second century BCE. Texts like the *Zhuangzi* and *Huainanzi* 淮南子 opposed the importance of traces of the past and proposed that sage rulership may only be achieved if the rulers forget about their human disposition and cover up (*yanji* 掩跡), eradicate (*mieji* 滅跡), or hide [their] traces (*cangji* 藏跡) so they may "embody the [traceless] Way" (*tidao* 體道).[16]

If we situate the *Huainanzi*'s discourse on the sage within this debate on the nature of traces and their value, we will see that a mere metaphorical reading of *wu ji* as an illustration of the Way (or, to be precise, of one of its features) reduces the term to a rhetorical ornamentation and therefore does not do justice to its allusive qualities, argumentative explosiveness, and complexity.[17] By introducing the term "tracelessness," these proto-Daoist texts justified their regime of body-politics that aimed at generating sage rulers in the erstwhile here and now and, at the same time, powerfully rejected the culture of remembrance (*Erinnerungskultur*) and reliance on sages of the past Ruists frequently promoted during the transitional phase from the Warring States (475–222 BCE) to the early imperial period.

The Trace as a Characteristic of the Myriad Beings

To better understand the discursive context of the *Huainanzi*'s illustration of the sage and the traceless Way, let us uncover in some detail the contexts in which Han (206 BCE–220 CE) and pre-Han writings utilized the term "*ji*."¹⁸ Early lexicographical texts like the *Approaching Elegance* (*Erya* 爾雅) from the third or second century BCE mainly used it to describe traces of animals. For example, the *Erya*'s penultimate section "Explaining Wild Beasts" ("Shishou" 釋獸) contains three depictions of animals, which are all defined by a sequence of characteristics: their species' name; the specific names for the species' male, female, and/or offspring; characterizations of their traces; and finally the name of a powerful subspecies.¹⁹ Thus, the *Erya* uses the term "*ji*" to describe the imprints of animals, valuable information for anyone who may want to track down and hunt them.²⁰ This utilization of *ji* as referring to the traces of game is quite rare in early Chinese texts, though. Instead, most writings use the terms "tracks" (*zong* 蹤) or "hoofs" (*ti* 蹄) to depict animal imprints and mainly refer to birds with the term "trace," to which I will return below.

The *Commenting Patterned Signs and Analyzing Characters* (*Shuowen jiezi* 說文解字), an early graphological dictionary attributed to Xu Shen 許慎 (ca. 58–147 CE), however, moves into a different direction.²¹ It leaves the realm of hunting and game and generalizes the *Erya*'s use of the term "trace."²² It says, "*ji* is the place of a step" (*ji buchu ye* 迹步處也),²³ claiming that it depicts any kind of imprint that has been left on the ground. By explicitly relating the trace with steps (*bu* 步),²⁴ the proto-dictionary associates the term with the motions of beings in the world,²⁵ as further reflected in its extension to "lifeless" objects in the entry on cart tracks (*zhe* 轍).²⁶ Hence, *ji* not only refers to the imprints of human or animal steps, but also to any form of impression left behind by a thing or being that has a form, walks (*xing*), and moves (*dong* 動).²⁷ If we follow the argumentative line laid out by the entries in the *Erya* and *Shuowen jiezi*, we may conclude that having a trace—as also reflected *ex negativo* in *Huainanzi* 14.2—was apparently an inherent feature of any Myriad Being during the Han dynasty.

Traces as Leftovers of Actions in Early China

This observation has profound consequences for the way early Chinese texts understood the cosmos and what it means to act in this world. Apparently, (human) beings were thought to inevitably inscribe themselves in the dust and dirt of the phenomenal world via their actions and deeds.²⁸ Early Chinese texts are filled with examples in which the actions of a human being were described with the term "*ji*." The poem

"Grieving at the Edifying Wind" ("Bei huifeng" 悲回風) from the *Elegies of Chu*'s (*Chuci* 楚辭) "Nine Pieces" ("Jiu zhang" 九章) cycle,²⁹ for example, conjures specific places (*chu* 處) in which the actions of figures like Bo Yi 伯夷 (trad. mid-eleventh century BCE) and his brother Shu Qi 叔齊 (trad. mid-eleventh century BCE) or Shentu Di 申徒狄 (trad. sixteenth century BCE) had been inscribed.³⁰ Bo Yi and his brother opposed King Wu of Zhou's 周武王 (trad. r. 1046–1043 BCE) martial advances against the Shang 商 dynasty (ca. 1600–1045 BCE) and took refuge in the wilds where they starved themselves to death. Shentu Di similarly drowned himself in remonstrance. Hence, the *Chuci* apparently describes their traces both as their (political) actions and the places (real and imagined) where these actions created some type of leftover,³¹ through which later generations may roam and therewith connect with them.³²

This discourse about traces as remnants of a (political) action prominently appears in several texts from the Han dynasty. The chapter on "The Principles of Government" ("Zhengli") 政理) from Liu Xiang's 劉向 (77–6 BCE) *Garden of Persuasions* (*Shuoyuan* 說苑), for example, uses the term "trace" to depict political actions and their outcomes. It illustrates two inherently different approaches to rulership: "the traces of a usurper" (*bazhe zhi ji* 霸者之跡), which refers to the policies of a "martial governance" (*wuzheng* 武政), and "the traces of a king" (*wangzhe zhi ji* 王者之跡), which connotes a ruler whose actions are "benevolent and kind" (*renhou* 仁厚).³³ Accordingly, the *Shuoyuan* explicitly relates the concept of traces to the actions of kings and other rulers and their evaluation by their successors as either rightfully or forcefully installed sovereigns.

Since traces seem to have frequently referred to the actions of a ruler, it is not surprising that *ji* were also closely related to the accumulation of a name/fame (*ming* 名), and, by extension, the practice of giving posthumous titles (*shi* 謚).³⁴ The *Discussion in the White Tiger Hall* (*Baihutong* 白虎通), for example, claims in its chapter "Appellations" ("Hao" 號) that "[a] posthumous name is the trace of one's conduct, by which one is distinguished for later generations" (謚者, 行之跡也, 所以別於後代).³⁵ For it defines *shi* as the "traces of one's actions" (*xing zhi ji* 行之跡) that are "handed down without cessation" (*chui wu qiong* 垂無窮), the *Baihutong* seems to directly relate the practice of posthumous titles back to the discourse on how (human) beings inevitably inscribe themselves in all under heaven (*tianxia* 天下) via their deeds.³⁶

The vision that a ruler's actions would leave behind traces in form of her or his posthumous titles and fame was so common that Wang

Chong 王充 (ca. 27–97 CE) would use it in one of the skeptical chapters of his *Balanced Discourses* (*Lunheng* 論衡) to argue against the apparently common narrative during the late Eastern Han dynasty (25–220 CE) that the legendary Yellow Emperor had been an immortal.[37] Hence, it seems as if several early texts considered names, appellations (*hao* 號), and posthumous titles to contain the traces of a person's past actions that led to her or his reputation, fame, and remembrance in the erstwhile present.

Traces and Their Relationship with Words and Writings

Since the term "trace" was directly associated with a ruler's actions, and by extension her or his name,[38] it is only logical that kings and other political actors would record their own deeds to safeguard their legacy and/or justify their legitimacy.[39] This practice finds its roots in the oracle bone inscriptions and later became institutionalized in the commissioning of Standard Histories (*zhengshi* 正史) and other records of historical events.[40] This royal concern about leaving behind a record of the traces of one's words and deeds is prominently displayed in the Feng 封 and Shan 禪 sacrifices. According to the *Baihutong*, emperors had to show gratitude and report their successes to Heaven and Earth as part of the rituals on Mount Tai (Taishan 泰山). They left their traces in this place by installing "an engraved stone [that] records the appellations [of the king and his predecessors]" (*keshi jihao* 刻石紀號) and by "writing down the traces of [their] accomplishments" (*zhu ji zhi gongji* 著己之功跡).[41]

However, the chapter does not only claim that the actions enshrined in the "traces of [their] accomplishments" were inscribed solely for reporting to Heaven and Earth so that emperors may proclaim their rulership over all under heaven.[42] Apparently, these engraved stone tablets were also open to the subjects.[43] For example, the *Grand Scribe's Records'* (*Shiji* 史記) "Basic Annals of the First Emperor of Qin" ("Qin Shihuang benji" 秦始皇本紀) contain an alleged transcript of the First Emperor's stone inscriptions from Mount Tai. According to this record, Qin Shihuang 秦始皇 (born Ying Zheng 嬴政; 259–210 BCE; r. 247–210 BCE) not only "for the first time . . . unified the world" (*chu bing tianxia* 初并天下). During the same ritual performance, his "accompanying ministers contemplated on the traces . . . and respectfully [chanted] his/their meritorious deeds" (從臣思跡 . . . 祗誦功德).[44] In other words, the ministers who eulogized the meritorious deeds engraved on the summit either observed the traces of Qin Shihuang or, as we will see in the next example, perhaps even engaged in the records left on Mount Tai by the former kings during their rituals.

This public component of traces, which we also encountered in the *Chuci*'s "Nine Pieces," is reflected in the continuation of the *Baihutong* passage. It includes a short comment attributed to Kongzi 孔子 (c. 551–479 BCE; latinized Confucius) that states, "When I climbed Mount [Tai] and made an inspection of the [number of] Kings who had [announced] the change of [the dynastic] name, [I discovered that] those who could be counted amounted to more than seventy Lords" (昇泰山，觀易姓之王，可得而數者七十有餘).[45] In other words, these royal traces of more than seventy rulers might have been accessible for at least a privileged portion of the population who could then trace back the sage kings' achievements (*gong* 功) and deeds in order to connect the past with the present (*tong gujin* 通古今)—for example, in form of eulogies (*song* 誦).[46]

As indicated by the texts left on Mount Tai, such traces of actions and deeds that were inscribed in the phenomenal world would regularly take on the form of writings.[47] In fact, the *Chuci*'s "Nine Pieces" explicitly mentions that both "words and actions may be traced back" (言與行其可跡兮).[48] Moreover, we have seen that the term "*ji*" is intricately related to the concept of names. Since the Chinese character *ming* not only refers to any name in our modern sense, but also to terms in general, it is not surprising that both actions and words were perceived to be traces. This twofold vision of traces as actions and words is clearly reflected in the famous myth that Cang Jie derived Chinese characters from bird tracks.[49] The *Lunheng*, for example, contains a short narrative in the chapter "Resonating Categories" ("Ganlei" 感類), in which Wang Chong argues in a typical manner for him that "the observation of bird traces gave rise to the invention of writing" (以見鳥跡而知為書) and not any supernatural commands (*ming* 命) from Heaven.[50] In fact, the *imaginaire* of the script as a sort of bird trace crystallized in the practice of bird writings (*niaoshu* 鳥書), which create characters out of bird motives (see figures 7.1 and 7.2).[51] Hence, early Chinese texts directly associated the script with the actions of animals (particularly birds) and their tracks in the universe (see figure 7.3).[52] Accordingly, *ji* referred to both the concrete actions and uttered words of beings in the phenomenal world and their recordings in form of writings.[53]

At the time of the *Lunheng*, this association of traces with writings became so ubiquitous that Wang Chong would refer to it in his discussion

Figure 7.1. Unknown maker, China, *Ying Gong Ritual Vessel*, detail of inscription that includes some bird script, Early Western Zhou dynasty, ca. 1046–771 BCE, bronze, H 7¼ × W 6 in. (18.4 × 15.2 cm). Courtesy of Art Properties, Avery Architectural & Fine Arts Library, Columbia University in the City of New York, Arthur M. Sackler Collections (S0283). The inscription says, "Ying Gong made this precious ritual vessel, saying, 'May [my son] Yan and [his] younger brother use [this vessel] morning and evening for sacrificial offerings of cooked foods.'"[54]

Figure 7.2. Rubbing of the Ying Gong vessel's inscription. After Luo Zhenyu 羅振玉, *San dai jijin wen cun* 三代吉金文存 (Shangyu: Luo shi bai jue zhai, 1936), 3.36.3. Fair use.

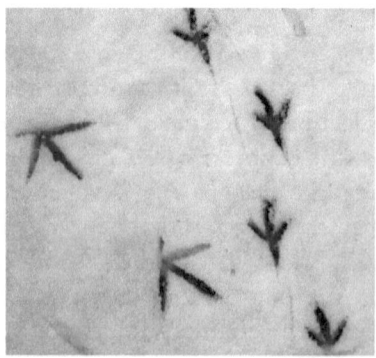

Figure 7.3. Bird tracks in snow that resemble the character *ge* 个 and its bronze script (*jinwen* 金文) version. Copyright Tony Hisgett.

of education in his chapter "Valuation of Knowledge" ("Liang zhi" 量知). Wang used the process of transforming bamboo and wood into refined writings (*wen* 文) as an image to illustrate the transformative powers of education. By comparing raw and crude writing materials with the human substance (*shi* 實), he argued that only training—and in this case practice with the very texts that had been written on the prepared bamboo slips and wooden boards—would generate properly cultivated officials:

> While bamboo is growing on mountains and wood in forests, their future use is still uncertain. Bamboo is broken into tubes, which are split into tablets. The traces made on these with styles and ink form [refined] characters. Big tablets become *Classics*, the smaller ones, records. Wood is cut into blocks, which are split into boards, which by dint of carving and planing become writing tablets for official memorials. Bamboo and wood are coarse things, but by cutting and polishing, carving and paring are wrought into useful objects. What about humanity, the noblest creature of all, whose nature encompasses heaven and earth? Unless people go to school to study the *Classics* and other works in order to enrich their uncarved substance, and unless they are imbued with propriety and righteousness, people would stand in the imperial court stiff like a lath or a tablet. What kind of use is this?
> 夫竹生於山，木長於林，未知所入。截竹為筒，破以為牒，加筆墨之跡，乃成文字，大者為經，小者為傳記。斷木為槧，析之為板，力加刮削，乃成奏牘。夫竹木、麤苴之物也，彫琢刻削，乃成為器用。況人含天地之性，最為貴者乎! 不入師門，無經傳之教，以郁樸之實，不曉禮義，立之朝庭，植笮樹表之類也，其何益哉? [55]

Here, we see an elaborate analogy that explicitly defines the *Classics* and any other text as an accumulation of brush and ink traces (*bimo zhi ji* 筆墨之跡).[56] Due to the paralleling of education and the inscription of traces on bamboo slips, it seems as if Wang Chong—like Mengzi (372–289 BCE)—suggests that self-cultivation imprints and refines "a coarse thing" (*cuju zhi wu* 麤苴之物) and "uncarved substance" (*pu zhi shi* 樸之實)—that is, the human physique—into a cultured (*wen* 文) body the same way ink inscribes bamboo slips and transforms them into refined, written patterns (*wen* 文).[57]

Memory, Traces, and the Preservation of the Teachings from the Past

So far, we have seen that various early Chinese texts associated the term "trace" with the motions of the Myriad Beings in general and the (recorded) actions and words of rulers, officials, and other human beings in particular. In this section, I will expand on how *ji* were accordingly considered to be valuable containers that enshrine the actions and words of the sages from the past, enabling their readers to temporarily recall or reexperience the originators and their teachings through the process of reception.[58] As we have seen in the example of the royal practices of engraving one's deeds on Mount Tai or the conferral of posthumous titles, traces were closely related to memory, commemoration, and contemplative practices (*si* 思). Since traces were the (written) leftovers of one's actions and words, they may also be used to envision the principles that guided the respective actions and words, as reflected in the ministers' contemplation on traces (*siji* 思跡) in the *Shiji* or the poetic egos engagement with the traces of political protests from the past in the *Chuci*. This discourse became particularly important in the late Warring States and early imperial period when writers wondered where they might find the teachings of the sage kings (*shengwang* 聖王).

The *Xunzi* 荀子 was particularly concerned with this question about the sources one might use to reconstruct the rituals of the glorious past. Since traces were perceived to be the leftovers of actions and words, the *Xunzi* developed an evaluation of the potential sources for reconstructing the true teachings of the sage rulers. In its chapter, "Contra Physiognomy" ("Fei xiang" 非相), Xun Kuang 荀況 (ca. 310–238 BCE) claims that the ability to create and act according to distinctions (*fen* 分) is what separates humans from animals. But how can we learn about these distinctions? The *Xunzi* argues in a typically Ruist fashion that distinctions are taught via rituals (*li* 禮), and rituals are again taught via the sage kings. This sequence, however, contains one salient problem: the sage kings had passed away a long time ago, so they could not personally teach the rituals anymore. So where might we find these paths (*dao* 道) to becoming human, then? Xunzi complains that his contemporaries searched for the sage king's teachings in the wrong place. Rather than expecting the traces of the sage kings to manifest in their leftover writings, as the "vulgar Confucians" (*suru* 俗儒) did,[59] one should better observe how their principles had been preserved in the actions of the later kings (*houwang* 後王) such as the "refined Ru" (*yaru* 雅儒) do.⁶⁰ Or in the *Xunzi*'s own allegorical voice: "If you want to observe a millennium, you must look at today" (欲觀千歲, 則數今日), since for the sage "the ancient and modern are one and the same [measure]" (*gujin yi du ye* 古今一度也).⁶¹ In other words, the *Xunzi* alludes here to the twofold meaning of the word traces as texts and actions and suggests that the real teachings of the past may not be found in arcane inscriptions and writings, since "what has been transmitted over a long span of time can be discussed only in broad outlines; what is recent can be discussed in greater detail" (傳者久則論略, 近則論詳).⁶² Hence, the real teachings, which are implemented and therewith commemorated in contemporaneous ritual practices and governance, may best be found in the lived memory of the sage's actions in the erstwhile here and now.⁶³

This discourse on where to find access to the teachings of the sage kings was continued, yet meaningfully altered in the famous Wheelwright Bian 輪扁 story from the *Zhuangzi*, a collection of anecdotes and short essays attributed to Master Zhuang Zhou 莊周 (fl. fourth century BCE). In this short vignette from the end of the "Way of Heaven" ("Tiandao" 天道) chapter, a conversation emerges between a craftsman and Duke Huan of Qi 齊桓公 (d. 643 BCE) who discuss the usefulness of language and texts. Duke Huan proclaims that he is reading "the words of the sages" (*shengren zhi yan* 聖人之言), which the wheelwright condemns immediately as "merely the dregs of the ancients" (*guren zhi zaopo* 古人之糟魄).⁶⁴ Since the duke considers his social status, intellect, and literacy superior to the "petty" craftsman, he is insulted by the subject's impudence and commands the wheelwright to explain himself, to which Bian responds with an allegory based on his own experience in wheel making. According to the wheelwright, the craft of making a wheel—like maintaining a sage governance—may not be transmitted and learned via written sources, a vision quite in line with the *Xunzi* and the *Han Feizi* 韓非子.⁶⁵ To substantiate his claim, Bian narrates his futile and finally fruitless attempts at teaching his son the arts of wheel making. Since "one achieves [this skill] with the hand and responds to it with the heart, [but] the mouth cannot put it in words" (得之於手而應於心, 口不能言), one may not learn the techniques from texts or speeches.⁶⁶ Only the repeated practice of making spokes with one's own hands and learning to respond to the distinct materials' varying conditions with one's heart might enable one to finally produce a wheel that perfectly links the hub with the spokes. Even though his son studied with a living teacher who could directly guide (*dao* 道 or 導) and speak (*dao* 道) to him, he was apparently unable to learn the craft. How could a dead, written record achieve such a feat and teach the arts of sage governance, then? *Ergo*, Bian called the writings of the sages "mere dregs of the ancients": that is, useless traces and mere leftovers of their sage rulerships that cannot transmit their embodied knowledge, experiences, and practices.[67]

If we read their critiques as reactions to prevalent contemporaneous concerns and "profound anxiety about the potential disappearance of knowledge" rather than isolated pronouncements, it seems as if a vivid discourse on the whereabouts of the teachings from the past evolved during the late Warring States and early imperial period, to which texts like the *Xunzi*, *Zhuangzi*, and *Han Feizi* responded.[68] Apparently, written traces of the sage kings were considered to be nodes or storage units that contain their words and teachings (*dao* 道) and therefore were valuable resources for commemoration and education. In fact, it seems as if some texts even described such traces as potential resources to reexperience or even conjure their originators, enabling the receiver to create a connection and continuity between the past and the present.[69]

Contrary to such a vision of traces, the two examples from the *Xunzi* and the *Zhuangzi* claimed that real learning may only be achieved in lived practices. In other words, rather than studying, memorizing, and implementing the stale messages of the remote past, it would be more beneficial to engage in the contemporaneous actualizations of their teachings. At the same time, however, the *Xunzi* and the *Zhuangzi* seem to disagree on the goal of such practices and their paths (*dao* 道). While the *Xunzi* thinks that the observance of contemporaneous practices may guide one's ritualistic behavior transforming one into a person that embodies sage virtues, the Wheelwright Bian's story and its direct textual context point toward a "transcendental" reading of the term "*dao*" and its relationship to the trace, on which I will elaborate in the next section.

The Discourse on the Tracelessness of the Way in the *Zhuangzi*

As we have seen so far, traces were commonly associated with four things in early China: tracks, actions, and words of Myriad Beings, as well as their recordings in form of writings. These traces were apparently thought to open up an avenue to events and people of the past that can be conjured, commemorated, and reexperienced in the process of reception.⁷⁰ By revisiting the places of the actions and words of people from the past (real and textual alike), the early Chinese texts consulted in this chapter, thus far, valued traces as powerful nodes that allow one to connect the past with the present.⁷¹ At the same time, however, a vivid debate arose in the late Warring States and early imperial period about the nature of traces in the phenomenal world and their proper allocation, as we have seen in the example of the *Xunzi*. Might the traces of the ancients be found in the writings associated with the Shang and Zhou dynasties? Or are they continuously actualized in the contemporaneous performance of sage rulership? Even though these texts disagreed on the very source that may be utilized to find the teachings from the past, they nonetheless offered a positive evaluation of human traces as a whole.

This self-affirmation that the connection to the past was not lost despite the vast destructions during the Warring States period came under fire during the third and second century BCE. As we have seen in the last subsection, proto-Daoist texts like the *Zhuangzi* and, as I will argue, the *Huainanzi* opposed such positive readings of traces as valuable records of the actions, words, and teachings/paths (*dao*) from the distant past. In fact, they claimed that no human device that is rooted in language would be able to uncover the workings of the only "real" Dao, which is the cosmic Way. To emphasize the difference between "Ruist" readings of traces as valuable containers of the teachings (*dao*) from the past and proto-Daoist concerns with a Way (*dao* 道) that transcends human faculties, texts like the *Zhuangzi* utilized encounters between Kongzi and Laozi 老子 (trad. fl. sixth century BCE) to drive home their point. For example, the chapter "Heavenly Revolutions" ("Tianyun" 天運) contains a short vignette, in which Kongzi complains to Laozi that no ruler followed his advice despite the fact that "I, Qiu, have been studying the Six Classics—the *Odes, Documents, Rituals, Music, Changes*, and *Spring and Autumn Annals*—for what I myself would consider a long time" (丘治詩書禮樂易春秋六經, 自以為久矣).⁷² Laozi responds to Kongzi's remorse that he should feel fortunate the rulers did not listen to him since he had studied the wrong sources.⁷³ According to Laozi,

> The Six Classics are the stale traces of the former kings, but they do not tell where these traces were coming from. Now, sir, what you talk about are traces. Traces, however, are the prints left by shoes—are the shoes the ones who produced them, though?

夫六經, 先王之陳跡也, 豈其所以跡哉! 今子之所言猶迹也。夫迹履之所出, 而迹豈履哉?⁷⁴

The *Zhuangzi* displays in this negative evaluation of the Six Classics (*liu jing* 六經) a clear illustration of traces as writings. These textual traces may contain human ideas about morality and order, yet they will inevitably fail to transmit the transformative powers of the cosmos. The Dao does not leave behind any traces and moral teachings (*fenghua* 風化; lit. windy transformations) in the universe, yet its powers trigger life and growth (*sheng* 生), as illustrated in the long list of impregnating animals Laozi incorporates in his argument that follows the quoted passage above.⁷⁵ Instead of studying the real effects of the Way's transformative powers that manifest in the procreation of the Myriad Beings, Kongzi spent all his time learning about the dead leftovers of human morality that the *Zhuangzi* oftentimes renders as the main reason for violence and untimely death in the world.⁷⁶ In short, this passage from the "Tianyun" chapter derides textual traces as static, useless, and even dangerous human remnants from the past.⁷⁷

Because of their negative evaluation of traces as a human and therewith limited avenue to the powers of the universe, texts like the *Zhuangzi*'s chapter "Knowledge Wanders North" ("Zhi beiyou" 知北遊) illustrated the cosmic Way as being traceless (*wu ji*) to create a contrast to the traceness of the Myriad Beings. This discourse seems to originate from *Laozi* 老子 27's depiction of the sage as a skillful traveler who "leaves [behind] no cart tracks" (*wu cheji* 無轍跡).⁷⁸ In one of "Zhi beiyou's" stories, Kongzi converses again with Laozi about the Dao. As both the *Laozi* and the *Zhuangzi* repeatedly express, "The Way is profound and difficult to describe" (夫道窅然難言哉), yet Laozi nonetheless attempts to circumscribe the parameters of this ineffable force in this short vignette.⁷⁹ At first, he decides to enumerate a sequence of births as if this series of creations captures an important aspect of the Dao, an idea we have already encountered in the passage from the "Tianyun" chapter above. It begins with the illustration of a process: "brightness is born out of darkness" (昭昭生於冥冥); "having relationships is born out of the formless" (有倫生於無形); "essence and spirits are born out of the Way" (精神生於道); and "bodily form and the trunk are born out of essence" (形本生於精), leading finally to the procreation of the Myriad Beings.⁸⁰

Following this depiction of the Myriad Beings' generation as a bodily realization out of the Dao, the text switches to a more explicit statement about the Way. It contrasts the physicality and spatial expansion of beings with the Dao's immaterial nature. While humans, animals, and spirits live in housings with entrances and are confined to a place due to their form, the passage claims that the Way "has neither gate nor house" (*wu men wu fang* 無門無房) and lodges in and connects with the Four Reaches (*si da* 四達), that is, the entire world.⁸¹ In other words, it depicts the Dao as a nonexistent "entity" (*wu* 無) that has neither spatial expansion nor a concrete location.⁸² The text asserts that these spatial implications are intricately related to the motions of the Way. As we have seen in the proto-dictionaries, the movements of the Myriad Beings were thought to inevitably produce tracks in the universe due to their corporeality. The *Zhuangzi*, however, creates a divergence to this "traceness" of beings and their disposition to leave behind tracks and offspring in its illustration of the Dao. It claims that the Way "comes without a trace" (*qi lai wu ji* 其來無跡) and "goes without a horizon" (*qi wang wu ya* 其往無崖).⁸³ Thus, this passage from the *Zhuangzi* clearly separates the Dao and its activities from beings that "with their [bodily] form reciprocally reproduce" (*yi xing xiangsheng* 以形相生).⁸⁴

Hence, it seems as if the *Zhuangzi* plays *ex negativo* with the intelligible association of the body with traces and movements that we also found in the early lexicographical and graphological texts. It associates the Way with superior motions and actions (particularly the ability to give birth without being affected by the transformative powers of life and death) and thereby contrasts its tracelessness with several characteristics ascribed to the Myriad Beings: their spatial expansion, temporal expression, and disposition to leave behind traces (*ji*) and offspring. As a result, it suggests that the real Dao is traceless and therefore may not be found in written leftovers. Such traces of human actions and words that rely on the discerning powers of language may be enough to transmit human, and therewith partial and limited teachings and ways of being as propagated by Ruists like Xunzi. However, they inevitably fail if one wants to engage in the transformative and procreative powers that govern the phenomenal world according to proto-Daoist sources.

The Discourse on Erasing, Covering, and Hiding Traces in the *Huainanzi*

Bearing in mind the debate on traces as human actions, words, and their written records from the past and proto-Daoist responses to it, in this section we may finally revisit *Huainanzi* 14.2, with which I began this chapter. As I have argued, proto-Daoist texts like the *Zhuangzi*—but also the *Huainanzi*—initiated a discursive shift during the late Warring States and early imperial period: from traces as records, through which we may access the teachings of the past, to hindrances that keep us from realizing the real power behind the organization of the universe.[85] This change had significant impact on the way texts like the *Huainanzi* construed sage rulers. Rather than following the ideals recorded in the textual and ritualistic traces attributed to the former kings, as presented in writings that Sima Tan 司馬談 (d. 110 BCE) would later categorize as Ruist, Liu An's text fashioned the ideal ruler as someone who should not simply follow (*xunji* 循跡) or adhere to any "singular trace" (*yi ji* 一跡).[86] In other words, the *Huainanzi* clearly picked up the discourse on traces as (written) leftovers from the past and questioned their universal applicability.[87]

Accordingly, it is not surprising that the *Huainanzi* is filled with passages that describe sages and True Persons as beings who should, rather, embody the Way's trace-, space-, action-, form-, speech-, and timeless qualities.[88] By having no trace and by embodying the Way (*tidao* 體道), their nonaction (*wuwei* 無為) would reinforce its powers, enabling them to govern all under heaven without causing any disturbances and unrest (*luan* 亂).[89] In other words, the idea of tracelessness was deemed an integral aspect of the *Huainanzi*'s vision of sage rulership.[90] How could a human being become traceless, though, if traces are a defining feature of the Myriad Beings? According to the *Huainanzi*, it may be achieved by erasing (*mieji* 滅跡), covering up (*yanji* 掩跡), or hiding one's traces (*cangji* 藏跡), transforming the sage into a supreme spirit being (*shen* 神) that may resonate with the entire phenomenal world.[91] Let us now return to the passage presented at the beginning.

Huainanzi 14.2 directly referred to a context we encountered several times throughout this chapter: the discourse on traces as records of a person's actions and fame. According to *Huainanzi* 14.2, however, the sage does not act "for the sake of fame and reputation" (*bu wei ming* 不為名), contradicting the sources we encountered in sections 3 and 4.[92] In fact, the continuation of the passage quoted at the beginning of this chapter picks up the theme of fame and remembrance, yet illustrates these two ideals as lethal aspirations for any (sage) ruler.

> Stars arrayed in the heavens are bright. Therefore people point at them. Rightness arrayed in one's Potency is obvious.

Therefore people observe it. What people point at has a manifestation because it moves; what people observe leaves a trace because it acts. When movements have manifestations, they will be criticized; when actions have traces, they will be appraised. Thus, the sage conceals her or his brilliance in the formless and hides her or his traces in nonaction.
星列於天而明, 故人指之; 義列於德而見, 故人視之。人之所指, 動則有章; 人之所視, 行則有跡, 動有章則詞, 行有跡則議, 故聖人掩明于不形, 藏跡于無為。[93]

Huainanzi 14.3 uses here celestial imagery to explain its concerns with fame and reputation. Famous people are like stars that people see (*jian* 見) and point at (*zhi* 指). But because their motions and actions can be perceived, for they have manifestations (*you zhang* 有章) and leave traces (*you ji* 有跡) in the phenomenal world, such famous people also are criticized (*ci* 詞) and praised (*yi* 議). Being praised and critiqued, however, does not pose a serious threat per se, so what is so problematic about being (in)famous, then?

Huainanzi 14.4 answers this question by providing several examples of people who perished because of their reputation. All of these individuals had particular strengths, yet by emphasizing their strengths, they inevitably pronounced their weaknesses, too. In other words, the discourse on hiding one's traces seems to be related to the discursive context we encountered above: that the traces of a ruler's actions were the basis for her or his posthumous titles and fame. However, the *Huainanzi* reassesses the vision enshrined in the *Baihutong* and other texts. Having a name makes one the target of other beings, just as the tracks of game makes them traceable for hunters. As *Huainanzi* 14.4 says by alluding to a passage from the *Zhuangzi*'s chapter "Responses from Emperors and Kings" ("Ying diwang" 應帝王), "the power of tigers and leopards attracts archers" (虎豹之強來射), and "the agility of monkeys and apes invites pursuit" (猨狖之捷來措), so that these magnificent beings often meet an untimely death.[94] The sage, however, should "not for the sake of a name/fame become a corpse" (聖人不為名尸) as *Huainanzi* 14.2 mentioned above,[95] so it is indispensable for a ruler to keep her or his underlings in the dark by outsourcing all actions and deeds to the officials and the subjects.[96] Consequently, *Huainanzi* 14.3 argued that "the sage conceals her or his brilliance in the formless and hides her or his traces in nonaction" (聖人掩明于不形, 藏跡于無為). In other words, the practice of hiding one's traces is the very means through which the ruler remains out of his subject's reach. Or as *Huainanzi* 14.45 argues, by "erasing one's traces in nonaction" (*mieji yu wuwei* 滅跡于無為) the ruler was thought to simply "follow the self-so-ness of Heaven and Earth" (*sui tiandi ziran* 隨天地自然) and remain dissociated with the important political practices of providing punishment (*zhu* 誅) and rewards (*shang* 賞) for the subjects.[97] As a result, the sage ruler would avoid any interference with the Myriad Beings and remain untraceable and intangible.[98]

This practice of erasing or hiding traces, however, does not only refer to the debate on *ji* as records of one's actions and fame. It also picks up the physiological connotations that we encountered throughout this chapter by claiming that erasing one's traces will result in an alteration of a sage's body and existence. As I have argued elsewhere, the *Huainanzi* contains an elaborate discourse on the sage as a traceless nonbeing who embodies the Way.[99] According to *Huainanzi* 13.8, the sage "achieves the root of the Way" (*de dao zhi ben* 得道之本) by "using the physique to embody it [i.e., the Way]" (*yi shen ti zhi* 以身體之).[100] By letting "one's disposition merge with the Dao" (*xing he yu dao* 性合于道), so one "exists yet seems to be nonexistent" (*you er ruo wu* 有而若無),[101] the sage would transform her- or himself into a nonbeing (*wu* 無) who could "use her or his nonexistence in order to resonate with those that exist" (聖人以無應有).[102] In other words, the practice of erasing one's traces, which effectively hides the ruler from its subjects' praise and blame, did not only refer to a governmental nonaction that would keep the sage ruler from building up a reputation (*ming*), a process several texts we discussed in the earlier subsections hailed as the very means through which the former kings may be commemorated and their teachings implemented.[103] In fact, it also referred to a vision that human beings may transform themselves into a receptacle of the Way in the phenomenal world, providing such sages with a far more direct access to a power that would transcend the human limitations of the former kings.[104] And to do so, the sage would need to erase her or his thingness (*wu*) by transforming her- or himself into a traceless nonbeing similar to the Dao that may reside in the hidden center of the imperial palace in order to function as the very pivot that provides all Myriad Beings with a place in the phenomenal world.[105] Or to use Michael Puett's words, the sage acts like a supreme spirit,[106] a traceless nonbeing that traverses within and beyond the limits of the cosmos without moving out of the center of all under heaven, and thereby "become[s] fully linked with the proper patterns of the universe . . . that any spirit inherently follows."[107]

Conclusion

As we have seen, having a trace was a defining feature of what it meant to be a Myriad Being. According to this vision, beings inevitably inscribed themselves in the phenomenal world via their actions and words. Such inscriptions could manifest in specific places and/or bodies associated with individual actors as reflected in the *Chuci*. However, it became more commonly identified with their recordings in form of written leftovers that enabled later generations to create a connection with the past. As a result, traces were oftentimes read as the textual and nontextual remnants of the sages and former kings that contained their paths (*dao*) of proper conduct and governance, which could be commemorated, memorized, and implemented via the reception process.

Proto-Daoist writings picked up this discourse yet turned its evaluation on the head. Rather than offering a valuable access to the knowledge of the sage kings, texts like the *Zhuangzi* and the *Huainanzi* argued that these traces of actions and words and their commemoration and veneration are hindrances for realizing the "real" Dao in the world. In these readings, the cosmic Way and its transformative and procreative powers may not be captured by the partial traces human beings inevitably create. Rather than following the teachings from the past, it would therefore be central for sage rulers to merge with the Way in order to embody its features.

Since such *ji* are insufficient to actualize the Way, these texts proclaimed a practical regime that could transform a human being into a traceless nonbeing like the Dao. Although the texts remained silent about what concretely the practical regime of nonaction (*wuwei*) and erasing traces would comprise, they nonetheless were quite vocal about its benefits. On the one hand, it would enable a sage ruler to avoid any praise and critique from the subjects, allowing her or him to evade early death by envious people. On the other hand, it would lead to a bodily transformation that converts the ruler into a traceless nonbeing that could universally resonate with the Myriad Beings. Hence, these proto-Daoist texts projected the discourse of tracelessness onto their constructions and reevaluations of sage rulers who were thought to have shed and transcended their human condition via various recipes and techniques (*fangshu* 方術).

At the end, the *Huainanzi*'s discourse on erasing traces and the tracelessness of the sage with which I began this chapter not only served as a metaphor for the Way, but also referred to the full discursive range of *ji* in early China: its association with the Myriad Beings and their bodily form (*xing*); its meaning as a written record, particularly in relationship to the concept of names and posthumous titles; and its connotation as a carrier of the sage teachings from the past. By introducing the Dao and the sage as traceless nonbeings that transcend the scope of human traces, proto-Daoist texts not only negated the usefulness of humanity's immediate and distant past, but also opposed all the institutions and practices associated with the retrieval, commemoration, and implementation of the former kings' teachings.[108] In other words, the *Zhuangzi* and *Huainanzi*'s refusal of traces as a valuable resource was not only a rhetorical move to emphasize the transcendental quality of the Way. By introducing the practice of erasing traces as a prerequisite for sage rulership, the *Huainanzi* presented a highly controversial and explosive rejection of humanity's reliance on the past as a model for the present, the very cultural practice various contemporaneous texts treated as the *sine qua non* of any governance.

Notes

1. For my reasonings why I think that the *Huainanzi* was construed to function as a powerful scripture, see Tobias Benedikt Zürn, "The Han *Imaginaire* of Writing as Weaving: Intertextuality and the *Huainanzi*'s Self-Fashioning as an Embodiment of the Way," *Journal of Asian Studies* 79, no. 2 (2020): 367–402.

2. For a discussion of the *Huainanzi*'s early textual history, see Charles Le Blanc, *Huai-Nan-Tzu: Philosophical Synthesis in Early Han Thought* (Hong Kong: Hong Kong University Press, 1985), 19–78; Judson B. Murray, "The Consummate Dao: The Way (Dao) and Human Affairs (Shi) in the *Huainanzi*" (PhD diss., Brown University, 2007), 42–57; Harold D. Roth, *The Textual History of the Huai-Nan Tzu* (Ann Arbor, MI: Association for Asian Studies, 1992), 9–26; and Tobias Benedikt Zürn "Writing as Weaving: Intertextuality and the *Huainanzi*'s Self-Fashioning as an Embodiment of the Way" (PhD diss., University of Wisconsin, Madison, 2016), 92–110.

3. For discussions of the *Huainanzi*'s vision of sages, see Tobias Benedikt Zürn, "Overgrown Courtyards and Tilled Fields: Image-Based Debates on Governance and Body Politics in the *Mengzi*, *Zhuangzi*, and *Huainanzi*," *Early China* 41 (2018): 297–332.

4. John S. Major, Andrew Seth Meyer, Sarah A. Queen, and Harold D. Roth, eds. and trans., *The Huainanzi: A Guide to the Theory and Practice of Government in Early Han China* (New York, NY: Columbia University Press, 2010), 528.

5. The *Huainanzi* frequently alternates between depicting the ideal ruler as a sage (*shengren* 聖人), a True Person (*zhenren* 真人), or a Thearch (*di* 帝). See *Huainanzi* 14.1 in Zhang Shuangdi 張雙棣, ed., *Huainanzi jiaoshi* 淮南子校釋 (Beijing: Beijing daxue chubanshe, 1997), 1469 and Major et al., *The Huainanzi*, 537. For a diverging interpretation, see Zhou Ying, "How to Live a Good Life and Afterlife: Conceptions of Post-Mortem Existence and Practices of Self-Cultivation in Early China" (PhD diss., University of Pennsylvania, 2019), 257–316.

6. Zhang, *Huainanzi jiaoshi*, 1469 and Major et al., *The Huainanzi*, 537.

7. Zhang, *Huainanzi jiaoshi*, 1469. The translations are altered from Major et al., *The Huainanzi*, 536.

8. Zhang, *Huainanzi jiaoshi*, 1469. The translation is altered from Major et al., *The Huainanzi*, 537.

9. I agree with most scholars of "religious" Daoism that we may only find a concrete community of people in the first and second century CE that formed a distinct group we may nowadays term Daoist. But unlike most scholars of early China or Michel Strickmann (1942–1994) and his students of later Daoist movements who see a strict division between what scholars in early China oftentimes call early "philosophical" Daoism and later "religious" Daoism, I perceive a discontinuous continuity between these two "movements" in form of shared terminologies, concepts, and practices. In other words, I follow Kristofer Schipper's (1934–2021) vision and call texts like the *Laozi*, *Zhuangzi*, or even in extension the *Huainanzi* proto-Daoist since they at least partially informed the lifeworlds and *imaginaires* of later Daoist practitioners.

10. The *Zhuangzi* uses a wide variety of expressions to depict this realm prior to and beyond the phenomenal world: "outside of the Four Seas" (*si hai zhi wai* 四海之外); "beyond the Six Coordinates" (*liu he zhi wai* 六合之外 or *liu ji zhi wai* 六極之外); "beyond the [Five] Quarters" (*fang zhi wai* 方之外); or simply, "beyond the world/age (*shi zhi wai* 世之外). For two discussions of the scholarly trend to reduce images to beautified supplements or substitutions for a term/concept, see Hans-Peter Hoffmann, *Die Welt als Wendung: Zu einer literarischen Lektüre des wahren Buches vom südlichen Blütenland* (Wiesbaden: Harrassowitz Verlag, 2001), 27–47 and Zürn, "Overgrown Courtyards and Tilled Fields," 297–305.

11. For an excellent explanation why early Chinese texts should be read within the context of contemporaneous debates, see Michael J. Puett, *The Ambivalence of Creation: Debates Concerning Innovation and Artifice in Early China* (Stanford, CA: Stanford University Press, 2001), 16–20. For another discussion of the term "erasure," see Esther Klein's contribution in this volume.

12. For a discussion of such engagements with traces, see Wu Hung, *A Story of Ruins: Presence and Absence in Chinese Art and Visual Culture* (Princeton, NJ: Princeton University Press, 2012), 62–91. The *Chart of the Sage's Traces* (*Shengji tu* 聖跡圖) in Kongzi's 孔子 (trad. 551–479 BCE) temple in Qufu 曲阜, Shandong 山東 province, may serve as a concrete albeit much later example of such engagements with traces. Julia K. Murray remarks regarding Confucian modes of venerating traces as relics that at least one writer considered these incised stone slabs that depict important episodes of Kongzi's life story and that are housed in the Hall of the Sage's Traces (*Shengji dian* 聖跡殿) as enabling "viewers to experience an 'audience' with Confucius." See Julia K. Murray, "A Heavenly Aura: Confucian Modes of Relic Veneration," *Journal of the British Academy* 2 (2014): 82.

13. For examples of the myth of Cang Jie, see *Huainanzi* 8.5, 19.5, and 20.12 in Zhang, *Huainanzi jiaoshi*, 828, 1982, 2059 and Major et al., *The Huainanzi*, 274, 778, 806.

14. The idea of traces as records and writings is reflected in the title of a chapter in Gongsun Long's 公孫龍 (ca. 325–250 BCE) collection of sayings and narratives, titled "The Storehouse of Traces" ("Jifu" 跡府).

15. For examples of the expression "traces of the sage kings" (*shengwang zhi ji*), see the passages from the *Xunzi's* 荀子 "Contra Physiognomy" ("Fei xiang" 非相) and "Contra Twelve Philosophers" ("Fei shier zi" 非十二子) in the section "Memory, Traces and the Preservation of the Teachings from the Past" and footnotes 59 and 60.

16. This vision of the traceless Way and sages gained so much prominence that it became projected onto any discourse of ascended beings in the Han dynasty who are repeatedly depicted as roaming in "the land of those who have cut off their traces" (*jueji zhi ye* 絕跡之野). However, the term "*jueji*" does not appear in the *Huainanzi*, so I excluded it from the discussion. For some references to usages of *jueji* in early China, see footnote 91.

17. For two classic studies that criticize scholars' tendency to read metaphors as ornamental replacements and substitutions of plain discourses, see Max Black, *Models and Metaphors: Studies in Language and Philosophy* (Ithaca, NY: Cornell University Press, 1962), 25–47 and Ivar Armstrong Richards, *The Philosophy of Rhetoric* (New York, NY: Oxford University Press, 1965).

18. The term "*ji*" plays an important role in ancient and early imperial Chinese texts. Aside from a few instances in the *Mozi* 墨子 (seven times) and

Guanzi 管子 (seven times) though, the term "*ji*" appears rarely in texts prior to the early third century BCE. As Mark Edward Lewis claims regarding the development of the library in the Han dynasty, "it is the product of a world where works are seen as traces of a vanished or vanishing era that must be maintained through *active* scholarly work" (*Writing and Authority in Early China* [Albany: State University of New York Press, 1999], 325–26). Hence, it seems as if the term "*ji*" only gained significance in the third century BCE, when scholars apparently became increasingly afraid of losing a connection to the past, as Newell Ann Van Auken also argues in her essay in this edited volume.

19. "Elk: male it is the Jiu; female it is the Chen; its offspring are the Yao; its tracks are those of a beastly [animal]; there is the extremely powerful Di [species]" (麋, 牡麔。牝麎, 其子麆, 其跡躔, 絕有力狄). See Liu Dianjue 劉殿爵 [D. C. Lau], ed., *Erya zhuzi suoyin; Xiaojing zhuzi suoyin* 爾雅逐字索引；孝經逐字索引 (Hong Kong: The Commercial Press, 1995), 123. For the other two examples, see Liu, *Erya zhuzi suoyin*, 123.

20. The specific animals that the chapter describes suggest that the *Erya* included depictions of their tracks since all these animals were common prey (elk, deer, and rabbit).

21. See William G. Boltz, "Shuo wen chieh tzu," in *Early Chinese Texts: A Bibliographical Guide*, ed. Michael Loewe (Berkeley, CA: Society for the Study of Early China, 1993), 429.

22. I follow here Françoise Bottéro and Christoph Harbsmeier's claim that "The *Shuowen* is not a dictionary of basic meanings [but] a dictionary of graphic etymology [that] provides only meanings that are relevant to the explanation of the graphs used to write words" (Françoise Bottéro and Christoph Harbsmeier, "The *Shuowen Jiezi* Dictionary and the Human Sciences in China," *Asia Major*, 3rd ser. 21, no. 1 [2008]: 249).

23. Xu Shen 許慎, *Shuowen jiezi zhenben* 說文解字真本, in *Si bu beiyao* 四部備要, vol. 75 (Taipei: Taiwan zhonghua shuju, 1965), 2b.2b.

24. Axel Schuessler claims that early forms of the character *ji* depict the visible signs of walking, scratching, or trampling that have been left behind on the ground. See Axel Schuessler, *ABC Etymological Dictionary of Old Chinese* (Honolulu: University of Hawai'i Press, 2007), 299.

25. An example of a story that employs the term "trace" in the sense of imprints resulting out of motions may be found in the *Zhuangzi*'s "An Old Fisherman" ("Yufu" 漁夫) when Kongzi laments that "I was twice driven out of Lu [and] had my traces obliterated in Wey [sic]" (丘再逐於魯, 削跡於衛). See Guo Qingfan 郭慶藩, ed., *Zhuangzi jishi* 莊子集釋, in *Zhuzi jicheng* 諸子集成, vol. 3 (Beijing: Zhonghua shuju, 1954), 446 and Victor H. Mair, trans., *Wandering on the Way: Early Taoist Tales and Parables of Chuang Tzu* (Honolulu: University of Hawai'i Press, 1994), 320.

26. See Xu Shen 許慎, *Shuowen jiezi zhenben* 說文解字真本, in *Si bu beiyao* 四部備要, vol. 76 (Taipei: Taiwan zhonghua shuju, 1965), 14a.15b. The category of *wu* includes both beings and things, blurring the boundaries between lifeless and living beings as it would be typical for a contemporary, English-speaking audience. This is not surprising since, as Robert Gassmann has argued, *wu* first and foremost means an aggregate or assembled thing that has a form, a name, and acts in a specific role (in our case moves and leaves traces)—a definition that fits to both things and human beings. See Robert Gassmann, "Getting to the Bottom of 'Things' (*wu* 物): Expanding on A. C. Graham's Understanding," in *Having a Word with Angus Graham: At Twenty-Five Years into His Immortality*, eds. Carine Defoort and Roger Ames (Albany: State University of New York Press, 2018), 120–25.

27. "If we look at what is most consistently used to characterize a *wu*, it is having a form, shape, or appearance" (Franklin Perkins, "What Is a Thing [*wu* 物]? The Problem of Individuation in Early Chinese Metaphysics," in *Chinese Metaphysic and Its Problems*, eds. Li Chenyang and Franklin Perkins [Cambridge: Cambridge University Press, 2015], 60). For another short summary of what defines *wu*, see Mercedes Valmisa, *Adapting: A Chinese Philosophy of Action* (Oxford: Oxford University Press, 2021), 2–3.

28. This understanding of the term "*ji*" partially explains why in later periods people who are about to ascend (*xian* 仙) always leave something behind. It is their last human imprint in the phenomenal world. See Guo, *Zhuangzi jishi*, 46, 122, and 291; Mair, *Wandering on the Way*, 21, 61, and 397; and Robert Ford Campany, *Making Transcendents: Ascetics and Social Memory in Early Medieval China* (Honolulu: University of Hawai'i Press, 2009), 57.

29. See Liu Dianjue 劉殿爵 [D. C. Lau], ed., *Chuci zhuzi suoyin* 楚辭逐字索引 (Hong Kong: The Commercial Press, 2000), 16. The translations are altered from David Hawkes, trans., *The Songs of the South: An Ancient Chinese Anthology of Poems by Qu Yuan and Other Poets* (London: Penguin Books, 1985), 183.

30. As Robert E. Harrist Jr. writes about stone inscriptions carved in landscapes (*moya* 摩崖 or *moya shike* 摩崖石刻) in early and medieval China, they "constitute a vast archive of writing. In a very real sense, visitors do not simply climb Mt. Tai—they *read* it, deciphering the written traces of those who traveled to the mountain before them and reanimating voices from the past that speak from the words of the carved texts" (*The Landscape of Words: Stone Inscriptions from Early and Medieval China* [Seattle: University of Washington Press, 2008], 17).

31. See Murray, "A Heavenly Aura," 67–68. I think that this vision of places as evocative nodes of human actions underlies the common literary practice of visiting places mentioned in poetic and artistic products in East Asian cultural history. For a discussion of the concept of *utamakura* 歌枕 (lit. poem pillow), a

poetic word/place name that creates an intertextual reference to other poems and the importance of (envisioned) visits of places mentioned in *waka* 和歌 poetry as a means to engage with one's poetic forebears, see Edward Kamens, *Utamakura, Allusion, and Intertextuality in Traditional Japanese Poetry* (New Haven, CT: Yale University Press, 1997). For another example of a literary place that serves as an evocative node of human action (in this case forgetting), see Michael Ing's contribution in this volume.

32. This vision that a trace may conjure a person of the past and her or his actions is also reflected in the myth of Hou Ji 后稷, whom Jiang Yuan 姜嫄 conceived by stepping into the footprint of the divine being Di 帝 or Emperor Ku (Di Ku 帝嚳). See Kong Yingda 孔穎達, ed., *Mao shi zhengyi* 毛詩正義, in *Shisan jing zhushu* 十三經注疏, vol. 2, ed. Ruan Yuan 阮元 (Taipei: Yiwen yinshu guan, 2001), 587a–96b and Jeffrey Riegel, trans., "Classic of Odes," in *The Columbia Anthology of Traditional Chinese Literature*, ed. Victor H. Mair (New York, NY: Columbia University Press, 1994), 163–65.

33. See Liu Dianjue 劉殿爵 [D. C. Lau], ed., *Shuoyuan zhuzi suoyin* 說苑逐字索引 (Hong Kong: The Commercial Press, 1992), 94. See also Eric Henry, trans., *Garden of Eloquence: Shuoyuan* 說苑 (Seattle: University of Washington Press, 2021), 400–3.

34. In fact, we find the expression "traces of fame" (*mingji* 名跡) in Eastern Han (25–220 CE) texts like the *Histories of the Han* (*Hanshu* 漢書) and the *Records of the Former Han* (*Qian Han ji* 前漢記).

35. See Liu Dianjue 劉殿爵 [D. C. Lau], ed., *Baihutong zhuzi suoyin* 白虎通逐字索引 (Hong Kong: The Commercial Press, 1995), 6 and Tjan Tjoe Som, trans., *Po Hu T'ung: the Comprehensive Discussion in the White Tiger Hall, Vol. 1: Introduction; Translation of Chapters I, II, XVIII, XL; Notes. A Contribution to the History of Classical Studies in the Han Period* (Leiden: Brill, 1952), 316.

36. See Liu, *Baihutong zhuzi suoyin*, 6 and Som, *Po Hu T'ung*, 316.

37. See He Zhihua 何志華 [Ho Che Wah], ed., *Lunheng zhuzi suoyin* 論衡逐字索引, 2 vols. (Hong Kong: The Commercial Press, 1996), 1.94. The translation is altered from Alfred Forke, trans., *Lun-Heng Part I: Philosophical Essays of Wang Ch'ung* (Leipzig: Harrassowitz, 1907), 333.

38. The *Mengzi* 孟子, a text attributed to Master Meng Ke 孟軻 (ca. 379–304 BCE), seems to utilize a string of arguments similar to my portrayal of traces in early China. In chapter 4B.21, it moves from "the traces of sovereign rule" (*wangzhe zhi ji* 王者之迹) via their crystallization in oral performance and songs of praise to their records in historical writings. See Jiao Xun 焦循, ed., *Mengzi zhengyi* 孟子正義, in *Zhuzi jicheng* 諸子集成, vol. 1 (Beijing: Zhonghua shuju, 1954), 337 and Bryan W. Van Norden, trans., *Mengzi: With Selections from Traditional Commentaries* (Indianapolis, IN: Hackett, 2008), 108.

39. For an example of such royal concern with one's legacy, see Olivia Millburn's discussion of King Fuchai of Wu 吳王夫差 (r. 495–473 BCE) in her contribution to this volume. If the funerary practice of removing the dead's traces from the *yang* world is accurate, as Li Xiang argues in his contribution, the royal concern with establishing and maintaining one's legacy via the recording of one's traces gains even more significance and urgency.

40. As it turns out, the *Grand Scribe's Records* (*Shiji* 史記) and the *Hanshu* frequently utilize the term "trace" in expressions such as "the traces of men" (*renji* 人跡), "the traces of great men" (*darenji* 大人跡), "the traces of Yin and Zhou" (*Yin Zhou zhi ji* 殷周之跡), "the royal traces" (*wangji* 王跡), or "the traces of the former kings" (*xianwang zhi ji* 先王之跡). In other words, *ji* is clearly a term closely related to early Chinese understandings of historiography and record-taking.

41. See Liu, *Baihutong zhuzi suoyin*, 38. The translation is altered from Som, *Po Hu T'ung*, 239.

42. "It was not just that the inscriptions, with their emphasis on the overall conquest, the foundation of the state, and the enforcement of social order, were basically political—the very act of erecting and inscribing stones constituted the fulfillment of the tour of inspection which was already well-established as a most noble demonstration of sovereignty" (Martin Kern, *The Stele Inscriptions of Ch'in Shih-Huang: Text and Ritual in Early Chinese Imperial Representation* [New Haven, CT: American Oriental Society, 2000], 109).

43. For a discussion of imperial stone inscriptions on Mount Tai, see Harrist Jr., *The Landscape of Words*, 219–70. For a short discussion of the practice "to give material form to intangible traces" by installing steles, see Murray, "A Heavenly Aura," 68.

44. Sima Qian 司馬遷, ed., *Shiji* 史記, 10 vols. (Beijing: Zhonghua shuju, 1987), 6.243. The translation is altered from Tsai-Fa Cheng, Zongli Lu, William H. Nienhauser Jr., Robert Reynolds, and Chiu-Ming Chan, trans., *The Grand Scribe's Records, Vol. 1: The Memoirs of Pre-Han China*, ed. William H. Nienhauser Jr. (Bloomington: Indiana University Press, 1994), 139.

45. See Liu, *Baihutong zhuzi suoyin*, 38–39. For the translation, see Som, *Po Hu T'ung*, 240.

46. Apparently, these records of kings' deeds were so important for their reputation that the *Spring and Autumn Annals of Mister Lü* (*Lü shi chunqiu* 呂氏春秋) would create a narrative in which the licentious King Zhuang of Chu's 楚莊王 (r. 613–591 BCE) reputation is saved by the virtuous deeds of his minister Sunshu Ao 孫叔敖 (ca. 630–593 BCE). See the chapter "On the Desires and Natural Emotions" ("Qingyu" 情欲) in Gao You 高誘, ed., *Lü shi chunqiu* 呂氏春秋, in *Zhuzi jicheng* 諸子集成, vol. 6 (Beijing: Zhonghua shuju, 1954), 18 and John Knoblock and Jeffrey Riegel, trans., *The Annals of Lü Buwei* (Stanford, CA: Stanford University Press, 2000), 86–87.

47. The vision of texts as traces extended far beyond the realm of literature. Early Chinese aesthetic writings, for example, utilize the term "trace" to illustrate brushstrokes (*biji* 筆跡; lit. traces of the brush), based on the brush's shared function as a tool in writing and painting. This idea derives from calligraphy and its vision of a person's handwriting as traces of her or his personality, which Xie He 謝赫 (fl. sixth century CE) incorporated in his understanding of early Chinese figure paintings. For a discussion of Xie He's *Record of the Classification of Old Painters* (*Guhua pinlu* 古畫品錄), the practice of physiognomy (*xiang* 相), and its manifestation in Xie He's vision of brushstrokes as expressions of a figures' inherent livelihood, see Mathias Obert, *Welt als Bild: Die theoretische Grundlegung der chinesischen Berg-Wasser-Malerei zwischen dem 5. und dem 12. Jahrhundert* (Freiburg: Karl Alber Verlag, 2007), 189–202.

48. Liu, *Chuci zhuzi suoyin*, 10. The translation is altered from Hawkes, *The Songs of the South*, 156.

49. Xu Gan's 徐幹 (171–218) *Balanced Discourses* (*Zhonglun* 中論), for example, contains a sequence of sages including Cang Jie, who developed technologies based on the observation of the cosmos. See He Zhihua 何志華 [Ho Che Wah], ed., *Xinyu zhuzi suoyin; Shenjian zhuzi suoyin; Zhonglun zhuzi suoyin* 新語逐字索引; 申鑒逐字索引; 中論逐字索引 (Hong Kong: The Commercial Press, 1995), 1. For some further references to the myth of Cang Jie in the *Huainanzi*, see Zhang, *Huainanzi jiaoshi*, 828, 1676, 1982, 2059 and Major et al., *The Huainanzi*, 274, 645, 778, 806.

50. See He, *Lunheng zhuzi suoyin*, 1.247. The translation is altered from Forke, *Lun-Heng Part II*, 27.

51. For a brief discussion of bird writings, see Susan Shih-Shan Huang, *Picturing the True Form: Daoist Visual Culture in Traditional China* (Cambridge, MA: Harvard University Asia Center, 2012), 154–64 and Tsuen-Hsuin Tsien, *Written on Bamboo & Silk: The Beginnings of Chinese Books & Inscriptions* (Chicago, IL: University of Chicago Press, 1962), 49–50.

52. The *Collected Writings of Court Gentleman Cai [Yong]* (*Cai zhonglang ji* 蔡中朗集) from the end of the Eastern Han dynasty further develops on this relationship between writings and the bodies of (mythological) animals and their traces in its chapter "The Power of Seals" ("Zhuanshi" 篆勢). See He Zhihua 何志華 [Ho Che Wah], ed., *Cai zhonglang ji zhuzi suoyin; Zhongjing zhuzi suoyin* 蔡中郎集逐字索引; 忠經逐字索引 (Hong Kong: The Commercial Press, 1998), 60.

53. Since traces were clearly thought to record actions and achievements of a person, it is not surprising that the term "*ji*" was also associated with erstwhile practices of physiognomy (*xiang* 相). Physiognomy refers to the evaluation of a person's skills and morality based on her or his physical appearance. For an insightful discussion of the materiality of virtue in the *Mengzi* and contempora-

neous practices of physiognomy, see Mark Csikszentmihalyi, *Material Virtue: Ethics and the Body in Early China* (Leiden: Brill, 2004), 101–60. This practice, which played a central role in early Chinese politics and was used by rulers to gauge the quality of their officials, prominently appears in the poem "Bei huifeng" from the *Chuci*'s "Jiu zhang" cycle. See Liu, *Chuci zhuzi suoyin*, 10 and Hawkes, *The Songs of the South*, 156. Interestingly, texts like Wang Chong's chapter, "A Definition of Worthies" ("Dingxian" 定賢), extended such a physiognomical reading of traces from human to textual bodies. According to Wang, Kongzi transmitted his greatness through the "leftovers and traces of ink and pencil left on boards and tablets" (筆墨之餘跡, 陳在簡笈之上). In his vision, the "[Chunchiu] was but a mere literary work, yet it showed that Confucius possessed the virtues qualifying him for an emperor" (春秋虛文業, 以知孔子能王之德), so that the writings of Kongzi served as a proxy for his missing body. See He, *Lunheng zhuzi suoyin*, 1.348–49 and Forke, *Lun-Heng Part II*, 150. In other words, one would not need to meet Kongzi in person to evaluate his emotional (*qing* 情) and/or physical disposition (*mao* 貌). It would be enough to just engage in his written *corpus*. Hence, it is not surprising that writings—like a person's physiognomy—were thought to be imbued with the traces of its producer's personality. Therefore, they may be used to recall her or his greatness/sagehood and to evaluate her or his skills, as it became typical practice in the reception of poetry and calligraphy in the Han and after. See Steven Van Zoeren, *Poetry and Personality: Reading, Exegesis, and Hermeneutics in Traditional China* (Stanford, CA: Stanford University Press, 1991) and Robert E. Harrist Jr., "Reading Chinese Calligraphy," in *The Embodied Image: Chinese Calligraphy from the John B. Elliott Collection*, ed. Robert E. Harrist (Princeton, NJ: Princeton University's Art Museum, 1999), 3. For a similar idea of recollection or evocation of an author based on their written traces as a central part of early Chinese reading practices, see Mercedes Valmisa's contribution in this edited volume.

  54. Jessica Rawson, *Western Zhou Ritual Bronzes from the Arthur M. Sackler Collections, Volume IIB* (Washington D.C.: The Arthur M. Sackler Foundation and the Arthur M. Sackler Museum, 1990), 226.

  55. He, *Lunheng zhuzi suoyin*, 1.172. The translation is altered from Forke, *Lun-Heng Part II*, 72–73.

  56. Further expressions of this vision in the *Lunheng* are "the leftover and traces of ink and pencil" (*bimo zhi yuji* 筆墨之餘跡) and "the scattered [footprints] of ink and pencil" (*bimo zhi shu* 筆墨之疏). See also footnote 53 above and the chapter "Literary Exaggerations" ("Yizeng" 藝增) in He, *Lunheng zhuzi suoyin*, 1.117 and Forke, *Lun-Heng, Part II*, 262.

  57. As I have discussed elsewhere, the *Mengzi* contains a similar discourse that parallels education with tilling, leaving incisions, furrows, and traces in the human body. For a discussion of this idea and various references to secondary

scholarship on agricultural imagery and education, see Zürn, "Overgrown Courtyards and Tilled Fields," 307–10 and 325–28. For more information on the relationship between traces and physiognomy, see footnote 53.

58. Robert Ashmore describes a similarly evocative process of reception in his reading of Tao Yuanming's 陶淵明 (365–427) intertextual engagement with the *Analects* and his later readers. See Robert Ashmore, *The Transport of Reading: Text and Understanding in the World of Tao Qian (365–427)* (Cambridge, MA: Harvard University Asia Center, 2010) and footnotes 12, 30–32, and 53.

59. See Wang Xianqian 王先謙, ed., *Xunzi jijie* 荀子集解, in *Zhuzi jicheng* 諸子集成, vol. 2 (Beijing: Zhonghua shuju, 1954), 51 and 88 and John Knoblock, trans., *Xunzi: A Translation and Study of the Complete Works*, 3 vols. (Stanford, CA: Stanford University Press, 1988), 1.206 and 2.79.

60. In the "Contra Twelve Philosophers" ("Fei shier zi" 非十二子) chapter, the *Xunzi* offers a less radical presentism, claiming that "the humane man . . . should model himself after the regulations of Shun and Yu [and] should model himself after the moral principles manifested by Confucius and Zigong" (仁人 . . . 法舜禹之制 . . . 法仲尼子弓之義). See Wang, *Xunzi jijie*, 61 and Knoblock, *Xunzi*, 1.225. For a discussion of the *Xunzi*'s discourse on vulgar and refined Ru and the former's reliance on ancient texts rather than current practice, see Anne Cheng, "What Did It Mean to Be A *Ru* in Han Times?," *Asia Major*, 3rd ser., 14, no. 2 (2001): 102–5 and Michael Nylan, "Han Classicists' Writing in Dialogue about Their Own Tradition," in *Philosophy East & West* 47, no. 2 (1997): 133–88.

61. See Wang, *Xunzi jijie*, 51–52 and Knoblock, *Xunzi*, 1.206–7.

62. See Wang, *Xunzi jijie*, 52 and Knoblock, *Xunzi*, 1.207–8.

63. For a discussion of the commemorative function of rituals and their mechanism of auxiliary memory that seems to be related to Xunzi's vision of rituals as the real source in which one may find sage teachings, see Paul Nicholas Vogt's contribution in this edited volume.

64. Guo, *Zhuangzi jishi*, 217. The translation is based on Mair, *Wandering on the Way*, 128.

65. Jean Levi summarizes the *Han Feizi*'s attitude toward the writings of the ancients as follows: "Officials of the State should be interested in the concrete and not search in dusty books for outdated models of action" ("*L'homme d'État doit s'intéresser au concret et non chercher dans les livres poussiéreux des modèles d'action périmés*"). See Jean Levi, "Langue, rite et écriture," in *Paroles à dire, paroles à écrire: Inde, Chine, Japon*, ed. Viviane Alleton (Paris: Édition de l'École des Hautes Études en Sciences Sociales, 1997), 161. Translated by the author. I would like to thank Albert Galvany for mentioning Levi's text to me and Dennis Schilling for making me aware of the *Han Feizi*'s critical stance toward texts and traces.

66. Guo, *Zhuangzi jishi*, 218. The translation is based on Mair, *Wandering on the Way*, 129.

67. The story right before Wheelwright Bian in the "Way of Heaven" ("Tiandao" 天道) chapter displays a similar skepticism toward language and writing. See Guo, *Zhuangzi jishi*, 217 and Mair, *Wandering on the Way*, 128.

68. For the quotation, see page 29 of Newell Ann Van Auken's essay in this edited volume.

69. See footnotes 12, 30–32, 53, and 58.

70. See footnote 53.

71. See footnotes 30–32.

72. Guo, *Zhuangzi jishi*, 234. The translation is altered from Mair, *Wandering on the Way*, 142.

73. For another discussion of this passage, see Levi, "Langue, rite et écriture," 163–66.

74. Guo, *Zhuangzi jishi*, 234–35. The translation is altered from Mair, *Wandering on the Way*, 142.

75. See Guo, *Zhuangzi jishi*, 235 and Mair, *Wandering on the Way*, 142. For an explanation of why the term *"fenghua"* alludes to both moral teachings and procreation, see Levi, "Langue, rite et écriture," 167.

76. For a discussion of the *Zhuangzi*'s negative vision of human virtues (*de* 德) and ritual propriety (*li* 禮), see Kim-chong Chong, *Zhuangzi's Critique of the Confucians: Blinded by the Human* (Albany: State University of New York Press, 2016), 123–40.

77. For similarly skeptical perspectives regarding textual memory, see Ken Brashier and Albert Galvany's contributions in this volume on the *Laozi* 老子 and *Liezi* 列子, respectively.

78. See Wang Bi 王弼, ed., *Laozi zhu* 老子注, in *Zhuzi jicheng* 諸子集成, vol. 3 (Beijing: Zhonghua shuju, 1954), 15 and D. C. Lau, trans., *Lao Tzu: Tao Te Ching* (London: Penguin Books, 1963), 32.

79. See Guo, *Zhuangzi jishi*, 323 and Mair, *Wandering on the Way*, 215.

80. See Guo, *Zhuangzi jishi*, 323. The translation is altered from Mair, *Wandering on the Way*, 215.

81. See Guo, *Zhuangzi jishi*, 324 and Mair, *Wandering on the Way*, 215.

82. The terms "gate" and "room" inevitably evoke connotations of a spatial expansion and corporeality. Especially the term "gate" would later become a central concept in Supreme Clarity (Shangqing 上清) Daoism and its understandings of orifices. If the *Zhuangzi* displays here a similar vision of the body as consisting of several gates (i.e., orifices and other openings), halls (*tang* 堂) and fields (*tian* 田), it is likely that the mentioning of *wu men wu fang* was understood as an allusion to the Dao's form- or bodyless (*wu xing* 無形) quality.

83. See Guo, *Zhuangzi jishi*, 323–24 and Mair, *Wandering on the Way*, 215.

84. See Guo, *Zhuangzi jishi*, 323. The translation is altered from Mair, *Wandering on the Way*, 215. For a discussion of the importance of *wu* in rela-

tionship to transformations, procreations and life and death, see Perkins, "What Is a Thing (*wu* 物)?," 56–63.

85. For an example in which Liu An's text follows the argumentation laid out in the two examples from the *Zhuangzi*'s "Tianyun" and "Zhi beiyou" chapters, see *Huainanzi* 1.13 in Zhang, *Huainanzi jiaoshi*, 87 and Major et al., *The Huainanzi*, 65.

86. *Huainanzi* 13.11 says, "sages . . . are not bound by the path of a single trace" (聖人 . . . 不結於一迹之塗). See Zhang, *Huainanzi jiaoshi*, 1403. The translation is altered from Major et al., *The Huainanzi*, 508.

87. For a similar conclusion regarding the *Huainanzi*'s vision of written leftovers and their various ways of action, see Franklin Perkins's contribution in this edited volume.

88. The discourse on embodying the Way crystallized in late Warring States texts such as the *Han Feizi*, *Xunzi*, and the *Zhuangzi*. The *Zhuangzi*'s "Zhi beiyou" 知北遊 chapter, for example, uses the expression "the ones who embody the Way" (*tidaozhe* 體道者) to depict the True Person. See Guo, *Zhuangzi jishi*, 329 and Victor H. Mair, *Wandering on the Way*, 219.

89. A paradigmatic illustration of such a glorious age is included at the beginning of the *Huainanzi*'s first chapter, "Originating the Way" ("Yuandao" 原道). See *Huainanzi* 1.2 in Zhang, *Huainanzi jiaoshi*, 1–2 and Major et al., *The Huainanzi*, 49–50.

90. *Huainanzi* 1.4, for example, depicts the two sage charioteers Feng Yi 馮夷 and Da Bing 大丙 as roaming the limits of the phenomenal world while leaving no traces behind. See Zhang, *Huainanzi jiaoshi*, 18 and Major et al., *The Huainanzi*, 51. For a more detailed discussion, see Zürn, "Overgrown Courtyards and Tilled Fields," 314–28.

91. Few texts used the expression "to cover up one's traces" (*yanji*) to illustrate a ruler's following of the sage kings' traces and the phrase "cutting off one's traces" (*xiaoji* 削跡 or *jueji* 絕跡) as a metaphor for the sudden disappearance and escape of a person; however, the terms "*mieji*," "*cangji*," and "*yanji*" mainly referred to the practice of embodying the Way during the Western Han dynasty. For the former use of *yanji*, see Wang, *Xunzi jijie*, 73 and Knoblock, *Xunzi*, 2.68. For an example of the latter use of *xiaoji* to illustrate Kongzi's sudden escape from the kingdom of Wei 衛, see footnote 25.

92. Zhang, *Huainanzi jiaoshi*, 1469 and Major et al., *The Huainanzi*, 537.

93. Zhang, *Huainanzi jiaoshi*, 1470. The translation is altered from Major et al., *The Huainanzi*, 538.

94. Zhang, *Huainanzi jiaoshi*, 1509 and Major et al., *The Huainanzi*, 538. For the textual parallel, see Guo, *Zhuangzi jishi*, 133 and Mair, *Wandering on the Way*, 68.

95. Zhang, *Huainanzi jiaoshi*, 1469 and Major et al., *The Huainanzi*, 537. Probably, the *Huainanzi* would have considered Qu Yuan's 屈原 (trad. 340–278 BCE) self-sacrifice in exchange for cultural immortality as an action close to the

tigers, leopards, monkeys, and apes' athletic bravado. See Esther Klein's essay for the discussion of Qu Yuan's story.

96. As the *Zhuangzi* concisely says, "The superior must subscribe to nonaction and use all under heaven; inferiors must subscribe to action and be used by all under heaven" (上必無為而用天下，下必有為為天下用). See Guo, *Zhuangzi jishi*, 208 and Mair, *Wandering on the Way*, 121. For an insightful discussion of the *Huainanzi*'s job-sharing strategy, see Roger Ames, *The Art of Rulership: A Study of Ancient Chinese Thought* (Albany: State University of New York Press, 1994), 58–62.

97. Zhang, *Huainanzi jiaoshi*, 1509. The translation is altered from Major et al., *The Huainanzi*, 560.

98. See *Huainanzi* 9.13 in Zhang, *Huainanzi jiaoshi*, 923 and Major et al., *The Huainanzi*, 306–7. The *Han Feizi* contains a similar discourse on nonaction (*wuwei* 無為) as a political undertaking in its "Explaining the *Lao[zi]*" ("Yu Lao" 喻老) and "Dissecting the *Lao[zi]*" ("Jie Lao" 解老) chapters. See Wang Xianshen 王先慎, ed., *Han Feizi jijie* 韓非子集解, in *Zhuzi jicheng* 諸子集成, vol. 5 (Beijing: Zhonghua shuju, 1954), 95–124 and Sarah A. Queen, "*Han Feizi* and the Old Master: A Comparative Analysis and Translation of *Han Feizi*, chapter 20, 'Jie Lao,' and chapter 21, 'Yu Lao,'" in *Dao Companion to the Philosophy of Han Fei*, ed. Paul R. Goldin (Dordrecht: Springer Verlag, 2013), 228–55.

99. See Zürn, "Overgrown Courtyards and Tilled Fields," 325–28.

100. Zhang, *Huainanzi jiaoshi*, 1368 and Major et al., *The Huainanzi*, 498–99.

101. See *Huainanzi* 7.7 in Zhang, *Huainanzi jiaoshi*, 747. The translation is altered from Major et al., *The Huainanzi*, 248.

102. See *Huainanzi* 7.6 in Zhang, *Huainanzi jiaoshi*, 745. The translation is altered from Major et al., *The Huainanzi*, 247.

103. A famous example of such a reading would be the Han reception of Kongzi as the Uncrowned King (*suwang* 素王) that crystallized, for example, in the *Guliang Commentary* (*Guliang zhuan* 谷梁傳) to the *Spring and Autumn Annals* (*Chunqiu* 春秋). See Mark Csikszentmihalyi, "Confucius," in *The Rivers of Paradise: Moses, Buddha, Confucius, Jesus and Muhammad as Religious Founders*, eds. David Noel Freedman and Michael J. Clymond (Grand Rapids, MI: William B. Eerdmans Publishing, 2001), 273–81 and Michael Nylan, "Kongzi, the Uncrowned King," in *Lives of Confucius: Civilizations Greatest Sage through the Ages*, eds. Michael Nylan and Thomas Wilson (New York, NY: Doubleday, 2010), 67–100. See also footnote 53 for Wang Chong's idea that Kongzi's writings enable a reader to glean at the master's superior personality.

104. The *Zhuangzi* calls this "returning to the one without a trace" (*fanyi wu ji* 反一無跡) in the chapter "Mending Nature" ("Shanxing" 繕性). See Guo, *Zhuangzi jishi*, 245. The translation is altered from Mair, *Wandering on the Way*, 150.

105. The *Zhuangzi* contains a similar discourse in its chapter "Seal of Integrity Fulfilled" ("Dechongfu" 德充符), which depicts the sage as a being

that has cast off portions of its human condition: "How insignificant and small is that part of him which belongs to humanity" (眇乎小哉! 所以屬於人也). See Guo, *Zhuangzi jishi*, 99 and Mair, *Wandering on the Way*, 49. For an example of someone who regressed to the primordial state expressed in the term "embodying the Way," see Albert Galvany's discussion of Huazi 華子 in this edited volume.

106. *Huainanzi* 15.19–20, for example, claims that a commander functions like a military sage who "can order the affairs of the five officers because (s)he cannot be surveyed or measured" (能治五官之事者, 不可揆度者也). Her or his "Way of using arms" (*yongbing zhi dao* 用兵之道) should be "like ghosts, leaving no [traces]; like water, bearing no scars" (若鬼之無跡, 若水之無創). See Zhang, *Huainanzi jiaoshi*, 1605 and Major et al., *The Huainanzi*, 605.

107. Michael J. Puett, *To Become a God: Cosmology, Sacrifice, and Self-Divinization in Early China* (Cambridge, MA: Harvard University Asia Center, 2002), 284.

108. In other words, the *Huainanzi* opposes here projects like the *Shiji*'s creative reconstruction as Esther Klein suggests in her contribution (particularly in the section "Obliteration and Creative Construction").

Chapter 8

The Oblivious against the Doctor

Pathologies of Remembering
and Virtues of Forgetting in the *Liezi*

Albert Galvany

Remembering is a malady for which forgetting is the cure.
—Georges Perec, *Species of Spaces and Other Pieces*

From Forgetting the *Liezi* to Forgetting in the *Liezi*

The idea of writing about the *Liezi* 列子 in an edited volume exploring the relations between forgetting and memory in ancient China would not, of course, seem out of place. No doubt because suspicions about both its doubtful nature and its late dating have had a dampening effect on its reception at least since the Tang dynasty,[1] this is a text that, even in recent times, has tended to be neglected by the community of scholars interested in elucidating and reconstructing the intellectual history of the early periods.[2] One only has to look at the academic production over recent decades to confirm that, with few exceptions, Western sinology has given it infinitely less attention than that accorded to other texts that are more or less thematically linked with it, the *Zhuangzi* 莊子,[3]

for example. In this regard, it has been scorned and almost invariably relegated to obscurity, when not to the most tenacious oblivion.

Although it is not the main aim of this chapter, it is still worth inquiring into the oblivion to which the *Liezi* has frequently been condemned—for mainly philological reasons—and assessing how far it can be justified. Is it perhaps a mere medieval falsification of little value? Is the *Liezi* a latterly composed text and therefore not worth analyzing if the purpose is to deepen knowledge about the history of ideas in ancient China? In the 1960s and 1970s, Yang Bojun 楊伯峻 (1909–1992) and Angus C. Graham (1919–1991) published some scholarly studies with results that seemed to confirm the long-held suspicions about the *Liezi* and thus ruled out its "authenticity" as a document dating back to the Warring States.[4] Ever since then, and despite recent attempts to reinstate the philological condition of the *Liezi*,[5] the academic community, and especially in the West, has accepted Graham's arguments and the discussion was therefore closed.[6] Nevertheless, the present response to these issues would seem to be much more cautious and nuanced than it was some decades ago when the seminal works of Yang Bojun and Angus C. Graham were published. With the proliferation of ancient manuscripts appearing with archaeological discoveries and looted tombs, the traditional approach of linking the composition of a text to a single author has now been superseded by a much more open and flexible representation of the processes of composition, formation, and circulation of early texts. Recovery of these materials in the last few years has led, among other things, to questioning and reevaluation of categories like "authentic," "original," and "authorship," which, until recently, were deemed to be appropriate tools of textual taxonomy.

Following some recent contributions by scholars working on unearthed materials and discussing text production in antiquity, it would be very risky to take an ancient text as a compact unit and pronounce categorically on its authenticity, originality, and dating since, in many cases, more than one person has intervened in its composition and construction in a process that can last for decades and even centuries.[7] The gestation of ancient texts should then be seen more as a choral, multifarious process whereby malleable materials of various origins[8] are deposited in the form of literary compilations or collages.[9] Even if one accepts the (in many respects debatable) approaches of some scholars regarding the late dating of certain parts of the received version of the *Liezi*, these conclusions should not be extrapolated to the text as a whole, for if the aforementioned processes of composition are accurate, such generalizations would not be acceptable in this case either. Agreeing with the hypothesis that the *Liezi* is a late compilation does not necessarily mean accepting that it is a forgery, or that one can dismiss in advance the possibility that some of the materials with no counterparts in pre-Han texts that are to be found in the received version of the *Liezi* were composed in early periods or copied from versions originally written in the Warring States period.[10]

At least, as far as I know, there are no conclusive philological arguments that would justify discarding the whole *Liezi* as an *unauthentic* or *unoriginal* piece, categories that are indeed completely alien to the textual production processes in ancient times and, hence, methodologically controversial. Rather, to the extent that the *Liezi* contains memorable anecdotes about forgetting, it would seem that there are very good reasons for reviving it and insisting on its relevance in this regard. In contrast to a good part of the ancient philosophical literature and, most particularly, writings that are classified as belonging to the so-called Confucian school (*ru jia* 儒家), where memory plays a crucial role and is given an explicitly positive treatment, the *Liezi*, in line with the subversive bent also shown by the *Zhuangzi* in this regard,[11] includes materials that suggest the need for critical revision of the idea of memory and its purported virtues.

The Dreadful Misleadings of Memory

It might be said that essential processes, in both individual and collective spheres, for example, the cult of ancestors, filial piety, self-cultivation, and interpersonal relations within a hierarchical order, require that nothing essential—the memory of one's progenitors, the words of the Master, instructions received from superiors, the codes of ritual behavior, the legacy of the sage-kings of antiquity, words pronounced, deeds done in the past, et cetera—can be forgotten. The crucial role played by memory in the writings of the Confucian school is clearly visible in a series of passages taken from the *Analects* where, by way of example, much emphasis is given to the negative character of forgetting or omission (*wang* 忘). In the first of these examples, and with reference to the characteristics of the morally accomplished or complete person (*cheng ren* 成人), it is stated that he always bears in mind words that have been spoken, even in the most adverse circumstances.

Zilu asked about the complete person. The Master said, "Take a person as wise as Zang Wuzhong, as free of desire as Gongchuo, as courageous as Zhuangzi of Bian, and as accomplished in the arts as Ran Qiu, and then acculturate them by means of ritual and music—such a man might be called a complete person." He continued: "But must a complete person today be exactly like this? When seeing a chance for profit he thinks of what is right; when confronting danger he is ready to take his life into his own hands; when enduring an extended period of hardship, he does not forget what he had professed in more fortunate times—such a man might also be called a complete person."

子路問成人。子曰：若臧武仲之知，公綽之不欲，卞庄子之勇，冉求之藝，文之以禮樂；亦可為成人矣！曰：今之成人者，何必然？見利思義，見危授命，久要不忘平生之言；亦可以為成人矣！[12]

In this passage, Confucius names, first of all, several individuals who he believes would incarnate the ideal image of the complete individual, after which he offers a more abstract description of certain values that could then be deemed as belonging to this morally accomplished person. Within this framework, and regarding commitment to previously uttered words, Confucius considers that the complete person does not forget what she has said and keeps her word, however much her circumstances vary or turn against her. Hence, any individual who aspires to become morally complete must conserve the memory of what she has said in favorable times and stay true to these earlier utterances even in adverse juncture. The project for political and moral restoration conceived by Confucius seems to have been largely shaped by clear awareness of the dangers associated with discourse, or with unseemly, careless use of language. One of the fundamental roles of the Master within the community of his disciples was to guarantee strict correspondence between the property of language and the property of action. It is not surprising, then, that both the complete person and the gentleman (*junzi* 君子)—the figure that paradigmatically embodies the moral standard compatible with the Confucian program—are ashamed of any word that exceeds their deeds, that is, any discourse that is not immediately and incontrovertibly translated into its corresponding action.[13] Confucius's project is articulated and organized around the notion of moral quality (*ren* 仁), which, with regard to one's relationship with words, goes back to a constellation of ethical concepts that validate an appropriate use of language, for example, the notion of credibility (*xin* 信).[14]

In this sense, and returning to the passage cited above, it can be said that commitment to complying with what is verbally agreed on depends on not forgetting what was promised in benign times, and this means preserving the undertaking in memory in order to be able to reactivate it fittingly when the time is ripe, and in adverse circumstances too.[15] In his construction of the complete person and with respect to her relationship with words Confucius, then, gives a key role to memory, making it an essential element in his program of moral renovation.

Memory, or better said, the duty of not forgetting, appears once again in another passage, this time referring to the process of refining the noble man through study or learning (*xue* 學). It now appears in words the *Analects* placed in the mouth of Zixia 子夏, one of the Master's disciples.

> Zixia said, "Being aware every day of what he still lacks, and after a month not forgetting what he is already capable of—such a person can be said to love learning."
> 子夏曰: 日知其所亡, 月無忘其所能, 可謂好學也已矣! [16]

By comparison with other more deliberative instances (*si* 思)[17] or those of conduct (*xing* 行),[18] learning (*xue*) refers to a prior process of gaining experience and acquiring knowledge. The inclination or propensity for study (*hao xue* 好學) is a recurring theme in the *Analects*,[19] and Confucius describes himself in one famous passage as someone who never tires of studying and learning.[20] Similarly, there are many examples of statements in Confucian literature, at least concerning the ideal embodied in the noble man, affirming that study is a process that is prolonged throughout one's existence, and only death puts an end to it.[21] This tireless devotion to learning is expressed in the passage from the *Analects* I have just cited, as a commitment to being aware of, and constantly checking the gaps one must aspire to fill, and the shortcomings, lapses, and omissions (*wang* 亡) that must be remedied. At the same time, together with mindfulness of these flaws, studying demands a permanent exercise of remembering, of recalling and reviewing what has been acquired so that it will not be lost by falling into oblivion (*wang* 忘). Self-cultivation, in which study and learning make up one of the most basic and indispensable phases, necessarily entails activation and strengthening of memory, inasmuch as this means a tenacious exercise of permanent introspective review.[22]

If one takes into account these passages where, in keeping with the conventional approaches of the tradition, Confucius emphasizes within his moral program the relevance of memory, which is so crucial for learning, and thereby accentuates by contrast the negative dimension of omission and carelessness, it is striking that, in another passage of the *Analects*, he makes no bones about presenting himself as someone abounding in forgetfulness. His comment here is made when Duke She 葉公, a high official from the state of Chu 楚, asks Zilu 子路, an outstanding member of the group of Confucius's disciples, about the figure of the Master, and the latter is unable to respond.

> The Duke of She asked Zilu about Confucius. Zilu had no reply. [Upon Zilu's return], the Master said, "Why did you not just say, 'He is the type of person who is so passionate that he forgets to eat, whose joy renders him oblivious to worries, and who grows old unaware of the passage of the years.'"
> 葉公問孔子於子路，子路不對。子曰：女奚不曰：其為人也，發憤忘食，樂以忘憂，不知老之將至云爾。[23]

Contrary to what might be expected after all of the above regarding the importance given to memory and the duty of not forgetting, in this passage, when it comes to defining Confucius as a person (*qi wei ren* 其為人), forgetting explicitly dominates in the first two of the three sentences, while unawareness prevails in the third. Nevertheless, and leaving aside hypotheses about Zilu's silence in response to the question of the dignitary from Chu, I believe that if this passage uses these paradoxical—or, at least, surprising at first sight—formulae, it is precisely with the intention of highlighting the intensity with which Confucius experiences his pedagogical vocation.[24] He goes to the extreme of neglecting the need for nourishment because his mind is wholly occupied with his fervor for teaching, and he forgets about worries because of the joys of his life as an educator, which also leads him to become impervious to the consequences of the inexorable passage of time. From this point of view, it should be said that if Confucius is portrayed in this passage as such a forgetful individual, it is because, in fact, he is presented as someone whose mental focus on his mission as a teacher is one of tremendous intensity or, in other words, a man whose mind is so wholly occupied with this pedagogical passion, that he neglects other important aspects of life. Despite the first impressions it might convey, the passage once again emphasizes the close links, in the Confucian school, between self-cultivation, learning, the pedagogical function, and memory.

I believe that three anecdotes about matters of omission and forgetting at the end of chapter 8 of the *Liezi* should be read bearing in mind this last passage from the *Analects*. The first one is about a man who loses his axe.

> There was a man whose axe went missing and suspected the boy next door. He watched the boy walking: he had stolen the axe! His expression, his speech, his behavior, his manner, and everything about him betrayed the fact that he had stolen the axe. Soon afterwards, the man was digging in his garden and found the axe. On another day he saw the boy next door again and there was nothing in his behavior and manner to suggest that he would steal an axe.
> 人有亡鈇者，意其鄰之子。視其行步，竊鈇也；顏色，竊鈇也；言語，竊鈇也；作動態度，无為而不竊鈇也。俄而抇其谷而得其鈇，他日復見其鄰人之子，動作態度，无似竊鈇者。[25]

The suspicions of the man who loses his axe, projected onto the young neighbor whom he believes has stolen it, change his perception as soon as prejudice takes root in his mind. Watching and judging the neighbor's gestures and demeanor only confirm what prejudgment has already dictated. After he is lucky enough to find the axe in his garden and realizes that its disappearance is due to his own absentmindedness, the man's perception of his neighbor is now altered in such a way that everything about him corroborates the innocence that finding the axe had proven. While his mind is fixed on an event that, owing to its subjective significance, tends to be projected onto objective fact, his perception of the surrounding world is also affected and deformed by obdurate memory. One might say that, in this case of the man who lost his axe, the memory of the first idea in which he associates his neighbor with the supposed theft completely colonizes his mind and warps his perception of things. From a similar point of view, the two following anecdotes more explicitly reinforce the correlation between memory centered on a single event or privileged object, and a series of omissions, lapses, and slips produced by this pathological regime of memory. In these stories, the distractedness and remissness described are not so much the result of what is known in psychology as transience, or the deterioration of a specific memory over time but, rather, they stem from a state of absentmindedness, which basically consists of interference between attention and memory. Attention is divided, giving rise to lapses of concentration and even a certain degree of unawareness as happens when, for instance, preoccupied by a professional problem and unable to override its memory, one leaves one's glasses in some odd place and, not being conscious of doing so, has to make a big effort to find them afterward.[26] These kinds of troubles that pervade our daily lives seem to comprise the fundamental theme in the second anecdote from the *Liezi*.

> Once there was a man of Qi who wanted gold. At dawn he put on his coat and cap and set out for the market. He went to the stall of a dealer in gold, snatched his gold, and fled. The guards caught him and questioned him. "Why did you snatch somebody else's gold in front of so many people?" "At the time I took it, I did not see the people. I only saw the gold." 昔齊人有欲金者, 清旦衣冠而之市, 適鬻金者之所, 因攫其金而去。吏捕得之, 問曰:「人皆在焉, 子攫人之金何?」對曰:「取金之時, 不見人, 徒見金。」[27]

Although it is not so much recall of something that happened in the past that obsessively takes hold in the mind of the gold thief but, rather, his yearning for an item he aspires to attain in a future action, the underlying scheme of this second story essentially coincides with what the first anecdote revealed. The hapless man from Qi longs to have gold and the intensity of his desire is such that it takes over his mind to the point that it pushes him into calamitous action in the hope of satisfying his craving. Dazzled by the presence of the golden treasure, now within easy reach, his perception of the reality of his surroundings at this critical point in the story is dominated by the overwhelming nature of his desire, and his mind, unable to take a distance from, forget about, or lose sight of its objective, even for a moment, cannot properly evaluate the situation. The result of this obstinate presence of gold in the man's mind is that his view or perception of the world is also circumscribed to the single aim of acquiring it, which, in turn, leads to error and disaster. As the version of this same story in the *Huainanzi* 淮南子 has it, "When will is subject to desire, it forgets the elementary principles of action" (志所欲, 則忘其為矣).[28]

If these first two anecdotes from the *Liezi* warn of the harmful consequences, at the level of action, which might be expected when a mind becomes dominated by the memory of a past event or a yearning, in the third apologue the damaging effects of the inability to forget are described much more explicitly and forcefully.

> Sheng, Duke of Bo, was pondering rebellion. Coming out of his court, he stood leaning on his horse goad without remembering to hold it the right way up. The point pricked his cheek and blood ran down to the ground, but he was not aware of it. "If he forgets his own head," said the people of Zheng when they heard about it, "is there anything he will not forget?" When a man's thoughts are fixed on something, he walks stumbling over tree stumps and holes, and knocking his head on doorposts and trees, without awareness of himself. 白公勝慮亂, 罷朝而立, 倒杖策, 錣上貫頤, 血流至地而弗知也。鄭人聞之曰:「頭之忘, 將何不忘哉?」意之所屬箸, 其行足躓株埳, 頭抵植木, 而不自知也。[29]

This third story is about a member of the ruling class of the state of Chu, Sheng 勝, Duke of Bo 白公, whose mind was totally occupied, to the point of obsession, with plotting a revolt. The background of the anecdote is that, according to some ancient texts, the duke's father, crown prince of the ruler of Chu, had been murdered by people from the state of Zheng 鄭.[30] After this, his son was determined to take revenge by punishing the killers. To this end, he tried unsuccessfully to convince the ruler of Chu to launch a punitive military attack on Zheng. After failing in this attempt, he then started plotting a rebellion with the aim of taking power in his own state so that he could proceed with his plans for revenge against the enemy state.

In the version told in the *Liezi*, the anecdote seems to fit with the divinatory approach that is so prominent in texts like the *Zuozhuan* 左傳 or the *Guoyu* 國語 where, thanks to interpretation of apparently insignificant gestures and somatic signs, which are taken as being revelatory portents, it is possible to predict the future of an individual or even of a whole state. For example, the *Zuozhuan*, which offers some of the earliest examples of percipient reading of somatic signs, describes the case of a military official who lifts his feet too high as he walks. Noting this kinetic symptom, an adviser at once pronounces that the official's intentions are suspect.[31] Something similar occurs when a ruler disdainfully receives a ceremonial piece of jade in an ancestral temple of his lineage. Having attentively observed the scene, one of his ministers predicts that his lord will end up childless.[32] In fact, the anecdote from the *Liezi* also appears in other ancient textual sources, among them the *Han Feizi* 韓非子 and the *Huainanzi*,[33] where it is used to comment on a sentence from the *Laozi* 老子: "The farther one goes out, the less one knows" (其出彌遠者, 其智彌少).[34] It seems evident, then, that the Duke of Bo's imperviousness to what was happening to him and around him also made him an open book to those who were watching, so the story would function to draw attention to close scrutiny of seemingly trivial, nearby details which, however, hold within them revealing information, at least for those people who are able to interpret them correctly.

The case of the Duke of Bo, as presented in the *Liezi*, makes it possible to establish a contrast of inverse symmetry with the story of King Fuchai of the state of Wu 吳王夫差 (r. 495–473 BCE). According to the telling in the *Zuozhuan* and other ancient textual sources, Fuchai, whose prominent natural tendency was to forgive and forget, needed an assistant to remind him every day that his father had been killed by King Goujian of Yue 越王勾踐 (r. 496–465 BCE) and to require from him a response in which he would proclaim that he would never dare to forget that his duty was to take revenge, which he did manage to achieve some time later. "Fuchai had someone stand in his courtyard to say to him whenever he went out or came in, 'Fuchai! Have you forgotten that the King of Yue killed your father?' Then he would reply, 'Very well. I dare not forget!'" 夫差使人立於庭, 苟出入, 必謂己曰: 夫差, 而忘越王之殺而父乎? 則對曰: 唯不敢忘.[35] In Fuchai's case, the success of his revenge for the murder of his father is somehow due to the fact of his having external support to make sure that he does not forget this painful past and that he constantly reactivates awareness of his duty to retaliate. To extrapolate from the lesson of Fuchai, it would seem that the failure of the Duke of Bo to take revenge is due to the fact that he has nobody from outside to help him to de-escalate his obsessive memory.[36] The contrast between the two stories draws attention to the fact that, while it is relatively simple to activate memory, it is much more complicated to bring about oblivion. The very effort of trying to shed a memory only intensifies its presence in our consciousness and automatically defers our desire for amnesia.[37] Since he does not have support that might help him to forget, the Duke of Bo's recurrent moments of inattention in the *Liezi* account make it clear to those observing his ungainly absentmindedness and bodily unawareness that his mind is occupied by brooding that is so obsessive that it demands his whole attention, to the point that he is unable to notice the visible physical consequences, even for himself, of his clumsy, distracted conduct. His vengeful project fails because, unable to forget what is troubling him, he forgets about everything else, thus allowing others to glimpse the plans and plots he is constantly fretting over. Far from embodying the positive value of a passionate vocation for study that, in its constancy, comes to disregard basic aspects of everyday life—as happens with Confucius in the passage from the *Analects* cited above—the obdurate memory of the death of his father turns the Duke of Bo into an imperceptive individual who is trapped in excessive recall, a victim of a hazy memory, constantly wallowing in the shattering emotions of the murder, and unable to distract his memories or to forget for a single moment his thirst for revenge. A prisoner of unrelenting memory, he appears, as a result, as someone prone to negligence and condemned to uneffectiveness in the ordinary course of his existence.

AMNESIA, MEMORY, AND LONGING: THE DIFFICULT REMEDY OF FORGETTING ABOUT FORGETTING

In the reading offered above, the three anecdotes which, successively linked, make up the end of chapter 8 of the *Liezi* stress the misfortunes and calamities deriving from hypertrophied recall, obsessively focused on a single memory that cannot be dispelled. Cognitive faculties such as perception, appropriate evaluation of the milieu, and judgment, but also movements and bodily sensations, are negatively affected by the obfuscating memory that is impervious to oblivion. The anecdote I shall now analyze comes from chapter 3 of the *Liezi* and continues, from a different though compatible standpoint, to relate the harmful consequences of memory while, at the same time, challenging the evident pathological dimension of amnesia. As a literary piece, the story is constructed with great narrative skill, full of humor, and provides, in my opinion, one of the most fertile accounts in the ancient literature of the complex relations between remembering and forgetting.

> In middle age Huazi of Yangli in the state of Song lost his memory. He would receive a present in the morning and forget it by the evening, give a present in the evening and forget it by the morning. In the street he would forget to walk,

at home he would forget to sit down. Today he would not remember yesterday, tomorrow he would not remember today. His family were troubled about it, and invited a diviner to tell his fortune, but without success. They invited a shaman to perform an auspicious rite, but it made no difference. They invited a doctor to treat him, but it did no good. There was a Confucian of the state of Lu who, acting as his own go-between, claimed that he could cure it; and Huazi's wife and children offered half of their property in return for his skill. The Confucian told them: "This is clearly not a disease which can be divined by hexagrams and omens, or charmed away by auspicious prayers, or treated by medicines and the needle. I shall try reforming his mind, changing his thoughts; there is a good chance that he will recover. Then the Confucian tried stripping Huazi, and he looked for his clothes; tried starving him, and he looked for food; tried shutting him up in the dark, and he looked for light. The Confucian was delighted and told the man's sons: "The sickness is curable. But my arts have been passed down secretly through the generations and are not disclosed to outsiders. I shall shut out his attendants and stay alone with him in his room for seven days."

They agreed, and no one knew what methods the Confucian used; but the sickness of many years was completely dispelled in a single morning. When Huazi woke up he was very angry. He dismissed his wife, punished his sons, and chased away the Confucian with a spear. The authorities of the state of Song arrested him and wanted to know the reason.

"Formerly, when I forgot," said Huazi, "I was boundless; I did not notice whether heaven and earth existed or not. Now suddenly I remember; and all the disasters and recoveries, gains and losses, joys and sorrows, loves and hates of twenty or thirty years past rise up in a thousand tangled threads. I fear that all the disasters and recoveries, gains and losses, joys and sorrows, loves and hates still to come will confound my heart just as much. Shall I never again find a moment of forgetfulness?"

Zigong marveled when he heard of it and told Confucius. "This is beyond the understanding of someone like you," said Confucius. He turned to Yan Hui and told him to note it down.

宋陽里華子, 中年病忘, 朝取而夕忘, 夕與而朝忘; 在塗則忘行, 在室則忘坐; 今不識先, 後不識今。闔室毒之。謁史而卜之, 弗占; 謁巫而禱之, 弗禁; 謁醫而攻之, 弗已。魯有儒生, 自媒能治之, 華子之妻子以居產之半請其方。儒生曰:「此固非卦兆之所占, 非祈請之所禱, 非藥石之所攻。吾試化其心, 變其慮, 庶幾其瘳乎!」於是試露之而求衣; 饑之而求食; 幽之而求明。儒生欣然告其子曰:「疾可已也。然吾之方密傳世, 不以告人。試屏左右, 獨與居室七日。」從之。莫知其所施為也, 而積年之疾, 一朝都除。華子既悟, 迺大怒, 黜妻罰子, 操戈逐儒生。宋人執而問其以。華子曰:「曩吾忘也, 蕩蕩然不覺天地之有無。今頓識, 既往數十年來, 存亡得失、哀樂好惡, 擾擾萬緒起矣。吾恐將來之存亡得失哀樂好惡之亂吾心如此也, 須臾之忘, 可復得乎?」子貢聞而怪之, 以告孔子。孔子曰:「此非汝所及乎!」顧謂顏回記之。[38]

The story presents what, from a conventional view of the values associated with memory and forgetting, would doubtless be regarded as a tragedy: a man from the state of Song 宋 is afflicted by a serious attack of amnesia. The mention of this place could have had humorous or parodic connotations for a reader of the time since the people from Song are often mocked and the butt of many a joke in the ancient literature.[39] In any case, according to the apologue, the man's crisis of forgetting afflicted him in his middle years, precisely when it is most necessary to have constant recourse to memory and remembering, when it is most essential to put into practice the ability to recall assigned precepts that are so carefully internalized in the learning stage, and when responsibilities toward those who are older, like parents and ancestors, and those who are younger, like children, are greater and more numerous. In particular, the anecdote from the *Liezi* highlights, among the actions affected by amnesia, exchange of goods, donations, and loans. This is no trivial matter. The deep oblivion into which Huazi has sunk as a result of this attack of amnesia destroys the effectiveness of regulated exchange which, in turn, involves and affects the logic of reciprocity, the very core of ritual action which, for many of the philosophical doctrines of ancient China, had to govern both individual and collective conduct.[40] And, here, it is worth citing a passage from the *Liji* 禮記 where this is explicitly stated.

> What the rules of ritual value is [reciprocity of] giving and receiving. If something is given and nothing is received in return, that contravenes the rites; if something is received and nothing is given back, that also contravenes the rites.

Those who know the rules of ritual enjoy tranquility while those who do not are in danger. It is therefore said, "Rites must necessarily be studied."
禮尚往來。往而不來, 非禮也; 來而不往, 亦非禮也。人有禮則安, 無禮則危。故曰: 禮者不可不學也。[41]

In ancient China, rule-governed exchanges of gifts required recall not only of what had been received but, also and especially, the debt incurred in these interactions, and how any gift, given or received, had to be reciprocated. The logic of reciprocity, a basic element in the regulation of conduct through rites and ceremonial actions, naturally entails remembering the obligations incurred by those who enter into these exchanges of gifts, but it also requires bearing in mind the hierarchical positions of participants, being aware of the value of items given and received, being sensitive to the expectations of others participating in the network of exchanges, et cetera. The reciprocity underlying this toing and froing of gifts is the very cement of social norms since it gives intersubjective relations a predictable orientation which, if it is to function, necessitates the effective intervention of memory.

As a result of his attack of amnesia, Huazi's erratic behavior therefore violates what is emphatically prescribed in the ritual treatises, while his apathetic, negligent demeanor jeopardizes the optimal functioning of the social, economic, and political resources of the whole family. To make matters worse, the unfortunate Huazi is also disoriented, so when he is away from home, he has no guiding principle to govern his behavior, and inside his house he does not know where he should be, what he should do, and what his position is. These symptoms associated with loss of coordinates, and such severe bewilderment that he does not know why, for what purpose, and where he is moving, connect the state of the amnesiac man with features that, in certain ancient texts, are also used to define an infant. In effect, the new-born is frequently described as a lost, aimless creature, unable to tell east from west, light from darkness, and so on, one that lacks a place and a purpose. Hence, for example, a passage from the *Zhuangzi*, has Laozi speaking of newborn babies in the following terms: "When moving, they know not where they are going; in repose, they know not what they are doing" (行不知所之, 居不知所為), and "the infant moves not knowing what he is doing, moves not knowing where he is going; his body is like the branches on a dry tree, and his mind like an extinguished fire" (兒子動不知所為, 行不知所之,

身若槁木之枝而心若死灰).⁴² Hence, it is possible to see Huazi's memory malaise as a kind of regression to babyhood, to the stage of life typical of the first two years and leaving no trace in later memory or, in other words, totally beyond memory's most tenacious efforts to recall it. This is what contemporary scholars in the cognitive sciences refer to as "childhood amnesia."⁴³

Given the seriousness of the consequences of Huazi's crisis of memory, it is understandable that the stricken man's family does not hesitate to consult an array of specialists, all skilled in different techniques that seek to detect the cause of the affliction and thus to cure him for once and for all. Seers, shamans, and physicians visit the man's home, one after the other, but all their efforts are in vain until, finally, there appears a literati from the state of Lu, the traditional bastion of the Confucian school. However, in the narrative logic of the anecdote, he is associated with and put on the same level as the other specialists in healing. At this point, then, there is an element of subtly and ironically expressed criticism when the story gives the impression that Confucian doctrines are just one kind among many ideas promising good health that are offered on the competitive market (and *the last* one that the family considers). Besides offering their healing skills to princes, dignitaries, and nobles, the members of the Confucian school also provided services to families that had suffered some kind of misfortune. This is perhaps a derogatory way of presenting the therapeutic vocation driving Confucian thought, and ironically discrediting its desire to transform and reorient the ideas of others since, as the story reveals, significant economic recompense is expected. And, in Huazi's case, it amounts to half his property.⁴⁴

In addition to the overlapping of a savior vocation and brazen financial ambition, the character of the Confucian literati from Lu exhibits, in the story told in the *Liezi*, certain features reflected in the way he presents himself to other people, which are not deemed seemly in moral terms. He is described as a man who appears on the scene acting as his own publicity agent, his own go-between (*zi mei* 自媒), unabashedly proclaiming his virtues, and exalting his ability to undo the damage. There are many ancient texts that severely criticize people who shamelessly parade around acting as their own promoters. Worthy of mention, here, is a refrain from the *Guanzi* 管子, but also appearing in other early documents, which observes that if a woman decides to act as her own advertiser, it is because she must be dreadfully ugly and not to be trusted (自媒之女, 醜而不信).⁴⁵

Nevertheless, despite the traits revealed by the Confucian's overweening demeanor, he still manages to convince Huazi's family and sets about curing him by means of a secret procedure, techniques he applies hidden away from view since the commercial success of his knowledge would certainly depend on secretiveness. How, then, did he manage to cure Huazi? What methods or formulae did the Confucian apply in order to achieve this? The way the story is told holds out some clues that would suggest the principles applied in the treatment with a certain degree of accuracy. First, it should be noted that if the Confucian is able to apply his healing methods to Huazi, it is partly because his amnesia, although profound, is not complete. Hope for his cure resides in the basic responses the Confucian can still detect in the behavior of Huazi when he tries to cover himself when unclothed or to look for food when he is hungry. The fact that he responds to the Confucian's stimuli suggests that although his mind (*xin* 心) is quite affected (even unlit, to use one of the analogies used to describe infants), his natural condition (*xing* 性) is not yet completely deactivated. The rudimentary mechanisms of "spontaneous" responses the Confucian detects in Huazi are viewed in a good part of Confucian doctrine as the basis on which it is possible to keep constructing processes that slowly become more sophisticated, conscious, and volitional. A passage from the *Xunzi* 荀子 offers a major clue for any attempt to ascertain the method used by the Confucian from Lu in curing Huazi.

> As for the modes in which different names are applied to human beings, the reason for which they are such from birth is called "natural condition." The close connection between stimuli and responses, which requires no effort, for it is spontaneous, is also called "natural condition."
> 散名之在人者：生之所以然者謂之性；精合感應，不事而自然謂之性。[46]

At first, the Confucian healer tests the oblivious man by means of a number of stimuli with the aim of observing whether he responds adequately to them, and thereby to establish whether Huazi's natural condition is gravely affected by the amnesia. Hence, when he sees that Huazi tries to cover himself when he feels cold, and to fill his belly when he is hungry,[47] he is sure that the affliction can be cured since, although the natural mechanism (*xing*) that contains the potential capacity for deploying emotional dispositions (*qing* 情) is fragile, the problem is not irreversible. Indeed, the passage from the *Xunzi* cited above extends and thus assumes continuity between these two phases or instances.

> The feelings of liking and disliking, happiness and anger, and sadness and joy in one's natural condition are called the "emotional dispositions." When there is a certain emotional disposition and the heart makes a choice on its behalf, this is called "reflection."
> 性之好、惡、喜、怒、哀、樂謂之情。情然而心為之擇謂之慮。[48]

With these two arguments in mind, it would not seem unreasonable to think that what the Confucian from Lu does when left alone with Huazi is to bring him back, starting out from this incipient, spontaneous, elemental behavior that is still discernible in the amnesia in its natural condition. Then, by submitting him to stimuli in the area of his emotional dispositions, he aims to eventually restore the reflective functions (*lü* 慮) and, with them, memory. This same sequence can be found, with minor variations, in manuscripts ascribed to Confucian ideology, which were exhumed in Guodian in 1993. For example, one text titled "Natural Condition Emerges from Mandate" (Xing zi ming chu 性自命出) states that, "Although people have a natural condition, the heart lacks stable commitment. [. . .] The vapors of pleasure, anger, grief, and sorrow constitute natural condition" (凡人雖有性, 心亡定志 [. . .] 喜怒哀悲之氣, 性也), and also that, "The emotional dispositions are born of natural condition" (情生於性).[49] These sources, which certainly predate and would have influenced the ideas expressed in the *Xunzi*,[50] include a general description of human psychology in which the natural condition is conceived of as a kind of innate, malleable, and originally passive potential that is only activated by way of contact with external stimuli and, once this occurs in any prolonged way, it opens out and crystallizes in the formation of emotional dispositions to develop, finally, into more complex mental processes.[51]

The ideas contained in these manuscripts suggest an optimal transition of human psychology going from an original, rudimentary state of immediate responsiveness where the emotions start to be deployed after being stimulated by contact with things and external reality, to a final state in which the mind, as a result of lengthy refinement, acquires a fixed purpose and reflective capacities.⁵² This is also the scheme that should be deduced—despite the ellipsis of Huazi's treatment hidden away from prying eyes—from the story told in the *Liezi*. The Confucian healer manages to channel Huazi's basic responses to the most elementary stimuli into a flow of emotions and, successfully reintroducing sadness and happiness, preferences and aversions, he then restores the deliberative functions.

Other hints in the description of Huazi's cure, like the duration of the treatment (seven days), the fact that the story relates at the beginning his inability to carry out duties pertaining to reciprocal gratitude and, even more important, the detail that he was not the one who sought the help of specialists, make it possible to find parallels between this anecdote and another famous story, this time from the *Zhuangzi*: the death of Hundun.

> The emperor of the Southern Sea was Lickety (Shu), the emperor of the Northern Sea was Split (Hu), and the emperor of the Center was Chaos (Hundun). Lickety and Split often met each other in the land of Chaos, and Chaos treated them very well. Wanting to repay Hundun's virtue, Lickety and Split said, "All people have seven holes for seeing, hearing, eating, and breathing. Chaos alone lacks them. Let's try boring some holes for him." So, every day they bored one hole, and on the seventh day Chaos died.
> 南海之帝為儵，北海之帝為忽，中央之帝為渾沌。儵與忽時相與遇於渾沌之地，渾沌待之甚善。儵與忽謀報渾沌之德，曰：「人皆有七竅，以視聽食息，此獨無有，嘗試鑿之。」日鑿一竅，七日而渾沌死。⁵³

In many ways like the amnesiac Huazi, the chaotic being Hundun is a magmatic mess wrapped around his own being, lacking identity—the seven orifices possessed by other individuals, and forcibly given by his comrades, outline a face—incapable of uttering words, and defined by an important degree of indifference to the external world which, since he has no sense organs, barely impinges on him. Hundun, too, is like a newborn baby. Unable to identify clearly the sensations he receives from outside himself and, lacking sense organs, he is immersed in a kind of primitive confusion. From the metaphorical standpoint, the death of Hundun signifies the end of this primeval state with the violent acquisition of specialized and hierarchized sense organs, which now allow him to perceive sensations as discrete and separate stimuli. He has become totally open to the outside world, which means the destruction of his almost hermetic consciousness, and abandoning the state of virtually total indistinction that reigned within him. As Jean Levi notes in this regard, once Hundun was forced to be open to the external world, the confusion that he had enclosed within himself was dissipated and scattered through the orifices that his comrades Shu and Hu had made in his amorphous body, one per day over seven days.[54]

If the story about Hundun in the *Zhuangzi* exemplifies the necessary, desirable (but not exempt from loss) step from infancy to adulthood—which is to say, the end of consciousness in which confusion and hermeticism prevail, leading to a fragmented consciousness that is open to one's own identity and to the outside world—then Huazi's affliction in the *Liezi* re-creates a surprising regression to this primordial state by way of the indifference of amnesia.[55] Hence, if Hundun is the victim of the lack of sensitivity of his comrades who, deciding that his extraordinary condition is pitiful, get carried away by the duty of reciprocity and gratitude and try to repair what, to their eyes, can only be a defective nature, Huazi is also a victim of the prejudices of his relatives who do not hesitate to see his state of oblivion as an unfortunate pathology and zealously seek to rid him of this state of amnesia. Hundun and Huazi were not the ones who asked for help from others. They received, without having sought them, the "caring" and "saving" actions of those around them, and they were the ones who suffered the consequences of these external decisions.

Nonetheless, at least from a certain point of view, the consequences of the "assault" on Huazi by his relatives through the Confucian healer can be understood as being more serious than those resulting from the homicide committed by Shu and Hu. After all, their reckless action ends Hundun's life, plunging him into the most radical of all the forms of indifference, namely death. Although lamentable, the shift from this primordial, infantile consciousness to one that is open to the world barely leaves, in his case, any traces in memory because everything is annulled with the advent of death and the suppression of consciousness. For Huazi, the consequences of healing are more detrimental than those of negligent homicide because, when he is rescued from his state of primordial indifference brought about by profound oblivion, he does not fall into an even more indifferent state but is ushered once again into a consciousness that is open to the world, and to memory, and this greatly upsets him. The vocabulary used in the anecdote from the *Liezi* when describing Huazi's state after recovering his memory reveals this contrast very well. The binomial used to describe the time when his consciousness is immersed in oblivion, indifferent to the existence or nonexistence of the external world is *dang dang* 蕩蕩, which evokes a serene, clear-headed state.⁵⁶ But once his memory and mind have been restored, and he is assailed by the clamor of emotions, the binomial *rao rao* 擾擾 is used, this time denoting a state of perturbation and distress.⁵⁷ The term *luan* 亂 also appears, indicating a profoundly negative and pathological disturbance of inner balance brought about by the avalanche of emotions.⁵⁸

Far from achieving the desired therapeutic results, the Confucian's healing process only makes Huazi suffer more. His pain is made more acute because, after he is returned to the regime of memory, he still has recall of the agreeable effects of the serene indifference endowed on him by the attack of deep amnesia, and this makes the sensation of its irreversible disappearance even more unbearable. In addition to the irruption into consciousness of all these gains and losses, and the unrestrained suffering and happiness that come with them, once again battering him and tormenting his existence, there is also the memory of the indifferent plenitude of oblivion, which is to say the excruciating yearning for a state that Huazi recognizes that he had enjoyed for a while but has now lost forever. The unexpected outcome of the healing and the fact that—in a twist that (although logical and coherent) has its funny side—he sets about attacking the people who have tried to help him, because not only have they brought back the disagreeable aspects of memory but they have also triggered this terrible yearning. Huazi thus moves from a regime of total forgetting, in which there is no awareness of one's own forgetting, to a regime of partial forgetting, in which one is able to register one's own forgetting.⁵⁹ Huazi cannot now forget his forgetting. He is unable to rid himself of the memory of having no memory. His bitter return to the regime of memory intensifies the calamity of being aware, of continually recalling the time when he was swaddled in the virtues of forgetting. It is then that Huazi runs the additional risk of being overwhelmed by obsessive memory of the stage when he had no memories, that is, of entering into the undesirable relationship with memory that is shown by the characters in the three anecdotes of the *Liezi* discussed earlier in this chapter.

One can only become aware of oblivion when trying to forget, when oblivion is not manifested. Its discernibility is, then, paradoxical. Huazi becomes aware of the deep oblivion when it is no longer possible to forget completely, when he is rescued from the deep oblivion of the time of his attack of amnesia and made to return to a regime of living in which memory plays its part. Cocooned in the absolute oblivion of amnesia, Huazi forgot about forgetting too but, once cured, the memory of forgetting becomes manifest and, with it, nostalgia for the condition that he describes as peaceable and serene. Only someone who has an existence marked by memory can be aware of oblivion, since both phenomena are bound together in the ordinary functioning of adult consciousness. From this perspective, Huazi's cure should be understood as an extreme experience where an individual, after having attained for a while the memoryless condition of early infancy, is brought back to the regime of memory associated with later stages of life, while still conserving the memory of the time without memory. So, for Huazi, the disaster of the healing action of the Confucian was not only the loss of all the good things associated with amnesia, but also the yearning, inevitably in vain, for something that was irrecoverable.

However, the story in the *Liezi* does not stop here since it concludes with a detail that shifts from Huazi's experience to introduce the outside perspective of the Confucian school. This external view, in the anecdote described above, plays a key role in the unfolding of the account inasmuch as it, at least partly, features an acolyte of Confucian doctrines from the state of Lu. However, now, right at the end, it is the founder of his school, Confucius himself, who takes center stage, even if indirectly. This is a narrative scheme that can also be found in other anecdotes of the ancient literature and in the *Zhuangzi* especially. The pattern is that, after some unusual event that flies in the face of the expectations and values prescribed in Confucian ideology, one of the Master's direct disciples, bewildered and unable to find a proper answer to explain the situation, seeks help from his mentor in the hope of finding some elucidation of the enigma.[60] The disciple baffled by the story of Huazi is Zigong 子貢 who, unable to extract a lesson from it by himself, goes to the Master and tells him about the astonishing situation, hoping thereby to obtain an explanation or to be offered a lesson. Yet, as the *Liezi* tells it, Confucius offers no teaching. His authority and pedagogical expertise are not displayed and, with a new paradoxical twist, he merely draws attention to Zigong's intellectual inability to understand what has happened.[61] However, although he offers no explanation, Confucius shows that he is sensitive to the deep lesson held out by Huazi's story regarding the benefits of forgetting and misfortunes of memory. Committed to his pedagogical mission and, thus to the moral transformation of others, he turns to his favorite and most gifted disciple, Yan Hui 顏回, and asks him to help by writing down the details of the story.[62]

It is probably no coincidence that, in the anecdote from the *Leizi*, it is Yan Hui who is entrusted with recording this episode, and this would seem to obey a deliberate narrative strategy. After all, Yan Hui is also the main character of a story in the *Zhuangzi* where, in a fictitious encounter with his master, he appears to be immersed in an unusual training process in which, encouraged by Confucius, he forgets more and more. In this story, Yan Hui is deemed by Confucius to be making good progress as he keeps forgetting some of the moral values that are essential in Confucian doctrine, among them benevolence, righteousness, and rituals. The training culminates when he tells Confucius that he can "sit in forgetfulness" (*zuo wang* 坐忘) and, at this point, Confucius asks his hitherto disciple to accept him as a pupil.[63] In the story from the *Liezi*, the person Confucius chooses to record the story of the amnesiac Huazi is someone who knows how to forget and, with this choice, he endorses a kind of paradoxical affiliation of oblivion.

Whatever the case, it would seem that caught up in the whirlwind of memory and the obligation to ensure its conservation and transmission, and fearing that the story of Huazi could be forgotten and lost forever, Confucius reiterates in his final sentence a request for a record (*ji zhi* 記之), in keeping with what tradition attributed to him on countless occasions throughout his career as a teacher and master of thought.[64] As the end of the story demonstrates, although he understands the ramifications of what happened to Huazi, or precisely because of this, Confucius shows that he is keen to ensure that his disciples to come will remember that it is not advisable to forget the value of forgetting, and to lead them by means of evoking this story to ponder, in turn, the paradox of the inextricable dilemmas of how to forget memory and, at the same time, forget about forgetting. By asking his cherished disciple to record the event concerning Huazi, Confucius dismisses the essential point of being submerged in unawareness, of living in oblivion, and thus he seems far away from some of the benefits of forgetting. He might be able to provide some teachings about forgetting but fatally unable to perform it and to be transformed by it.

Notes

1. For a complete study of the textual history, the commentary tradition, and the reception of the *Liezi* throughout the history of China, see Liu Peide 劉佩德, *Liezi xue shi* 列子學史 (Beijing: Xueyuan chubanshe, 2015).
2. As Xiaofan Amy Li puts it, "This lack of scholarly attention and exegeses is mainly due to the perception of the *Liezi* as a ragbag of miscellaneous writings that are not authentic or "original," and which lack the philosophical depth and linguistic complexity of earlier literature. [. . .] These established views that predominantly valorize textual authenticity and antiquity have discouraged scholars from engaging with the *Liezi* on a deeper level, for its intellectual depth and textual complexity are in fact far from superficial and many of its sections merit detailed examination, as recent studies increasingly show" (Xiaofan Amy Li, "The Notion of Originality and Degrees of Faithfulness in Translating Classical Chinese: Comparing Translations of the *Liezi*," *Early China* 38 [2015]: 109–28, 112). The *Liezi* is not the only case, as the same thing happened to other ancient "suspicious" texts, the *Wenzi* for instance. For previous generations of scholars what appeared to them as miscellaneous and unoriginal (that is, with an important number of parallels elsewhere) was almost a synonym of copy, forgery, or fake. As a more nuanced study of the *Wenzi* by Paul van Els has demonstrated, it was not so miscellaneous as it appeared at first sight, there is more coherence and cogency to its themes and arguments than expected, and, importantly, before neglecting and ignoring it we need to rethink our notions of "originality" and "authenticity." See P. van Els, *The Wenzi. Creativity and Intertextuality in Early Chinese Philosophy* (Leiden: Brill, 2018).
3. After several decades of silence in Western sinology and although there is not, as yet, any monographic study on the *Liezi*, some relevant contributions have been published in recent years, as well as translations that have helped to give the text a new lease on life. Notable among these works are the volume edited by Ronnie Littlejohn and Jeffrey Dippmann, *Riding the Wind with Liezi: New Perspectives on the Daoist Classic* (Albany: State University of New York Press, 2011); the French translations, *Lie Tseu. L'Authentique Classique de la Parfaite Vacuité* (Paris: Éditions Entrelacs, 2012) and *Les Fables de Maître Lie* (Paris: Éditions de l'Encyclopédie des Nuisances, 2014), by Rémi Mathieu and Jean Levi, respectively; and two doctoral dissertations, one by June Won Seo, "The Liezi: The Vision of the World Interpreted by a Forged Text" (School of the Oriental and African Studies, University of London, 2000), and the other

by Wayne Kreger, "Echo of the Master, Shadow of the Buddha: The Liezi as a Medieval Master Text" (University of British Columbia, 2016).

4. The philological studies by Yang Bojun are included as appendixes in his edition of the *Liezi*, which was first published in 1958. I have used the subsequent reedition, *Liezi jieshi* 列子集釋 (Beijing: Zhonghua shuju, 1979). Graham's study, "The Date and Composition of the Liehtzyy," was originally published in 1961 (*Asia Major* 8, no. 2 [1961]: 139–98) and was reprinted, in a revised version, in *Studies in Chinese Philosophy and Philosophical Literature* (Albany: State University of New York Press, 1986), 219–82.

5. In this regard, special emphasis should be given to the contributions of Chen Guangchong 陳廣忠, "Cong gu ciyu kan Liezi fei wei—Liezi fei wei shu kao zhi san 從古詞語看《列子》非偽—《列子》非偽書考之三," *Daojia wenhua* 道家文化 10 (1996): 289–99; Ma Da 馬達, *Liezi zhen wei kaobian* 列子真偽考辨 (Beijing: Beijing chubanshe, 2000); Jean Levi, "La question de l'authenticité du Lie-tseu," in *Les Fables de Maître Lie*, 153–78; and Cen Zhongmian 岑仲勉, "Liezi fei jinren weizuo 列子非晉人偽作," in *Liang Zhou wenshi luncong* 兩周文史論叢 (Beijing: Zhonghua shuju, 2014), 313–33.

6. Graham's conclusions were accepted by T. H. Barrett in the text he wrote on the *Liezi* in *Early Chinese Texts: A Bibliographical Guide*, ed. Michael Loewe (Berkeley: The Society for the Study of Early China/University of California, 1993), 298–308. Nor were they questioned more recently when cited by Roger T. Ames in his Introduction to the volume edited by Littlejohn and Dippmann: *Riding the Wind with Liezi*, 2–3.

7. I refer here, among many others, to the study by Zhang Hanmo, *Authorship and Text-Making in Early China* (Berlin: De Gruyter, 2018).

8. Li Ling 李零, "Chutu faxian yu gushu niandai de zairenshi 出土發現與古書年代的再認識," in *Li Ling zixuan ji* 李零自選集 (Guilin: Guangxi shifan daxue, 1998), 27–31. In the same vein, Erik W. Maeder, basing his comparison on observations concerning recently excavated texts, likened early Chinese texts to "the looseleaf ring binder into which miscellaneous material, including both class notes by different hands and documentary handouts, can be entered" ("Some Observations on the Composition of the 'Core Chapters' of the *Mozi*," *Early China* 17 [1992]: 27–82, 28). Finally, Zhang Hanmo also states: "Reliance on pre-existing materials (i.e., textual building blocks), to produce new text was the norm. This process may have been responsible for popular aphorisms, anecdotes, and other short pieces of material preserved either orally or in written form" (*Authorship and Text-Making in Early China*, 222).

9. For an analysis of the use of the technique of collage in the texts of ancient China, based precisely on a study of a chapter of the *Liezi*, see Christian Schwerman, "Collage-Technik als Kompositionsprinzip klassicher chinesischer Prosa: Der Aufbau des Kapitels 'Tang Wen' (Die Fragen des Tang) im *Liezi*," *Bochumer Jahrbuch zur Ostasienforschung* 29 (2005): 127–57, esp. 127–30.

10. As Wayne Kreger notes in this regard, "To say that the *Liezi* was 'compiled' is very much a calculated suggestion; even in light of the evidence that suggests the *Liezi* reached something closely resembling the received version in the early medieval period, there is also much evidence that a great deal of the material in the *Liezi* could be traced legitimately to the Warring States period" (*Echo of the Master, Shadow of the Buddha*, 55–56). Jean Levi comes to a similar conclusion when he writes, "Il est probable que la date définitive de la constitution de l'ouvrage [. . .] soit relativement tardive: vers la toute fin des Royaumes Combattants ou le début des Han. Mais le fait que celle-ci soit postérieure de plusieurs siècles à la période où est censé avoir vécu le personnage mythique sous le patronage duquel le livre est placé ne saurait être retenu comme preuve d'une falsification perpétrée par un auteur de la Chine médiévale" (J. Levi, *Les Fables de Maître Lie*, 177).

11. The important role played by forgetting in the thought of the *Zhuangzi* has been approached from different perspectives in recent contributions. See among them the studies by Romain Graziani, "Optimal States and Self-Defeating Plans: The Problem of Intentionality in Early Chinese Self-Cultivation," *Philosophy East and West* 59, no. 4 (2009): 440–66; Livia Kohn, *Sitting in the Oblivion: The Heart of Daoist Meditation* (Honolulu: University of Hawai'i Press, 2010); Chris Fraser, "Heart-Fasting, Forgetting, and Using the Heart Like a Mirror: Applied Emptiness in the Zhuangzi," in *Nothingness in Asian Philosophy*, ed. J. Liu and D. Berger (New York: Routledge, 2014), 197–212; and Franklin Perkins, "So Comfortable You'll Forget You're Wearing Them: Cultivating Oblivion in the Zhuangzi," which is included in this volume.

12. *Lunyu* 14/12; Edward Slingerland, *Confucius Analects: With Selections from Traditional Commentaries* (Indianapolis, IN: Hackett, 2003), 158.

13. *Lunyu* 14/27; see also *Lunyu* 5/25. For an analysis of Confucius's use and conception of language, see Jean Levi, *Confucius* (Paris: Éditions Pygmalion, 2002), 90–130.

14. See *Lunyu* 1/3, 1/7, 13/20, and 15/6. Credibility is given enormous importance in the moral scheme, not only of the *Analects*, but in a good part of Confucian literature. For example, a manuscript exhumed in 1990 in Guodian 郭店, and titled by the editors "The Way of Loyalty and Credibility" (Zhong xin zhi dao 忠信之道), contains the following fragments, "Letting the mouth utter kind words and then not following them through in the facts, is not the way the noble man uses words (口惠而弗從，君子弗言爾)," and "Credibility is the foundation of righteousness (信，義之基也)": Jingmenshi bowuguan 荊門市博物館, *Guodian Chu mu zhujian* 郭店楚墓竹簡 (Beijing: Wenwu chubanshe, 1998), 163.

15. Of course, it is highly probable that, in the passage from the *Analects* that I have just cited, Confucius would be condemning not so much a lack of memory as not keeping one's word. Rather than amnesiac loss of memory, not

remembering what one has said when times are good signals moral forgetting, which would be akin to bad faith. In any case, it seems evident that, in order to attain the virtue of credibility (*xin*), one must preserve the memory of the proffered word, which would counteract both these forms of laxness.

16. *Lunyu* 19/5; Slingerland, *Confucius Analects*, 222.

17. *Lunyu* 15/31.

18. *Lunyu* 11/22.

19. See, for instance, *Lunyu* 6/3 and 19/6.

20. *Lunyu* 7/2. See also Chen Qiyou 陳奇猷, *Lüshi chunqiu xin jiaoshi* 呂氏春秋新校釋 (Shanghai: Shanghai guji chubanshe, 2002), 4.3.209 ("Zun shi" 尊師); and Sima Qian 司馬遷, *Shiji* 史記 (Beijing: Zhonghua shuju, 1963), 47.1928.

21. See Wang Xianqian 王先謙, *Xunzi jijie* 荀子集解 (Beijing: Zhonghua shuju, 1988), 1.1 ("Quan xue" 勸學); and Wang Pinzhen 王聘珍, *Da Dai liji jiegu* 大戴禮記解詁 (Beijing: Zhonghua shuju, 1983), 64.130 ("Quan xue" 勸學).

22. For the importance of introspection, see *Lunyu* 1/4 and 5/27.

23. *Lunyu* 7/19. This is a slightly modified version of the translation by Slingerland, *Confucius Analects*, 70. A version of this same anecdote appears in *Shiji*, 47.1928 ("Kongzi shi jia" 孔子世家). A passage from the *Liji* also presents Confucius as stating that the ideal student is someone whose passion for learning the way makes her to forget her old age (鄉道而行, 中道而廢, 忘身之老也): Sun Xidan 孫希旦, *Liji jijie* 禮記集解 (Beijing: Zhonghua shuju, 1996), 32.1304 ("Biao ji" 表記). See the alternative reading by Klein in this volume.

24. I believe that the term *fen* 憤, which refers to intense emotion that could signify "indignation," "resentment," or "affliction" should be understood here in the light of another, nearby passage in the *Analects* (7/8), where the term is used to convey a desire for learning: "If they are not eager I do not explain" (不憤不啟). As for this sentence, in the annotated edition of the *Analects* (*Lunyu zhengyi* 論語正義), edited by Liu Baonan 劉寶楠 (1791–1855), there is mention of a dictionary of regional usage, *Fangyan* 方言 by Yang Xiong 揚雄 (53 BCE–18 CE), where the term *fen* is presented as being equivalent to *ying* 盈 ("complete," "full," "overflowing," "brimming over"). The readings suggested by Huang Kan 皇侃 (488–545) and Huang Huaixin 黃懷信 (1951–) are along similar lines since, for them, the term designates the intention of students who, not yet having managed to understand the teachings, ardently throw themselves into the attempt: see Huang Huaixin 黃懷信, *Lunyu huijiao jishi* 論語彙校集釋 (Shanghai: Shanghai guji chubanshe, 2008), 580–81. To return to the passage quoted in the body of the present text, the term *le* (*pleasure* or *joy*) is, from the very beginning of the *Analects* (1/1) repeatedly linked with Confucius's pedagogical activity and vocation.

25. Yang Bojun 楊伯君, *Liezi jishi* 列子集釋 (Beijing: Zhonghua shuju, 1976), 8.271–72 ("Shuo fu" 說符). This is a slightly modified version of the translation

by Angus C. Graham, *The Book of Lieh-Tzu* (New York: Columbia University Press, 1990), 180. The same anecdote also appears in *Lüshi chunqiu xin jiaoshi*, 13.3.693–94 ("Qu you" 去尤).

26. On this issue, see Daniel L. Schacter, *The Seven Sins of Memory: How the Mind Forgets and Remembers* (Boston, MA: Houghton Mifflin Company, 2001), esp. 41–50.

27. *Liezi jishi*, 8.272–73. This is a slightly modified version of the translation by Angus C. Graham, *The Book of Lieh-Tzu*, 180–81. The same anecdote appears, with some small variations, in *Lüshi chunqiu xin jiaoshi*, 16.7.1024 ("Qu you" 去宥); and Zhang Shuangdi 張雙棣, *Huainanzi jiao yi* 淮南子校譯 (Beijing: Beijing daxue chubanshe, 1997), 13.1447 ("Fan lun" 氾論).

28. *Huainanzi jiao yi*, 13.1447.

29. *Liezi jishi*, 8.272. This is a slightly modified version of the translation by Angus C. Graham, *The Book of Lieh-Tzu*, 180.

30. The story of the circumstances of the murder of Sheng's father Jian 建 and Sheng's attempts at revenge is told in the *Zuozhuan* 左傳: Yang Bojun 楊伯君, *Chunqiu Zuozhuan zhu* 春秋左傳注 (Beijing: Zhonghua shuju, 1995), 1700–01 (Ai 16).

31. *Chunqiu Zuozhuan zhu*, 136–37 (Huan 13).

32. *Chunqiu Zuozhuan*, 338 (Xi 11). For a detailed discussion of the divinatory reading of bodily gestures in the *Zuozhuan*, see Zhang Duansui 張端穗, *Zuozhuan sixiang tanwei* 左傳思想探微 (Taipei: Xuehai, 1987), 134–36; Wai-yi Lee, *The Readability of the Past in Early Chinese Historiography* (Cambridge, MA: Harvard University Asia Center, 2007); and Albert Galvany, "Signs, Clues and Traces: Anticipation in Early Chinese Political and Military Texts," *Early China* 38 (2015): 151–93.

33. Chen Qiyou 陳奇猷, *Han Feizi xin jiao zhu* 韓非子新校注 (Shanghai: Shanghai guji chubanshe, 2000), 21.454 ("Yue lao" 喻老); *Huainanzi jiao yi*, 12.1305 ("Dao ying xun" 道應訓).

34. Gao Ming 高明, *Boshu Laozi jiao zhu* 帛書老子校注 (Beijing: Zhonghua shuju, 1996), 52.

35. *Chunqiu Zuozhuan zhu*, 1596 (Ding 定 14); translation by Stephen Durrant, Wai-yee Li and David Schaberg, *Zuo Tradition: Commentary on the Spring and Autumn Annals* (Seattle: University of Washington Press, 2016), 1819. See also Xiang Zonglu 向宗魯, *Shuoyuan jiaozheng* 說苑校證 (Beijing: Zhonghua shuju, 2000), 228 ("Zhengjian" 正諫); and *Shiji*, 41.1740. For a detailed discussion of this story, see the contribution by Olivia Milburn "The Ice of Memory and the Fires of Forgetfulness: Traumatic Recollections in the Wu Yue chunqiu," included in this volume.

36. On the beneficial role of distraction for regulating the negative consequences of intense emotions, from the perspective of social psychology, see C. L. Rusting and S. Nolen-Hoeksema, "Regulating Responses to Anger: Effects of

Rumination and Distraction on Angry Mood," *Journal of Personality and Social Psychology* 74 (1998): 790–803.

37. On the paradoxical condition of oblivion and other optimal states of consciousness that are unyielding to the will, see the excellent essay by Romain Graziani, *L'usage du vide: Essai sur l'intelligence de l'action, de l'Europe à la Chine* (Paris: Gallimard, 2019).

38. *Liezi jishi*, 3.108–110 ("Zhou mu wang" 周穆王). The translation is by Angus C. Graham, *The Book of Lieh-Tzu*, 70–72. This anecdote from the *Liezi* has been analyzed by specialists in philology who have sought to demonstrate that it is a piece of late composition. Among these studies, first emphasis should be given to an article signed by Xu Manman 徐曼曼 and Wang Yili 王毅力, "Cong ci hui shi kan Liezi de chengshu niandai bulue 從詞匯史看《列子》的成書年代補略," *Xinan Jiaotong daxue xuebao* 西南交通大學學報 12, no. 2 (2011): 25–30. They consider that expressions like *ji nian* 積年, *ju chan* 居產, *shi wei* 施為, et cetera, whose use is limited to texts of relatively late dating (the Han dynasty and afterward) and that do not appear in texts dated in the preimperial period, means that early composition of the story can be discarded. Also noteworthy along similar lines of inquiry, is the analysis by Wei Peiquan 魏培泉, *Liezi de yuyan yu bianzhu niandai* 列子的語言與編著年代 (Taipei: Academia Sinica, 2017). Nevertheless, these conclusions require some caution since, as Esther Klein shows for the *Zhuangzi*—with findings that, in my opinion, can be extrapolated to the case of the materials included in *Liezi*—the scope of this kind of terminological analysis is limited. As it is very likely that this anecdote was not included in a text that enjoyed canonical status in the eyes of ancient transmitters and commentators, it might have remained less stable and thus more open to being interpolated or even rewritten in later periods (Esther Klein, "Were there 'Inner Chapters' in the Warring States? A New Examination of Evidence about the *Zhuangzi*," *T'oung Pao* 96, no. 4–5 [2011]: 299–369, esp. 311–12). It would be plausible to consider a scenario in which, for example, the story could have been composed during the Warring States period but would end up being rewritten and compiled in a later version, using a less archaic vocabulary. I believe, then, that there are no irrefutable philological arguments that would definitively establish that this piece was composed at a later time or, to put it slightly differently, there are no elements that would make it possible to rule out an ancient origin of this story.

39. On this issue, see for instance Wang Yong 王永, "Xianqin 'yu Song' xian xiang yu 'Hanshu dilizhi' zhi diyu wenhua guan 先秦「愚宋」現象於《漢書·地理志》之地域文化觀," *Ningxia daxue xuebao* 寧夏大學學保 30, no. 2 (2008): 57–63.

40. See Eric C. Mullis, "Ritualized Exchange: A Consideration of Confucian Reciprocity," *Asian Philosophy* 18, no. 1 (2008): 35–50.

41. *Liji jijie*, 1.2.11–12 ("Qu li shang" 曲禮上).

42. Guo Qingfan 郭慶藩, *Zhuangzi jishi* 莊子集釋 (Beijing: Zhonghua shuju, 1989), 23.784–85 ("Gesang Chu" 庚桑楚). The same terms are employed

in a passage from the *Huainanzi* to define the authentic man (*shen ren* 慎人): *Huainanzi jiaoyi*, 7.747.

43. See, for instance, M. Hayne and F. Jacks, "Childhood Amnesia," *Cognitive Science* 2. no. 2 (2011): 136–45.

44. With parodic and critical intention, several ancient texts draw attention to the financial motivation of the members of the Confucian community. See, for instance, Sun Yirang 孫詒讓, *Mozi jiangu* 墨子閒詁 (Beijing: Zhonghua shuju, 2001), 38.198 ("Fei ru" 非儒); and *Zhuangzi jishi*, 26.927 ("Wai wu" 外物).

45. Li Xiangfeng 黎翔鳳, *Guanzi jiaozhu* 管子校注 (Beijing: Zhonghua shuju, 2004), 2.45 ("Xing shi" 形勢).

46. Wang Xianqian 王先謙, *Xunzi jijie* 荀子集解 (Beijing: Zhonghua shuju, 1988), 22.412 ("Zheng ming" 正名). This is a slightly modified version of the translation by Eric L. Hutton, *Xunzi. The Complete Text* (Princeton, NJ: Princeton University Press, 2014), 236.

47. Seeking food when one is hungry, or covering oneself when one is cold are examples that also appear in the *Xunzi*, where the spontaneous natural condition, common to all human beings, is described: *Xunzi jijie*, 5.78 ("Fei xiang" 非相).

48. *Xunzi jijie*, 22.413 ("Zheng ming" 正名). This is a slightly modified version of the translation by Eric L. Hutton, *Xunzi*, 236. In this very same chapter, the *Xunzi* also states: "Natural condition is Heaven's accomplishment and emotional dispositions are the material foundation of natural condition" (性者天之就也, 情者性之質也): *Xunzi jijie*, 22.428. According to this passage, natural condition would be the original, inborn, elementary capacities of human (and other) beings, whereas emotional dispositions would be actualized qualities, manifested when confronted to the external stimuli.

49. *Guodian Chu mu zhujian*, 179. Along very similar lines, one finds in the collection titled "Thickets of Sayings" (Yu cong 語叢) the statement, "The emotional dispositions emerge from natural condition" (情出於性): *Guodian Chu mu zhujian*, 216.

50. See Paul R. Goldin, "*Xunzi* in the Light of the *Guodian* Manuscripts," *Early China* 25 (2000): 113–46.

51. Ding Sixin 丁四新, *Guodian Chumu zhujian sixiang yanjiu* 郭店楚墓竹简思想研究 (Beijing: Dong fang chubanshe, 2000), 173–76.

52. See Michael J. Puett, "Theodicies of Discontinuity: Domesticating Energies and Dispositions in Early China," *Journal of Chinese Philosophy* 37 (2010): 51–66, esp. 58.

53. *Zhuangzi jishi*, 7.309 ("Ying di wang" 應帝王). This is a slightly modified version of the translation by Victor H. Mair, *Wandering the Way: Early Taoist Tales and Parables of Chuang Tzu* (New York: Bantam Books, 1994), 71.

54. Jean Levi, *Propos intempestifs sur le Tchouang-tseu* (Paris: Allia, 2007), 22–23.

55. It should be noted that if Huazi's recovery of memory is due to the fact that his amnesia is not absolute, in Hundun's case it is because the confusion

of his consciousness is not total, since he has been able to have a relationship with his unwitting killers, Shu and Hu.

56. See, for instance, *Lunyu* 7/37 and *Xunzi jijie*, 3.40 ("Bu gou" 不苟).

57. See *Zhuangzi jishi*, 12.416 ("Tian di" 天地).

58. On the pathological consequences of uncontrolled emotions, see Elisabeth Hsu, "Outward Form (*xing* 形) and Inward Qi 氣: The Sentimental Body in Early Chinese Medicine," *Early China* 32 (2008–2009): 103–24.

59. I take the distinction between total forgetfulness and partial forgetfulness, which already appears in Augustine, from Aleida Assmann's analyses in her book *Formen des Vergessens* (Göttingen: Wallstein Verlag, 2016), 18–19.

60. See, for instance, *Zhuangzi jishi*, 6.266–67 ("Da zong shi" 大宗師).

61. The words used by Confucius to ignore Zigong (此非汝所及乎) in the story in the *Liezi* appear in several early textual sources, replacing the term *nai* 及 with *zhi* 知 in situations where Confucius himself or other figures of authority refer to the inability of their interlocutors to understand a given circumstance. See *Xunzi jijie*, 15.280 ("Yi bing" 議兵); and Chen Shike 陳士珂, *Kongzi jiayu shuzheng* 孔子家語疏証 (Shijiazhuang: Shanghai shudian, 1987), 15.96 ("Bian wu" 辯物).

62. Yan Hui is portrayed in the Analects as the one who approaches the most among the disciples the perfect condition of a sage: see *Lunyu* 4/7, 5/9, and 11/19.

63. *Zhuangzi jishi*, 6.282–85 ("Da zong shi").

64. See, for instance, *Han Feizi xin jiao zhu*, 32.709 ("Wai chu shuo zuo shang" 外儲說左上); *Lüshi chunqiu xin jiaoshi*, 17.3.1077 ("Ren shu" 任數); *Shuoyuan jiaozheng*, 7.148 ("Zheng li" 政理), and 10.259 ("Jing shen" 敬慎).

Chapter 9

Wang Bi and the Hermeneutics of Actualization

MERCEDES VALMISA

A Theory on Understanding

I was unsure whether I should take on this new project—so I confided in a Spanish friend in a recent conversation. After reluctantly listening to my complaints about overloads and overwork, she settled the issue with the cutting saying, "Camarón que se duerme se lo lleva la corriente," which literally translates into "A shrimp that sleeps gets carried by the tide," and approximates the meaning of "You snooze, you lose." Obviously, my friend had no interest in discussing shrimp, yet I effortlessly understood her position regarding my hesitation. Reflecting on the process of understanding, I had to forget the literal nonsense of her uttered words referring to sleeping shrimp and tides in order make room for her intention. Although she chose a proverb to caution me of the dangers of not actively making timely decisions and missing opportunities, she

---

I presented an early version of this manuscript at the reading workshop "The Global Reception of the Classic *Zhuangzi*: Han to Tang," March 8–9, 2019, at the University of California, Berkeley. I thank Tobias Zürn and Mark Ciskszentmihalyi for their kind invitation and all the workshop participants for their interesting comments.

could have expressed her opinion in a variety of other ways. I was able to understand her meaning by virtue of her words, but only by letting the specific referents of her words go. Later that day, still not entirely persuaded that I should accept the new project, I decided to consult the *Zhouyi* 周易 (also known as *Yijing* 易經). I asked my question and got the following line in *Kun* 坤: "A sack tied up: no fault, no praise" (括囊; 无咎无誉).[1] This was a more conservative suggestion. I should probably be careful about how much work I can account for if I want to avoid disappointing myself and others. After all, one should never bite off more than one can chew. All these words and images—the shrimp, the sack, biting and chewing—are evocative signs that succeed in conveying meaning. And yet, without a doubt, the ideas that they convey can be illustrated through a multiplicity of different signs that do not necessarily involve tides, ties, and full mouths. Moreover, we could never understand the intentional meaning of these words were we to take them literally as opposed to pragmatically. That is, if we did not move beyond what the phrase says in an attempt to grasp the intention of the speaker in uttering it.[2]

This preoccupation lies at the core of "Clarifying the Images" ("Ming xiang" 明象), a concise and influential essay written by Wang Bi 王弼 (226–249), which alerts us against being too literal in understanding what others have said.[3] "Clarifying the Images" is part of Wang Bi's longer commentary to the *Zhouyi* 周易 titled "General Remarks on the Changes of Zhou" ("Zhouyi lüeli" 周易略例). Its central preoccupation lies not with oral communication but with written one—more specifically, the recorded words (statements) and images (hexagrams) of the ancient sages who are traditionally believed to have authored the *Zhouyi*. After all, had I needed clarification, I could have asked my friend to reformulate her ideas. But when the oral context of utterance is lost and all we have left is a written record, a pragmatic reading in search of intentions becomes more complicated. Reacting against the symbolic closure of the Image-Number (*xiang shu* 象數) exegetical methods that had become popular during the Han dynasty (202 BCE–202 CE), Wang Bi came to challenge a centuries-long standing tradition of reading the *Zhouyi* through a closed self-referential system of images and their numbers.[4]

The mistake at the heart of these methods, Wang Bi diagnoses, consists in treating contingent and eventful correlations as relations of identity and necessity. As Zhu Xi said: "When the *Zhouyi* mentions something, it does not really refer to that thing; for example, when it mentions a dragon, it is not referring to a real dragon. This contrasts with other writings where what is mentioned is what is meant: filial piety is simply filial piety; humanity is simply humanity" (易說一個物非真是一個物,如說龍非真龍。若他書則真是實物,孝悌便是孝悌,仁便是仁).[5] Namely, the signs registered in the *Zhouyi*, such as "horse" or "ox," are not identical to their direct referent, for they point not at physical horses and oxen but at other ideas. The sages' intentions befall locally in contingent signs that are historically, culturally, and contextually constituted. Wang Bi explains that the relationship between the signs and the intentions is not one of identity, but one of equivalence or commonality between the valence of their elements: "Anything that touches upon its category can act as its image" (觸類可為其象).[6] While the signs used to convey intentions are local and linked to particular events, times, and contexts, the Image-Number form of exegesis turned them into a closed system of necessity. The problem with these "overflowing artificial theories" (偽說滋漫) is that they exploit identity, making it explode into meaningless numerical profusion, with the result that the intentions are lost in the process ("they got horse and lost Qian" 有馬无乾). As T'ang has humorously commented, "Han scholars could not get concrete things out of their mind."[7]

Wang Bi offers a theory for interpreting the *Zhouyi* and, more generally, a semiotic analysis with implications for the act of understanding. This theory revolves around the concept of forgetting (*wang* 忘). There is a general agreement that Wang Bi's hermeneutics can be summarized in a call to forget (i.e., dismiss) the words after getting their meaning, which points at the insufficiency of words and other signs as tools for expression. I propose a reading of Wang Bi's hermeneutic theory wherein language and other signs are *not* insufficient and *must not* be dismissed, despite Wang Bi's urge to forget them. I also propose a reading of Wang Bi's essay that prevents a Barthesian death-of-the-author approach to interpretation, because in Wang Bi the ultimate act of understanding consists in recovering (a sort of remembering) the original authorial intentions.[8] If forgetting does not consist in abandoning signs and liberating the reader from the tyranny of the author, what is the role of forgetting words and images in getting their intentional meaning? This is the question that I take on in the next few pages.

Hermeneutics of Actualization

"Clarifying the Images" puts forward a theory of interpretation for the *Zhouyi*, where the guiding problem is how to read a text that is extremely subtle and has an immense sociopolitical and ethical guiding value in a way that (1) is meaningful and relevant for current readers in their shifting contexts, hence the system of signs cannot be purely self-referential, fixed, and closed; and that simultaneously (2) preserves and actualizes the intentions of the sages who created the text, hence the interpretation cannot be fully free, unbound, and open. Against the self-referential closure of Image-Number exegeses, Wang Bi advocates for the openness of the text. Yet the openness and flexibility of the sign does not lead him to the opposite extreme—a death-of-the-author reader-oriented radical hermeneutic freedom where any interpretation is possible and valid. In reading a text such as the *Zhouyi*, there is an interpretive constraint that cannot be overcome: the intentions of the authors-sages. Hence, Wang Bi's method is neither purely author-oriented nor reader-oriented. He proposes something more sophisticated: reading is always an exercise of actualizing meaning with different enabling and constraining aspects at play.

In this way, "Clarifying the Images" is a self-aware, complete, and systematic exposition of an interpretive trend in reception theory that I call the *hermeneutics of actualization*. As a theory on how to receive texts, the hermeneutics of actualization deal with the reader's method to properly understand the meaning of a text that has been inherited from the authoritative past. As a poetics, the reader's method will be an intimate response to the author's strategies to construct meaning and the semiotic relation between signs, signifiers, and intentions. From this perspective, and strictly speaking, Wang Bi's essay "clarifies" not the *Zhouyi*'s images per se, but their role in expressing and helping the reader grasp the sages' intentions: the nature of the relation between intentions, images, and words, and the implications of this relation for properly understanding the text.

A word on "images" is necessary. Traditionally, the authors of the *Zhouyi* are the sages whose intentions reflect a privileged understanding of cosmic and world order. According to the literature on the origins of the *Zhouyi*, such as the well-known section in the *Hanshu* "Yiwenzhi" 漢書藝文志, the sages achieved this understanding by looking up to the sky and down to the earth, that is, by observing the figures of natural entities and comprehending their shared patterns of order and disorder, movement and stillness, growth and decay.⁹ The attached commentary that transformed the divination manual into a foundational philosophical text, the *Xici zhuan* 繫辭傳, also presents the *Zhouyi* as a visual system of representation. In the narrative, Fuxi 伏羲 extrapolated the trigrams to be a transcription of the relational and mobile structure of the world in its multiple configurations, thereby transferring for humankind's benefit the knowledge he had acquired through observation.¹⁰ A world comprehended through the visual observation of figures—including the shapes of celestial bodies (*tian xiang* 天/象), the patterns of earth (*di fa* 地/法), and adaptive designs of animals in correspondence with the patterns of earth (*wen yi* 文/宜)—is first translated into symbolic visual signs or images for human use, only adding words at later stages for further elaboration.¹¹ Images and words are the material means of transmission of the intentions generated in the sages by visually comprehending the world. As a result, it is by means of observing these images and words that readers can reach the immaterial and invisible intentions therein stored. We find the criterion to judge the validity of an interpretation in the authorial intention contained in the material means of transmission.¹² If in the absence of the authors we can still make sense of their intentions via the "traces" they have left behind, it must be because there is something in their words and images worth keeping, capable of communicating meaning despite time and context.¹³ A good reading is the one that recovers this initial intention in the act of communication through interacting with words and images. But the act of recovery is not a passive task: in being recovered, intentions become actualized.

We are to understand actualization in its two senses of bringing to the present and realizing what remains in potency. In order for signs to be correctly interpreted, the reader must deny a relation of identity where the sign is equal to itself, and hence welcome the gap onto which a new actualization of meaning can be grounded into the present. The hermeneutics of actualization will celebrate the gap as the condition of possibility of true understanding. It is the gap that allows for the sign to manifest its guiding force regardless of shifting contexts and the passage of time, and hence it is the gap that creates the classic—the text whose lasting relevance and universality invites rereading and reinterpreting. The classic has an abstract quality, where the abstract is to be understood as an unfinished potentiality that simultaneously permits and demands new concrete actualizations. Nevertheless, these actualizations of meaning are not fully dependent on the reader. While the gap allows and demands for the reader to complete its meaning, the completion must not be arbitrary. The works of the sages—the classics—contain normative guiding principles that ensure sociopolitical peace and order. Actualizing their meaning into the present must follow a criterion for proper understanding found in the correct contextualization of the speech acts that reveal the original intentions embodied in local and historical tools of meaning construction. In this way, each proper understanding of the classic is an act of remembrance: the recovery of a memory that one individually never had. This act of remembrance necessitates an exercise of forgetting, where forgetting is not mere lapse of the recollecting capacity of the mind but an active exercise of displacement and gap-opening. Actualization is hence to be defined as an exercise of forgetting for the sake of remembering.

The Fishnet Allegory

Wang Bi found some keys to formulate his hermeneutic theory in the *Zhuangzi*'s fishnet allegory and concept of forgetting. "Clarifying the Images" uses a couple of lines from "External Entities" ("Wai wu" 外物), which are part of what has come to be known as the fishnet allegory, here transcribed in full (Wang Bi uses lines 2 and 1, which is a significant choice, as we will see).

(1) 荃者所以在魚，得魚而忘荃

(2) 蹄者所以在兔，得兔而忘蹄

(3) 言者所以在意，得意而忘言

(4) 吾安得忘言之人而與之言哉[14]

As it happens with other *Zhuangzi* passages that have enjoyed popularity among contemporary readers, different interpretations of the fishnet allegory have produced radically different translations. By taking a look at some of the most prominent interpretations by ancient and modern scholars, we will be better equipped to appreciate Wang Bi's originality and creativity, even his intentions, in using this passage.

The standard interpretation, to which readers of English are accustomed by the translations of Burton Watson and James Legge, emphasizes the elusiveness of meaning and ideas, and the inadequacy of language to fully capture reality, inaugurating an interpretational framework where "the signified outplays the signifier."[15] Just as the tools for fishing and hunting rabbits are mere instruments to reach a goal and cease to be relevant once we have caught our prey, the tools that we use to catch meaning (words) should also be left behind once communication has been accomplished. The standard interpretation introduces a logic of subordination of instruments to goals: "The purpose of nets is catching fish; get the fish and forget the net. . . . The purpose of words is catching ideas; get the meaning and forget the words."

Principal *Zhuangzi* editor and commentator Guo Xiang 郭象 (252–312) offers the following comments on this passage: "When it comes to two sages having no intentions, they will have nothing to talk about" (至於兩聖無意, 奶都無所言也).[16] Hans-Georg Möller takes a renewed interest in Guo Xiang's interpretation of the fishnet allegory by reading *de yi* 得意 as a play on words that breaks with the structure of the previous two parallel lines. *De yi* would depart from its ordinary meaning of getting intentions to mean "satisfied," a state that would indicate complete lack of intentional activity. This reading suggests that the Daoist sage forgets both words and intentions: "Words are the means to get hold of intentions. [Only] by getting what is intended (that is, by being content and thus having no intentions anymore), [can] you forget the words."[17]

Jane Geaney takes the fishnet allegory's image of the hunting trap literally and looks at spoken words (*yan* 言) as traps for speakers in sociopolitical contexts. Those who speak alternatively snare themselves by showing their true colors (the intentions-*yi* 意 in their heart-minds-*xin* 心), or have the capacity to ensnare others, particularly rulers, by uttering deceiving and manipulative words. The allegory's last sentence refers alternatively to speakers who do not trap themselves by speech, hence, they are still free rabbits, or to rulers who "should cease being impressed by the rhetoric of dispute" and by the cleverness of the ministers (*wang yan* 忘言): "Where can I get someone who has forgotten the speaking and speak with him?"[18]

Wim De Reu contextualizes the fishnet allegory within the "External Entities" chapter of the *Zhuangzi*, looking for connections between key terms. In the chapter, De Reu remarks, *yi* does not refer to thoughts in general but to commonly held opinions, whereas *yan* does not refer to speaking in general but to the use of fixed evaluative terms. Thus, the allegory would argue that speaking in the *yan* evaluative mode (De Reu also calls it "divinatory") needs to be abandoned, for it creates patterned habits of thinking and acting that do not allow the necessary flexibility and awareness to respond adaptively to each situation as it arises. By abandoning this mode of speaking through fixed value judgments people can *really talk* (in a different mode): "[Divinatory-style] term-words are that by which [those who strain themselves] get a hold on opinions. [Alternatively,] in winning over opinions, disregard [divinatory-style] term-words!"[19]

As different as they are, all these interpretations of the fishnet allegory have one feature in common. They all portray the forgotten entities (tools, words, intentions, speech, fixed evaluative terms) as unidimensional and negative: something that needs to be overcome in order to achieve the ultimate goal (true understanding, sagely satisfaction, communication without self-entrapment, situational awareness, and expressive flexibility). Furthermore, all of these interpretations but De Reu's assume a logical prioritization of getting over forgetting (get *and then* forget). De Reu, in turn, understands forgetting as pragmatically significant for the activity of getting, thereby anticipating the relation of simultaneity between forgetting and getting that Wang Bi will make explicit in his hermeneutic theory.[20]

Wang Bi's Sampling

Many consider Wang Bi's essay on "Clarifying the Images" the source of the standard interpretation of the fishnet allegory, the one that most strongly showcases the insufficiency of language to convey reality. In this reading, the trap-net images that Wang Bi samples from the allegory are taken to represent the entirety of Wang Bi's hermeneutic theory, and then they are read back into the *Zhuangzi* as manifesting a suspicious and negative attitude toward language where words must ultimately be rejected or abandoned (i.e., forgotten). To obtain this reading of both Wang Bi's hermeneutic theory and the *Zhuangzi*'s fishnet allegory, two assumptions must be at work. One is that Wang Bi's essay offers an interpretation of the fishnet allegory. Another is that the trap-net images that Wang Bi takes from the allegory encapsulate the essence of his approach to reading and interpreting.

None of these assumptions stand. The first assumption has been challenged by Möller and others when they point out that Wang Bi is not interested in clarifying, reading, or interpreting the allegory; rather, he instrumentalizes the *Zhuangzi* lines that he cherry-picks to illustrate his own theory on how to read the *Zhouyi*.[21] Here, Mattice's notion of *sampling* as a specific form of intertextual practice with the potential to act as a model for textual composition and hermeneutic paradigm proves useful. In music, sampling is the practice to use a portion (sample) of someone else's song/composition in a different song/composition, recontextualizing it in a new setting.[22] Translated into a means of intertextual composition, sampling becomes a creative way to use a passage that departs from the source text by providing a new framework and conveying new meaning with a new textual goal. The sampled lines from the allegory in Wang Bi's essay introduce a creative element that plays a meaningful role in his new composition. They do not look back to the *Zhuangzi* in order to explicate the source text. Rather, they use the preexisting text in order to illustrate, expose, and explicate the text that the sampling author is writing and/or a third target text (such as the *Zhouyi*). Sampling does not give primacy to the sampled passage, but to a different text, whether this is the text that samples or yet another text that is discussed through the sampling. Likewise, the weight is put on the sampling author's thinking, not the sampled author's one, and hence sampling does not involve the interpretation of the source text in and of itself.

The second assumption takes the sampled trap-net images as the core of Wang Bi's hermeneutic theory. In doing so, it denies the role of context and structure in the intentional composition of meaning. When ancient and current interpreters portray Wang Bi as an advocate for getting rid of language and/or purely relying on the reader's interpretive capacity to understand a text, they are taking his two sampled sentences too literally—precisely the heart of Wang Bi's critique against the previous exegetical tradition—and losing the total intended meaning.[23] When contextualized within the full hermeneutic theory exposed in Wang Bi's essay, we see that the trap-net images serve only to illustrate *one* aspect of his semiotic analysis (the trapping aspect of the sign, as we discuss below). It is only by taking these lines in isolation and not contextualizing them within "Clarifying the Images" that we may read them as manifesting Wang Bi's overall suspicious attitude toward language. In order to understand Wang Bi's hermeneutic theory, let us follow his pragmatic method: do not take his words too literally and search instead for his intention in sampling from the fishnet allegory by locating those lines within the structure of the full essay. By doing so, we reach the conclusion that Wang Bi does not turn the forgotten entities (in this case, *Zhouyi* hexagrams and their attached verbalizations) into something inherently negative, and that he proposes a logic of simultaneity between forgetting and getting the intention (getting by forgetting).

The Two Aspects of the Media: Enabling and Trapping

In hermeneutical theory, Wang Bi's ontological concept of the *suoyi* 所以 becomes a mediation notion that enables the communication and reception of ideas.[24] "Clarifying the Images" begins by introducing the semiotic relation between intentions (*yi* 意) and the material means by which these are made explicit and transmitted: images (*xiang* 象) and words (*yan* 言), to which I will alternatively refer as the media or the signs. Wang Bi's first exposition of the media is entirely positive, declaring its enabling aspect at both the levels of the author, as the producer and conveyor of meaning, and reader, as the receiver and interpreter of meaning. The enabling aspect of the media is such that authors can, thereby, fully express and transmit their intentions: "Images put forth intentions; words clarify images. To fully express intentions there is nothing like images; to fully express images there is nothing like words" (象者, 出意者也。言者, 明象者也。盡意莫若象, 盡象莫若言).[25] The enabling aspect also involves the reader's understanding, insofar as readers can grasp the intentions of the author by retracing the media's order of production (intentions-images-words): "The words are generated from the images, and thus it is possible to seek the words in order to comprehend the images. The images are generated from the intentions, and thus it is possible to seek the images in order to comprehend the intentions" (言生於象, 故可尋言以觀象; 象生於意, 故可尋象以觀意).

There are several points to notice in this opening passage. First, there is a logical and temporal sequence between intentions, images, and words. Intentions, as thoughts and ideas, are invisible and immaterial insofar as they are prelinguistic. Wang Bi differentiates between language and thought, establishing the basis that not all thought is linguistic. Language is presented as a sophisticated means to express our intentions and impressions on the world, but the world and our thoughts about it predate language.[26] Second, if words are generated from images in order to fully express them, and images are generated from intentions in order to fully express them, the media is necessary for intentions to shine forth beyond the thinker's mind and to be externally communicated, received, and interpreted. Notice that the verb used for "comprehending" images and intentions is *guan* 觀, which also means to visually observe—the same verb used in the *Xici zhuan* with regard to the sage's observation and comprehension of natural patterns. Immaterial hence invisible intentions become observable via images. Third, as a result, intentions become ultimately dependent on the media, despite their ontological priority, given that they could never appear beyond the author's mind without their symbolic particularization and determination into visual and aural means. Finally, a reader's "understanding" of a text cannot be the free and unbound creation of meaning, but the restricted assimilation of its author's intentions as facilitated by linguistic and/or nonlinguistic signs.

The opening of Wang Bi's essay argues for the enabling aspect of the media. Far from a suspicion of language theory, whether it is in ancient or modern terms, we find here an evaluation of signs as the unmatched bridge that allows a transmission of thoughts from one person to another, even between persons born with hundreds of years in between. By using linguistic and nonlinguistic signs, the authors of the *Zhouyi* built a bridge to their intentions, and it is only by walking this bridge back that we can reach their thoughts. The enabling aspect of the media is the basis on which we are to build the next step of the theory ("this being settled" *gu* 故). Nevertheless, we are about to witness a shift in perspective. The sampling from the *Zhuangzi*'s fishnet allegory in the second section of the essay is used to examine the media from a different angle.

言者所以明象	Words are the means to clarify the images;
得象而忘言	get the images and forget the words.
象者所以存意	Images are the means to preserve the intentions;
得意而忘象	get the intentions and forget the images.
猶	Similarly,
蹄者所以在兔	"Snares are the means to get rabbits;
得兔而忘蹄	get the rabbit and forget the snare.
筌者所以在魚	Fishnets are the means to get fish;
得魚而忘筌也	get the fish and forget the net."

Wang Bi's choice of lines from the fishnet allegory is a declaration of his intentions in sampling the *Zhuangzi*. He uses the visually and conceptually memorable images of the rabbit snare and the fishnet to portray a different aspect of the media that is not enabling, but trapping. The trapping aspect, which affects only readers, implies the risk of getting stuck in the words as opposed to using them to access the images, and getting stuck in the images as opposed to using them to access the intentions, which are the ultimate object of understanding. Far from the unmatched enabling means of the first section (*mo ruo xiang/yan* 莫若象/言), the second section describes words and images as hunting traps: "Words are snares for the images; images are nets for the intentions" (言者, 象之蹄也。象者, 意之筌也). The trap consists in a certain call for the sign to be read too literally, to find its significance in its own referent, neglecting the gap between the two. As we have seen, this is the problem with computational exegetes who read "horse" as "horse" instead of, say, "strength," getting stuck in a relation of identity of the sign with itself. The connector *you* 猶, here translated as "similarly," denotes that the following lines introduce an equivalent idea to what has previously been asserted by using different phrasing. Like dragons in *Qian* 乾, the lines that Wang Bi samples from the *Zhuangzi* should not be read literally but for their implications. Interestingly, the fact that we must negotiate between different possible meanings while reading proves once again that thought is partially independent from language, and that linguistic and nonlinguistic signs have correlations with meanings but not necessarily in an unequivocal or literal way.

Were we to take Wang Bi's words literally in section 2, the inadequacy of language theory would seem to be an appropriate way of approaching his essay. He literally writes that one is to forget words after getting their meaning, which he then reinforces by using an equivalent formulation from the *Zhuangzi*. Yet this literal reading of section 2 does violence to the overall structure of the essay. Wang Bi uses the Zhuangist images of the trap and net to highlight an important point in his theory: the media have a trapping aspect that readers must take into account. However, this new claim regarding the trapping aspect of the media should not invalidate the enabling evaluation offered before. The first and second sections enjoy a perfect parallelism in distinctly exposing each aspect of the media. Where the first section established the logic "intentions-images-words" to express how authors take advantage of the media to put forward their intentions, section 2 uses a reverse-order opening that mirrors back this logic, "words-images-intentions," highlighting the process that a reader must follow to reach the intentions and the risks involved in such process. Through this parallelism, Wang Bi invites us to consider both claims as simultaneously valid, none of them taking priority over the other. Namely, images and words, the *suoyi* or media, have both aspects at the same time: one enabling, the other trapping. These aspects coexist and neither one has primacy over the other.

The third section of "Clarifying the Images" confirms that this is the case by drawing out the consequences of the previously established premises in a synthetic exercise that comprises what we have learned from sections 1 and 2. Since the media has an enabling aspect, authors can use it in conveying their intentions; since it also has a trapping aspect, readers must not remain at the literal level of the media, but "forget" it in getting the message. Section 3, discussed below, resolves this tension and offers precise instructions on how to properly read given the two conflicting aspects of the media.

Forgetting for Getting

Throughout "Clarifying the Images," Wang Bi amazes us with his insights into semiotics, language, signs, and their relation to ideas and meaning. He first advanced the claim that not all thought is linguistic, a thesis that did not enjoy so much popularity in the second half of the twentieth century with poststructuralist and deconstructionist philosophy but has more recently resurged due to advances in neuroscience.[27] He then announced the gap between the sign and its direct referent, welcoming nonliteral correlations and equivalences as necessary for interpretation and the creation of meaning. In section 3, Wang Bi surprises us again when he explains that both linguistic and nonlinguistic signs, the media, have a function beyond communication whose purpose is to store ideas: "Images are generated from the intentions and [intentions] are preserved in the images. . . . Words are generated from images and [images] are preserved in the words" (象生於意而存象焉. . . . 言生於象而存言焉). As a logical consequence of the media's storing function, we must not confound the media with what it is storing, which is the mistake of all literalist approaches to interpretation: "What is to be preserved is not the same as its image/words" (所存者乃非其象/言也). Given that what is preserved necessarily differs from the means by which it is preserved, "those who preserve the words do not get the images" (存言者,

非得象者也) and "those who preserve the images do not get the intentions" (存象者, 非得意者也).

Wang Bi's innovation lies with the apparently simple suggestion that both dimensions of the media, enabling and trapping, coexist, an insight that he fruitfully employs to establish practical implications for both authors and readers. Namely, the poetics of a text and the semiotic analysis of the sign both inform and impose normative constraints on reading practices. Signs store and communicate the author's intentions but, in receiving them, the reader cannot stay at the superficial level of what the sign literally says. In a way, the reader must search for the meaning that is preserved in between the lines by paying attention to equivalences and structure. This reading in between lines that allows a reader to get the intention is conceptualized as an exercise of forgetting. However, where in section 2 Wang Bi read the *Zhuangzi* lines as "get and then forget," he will introduce now a logical difference turning the relation between getting and forgetting into a relation of simultaneity: getting by forgetting, or forgetting for getting.

然則	This being so,
忘象者乃得意者也	those who forget the images, thereby get the intentions;
忘言者乃得象者也	those who forget the words, thereby get the images.
得意在忘象	Getting the intentions lies with forgetting the images;
得象在忘言	getting the images lies with forgetting the words.

Sections 1, 2, and 3 of Wang Bi's essay can be read as thesis, antithesis, and synthesis in a dialectical model. The newly proposed relation of simultaneity between forgetting and getting is not a simple negation of forgetting's priority with regard to getting that had been established in section 2 through the sampling of the fishnet allegory. Rather, it is a synthetic result of the integrative analysis of the dual aspect of the media explored in sections 1 and 2. Section 3 synthesizes these conflicting aspects (enabling versus trapping) in a new proposition that relies on, yet necessarily qualifies, both of them. The codependency of the thesis and the antithesis plays out into a resolution that combines both statements while excluding the possibility of their radicalization.

On the one hand, if we focused exclusively on section 1, we could be led to remain at the level of the sign, given that the sign is presented as unproblematically emerging from intentions and the unmatched bridge that brings us back to them. On the other hand, if we focused exclusively on section 2 with the sampling from the fishnet allegory, we could be led to fully abandon the sign, for there it is presented as a tool that, if reified or hypostasized, becomes a trap that encages the intention: the trap of literalness that makes us mistake the intention for the sign that conveys it. By integrating both claims and taking seriously the coexistence of both aspects of the media, we conclude with Wang Bi that, while forgetting is necessary (consequence of claim 2), forgetting is not an abandonment of the sign, for the sign is the only carrier of the intention and the locus of any possible interpretation (consequence of claim 1). Hence we learn that forgetting is inherent to getting (notice that *zai* 在 works both to express method and simultaneity); not the instrumental approach to a tool that has fulfilled its purpose, but the very exercise of displacement by which the intention that the sign has stored becomes actualized. In this way, the conflicting aspects of the media are not so much resolved or dissolved as they are accounted for in Wang Bi's proposal for reading the *Zhouyi*, which can be extrapolated to a more general theory of interpreting and understanding.[28]

We must remember that, in approaching the *Zhouyi*, readers must reach the intentions of the sage-authors who composed it while making room for actualizing the relevance of its meaning to contemporary contexts. In forgetting words and images to get the intentions, the reader lets go of identity and apprehends equivalence by thinking of one element of the relation in terms of the other. The exercise of forgetting is necessary because, as Wang Bi has already argued: (1) There is a gap at the heart of the semiotic relation: immaterial and invisible intentions always depend on some material means to be externalized, stored, and conveyed, with the result that intentions cannot be found in the intentions themselves but in their signs. (2) And yet, even though intentions are always discovered in the signs used to convey them, they are not identical to the signs. These two facts lead readers to two risks that they must avoid: (1) They should not mistake the signs for the intentions themselves (remember that "what is to be preserved is not the same as its image"); and (2) they should not do away with the signs either, for intentions can only be discovered in the signs that preserve them. In short, the intentions are always revealed in a sort of a relational tension between signs and meaning.

We are coming closer to understanding the concept of forgetting. Forgetting the signs in getting the intentions suggests a technical sense of forgetting that finds resemblances with the Zhuangist art of active oblivion, a technique to progressively let go of certainties, patterns of thinking, feeling and interacting, and spontaneous tendencies.[29] As Kohn has argued, as a meditation and self-cultivation practice, *wang* 忘 is better translated as oblivion, "because the connotation of forget in English is that one *should* remember but doesn't do so."[30] Wang Bi's forgetting is an intentional letting go of the reader's tendency to cling to particular signs as if they were literal, absolute, and necessary, in a movement to favor flexible correlations and semantic openness. In this way, Wang Bi's forgetting can be compared with the meditational/self-cultivational *wang* in its function of decentering the self. A desired effect of "sitting in oblivion" (*zuo wang* 坐忘) is ceasing to see the world in self-referential terms. Similarly, forgetting the sign in getting the intention decenters the reader as the main source of meaning. In Wang Bi's semiotic analysis, the relation between intentions, images, and words cannot be overcome. Intentions only come to light through images and words, which preserve and enable the intentions. Therefore, when readers *forget* the visible signs in order to get the intentions, they are not fully abandoning the signs, but actively letting go of the literalist view that establishes their character as necessary and their relation as one of identity. By getting rid of this conception, readers are able to travel through the relational tension between sign and intentions toward comprehending the intended meaning of the signs.[31]

Wang Bi's hermeneutics does not condemn the particular, local, and contingent; it does not reject language or any other means of semantic particularization such as symbols and images. What Wang Bi's hermeneutics does is caution readers against the trapping and misleading aspect of the particular, the singular, the determinate, the given word, the name, and the visible entity because their seemingly finished character makes us think that there is no more to it than what we perceive. Things that are determinate may lead to a repetition of the same where meaning is lost and signs turn flat and shallow. Thus, Wang Bi's hermeneutics vindicates the fundamental value of determinate signs in storing meaning, and the crucial need for readers to rely on them to actualize meaning, but he must do so with these caveats in mind. Forgetting leads in Wang Bi's hermeneutics to a sort of remembering: the exercise of displacement both of the sign and the self through which the memory of what the author intended in the sign becomes actualized.

Relational Codependency

I am presenting the relation between intentions, images, and words as one of codependency, where intentions and signs need each other to come to fruition. A minimal approach to ontological priority entails that *a* is prior to *b*, or that it is more fundamental. This is certainly the case with the intentions, which are not only prior in time to the signs, but also necessary while the signs chosen to convey them are contingent. However, in a more demanding approach, ontological priority may entail that in a claim where *a* is prior to *b*, *b* depends on *a* for its existence, while *a* is independent from *b*. While it is the case that images and words depend on intentions for their existence (they emerge from intentions), we should also notice that intentions depend, materially or symbolically, on the media—not to arise, but to exist beyond the author's mind, and to be preserved and conveyed. We may therefore argue that the relation between intentions and signs is one of codependency.

In the standard reading of the fishnet allegory, a relation of instrumentality is at work: words and images are tools subordinated to intentions, and accessorial with respect to the fundamental reality of the intentions. Therefore, they can be easily disposed of after use. Wang Bi, in turn, corrects the instrumentality of the sign in order to create a relational codependency that can never be overcome. In Wang Bi's model, words, images, and intentions become an ongoing resource for one another. Intentions are a resource for the proliferations of signs, while images and words are resources available for the actualization of intentions—something that lies within easy reach for the author of intentions, to the service of thinking. In summary, signs are not to be reified and fixated into a relation of self-referential identity, which would lead to a loss of potentiality to signify and capacity to remain relevant. Nor are signs to be dismissed as disposable instruments. Forgetting the signs in getting the intentions does not imply a disparaging treatment of the signs. On the contrary, it suggests the most appropriate and respectful way to treat the sign, as the sign constantly demands to be forgotten in this technical sense of displacement and gap-opening. Through the concept of forgetting, Wang Bi recovers the semantic richness of the sign, which, being local and particular, points beyond itself. The reader forgets in order to make room for a difference and allow intentions to be continuously actualized in new signs by using new local resources.

The last line of the essay summarizes the central idea by toying with the notions of visibility and invisibility: "Only by forgetting the images in reaching to their intentions (yi 意), the meaning (yi 義) makes itself apparent" (忘象以求其意, 義斯見矣). By forgetting that which can be seen, what cannot be seen appears visible. One can only see by unseeing, get by not clinging, and remember by forgetting. Tang Jungyi 唐君毅 (1909–1978) has interpreted the difference between "intentions" and "meaning" as one between private and personal thoughts versus public and general concepts that have already been expressed and articulated (意知所知即義).[32] The meaning that makes itself apparent through the exercise of forgetting is indeed the author's intention as conveyed through the sign and activated by a new reader. Drawing on the dichotomy visible/invisible, the essay closes with a renewed emphasis on the importance of forgetting the sign in actualizing its meaning.[33] Unlike rabbits and fish, intentions are not visible material entities. They belong to the formless realm of thought, and must dwell with signs on which they rely to be materialized, preserved, conveyed, and made explicit. The reliance of thought on signs radically amplifies the risk to mistake the sign for the intention, which led Wang Bi to paradigmatically illustrate the trapping aspect of the sign through the fishnet allegory and to version the self-cultivational concept of forgetting to serve at the core of his hermeneutical theory. Nevertheless, as we have seen, it would be a mistake to take the part for the whole. Wang Bi's synthesis of the dual aspect of the media and his analysis of the codependency between thought and sign lead not to the abandonment of the sign but to its actualization into new forms of meaning articulation that properly express the intentions of the sages and renovate their relevance into a new context.

Forget, Actualize, Remember

Wang Bi's proposal is not rare compared with other hermeneutic practices in those times. What is unique in "Clarifying the Images" is the succinct, theoretical, and systematic articulation of the theory, which we had not found before. But already in Han times we find scholars who approach the classics in just the way that Wang Bi would theorize centuries later. A privileged example is the Han poet and philosopher Yang Xiong 楊雄 (53 BCE–18 CE), who believed that the most respectful and accurate strategy to actualize the intentions of the sages was not to comment on the classics but to rewrite them entirely. The rewriting of the *Analects* (*Lunyu* 論語) gave way to *Model Sayings* (*Fayan* 法言), while the rewriting of the *Zhouyi* produced *The Canon of Supreme Mystery* (*Taixuan jing* 太玄經).³⁴ Much as Wang Bi would theorize later, the goal of Yang Xiong's hermeneutical practice is neither to fully abandon the transmitted sign (the recorded words of the sages) nor the authors' intentions in a move toward favoring reader-created meaning. On the contrary, translating the transmitted signs into new ones actualizes the original intention of the sages into new media that can convey it more accurately and efficaciously for the new audiences. Rewriting the classics saves them from the risk of being taken literally, hence from becoming either shallow and irrelevant or cryptic and devoid of guiding value. Although sharing the same assumptions regarding the dialectics of forgetting and remembering in the act of interpretation, Wang Bi proposes not to rewrite the classics but to learn to read them properly in order to actualize their meaning. A few years after Wang Bi's premature death, the poet Shu Xi 束皙 (263–302) rewrote six *Lesser Elegantiae* 小雅 odes that had been cataloged yet lost in transmission in his influential "Filling Out the Missing Odes" ("Bu wang shi" 補亡詩).³⁵ In this scenario, it is not the case that some particular words need to be forgotten in order to make room for the intention, but rather the opposite: some words have de facto been forgotten and urgently need to be remembered for the completion of this important cosmic and political ritual and the sociopolitical order that results from its performance. Interestingly, Shu Xi does not claim to invent these odes, but to remember them, as they would have been written, in accordance with the intentions of the sages: "Fixing our thoughts on what had come before, and setting our minds upon the past, we [Shu Xi and his peers] filled out the words in order to stitch together the old institutions" (遙想既往, 存思在昔, 補著其文, 以綴舊制).³⁶

Overall, we find two reverse phenomena. In the case of Shu Xi's odes, we have the meaning but the words themselves were lost (summarized as 有其義而亡其辭). In the case of Yang Xiong and Wang Bi, we have words and images, but their meaning is lost (summarized as 有其象言而亡其義). In all three cases there is something found, something lost; something forgotten or to forget, something to be remembered. Remembering in this context is a different activity than recalling or bringing images to mind. Remembering the intentions of the ancient sages involves an exercise of actualization: a revitalized realization of the original, a restoring hermeneutic exercise that challenges the distinction between reception and creation. Understanding, then, whether it is a text, an image, or a person, consists in remembering a memory that one never individually had.

Notes

1. Wang Bi 王弼, Han Kangbo 韓康伯, and Kong Yingda 孔穎達 ed., *Zhouyi zhushu* 周易注疏 (Taipei: Taiwan xuesheng, 1998), 96. The commentary to the image (*xiang zhuan* 象傳) reads: "'A sack tied up: no fault' means that being careful leads to no harm/trouble" (括囊无咎, 慎不害也). *Zhouyi zhushu*, 97.

2. Herbert Fingarette introduced the first pragmatic reading of the *Analects* in his groundbreaking work, *Confucius: The Secular as Sacred* (San Francisco, CA: HarperCollins, 1972). On pragmatic readings of the Chinese classics, see also Yang Xiao, "How Confucius Does Things with Words: Two Hermeneutic Paradigms in the *Analects* and Its Exegeses," *Journal of Asian Studies* 66, no. 2 (2007): 497–532.

3. Wang Bi was posthumously characterized as a scholar of the Dark or *Xuanxue* 玄學, a category first used in the *Jinshu* 晉書 (Tang period, 618–907), and which took the term *xuan* 玄 (darkness, mystery, profound) from the *Laozi* 老子 as central to a series of philosophical exercises and exchanges in the third century.

4. As Richard Lynn, Rudolf Wagner, Chen Guying, Edward Shaughnessy, Ming Dong Gu, and others have explained, Wang Bi changed the course of *Zhouyi* exegesis to put the emphasis on disclosing and reinterpreting intentions and meaning, a trend of reading the *Zhouyi* as a philosophical text already started by the *Xici zhuan* 繫辭傳. My reading of "Clarifying the Images" owes much to the insightful previous scholarship on Wang Bi and the *Zhouyi*.

5. Zhu Xi 朱熹, *Zhuzi yulei* 朱子語類, juan 67, 13b–14a. I discovered this Zhu Xi passage in Ming Dong Gu, *Chinese Theories of Reading and Writing: A Route to Hermeneutics and Open Poetics* (Albany: State University of New York Press, 2005), 101–2.

6. All my quotes from "Clarifying the Images" are in Lou Yulie 楼宇烈, *Wang bi ji jiaoshi* 王弼集校釋 (Beijing: Zhonghua shuju, 1980), 609.

7. T'ang Yung-t'ung and Walter Liebenthal, "Wang Pi's New Interpretation of the I Ching and Lun-yü," *Harvard Journal of Asiatic Studies* 10, no. 2 (1947): 124–61, 143.

8. Roland Barthes, *La mort de l'auteur*. In *Le bruissement de la langue: Essais critiques IV* (Paris: Seuil, 1984), 63–69. Ming Dong Gu argues that Wang Bi inaugurates a reader-oriented trend of open interpretation that presupposed the death of the author throughout his Wang Bi chapter in *Chinese Theories of Reading and Writing*, 81–150.

9. There are versions of this text in the *Xici zhuan* 繫辭傳, *Hanshu* "Yiwenzhi" 漢書藝文志, *Shiji* 史記, *Hou hanshu* 後漢書, *Shuowen jiezi* 說文解字, *Fengsu tongyi* 風俗通義, and *Baihutong* 白虎通. Each of these sources utilizes the story of the origins of the trigrams for a different purpose, such as a genesis of civilization and cultural achievements in the *Xici zhuan*, or an explanation of the origins of writing in the *Shuowen jiezi*.

10. Willard Peterson, "Making Connections: 'Commentary on the Attached Verbalizations' of the Book of Change," *Harvard Journal of Asiatic Studies* 42, no. 1 (1982): 67–116. See pp. 80–81 for a discussion on translating *xiang* 象 as either image or figure. I do not translate the term *xiang* as figures in "Clarifying the Images" because Wang Bi does not portray *xiang* as observer-independent in the way that natural entities often are thought to be. While natural entities are figures, they become images when comprehended, and visual signs when represented.

11. *Zhouyi zhushu*, 674.

12. As Albert Galvany has noted, Wang Bi assumes the logic underlying divination languages such as the *Zhouyi*'s: thanks to the equivalence between language/signs and reality, it is possible to trace the path from the written sign back to natural signs/patterns (*wen* 文); and thereby to reveal inner and invisible intentions (*yi* 意) by means of external and visible signs (*xiang/yan* 象言). We also find this logic in morphoscopic practices and physiognomic techniques: it is possible to identify inner characteristics and tendencies in humans by means of the observation of their physical forms. Galvany, "Signs, Clues, and Traces: Anticipation in Ancient Chinese Political and Military Texts," *Early China* 38 (2015): 151–93.

13. The sages have left traces (*ji* 跡) behind in the form of writings, by means of which their intentions and teachings can potentially be recovered. On the question of traces from a wiser past, how to recover them, and whether it is even possible to recover them, read Tobias Zürn's chapter in this volume. As we will see, Wang Bi participates in the philosophical project of trace-recovery that we most commonly associate with "Confucian" scholars and thinkers. But he also understands the merits of the critical premise that writings and other traces are but "dregs" or "residues" (*zaopo* 糟魄) from the past, most prominently developed in the *Zhuangzi* and the *Han Feizi*. Toward the end of recovering the traces from the past and actualizing their meaning and significance into the present, Wang Bi offers a third path that harmonizes (or fruitfully synthesizes) the two previous opposite attitudes. Scholars have discussed this syncretic or pluralistic element—particularly as a synthesis of Daoism and Confucianism—as one of the most characteristic elements of Wang Bi's thought. See, among others, Tang Yongtong 湯用彤, *Wei jin xuanxue lungao* 魏晉玄學論稿 (Shanghai: Shanghai renmin chubanshe, 1957), 83–85; Rudolf Wagner, *The Craft of a Chinese Commentator: Wang Bi on the Laozi* (Albany: State University of New York Press, 2000), 133.

14. Guo Qingfan 郭慶藩, *Zhuangzi jishi* 莊子集釋 (Beijing: Zhonghua shuju, 2004), 944.

15. Hans-Georg Möller, "Zhuangzi's Fishnet Allegory: A Text Critical Analysis," *Journal of Chinese Philosophy* 24, no. 7 (2000): 489–502, 491.

16. Reference and translation in Möller, "Zhuangzi's Fishnet Allegory," 494. *Zhuangzi jishi*, 946.

17. Möller, "Zhuangzi's Fishnet Allegory," 498.

18. Jane Geaney, *Language as Bodily Practice in Early China: A Chinese Grammatology* (Albany: State University New York Press, 2018), 114–21.

19. Wim De Reu, "A Ragbag of Odds and Ends? Argument Structure and Philosophical Coherence in *Zhuangzi* 26," in *Literary Forms of Argument in Early China*, ed. Joachim Gentz and Dirk Meyer (Leiden: Brill, 2015), 271–77.

20. De Reu, "A Ragbag of Odds and Ends?," 275.

21. Möller, "Zhuangzi's Fishnet Allegory," 492; De Reu, "A Ragbag of Odds and Ends?," 247–48.

22. Sarah Mattice, *Exploring the Heart Sutra* (New York: Lexington Books, 2021), ch. 1, "Sampling Authenticity."

23. For ancient literalist interpretations of Wang Bi's essay, see Gu, *Chinese Theories*, 124.

24. On the ontological *suoyi*, see Rudolf Wagner, *Language, Ontology, and Political Philosophy in China: Wang Bi's Scholarly Exploration of the Dark (Xuanxue)* (Albany: State University New York Press, 2003).

25. Compare with the *Xici*: "The sages established the images as means to fully express their intentions, set forth the hexagrams as means to fully express natural and created tendencies, attached verbalization as means to fully express what they said, and made them all in flux and comprehensive as means to fully express their utility" (聖人立象以盡意, 設卦以盡情偽, 繫辭以盡其言, 變而通之以盡利), *Zhouyi zhushu*, 641; Peterson, "Making Connections," 98–99.

26. Compare Wang Bi's realist attitude with Wittgenstein's "the limits of my language are the limits of my world" (*Tractatus Logico-Philosophicus* 5.6) and the linguistic turn in twentieth-century European and analytic philosophy. Wang Bi's approach to thought and language is shared by other Classical Chinese philosophers. See, for instance, the *Guanzi* 管子, when it says that "thoughts/intentions are prior to speaking/words" 意以先言. Li Xiangfeng 黎翔鳳, *Guanzi jiaozhu* 管子校注 (Beijing: Zhonghua shuju, 2009), 37, 786.

27. Among many other studies, I refer here to the important contributions by Evelina Fedorenko and Rosemary Varley, "Language and Thought Are Not the Same Thing: Evidence from Neuroimaging and Neurological Patients," *Annals of the New York Academy of Science* 1369, no. 1 (2016): 132–53; Steven Pinker, *The Blank Slate: The Modern Denial of Human Nature* (New York: Penguin Books, 2002), 207–13; Michael Siegel, Rosemary Varley, and Stephen C. Want, "Mind

over Grammar: Reasoning in Aphasia and Development," *Trends in Cognitive Sciences* 5 (2001): 296–301; Steven Pinker, *The Language Instinct* (New York: HarperCollins, 1994), ch. 3.

28. On Wang Bi's use of "interlocking parallel style," which has a similar effect as a dialectic method, see Wagner, *The Craft of a Chinese Commentator*.

29. See Franklin Perkins's chapter in this volume for an exploration of the Zhuangist art of forgetting.

30. Livia Kohn, *Sitting in Oblivion: The Heart of Daoist Meditation* (Dunedin, FL: Three Pines Press, 2010), 1.

31. We may say that Wang Bi's forgetting differs from the meditational "sitting in oblivion" insofar as it is an intentional activity that does not involve an ultimate suspension of consciousness. However, interpretations of *zuo wang* vary.

32. Tang Junyi 唐君毅, *Zhongguo zhexue yuanlun: yuandao pian* 中國哲學原論: 原道篇 (Hong Kong: Xinya yanjiusuo, 1973), 2.885. Cited by Richard Lynn, "Wang Bi and *Xuanxue*," in *Dao Companion to Daoist Philosophy*, ed. Liu Xiaogan (New York: Springer, 2016), 389.

33. This dichotomy has been explored by Jane Geaney, *On the Epistemology of the Senses in Early Chinese Thought* (Honolulu: University of Hawai'i Press, 2002); Geaney, *Language as Bodily Practice*.

34. On Yang Xiong, see Michael Nylan, *Yang Xiong and the Pleasures of Reading and Classical Learning in China* (New Haven: CT: American Oriental Society, 2011).

35. *Wang* 亡 either refers to odes that had music and titles but no lyrics, or odes that originally had lyrics which were lost in transmission. The latter is the preferred theory for most scholars and favored by Shu Xi himself. Zhao Jing 趙婧, *Lun shu xi de shijing xue ji qi buwangshi chuangzuo* 論束皙的詩經學及其補亡詩創作, *Xinyang shifan xueyuan xuebao* 35, no. 2 (2015): 127–30; Tom Mazanec, "Righting, Riting, and Rewriting the *Book of Odes* (*Shijing*): On 'Filling Out the Missing Odes' by Shu Xi," *Chinese Literature: Essays, Articles, Reviews* 40 (2018): 5–32.

36. Reference and translation in Mazanec, "Righting, Riting, and Rewriting," 12.

PART III
RITUAL AND LITERARY TEXTS

Chapter 10

Embodied Memory and Natural Forgetting in Early Chinese Ritual Theory

Paul Nicholas Vogt

Remembering and forgetting constitute rather than negate each other. In order to "recall" something, that something must have passed from the conscious mind, however that mind is constituted; and for this recall to differ perceptibly and in its own right from the state of consciousness in other circumstances, it must accommodate the possibility of failure.[1] What form that failure takes, and, by extension, what forgetting is, depends on how the relationship between the state of consciousness and the contents of memory is construed. This problem lies at the center of the phenomenology of memory in its colloquial sense, that is, the study of the experience of remembering.[2]

That such a field has come to exist attests that memory is different from other mental processes in a recognizable way. One senses when one is remembering, rather than perceiving or imagining, an entity or event (though that sense can be manipulated with relative ease).[3] Beyond this basic point, various questions remain open. Is remembrance different from imagination, or is it only the mind's perception of the truth-value of the remembered content that distinguishes the two?[4] Does one experience the recall of information as a subjectively embodied experience—through the sense-memory of hearing a lecture, reading a book, or learning a song—or is there a different mechanism of recall at work?[5] To what degree is memory fundamentally a visual phenomenon?[6]

Classical Western philosophers such as Aristotle and Augustine struggled with these problems, as Ricoeur has elaborated in depth.[7] So too did the ritual theorists of early China, for whom the role of memory in ritual drove the operation of a very large and expensive state apparatus and underlay both personal and collective claims to legitimacy. Evidence on early Chinese ritual theory is spread across a bewildering array of sources, but finds its most concentrated form in the ritual collections of the Han dynasty. The following analysis traces the discourse of forgetting through one such collection, known as the *Liji*. It will not solve any of the long-standing problems mentioned above, but it will show how the intellectual assumptions underlying much of the *Liji* collection dealt with embodied memory, learned principle, and sentiment as interrelated aspects of the decision-making process; how they approached forgetting as a natural but alterable aspect of human nature, alternately threatening and, when guided by ritual, facilitating social existence; and how the need to deal with forgetting shaped the justification of ritual in early imperial China.

The *Liji* as a Source on Forgetting

The *Liji* 禮記, or *Ritual Records*, is a compendium of forty-nine essays, dialogues, and commentaries on the theory and practice of early Chinese ritual. Its origins and the dating of its components, as with many early Chinese collections, are complex and still debated. Scholarly consensus places its redaction sometime in the last three-quarters of the Han dynasty (206 BCE–220 CE), but outlying opinions exist, and many or all of its component chapters may have their own textual histories reaching back before the Han—as recent archaeological discoveries have attested.[8] Its editing was once commonly attributed to the Han scholar Dai Sheng 戴聖, who, along with his cousin Dai De 戴德, was active during the last century before the Common Era.[9] Its textual history is therefore connected with that of the *Da Dai Liji* 大戴禮記, another ritual compendium sometimes attributed to Dai De, with which it shares some content. However, Riegel and others have questioned this attribution; the issue remains open.[10]

In terms of both content and form, the *Liji* is the most internally diverse of the three works often grouped under the umbrella term *Sanli* 三禮, or *Three [Books on] Rites*. It contains lofty theorizations and practical advice; narrative histories and invented dialogues; highly original conceits and derivative commentaries. Moreover, as Ing has noted, the *Liji* collection, unlike some other roughly contemporary compendia, does not seek to create a textual microcosm reflecting a particular vision of the phenomenal universe.[11] Its chapters are loosely connected by shared vocabulary, common arguments weaving through multiple chapters, and the overarching topic of ritual in general and mortuary ritual in particular. Effectively, the *Liji* sets the bounds for an area of discussion rather than building a specific, individual argument. It preserves room for inconsistency on particular philosophical and doctrinal points, making it somewhat complicated to follow a particular intellectual thread through the entire collection.

Some mitigating factors, however, make the *Liji* an appealing target for the present inquiry. The loose network of knowledge that the *Liji* collection builds is well suited for an intellectual-historical project on forgetting, which, as noted below, comprises a range of diverse but related phenomena. Few portions of the collection address the nature and implications of forgetting directly; many, however, argue against a background of assumptions about the role of forgetting in formal interactions, creating a relatively detailed basis for comparison. The individual chapters of the *Liji* show a high degree of internal intellectual coherence; generally speaking, individual chapters rarely contradict themselves in major ways. Moreover, though chapters do sometimes differ among each other on specific points, it has been my experience that the *Liji* as a compendium is, despite its formal and rhetorical diversity, relatively intellectually consistent.[12] It therefore presents an attractive environment for considering attitudes toward forgetting in early Chinese ritual—varied enough to hint at a realistically diverse discourse, but consistent enough in its main points to allow comparison of a background phenomenon like forgetting, which is peripheral to the chapters' main arguments and yet vital to their intellectual coherence.

This observation does not, of course, exclude the occasional ambiguity on a particular point, either within a particular chapter or between chapters of the work. Many of the *Liji* chapters are clearly composites, as was normal for texts produced in early China, and the prioritization of certain editorial motives over others sometimes led their composers to include contradictory but related passages.[13] However, the general trend toward consistency suggests that apparently contradictory passages in the same chapter may in fact be reconcilable through a close reading of other passages dealing with similar points. The present work takes the phenomenology of forgetting as the anchor point for such a hermeneutical attempt; other entry points are of course possible.[14]

The Basics of "Forgetting" (*wang* 忘): Destruction or Distraction?

Like its complement, "memory," the concept of "forgetting" comprises a broad range of related but distinct cognitive phenomena.[15] Such was also true of the term *wang* 忘, the most common expression of closely equivalent meaning in early Chinese materials. The *Ritual Records*, in particular, has an intense concern with the inculcation of appropriate dispositions through ritual, as well as the opposite side of the coin—the maintenance of the emotional and mental attitudes necessary to make ritual effective. The "forgetting" warned against in the *Ritual Records* thus often refers to temporary distraction from some otherwise enduring disposition, to deleterious consequences.

> Thus it is said: "Music (*yue*) is delight (*le*)." The gentleman delights in attaining his Way; the petty man delights in attaining his desires. If one orders one's desires by means of the Way, then one is delighted without being chaotic; if one forgets the Way by means of desires, then one becomes confused and so does not experience delight.
> 故曰：「樂者，樂也。」君子樂得其道；小人樂得其欲。以道制欲，則樂而不亂；以欲忘道，則惑而不樂。[16]

As usual in Confucian texts, the "Way" (*dao*) here refers to a system of behavior associated with the ideal practice of the rites, something that a "gentleman" (*junzi*) has internalized through both learning and practice and that is therefore constantly present, if not front-of-mind, in his psychic makeup.[17] The "forgetting" of this Way that desires (*yu*) may engender refers not to its total effacement, a la Ricoeur, but to a temporary blocking from the conscious mind of something that should be a factor in all of its decisions.[18]

This brand of forgetting as distraction appears in various *Liji* passages as a constant danger to moral conduct. It can appear in almost any context and affect almost any element of the psyche. Hence, in the "Tan gong xia" 彈弓下, for example, Zhao Wenzi 趙文子 praises Sui Wuzi 隨武子 for his ability to integrate personal interest with social concern.

> "Personally, I would follow Wuzi! In bringing profit to his lord, he did not forget himself, and in planning for himself, he did not leave his associates behind."
> 「 . . . 我則隨武子乎! 利其君, 不忘其身, 謀其身, 不遺其友。」 [19]

One must thus guard against forgetting "oneself," that is, one's personal interests, in rendering service. However, even in the heights of ritual, one must guard against forgetting others as well.

> The stand-in was revered to an even greater extreme. This extreme reverence lasted through the end of the ritual, but not forgetting the lowliest, [the revered participants] gave them the leftovers.
> 尸又至尊。以至尊既祭之末而不忘至賤, 而以其餘畀之。[20]

This line derives from the "Ji tong" 祭統 chapter, which comprises a coherent and (relatively speaking) brief essay on the use of sacrificial ritual as a medium to establish social hierarchy. "Ji tong" is much concerned with the relative degrees of reverence paid to different kinds of people during the performance of rituals; the particular passage containing this line deals with various low-status support staffers whose treatment not only made the ritual itself possible, but established an analogy between the body of persons involved in the ritual at all levels and the total social composition of the state. "Not forgetting the lowliest" thus refers to the idea that the stand-in, understood as the moral center of ancestral ritual and the analogue of the ruler, should keep the well-being and proper privileges of all participants in mind at all times, just as a ruler should always be driven by the consciousness of his people's needs. The potential "forgetting" against which the "Ji tong" warns is thus another case of distraction from what is expected to be an ongoing and conscious element of the subject's psyche—inasmuch as seeing to the well-being of the populace is, elsewhere in early Chinese texts, part and parcel of being a ruler.[21]

Generally speaking, concern about forgetting in the *Liji* follows the model of the above examples—that is, warnings against apparently temporary distraction from principles that otherwise form permanent parts of the ritually informed psyche. Variation between the chapters' statements on forgetting tends to pertain to the causes of such distraction (internal or external) and the efficacy of methods (ritual, physical commemoration through objects) used to combat it. Relatively little time is given to the question of the duration of the forgetting (short term, long term, or permanent), though the collection seems often to assume that the principles in question are too deeply ingrained in the ritual practitioner's psyche to be completely lost.[22] The *Liji*'s "forgetting" thus departs somewhat from both of the models of forgetting with which Ricoeur, for example, treats; that is, whether it is a permanent damaging of the deep traces that support the integrity of the self over time, or a temporary relegation of experiential content to a theoretically accessible "reserve," plays little role in the collection's standpoint.[23] More relevant to the *Liji*'s theorizations of ritual are the physical causes of the distractive mode of forgetting; the relationship of emotion to memory, and thus to ritual as a form of auxiliary memory; and, especially, the particular content most likely to be forgotten, and the effects of that forgetting on the efficacy of ritual as a vehicle of moral education.

Embodied Memory and Physical Forgetting

That the construct of memory, and therefore the process of forgetting, was physically embedded is most forcefully stated early in "Ji yi" 祭義 ("The Meanings of Sacrifices"), one of the most explicitly theoretical chapters of the *Liji*. "Ji yi" is rhetorically diverse, combining recommendations about the conduct of ritual, anecdotes about culturally weighty figures such as King Wen and Confucius, and general references to the ritual conduct of the former kings. Among the latter appears the following take on parental memory in ritual:

> Thus the filiality of the former kings was such that the appearance [of deceased parents] was not forgotten from their eyes;

the sound [of deceased parents] was not cut off from their ears; and the hearts, wills, tastes, and desires [of deceased parents] were not forgotten from their hearts. Through the extreme of caring, [the qualities of their parents] endured; through the extreme of earnestness, [they] were made manifest.[24] If something is manifest, endures, and is not forgotten from the heart, how could it not be revered?
是故先王之孝也，色不忘乎目；聲不絕乎耳；心志嗜欲不忘乎心。致愛則存；致愨則著。 著、存不忘乎心，夫安得不敬乎？[25]

The various facets of the experience of parental memory are assigned to the corresponding sensory organs: vision to the eyes, sound to the ears, and elements requiring reason or predictive capacity to the heart, that is, the mind. I am inclined to take these attributions literally, as locating the experience of memory in the organs of perception themselves—including the heart/mind, in its capacity as a portion of the human organism that forms preconscious responses to the external environment.[26] That forgetting is placed in opposition to the filiality of the former kings seems to hint that it is an expected aspect of human existence against which the special habits of the early paragons—described as "utmost" or "extreme" (*zhi* 致)—had the capacity to mitigate. The act of forgetting (here, *wang* 忘) then becomes a function and a vulnerability of the body, including the heart/mind, in all areas in which it is influenced by outside stimuli. Within the *Liji*, the most frequently discussed such stimulus is consumption. A substantial portion of the collection addresses its management as an expression of moral quality, in both its positive aspects—as, for example, in the "Wen Wang shizi" 文王世子 chapter's discussions of the feeding of parents, or the "Wang zhi" 王制 chapter's specifications to keep elders from going hungry—and its negative ones, embodied in the austerity measures that are assumed to accompany mourning.[27] A few passages spread across the collection address the potential of consumption behaviors as drivers of forgetting, sketching a vision of forgetting as dependent on the state and needs of the body. Hunger posed perhaps the greatest immediate corporal threat to memory, as it was a likely result of the very devotional practices prescribed throughout the *Liji*. The "Za ji xia" 雜記下 ("Miscellaneous Records 2") chapter touches on the inherent dangers of dietary austerity as a facet of mourning.

When mourning, one must eat enough to stave off hunger even if one dislikes the food. Allowing a [devotional] matter to fall by the wayside due to hunger is counter to the rites; so too is forgetting (*wang* 忘) one's sorrow due to being full. If one's vision does not see, one's hearing does not perceive, and one's behavior is not correct, one does not know grief; the gentleman considers this an illness. Thus the infirm drink liquor and eat meat [when mourning]; those in their fifties do not harm [themselves] severely [through starvation]; those in their sixties do not harm [themselves] [at all]; and those in their seventies drink liquor and eat meat. All [of this] is done out of concern about [the mourner's] death.
喪食雖惡，必充饑。饑而廢事，非禮也；飽而忘哀，亦非禮也。視不明，聽不聰，行不正，不知哀；君子病之。故有疾飲酒食肉；五十不致毀；六十不毀；七十飲酒食肉。皆為疑死。[28]

This passage makes explicit several assumptions about the connections between physical well-being, sensory perception, and mental faculties. Should one's hunger become too severe, it claims, the ill effects that one's body experiences will interfere with one's power of perception, which may in turn lead one to perform ritual actions either incorrectly (*buzheng* 不正) or not at all.[29] Yet the opposite is just as dangerous. Consumption to the level of fullness (*bao* 飽) may dampen one's feelings of grief—a state that the following lines suggest is as morally dangerous as a lack of vision, hearing, or proper behavior. A certain amount of physical deprivation is, by implication, necessary in order to match the mental deprivation of grief, allowing one's conscious mind to experience it in a full and sustaining fashion. Should one take privations to an extreme, one may falter in the physical performance of the rites; on the other hand, without the physical reminder of hunger, one may fail ritual responsibilities on an emotional level by losing the single-minded focus on feelings of loss that is implied, here and elsewhere in the *Liji*, to power effective mourning.[30]

Forgetting One's Parents

Forgetting one's parents is a preoccupation of the *Liji*; yet the treatment of parental memory varies across passages in both its ontological and normative elements. The *Liji* authors seem to have disagreed about whether forgetting one's parents was a real concern, or even possible; whether forgetting or remembering them posed the greater danger; and whether the role of mourning ritual was to facilitate the latter or the former. Concerning the danger of forgetting one's parents, a quotation attributed to Zisi 子思 in the "Tan gong shang" 檀弓上 chapter stakes out the most optimistic position.

> Zisi said, "In mourning, after three days, one arranges the body in the coffin. Everything that goes along with the body must be sincere[ly] and reliabl[y deployed], simply because one must have no regrets about it.[31] After three months, one conducts the burial. Everything that goes along with the coffin must be real and earnest, simply because one must have no regrets about it. Mourning for three years is considered the utmost limit, [but] although the deceased are gone, one does not forget them. Thus the gentleman bears a lifetime of sorrow, but not a single morning's worth of debilitation. One therefore enjoys no music on the taboo day (associated with the death of one's parent).
> 子思曰：「喪三日而殯。凡附於身者，必誠必信，勿之有悔焉耳矣。三月而葬。凡附於棺者，必誠必信，勿之有悔焉耳矣。喪三年以為極，亡則弗之忘矣。故君子有終身之憂，而無一朝之患。故忌日不樂。」[32]

Speaking very generally, the *Liji*'s prescriptions attempt to ensure that mourners maintain the appropriate emotional attitude throughout the process. Failure to do so seems to imply inefficacy of the rites themselves.[33] For the short- and medium-term stages of mourning, then, in which the remains of the deceased are still theoretically visible (either directly or as part of the coffin setup), the passage warns against materialistic impulses that might give rise to "regrets" (*hui* 悔) and disrupt the focused sorrow of mourning. In the long term, however, the emotional problematic is reversed. The memory of one's parents, Zisi informs us, will never disappear, and so the sorrow that their memory engenders requires compartmentalization rather than maintenance. The exemplary gentleman's skill at managing it ensures that he will suffer no catastrophic effects from his lasting sadness. That no music brightens his parents' death day implies that he does partake of music the rest of the time.

The key point, then, is that the gentleman manages to cope with the constant memory of his lost loved ones without his emotional health and his efficacy as a social actor becoming compromised.

On the opposite side of the coin lie certain assertions in the "Fang ji" 坊記 ("Record of Bulwarks") chapter. "Fang ji" presents itself as a collection of sayings attributed to a certain unnamed "Master" (*zi* 子)—much in the style of the received *Analects*—that record both methods for dealing with the shortcomings of the people and strategies for coping with the inevitable failure of those methods. The premise of the chapter is thus fundamentally pessimistic. Small wonder, then, that its sparse commentary on the problem of forgetting one's parents emphasizes inevitability.

> The Master said, "The [stand-in for the] deceased appears in sacrificial offerings, and the host in the ancestral temple, to demonstrate [an attitude of] service to the people.[34] Keeping up the ancestral temple and showing reverence in the affairs of sacrifice instructs the people in pursuing filiality.[35] But although the people are shored up in this way, they still forget their parents."
> 子云：「祭祀之有尸也，宗廟之有主也，示民有事也。修宗廟，敬祀事，教民追孝也。以此坊民，民猶忘其親。」[36]

By the time of composition of "Fang ji," the common understanding, whether or not it represented either contemporary or historical practice, was that certain ancestral rites employed a living individual to substitute for the deceased.[37] The unnamed Master laments that people will forget their parents despite the physical presence of a figure meant to evoke them, as well as direct instruction about how to commemorate them, all held in a physical infrastructure tailored for the purpose—that is, under virtually the most conducive conditions imaginable.[38]

Can one reconcile the "Tan gong shang" passage's concern about parental forgetting with the pessimistic model of "Fang ji"? The contrast between the ideals of the ancients and the flaws of the people in general (*min* 民) is a key rhetorical conceit of "Fang ji." Might such forgetting, then, be a foible of lesser persons, in contrast with the burdensome memory experienced by those of superior cultivation? A passage from "San nian wen" 三年問 offers this interpretation a bit of support.

What if one means to associate with men who are plagued by wicked licentiousness (*yin* 淫)? Then if someone [to be mourned] dies in the morning, one will forget him by the evening. If one follows [such men], one has already fallen short of bird or beast. How could they gather or live together and not cause chaos? What if one means to associate with cultivated gentlemen? The three years of mourning will come to a close after the 25th month like a team of horses crossing a gorge.[39] Thus if one left it unfettered, it would never end. This is why the former kings established moderation and prescribed restraint [in mourning]. Once one had mourned enough to complete the patterning of one's principles, then one let it go.

將由夫患邪淫之人與？則彼朝死而夕忘之。然而從之，則是曾鳥獸之不若也。夫焉能相與群居而不亂乎？將由夫修飾之君子與？則三年之喪，二十五月而畢，若駟之過隙。然而遂之，則是無窮也。故先王焉為之立中、制節，壹使足以成文理，則釋之矣。[40]

Both extremes, the passage suggests—rapid forgetting versus unfettered memory of one's deceased parents—are possible, dependent on one's social environment; the company one keeps will determine the length of grief's hold on one's heart. Notably, the former kings appear not as an example of those in whom the sorrow of morning lingers, but as the source of the rules that help manage it and resocialize those who experience it. We might, then, logically assume that the passage's author(s) considered their environment rich in the sort of refined company that made the curtailment of mourning necessary. We might equally well imagine that the author(s), as real people, saw around them a world somewhere between the two extremes described in the passage and felt the need to account for it. A logical connection thus exists between this portion of "San nian wen" and "Fang ji," which leans so heavily into the ironic contrast between the former kings' prescriptions and the problematic human world. Both celebrate the virtuous quality of the ancients' rules while recognizing that many will fall short of them.

Although the *Liji* chapters mostly share the assumption that parents should be remembered, passages like the "San nian wen" warning recognize, if not favor, the standpoint that such memory may be socially dangerous if improperly managed.[41] A single location in the "Ji yi" chapter admits a further possibility: that the memories of *particular* parents may fall short of ideal. The passage in question offers the comments of Zengzi 曾子 on a statement, attributed to Confucius, about the relationship between filiality and the natural world.

> To cut a single tree or kill a single animal out of season is not filial.
> 斷一樹, 殺一獸, 不以其時, 非孝也。⁴²

Zengzi's commentary on this laconic statement proposes a hierarchy of filiality in which the highest degree, "great filiality" (*da xiao* 大孝), is characterized by a constant, broad-based (*bo* 博), and generous consciousness of the acts and needs of one's parents over the full course of their lives.⁴³ His explanation of "great filiality" later in the passage offers advice on dealing with a suboptimal parental relationship.

> To rejoice in the care that one's parents show one, and not to forget it; to fear the evil that one's parents show towards one, but not to resent it; if one's parents transgress, to remonstrate with them, but not to go against them; once one's parents are gone, to always seek the grain of the humane with which to make offerings to them; this is called the full course [lit. "end"] of filiality.
> 父母愛之, 嘉而弗忘; 父母惡之, 懼而無怨; 父母有過, 諫而不逆; 父母既沒, 必求仁者之粟以祀之; 此之謂禮終。⁴⁴

Poor treatment of children by parents appears elsewhere in the *Liji* as a reality that must be dealt with on the way toward moral behavior. The "Nei ze" 內則 ("Domestic Principles") chapter, for example, counsels sons' forbearance in the face of what can only be termed severe physical abuse.⁴⁵ The "resentment" (*yuan* 怨) that such treatment would naturally engender presented an obstacle, it was recognized, to earnest devotion in the realm of ancestral ritual. The recommendation of "Ji yi," perhaps shocking to those of us with modern parental sensibilities, is that one should strive simply to *fear* (*ju* 懼) rather than *resent* one's parents for this ill usage. Doing so forms part of a spectrum of filial conduct that strives to maintain a positive cast for the parent-child relationship throughout its existence, even posthumously. Hence, one is to "seek only the grain of the humane for offerings to [one's parents]," which I understand to mean ensuring that one's professional conduct as a fully actualized adult includes no service to a morally questionable employer—and that the needs of one's deceased parents thus cause no broader ill effects in the world.

Resentment is not identical to memory. It includes both a mechanical element of recall and an emotional orientation toward the content recalled. Yet the passage's opposition of "resentment" (*yuan*) to "forgetting" (*wang*) suggests that some portion of the latter is necessary to avoid the former; and the factual content of memory and the emotional state it engenders are not consistently differentiated throughout the *Liji*.[46] "Ji yi" implicitly recognizes the danger inherent in the emotional effects of the memory of specific parents and recommends what might charitably be called editing it, protecting the positive role of the idealized parent-child relationship—extended into a lifelong scale through the mechanism of mourning ritual—as a linchpin of social organization. It thereby hints that the character of a parent's memory may be changed both through and to fit the needs of ritual. Such, in other words, is the creation of ancestors; and as we will shortly see, the forgetting of one's ancestors was a focus of anxiety to the *Liji* contributors in its own right.[47]

Forgetting Origins

Ritual theorists' anxieties about loss of self and loss of history meet in the *Liji*'s many warnings against forgetting one's origins. Multiple passages approach ritual as a mechanism of auxiliary memory, keeping one in an appropriate relationship with one's past.[48] The ongoing awareness of one's social inheritance—that is, the role played by one's lineage relations in the broader social milieu—brought individual identity into alignment with the hierarchical concerns of society. Maintaining that awareness across generations was a prerequisite for moral education and, therefore, a primary focus of ritual activities as certain parts of the *Liji* construed them.

A sequence tucked in among the "Ji yi" chapter's theorizations tries to contextualize these activities historically. Beginning with a dialogue between Confucius and the disciple Zai Wo about the difference between *gui*-spirits 鬼 and *shen*-spirits 神, it segues into a quasi-historical account of the conceptual roots of ancestral ritual.

> The sages found this insufficient. [They] built palatial halls and called them ancestral temples and ancestral chambers, in order to differentiate close and distant degrees of kinship and to instruct the people in returning to the ancient, restoring the initial, and not forgetting from whence they sprang. The submission of the multitudes came from this; thus they were quicker to hear [commands].
> 聖人以是為未足也。筑為宮室,謂為宗、祧,以別親疏遠邇,教民反古復始,不忘其所由生也。眾之服自此;故聽且速也。[49]

The initial creation of ancestral ritual, we are told, served not merely to see to the needs of the deceased, but to train the populace in maintaining cultural and social continuity. Inculcating this habit of memory in turn rendered the populace more receptive to the words (and orders) of the sages. Social order thus arose from the struggle against forgetting. Moving forward, "Ji yi" ties this history into a general recommendation.

> The gentleman returns to the ancient and restores the beginning, not forgetting from whence he sprang. This is how he maximizes his reverence, brings forth his sentiments, and exhausts his power in performing service, in order to repay his relatives. He does not dare to give less than his all. Thus in the old days, when the Son of Heaven ploughed the Thousand Acres, he wore a cap with red strings and grasped the plough himself. When the many lords ploughed the Hundred Acres, they wore caps with green strings and grasped the plough themselves, in order to render service to the Sky and the Earth, the mountains and rivers, the altars of soil and grain, and the former ancients by providing wine, milk, and full vessels [of grain].[50] Obtaining [these goods] in this way [i.e., by doing the ploughing themselves] was the height of reverence.
> 君子反古復始,不忘其所由生也。是以致其敬,發其情,竭力從事以報其親。不敢弗盡也。是故昔者天子為藉千畝,冕而朱紘,躬秉耒。諸侯為藉百畝,冕而青紘,躬秉耒,以事天地、山川、社稷、先古,以為醴、酪、齊盛。於是乎取之,敬之至也。[51]

The "Thousand Acres" (*qianmu* 千畝) plays a complicated role in the historical construct of Zhou ancestral ritual. In a recently discovered manuscript, the "Thousand Acres," and its ploughing by the Zhou king as described above, stands in for the ritual heritage of Zhou in general, and forgetting it leads to the ultimate downfall of the Zhou royal house at the end of the Western Zhou period.[52] In the context of the "Ji yi," these associations help tie the construct of ritual history in with the practicalities of contemporary ancestral-ritual practice. Ancestral ritual is a legacy of the ancient sages; thus when the gentleman "returns to the ancient and restores the beginning, not forgetting from whence he sprang," he is at once maximizing his attitude of filiality and continuing historical precedent. Remembering one's parents appropriately, through complete devotion to their offerings, is also an act of restoration, recalling the ways of the ancient sages to the contemporary world. The place "from whence one sprang" comes to mean both one's parents and the social history that one's relationship with them evokes, and the act of remembering this dual place through ritual becomes the act of perpetuating civilization. In the *Liji*, to remember one's origins is thus to maintain the historically informed theorization of ritual as a mental orientation toward its performance in the present.[53]

Ritual as (Failed) Memory: The Threat of Forgetting the Rites

Ritual can help manage the social danger of both memory and forgetting.[54] Yet the rites were not, to certain *Liji* authors, a *sui generis* part of human existence. They had to be created as part of the activities of early sages that laid the groundwork for human civilization.[55] Proper training in and repetition of the rites, in the *Liji* construct, thus ensured the continuation of a teleological sequence of human development. Certain theorists recognized that this repetition had its limits. Even the rites themselves could threaten the delicate emotional balance needed for efficacious ritual performance, if taken beyond their natural bounds.

> One does not want to conduct offerings too often. If conducted often, they become troublesome, and if troublesome, they will not be reverent[ly performed]. One does not want to perform offerings too rarely. If rare, they will be lax, and if lax, they may be forgotten [altogether]. Thus the gentleman matches [offerings] to the Way of Heaven; in the spring he conducts the *di*-offering, and in the autumn he conducts the *chang*-offering.[56] Once the frost descends, the gentleman, stepping

on it, inevitably feels dreary and disconsolate, though not due to its chill. In the spring, when rain and dew have made [the ground] slick, the gentleman, stepping on it, inevitably feels timid and alert, as though about to see [his ancestor(s)].[57] One welcomes something with joy and sees it off with sorrow; thus the *di*-offering involves joy, while the *chang*-offering is without joy. ("Ji yi")

祭不欲數。數則煩，煩則不敬。祭不欲疏。疏則怠，怠則忘。是故君子合諸天道，春禘、秋嘗。霜露既降，君子履之，必有淒愴之心，非其寒之謂也。春雨露既濡，君子履之，必有怵惕之心，如將見之。樂以迎來，哀以送往，故禘有樂而嘗無樂。[58]

Ritual seems here to occupy a mediating space between the natural world and the world as structured by human social endeavor. The passage's insistence on regular repetition suggests that the rites are a foreign, if beneficial, addition to the natural human state, one that may subside without constant reinforcement and conditioning.[59] The default state of humanity, by implication, is one of unfettered forgetting, in which the key principles of social order may at any point be lost. Avoiding this fate requires a certain amount of risk, as the repetition necessary to maintain the embodied memory of the rites threatens to lead to contempt. The surest guide against this is the cycle of the surrounding phenomenal world, which produces certain emotional responses in the human body. By organizing the performance of ritual in accordance with this cycle, one can ensure that the emotional state it demands aligns with that evoked in its performers by the environment, reducing the overall mental burden. Ritual, the environment, and humanity are thus entangled in a complex relationship, in which ritual offers correction to the "natural" state of humanity but depends on the guidance of the surrounding world for its efficacy. The potential for humans to "forget" the rites is thus both "natural," that is, the default situation, and in opposition to a deeper vision of the state of humanity.

Conclusion: The Phenomenology of Forgetting in Early Chinese Ritual Theory

In the ritual theories articulated within the *Liji*, the "forgetting" that draws the most concern is the passage of motivating phenomena out of the web of factors making up the decision-making process of the mind.

These motivations may include emotions, historical constructs, moral principles, or the sense-memories of individuals. Little differentiation is made between emotional content (i.e., "feeling"), direct sensory experience (e.g., memories of one's parents), and second-order mnemonic content (e.g., learned principles or historical example); the construct of "memory" that emerges as the opposite of "forgetting" (*wang* 忘) in the *Liji* is thus akin to what might be called "awareness." This "forgetting" is generally temporary, judging from the capacity of ritual, conversational content, and even deftly chosen objects to counteract it.[60] It does not seem to imply the complete loss of its object from the mind as a whole; it might be considered a strong form of distraction.

Though one point in the collection acknowledges the theoretical possibility that the rites could be forgotten, the *Liji* compilers do not, in fact, seem to have spared much concern for the permanent forgetting of information—perhaps because they found themselves in a world where the value of preserving ritual knowledge seemed to be commonly accepted. Nonetheless, the forgetting addressed in the collection still poses a severe potential danger to social order, through its capacity not only to temporarily obscure the principles and historical examples that guide moral behavior, but also to disrupt the emotional states—such as sorrow due to the loss of one's parents—that drive the efficacy of ritual. The theorists of early China whose work is represented in the *Liji* collection thus spilled more than a little ink over the question of how to manage it.

Yet though forgetting can compromise the social order, unrestrained memory poses as much of a threat. The distraction of which forgetting consists is often brought on by sensory input, be it sensual—in the form of overindulgence, or hunger in the negative—or the lingering sense-impression of one's deceased parents. In the construct of "Ji yi," sense-memory is not fundamentally distinguished from emotion and recognition; all have the capacity to occupy mental bandwidth and thus to bring on the "forgetting" that consists of the crowding out of dispositions that normally occupy space in the decision-making portion of the mind.[61] Through sorrow, the memory of relatives can overwhelm, driving one to abandon social obligations and mistreat one's own body. Mourning ritual in its ideal form corrects this danger by compartmentalizing memories of the deceased, and the emotions that they bring on, in time and space, freeing the bereaved to devote their time and mental energy to existence among the living. Maintaining the proper mental and emotional state during ritual offerings, as the *Liji* chapters propound time and time again, is thus vital to the efficacy of ritual not just because it displays the participant's moral development and emotional maturity, but also because it allows—or rather *is*—the catharsis that enables the bereaved to fulfill their expected roles as social beings.

Beyond its other benefits for social organization and moral development, then, ritual converts the unruly recollections to which the physical being is prone into the right kind of memories. Through ritual, the memory of the deceased, and the feeling of disjunction provoked when the deceased are not present, is relegated to a controlled space in the psyche, to be harnessed and brought forth at regular intervals and under orderly conditions. Ancestral sacrifice thus both enables and combats the distractive forgetting of early Chinese ritual theory. It helps remove the pain of bereavement from everyday life, lessening the burden of the knowledge of one's origins on which moral decision-making is predicated. Through ritual, one can live in the awareness of one's history without being emotionally damaged by it.

A complex network of conceptual interdependencies thus pertains between memory, as a driver of ritual, but dangerous to it if maintained either too tightly (as when the memory of one's family members pushes one beyond the bounds of proper ritual)[62] or too loosely; emotion, as an effect of and threat to memory, as well as a necessary component and potential spoiler of ritual; and ritual itself, a vehicle for managing dangerous memories that depends on an unbroken memory of the past; a way to compartmentalize emotion, but reliant on the proper emotional state for its efficacy. The complexity of these relations no doubt stems in part from the nature of the *Ritual Records* as a composite text that acts more to define a realm of discourse than to create a coherent, exclusive thesis.[63] Minor and apparent conflicts between portions of such texts—the question of whether forgetting one's parents is a natural process, for example—can in fact be a feature rather than a bug, creating ambiguities that support rhetoricians in their discursive efforts.

Yet I think not all these complexities can be chalked up to the natural variance of composite texts. The *Liji* passages we have seen sketch out the bounds of a phenomenology of memory as one among a variety of mental dispositions, connected with and dependent on all the other such dispositions—conscious or unconscious, mnemonic, somatic, or otherwise—that occupy bandwidth in the operational construct of the self. In this phenomenological environment, forgetting then becomes a selective interruption of one of these dispositions, through which we can glimpse the others flow as the first ebbs; and mental functioning requires an ongoing, complex balancing of these dispositional tides through the structured remembrance—and forgetting—that ritual affords.

Notes

1. See Paul Ricoeur, *Memory, History, Forgetting*, trans., Kathleen Blamey and David Pellauer (Chicago, IL: University of Chicago Press, 2004): 19, 27–28, 30, 413, 426–27, 442–43; Mark Rowlands, *Memory and the Self: Phenomenology, Science, and Autobiography* (Oxford: Oxford University Press, 2017), 8.

2. Useful introductions to the phenomenological study of memory include David Farrell Krell, "The Phenomenology of Memory from Husserl to Merleau-Ponty," *Philosophy and Phenomenological Research* 42, no. 4 (June 1982): 492–505; Edward S. Casey, *Remembering: A Phenomenological Study*, 2nd ed. (Bloomington: Indiana University Press, [2000] 2009); Alexangre Dessingué, "Towards a Phenomenology of Memory and Forgetting," *Études Ricoeuriennes/ Ricoeur Studies* 2, no. 1 (2011): 168–78; Fabrice Teroni, "The Phenomenology of Memory," in *The Routledge Handbook of Philosophy of Memory*, ed. Sven Bernecker and Kourken Michaelian (London: Routledge, 2017), 21–33; Rowlands, *Memory and the Self*. Rowlands, I should note, objects to the above characterization of phenomenology; see 20–27.

3. On the distinguishability of memory and imagination, see, for example, Ricoeur, *Memory, History, Forgetting*, ch. 1, 5–55; on the phenomenology of memory versus that of perception, see, for example, Fabrice Teroni, "The Phenomenology of Memory," in *The Routledge Handbook of Philosophy of Memory*, ed. Sven Bernecker and Kourken Michaelian (London: Routledge, 2017), 24–26. On the manipulation of that distinction, see, for example, Maria S. Zaragoza, Patrick Rich, Eric Rindal, and Rachel DeFranco, "Forced Fabrication and False Eyewitness Memories," in *False and Distorted Memories*, ed. Robert A. Nash and James Ost (New York: Routledge, 2017). And on falsified memories, see the rest of that volume.

4. See, for example, Jean-Paul Sartre, *The Imaginary: A Phenomenological Psychology of the Imagination* (revised by Arlette Elkaim-Sartre, trans. Jonathan Webber) (London: Routledge, 2004), 191–93 (with respect to hallucination specifically), 194; Felipe de Brigard, "Memory and Imagination," in *The Routledge Handbook of Philosophy of Memory*, 127–39; Emily Keightley and Michael Pickering, *The Mnemonic Imagination: Remembering as Creative Practice* (Houndmills: Palgrave Macmillan, 2012), 43–80.

5. This is what Teroni refers to as the difference between "nonexperiential" versus "experiential contents" of memory; see "The Phenomenology of Memory,"

22–27. Nicolas Russell, "Collective Memory before and after Halbwachs," *The French Review* 79, no. 4 (2006): 796–800, summarizes several recent theorists' approach to this distinction, there termed "semantic" versus "episodic" (798).

6. Ricoeur treats the problem of memory as visual phenomenon in *Memory, History, Forgetting*, ch. 1, and especially 44–55; see also Elizabeth Irvine, "Memory images," in *The Routledge Handbook of Philosophy of* Memory, 127–39. Henri Bergson speaks of the "images" of memory throughout the classic *Matter and Memory*, but his concept thereof includes nonvisual sensory experiences; see Bergson, *Matter and Memory*, trans. Nancy Margaret Paul and W. Scott Palmer (London: George Allen, [1911], 1913), 1 and throughout.

7. See Ricoeur, *Memory, History, Forgetting*, 7–21, 30–32. Dessingué, 170–71, touches on this ground as well; see also Bernecker, "A Causal Theory of Mnemonic Confabulation," *Frontiers in Psychology* 8, no. 1207 (July 2017): 3.

8. Michael David Kaulana Ing, *The Dysfunction of Ritual in Early Confucianism* (Oxford: Oxford University Press, 2012), 220–21. Pages 219–23 of that work provide a detailed overview of the textual history of the work, complementing Riegel's chapter in *Early Chinese Texts* (Jeffrey K. Riegel, "Li chi 禮記," in *Early Chinese Texts: A Bibliographical Guide*, ed. Michael Loewe [Berkeley, CA: Society for the Study of Early China, 1993], 293–97). The summary here is based mainly on those two sources. See also E. Wang, 王锷, "*Liji*" *chengshu kao* 《礼记》成书考 (Beijing: Zhonghua shuju, 2007), 283–99, 314–37.

9. Riegel, "Li chi," 294.

10. Riegel, "Li chi," 294; Riegel, "Ta Tai Li chi," in *Early Chinese Texts*, ed. Loewe, 456; Ing, *Dysfunction*, 222.

11. Ing, *Dysfunction*, 223. Ing cites the *Lüshi chunqiu* 呂氏春秋 and *Huainanzi* 淮南子 as examples of this phenomenon; one might include the *Zhouli* 周禮, as well.

12. Compare, however, the apt warning about projecting intellectual coherence onto the collection given in Ing, *Dysfunction*, 5.

13. On the prevalence of composite textual production in early China, see William G. Boltz, "The Composite Nature of Early Chinese Texts," in *Text and Ritual in Early China*, ed. Martin Kern (Seattle: University of Washington Press, 2006), 50–78.

14. See, for example, Ing, *Dysfunction*. Throughout this work, references to the *Liji* are drawn from Sun Xidan 孫希旦, *Liji jijie* 禮記集解, ed. Shen Xiaohuan 沈嘯寰 and Wang Xingxian 王星賢, 3 vols. (Beijing: Zhonghua shuju, 1998 [1989]) (hereafter *Liji jijie*). The Chinese text of all excerpts follows that source. However, I have derived the initial digital texts from Ctext.org and adjusted them to match the *Liji jijie* version where necessary; and I have adjusted the punctuation of the Chinese text to correspond better with that of the English translations. I have referred to various other editions of the text, both premodern and modern; these are noted explicitly only when the punctuation or translation

of the text follows their assertions. Apart from *Liji jijie*, the main editions consulted include Chen Shuguo 陈成果, ed., *Liji jiaozhu* 礼记校注 (Changsha: Yuelu, 2004); Wang Meng'ou 王夢鷗 and Wang Yunwu 王雲五, *Liji jin zhu jin yi* 禮記今註今譯, 2 vols. (Taipei: Taiwan Shangwu, Minguo 58 [1969]); Yang Tianyu 扬天宇, *Liji yizhu* 礼记译注, 2 vols. (Shanghai: Shanghai guji, 2004); Zheng Xuan 鄭玄, *Liji Zheng zhu* 禮記鄭注 (Taipei: Xinxing, Minguo 66 [1977]); Ruan Yuan 阮元, ed., *Shisanjing zhushu* 十三经注疏, 2 vols. (Beijing: Zhonghua shuju, 1980) (hereafter *Shisanjing zhushu*), *Liji zhengyi* 礼记正义: 1221–696. The translations throughout are my own, but I have consulted Legge's full translation of the text closely in preparing them, and my points of agreement with Legge are much more numerous than those of disagreement. See James Legge, *The Sacred Books of China: The Texts of Confucianism, Part III: The Lî Kî, I–X* (Oxford: Clarendon Press, 1885) and *Part IV: The Lî Kî, XI–XLVI* (Oxford: Oxford University Press, 1885).

15. On the diversity of memory, see Sven Bernecker, *Memory: A Philosophical Study* (Oxford: Oxford University Press, 2009), 11.

16. *Liji jijie*, 1005 ("Yue ji" 樂記).

17. On ritual and the Confucian "Way" in the *Analects*, for example, see A. C. Graham, *Disputers of the Tao: Philosophical Argument in Ancient China* (La Salle, IL: Open Court, 1989), 13–14; Herbert Fingarette, *Confucius: The Secular as Sacred* (Prospect Heights, IL: Waveland Press, 1998 [1972]), 1–36.

18. Ricoeur, *Memory, History, Forgetting*, 8, 13. In comparing their takes on the failure to act morally, Nivison describes Aristotle's approach—in contrast, he suggests, to that of Mencius and his intellectual inheritors—as something like what is implied here, in that an error in "minor premise" (i.e., understanding of the immediate environment) can obscure a broadly held "universal" one and thus lead one to act against one's principles. See "Weakness of Will in Ancient Chinese Philosophy," in David S. Nivison, *The Ways of Confucianism: Investigations in Chinese Philosophy*, ed. and intro. by Bryan W. Van Norden (La Salle, IL: Open Court, 1996), 87–90. I am indebted to Michael Ing for this reference.

19. *Liji jijie*, 304 ("Tan gong xia" 彈弓下); the full anecdote appears on pp. 303–4.

20. *Liji jijie*, 1248 ("Ji tong" 祭統).

21. On the widespread acceptance of this concept in early Chinese materials, see, for example, Benjamin I. Schwartz, *The World of Thought in Ancient China* (Cambridge, MA: Belknap, 1985), 46–47. This forgetting of established social roles is a danger not just for the ruler himself, however, but also those whose duties place them in a position of service, who might forget the practices of their present and former rulers; see "Tan gong xia" 彈弓下 (*Liji jijie*, 295–96) on the figure Rong Ju 容居 of Xu 徐.

22. A single passage in which this type of "forgetting" receives a positive spin hints at this; see *Liji jijie*, 1304 ("Biao ji" 表記), in which Confucius suggests

that the devoted student of the way "forgets [his] old age" (*wang shen zhi lao* 忘身之老). Confucius describes himself as such a person in *Analects*, "Shu er" 述而 (see *Shisanjing zhushu*, 2483). I am indebted to Albert Galvany for this observation.

23. See Ricoeur, *Memory, History, Forgetting*, 413–43, esp. 414, 417.

24. I understand the subject of the two verbs following *ze* 則 in these clauses to be the various facets of the former kings' sense-memory of their parents and, by extension, the parents themselves.

25. *Liji jijie*, 1209 ("Ji yi" 祭義).

26. On the "Confucian heart" as a source of preconscious responses to the surrounding environment, see Bongrae Seok, *Embodied Moral Psychology and Confucian Philosophy* (Lanham, MD: Lexington Books, 2013), 160.

27. See *Liji jijie*, "Wen Wang shizi," 551–52, 579–580; "Wang zhi," 382–83; "Tan gong shang," 173–74.

28. *Liji jijie*, 1100–1 ("Za ji xia" 雜記下).

29. I understand *fei shi* 廢事 to include both neglecting to carry out an action and carrying it out so incorrectly as to be useless.

30. See, for example, *Liji jijie*, 79–81 ("Qu li shang" 曲禮上); 202 ("Tan gong shang" 彈弓上); 943 ("Shao yi" 少儀); 1089 ("Za ji xia" 雜記下); 1269 ("Zhongni yan ju" 仲尼燕居).

31. I take this to mean that one should not hold back any of the burial accoutrements due to one's parent out of greed, nor should one include overly valuable materials that misrepresent the status of one's parent.

32. *Liji jijie*, 170 ("Tan gong shang" 彈弓上).

33. See the discussion of an excerpt from the "Za ji xia" 雜記下 chapter above.

34. The previous clause follows Zheng Xuan as cited in *Liji jijie*, 1289 ("Fang ji" 坊記). See also Wang and Wang, *Liji jin zhu jin yi*, 680.

35. The translation of this sentence closely follows the commentary in Wang and Wang, *Liji jin zhu jin yi*, 680.

36. *Liji jijie*, 1289 ("Fang ji" 坊記).

37. For a dedicated treatment, see Michael Carr, "The *Shi* 'Corpse/Personator' Ceremony in Early China," in *Reflections on the Dawn of Consciousness: Julian Jaynes's Bicameral Mind Theory Revisited*, ed. Marcel Kuijsten (Henderson, NV: Julian Jaynes Society, 2006), 343–416 (esp. 364–75, for a review of early Chinese sources). I favor the term *stand-in*, since the customary use of a descendant from two generations after the deceased suggests that resemblance was not a priority; see *Liji jijie*, 72–73 ("Qu li shang" 曲禮上); 542 ("Tan gong shang" 彈弓上); both points cited in Carr, 372–74.

38. A later passage in "Fang ji" 坊記 confirms that this pessimistic view of attitudes toward "relatives" (*qin*) is indeed meant to encompass deceased parents; see *Liji jijie*, 1292.

39. The reading of the preceding two sentences follows the Zheng Xuan commentary as quoted in *Liji jijie*, 1374 ("San nian wen" 三年問).

40. *Liji jijie*, 1374–75 ("San nian wen" 三年問).

41. A passage in "Tan gong shang" 彈弓上 featuring the Confucian disciples Zizhang 子張 and Zixia 子夏 illustrates the possibility of different standards for the management of parental memory. See *Liji jijie*, 205; on the careers of Zizhang and Zixia, see Sima Qian 司馬遷, *Shiji* 史記 (Beijing: Zhonghua shuju, 1959), 144–45 ("Zhou ben ji 周本纪"); 2185, 2202–5 ("Zhongni dizi liezhuan" 仲尼弟子列传).

42. *Liji jijie*, 1227 ("Ji yi" 祭義). *Da Dai Liji*, "Zengzi da xiao" 曾子大孝, closes with the same quote, albeit with slightly different wording; see Huang Huaixin 黃懷心, Kong Deli 孔德立, and Zhou Haisheng 周海生, *Da Dai Liji huijiao jizhu* 大戴禮記彙校集注, 2 vols. (Xi'an: Sanqin, 2005), 542.

43. Zengzi, an important character in and one putative author of the *Classic of Filial Piety* (*Xiaojing*), was strongly associated with the concept of *xiao*; see William Boltz, "Hsiao ching 孝經," in *Early Chinese Texts*, ed. Loewe, 141–42; Soon-ja Yang, "The Reconciliation of Filial Piety and Political Authority in Early China," *Dao* 16, no. 2 (2017): 192n5.

44. *Liji jijie*, 1228 ("Ji yi" 祭義).

45. *Liji jijie*, 737–38 ("Nei ze" 內則).

46. In this regard, it is of note that *ai* 愛, "caring," and *ju* 懼, "fear," are characterized as opposing sentiments elsewhere in the *Liji*; see *Liji jijie*, 606–7 ("Li yun" 禮運).

47. On creating socially efficacious ancestors from the dead, see, for example, Meyer Fortes, "Some Reflections on Ancestor Worship in Africa," in *African Systems of Thought*, ed. Fortes and Germaine Dieterlen (Oxford: Oxford University Press for the International African Institute, 1965), 124–29 (cited in Jon B. Hageman and Erica Hill, "Leveraging the Dead: The Ethnography of Ancestors," in *Archaeology of Ancestors: Death, Memory, and Veneration*, ed. Hill and Hageman [Gainesville: University Press of Florida, 2016], 6); Rosana Waterston, *Paths and Rivers: Sa'dan Toraja Society in Transformation* (Leiden: Brill, 2009), 374.

48. Typically, this takes the form of appeals to maintain the organizational force of kinship; see, for example, *Liji jijie*, 575 ("Wen Wang shi zi" 文王世子).

49. *Liji jijie*, 1220 ("Ji yi" 祭義); the dialogue begins on p. 1218.

50. The translation of this sentence follows the commentary in *Liji jijie*, 1222 ("Ji yi" 祭義), as well as the gloss of 齊 as 齍 quoted from the *Shiwen* therein.

51. *Liji jijie*, 1222 ("Ji yi" 祭義). The combination of these lines into one paragraph follows the Ctext.org version.

52. The "Thousand Acres" (*qian mu* 千畝) was, in theory, an agricultural facility established at the beginning of the Western Zhou to provide for state

sacrifices. Centuries later, it would become the site of a disastrous battle that ushered in the end of Zhou power. Thanks to this juxtaposition, it eventually came to represent the dangers of forgetting ritual traditions. Chapter 2 of Vogt, *Kingship, Ritual, and Royal Ideology in Western Zhou China*, forthcoming from Cambridge University Press, addresses this phenomenon in some detail and translates the relevant portion of the *Xinian manuscript. The full manuscript is available in Qinghua daxue chutu wenxian yanjiu yu baohu zhongxin 清華大學出土文獻研究與保護中心 (Li Xueqin 李學勤, ed.), *Qinghua daxue cang Zhanguo zhujian* 清華大學藏戰國竹簡, vol. ("Xinian" 系年) (Shanghai: Shanghai wenyi, 2011). Yuri Pines, "Zhou History and Historiography: Introducing the Bamboo Manuscript Xinian," *T'oung Pao* 100, no. 4–5 (2014): 287–324, provides a detailed English-language introduction. (The title is here prefaced with an asterisk to indicate that it was set by modern editors, a practice originating, I believe, with Richter; see e.g., Matthias L. Richter, *The Embodied Text: Establishing Textual Identity in Early Chinese Manuscripts* [Leiden: Brill, 2013]).

53. Occasionally, the metaphor of the "root" (*ben* 本), rather than "from whence one sprang" (*qi suo zi sheng* 其所自生), expresses this idea in the *Liji*. See, for example, the account of the burial of Taigong Wang 太公望 and the first several lords of Qi 齊 in *Liji jijie*, 183–85 ("Tan gong shang" 檀弓上); as well as 1213–14 ("Ji yi" 祭義) and 1001–2 ("Yue ji" 樂記). The latter two locations are somewhat less clear-cut; the phrasing leaves open the possibility that the "root" there refers to the basic principles driving ritual and music, respectively.

54. On ritual as an aid to memory, see, for example, Jan Assmann, *Cultural Memory and Early Civilization: Writing, Remembrance, and Political Imagination* (Cambridge: Cambridge University Press, 2011), 3–4, 39–44. On the ritual management of forgetting in an early Chinese context, see Brashier, *Ancestral Memory*, 64–65.

55. See, for example, *Liji jijie*, 587–88 ("Li yun" 禮運); the relevant passage is translated in Ing, *Dysfunction*, 108–9.

56. The rites known as *di* and *chang* were understood, here and elsewhere in the *Liji*, to mark the chronology of state ritual through their associations with the seasons; see also *Liji jijie*, 902–04 ("Da zhuan" 大傳); 346–47 ("Wang zhi" 王制). On the earlier history of these terms for ritual techniques—which, especially in the case of *di*, can vary substantially from their *Liji* constructs—see Vogt, *Kingship, Ritual, and Royal Ideology*; see also Liu Yu 刘雨, "Xi Zhou jinwen zhong de jizuli" 西周金文中的祭祖礼, *Kaogu xuebao* 考古学报, no. 4 (1989): 496–98, 511, 515.

57. This reading of the pronoun *zhi* in the phrase 如將見之 follows Kong Yingda's commentary as quoted in *Liji jijie*, 1208.

58. *Liji jijie*, 1207–1208 ("Ji yi" 祭義). The combination of these lines into one paragraph follows the Ctext.org edition.

59. This basic standpoint on ritual—that it is not innate to humanity but acts to improve humanity's state within the world—enjoys its clearest expression in "Li yun" 禮運 (*Liji jijie*, 581–99), but is a background assumption for most theoretically oriented parts of the collection (see, e.g., 662–63 ["Li qi" 禮器]).

60. The use of objects to supplement memory is attested in, for example, *Liji jijie*, 274–76 ("Tan gong xia" 彈弓下), in which a liquor cup becomes a traditional reminder of a famous minister's remonstrance against his ruler.

61. The senses can, however, contribute to the process of memory by inducing the proper state of mind to coincide with the emotional state that memories are supposed to bring on. This logic underlies the deprivations of the mourning period, which not just prevent memory from being overwhelmed by sensual indulgence, but also induce a feeling of deprivation that goes along with the sorrow that the memory of one's loved ones brings on.

62. Ing, *Dysfunction*, 99–101, examines examples of this from the *Liji* collection in detail.

63. On the prevalence of composite texts in early China (up through the Han) and the textual implications of their physical qualities, see Boltz, "The Composite Nature of Early Chinese Texts." On the degree of consistency in the *Liji*, see Ing, *Dysfunction*, 223.

Chapter 11

Exile and Return

Oblivion, Memory, and Nontragic Death in Tomb-Quelling Texts from the Eastern Han Dynasty

XIANG LI

In an entombed epigraph excavated from Nanyang 南陽 in 1973, it is written:

> [Your] spirit wanders alone, in eternal darkness underground, and cuts [its] connection with this family forever. How can we still hope to glimpse [your] face again? As we visited [the tombs of] former ancestors, we longed for you with all our hearts. Several times we increased offering and incense, mourning for our deceased kin. Qu, you did not recognize your ancestors, only running east and west, crying and weeping; after a long time, you began to follow them, while still turning back from time to time. Deeply moved, we your father and mother. . . . We are exhausting our savings [to build your shrine and to make offerings], hoping your spirit will last forever.
> 神靈獨處, 下歸窈冥, 永與家絕, 豈復望顏。謁見先祖, 念子營營, 三增仗火, 皆往吊親, 瞿不識之, 啼泣東西, 久乃隨逐, 當時複遷。父之與母, 感□□□, . . . 投財連篇, 冀子長哉。[1]

The text was written for a boy, Xu Aqu 許阿瞿, who lived in the Eastern Han period and died at the year of five (around 170 CE), almost 1,900 years ago. Just as with many modern-day authors of elegies, the producer of this text uses specific rhetoric skills and speaks in the voice of Xu's sorrowful parents. The whole paragraph expresses their missing the premature dead—the little one who has been exiled from the happy earthly life but has left his traces for the living. His soul whined and murmured, which made an island of memory rise in his parents' minds.

Yet, since the dead child was buried deep in the earth, his parents also acknowledged that their son had "cut his connection with the family forever" (*yong yu jia jue* 永與家絕). The image of the boy was erased from their memories ("How can we still hope to glimpse your face again?" [*qi fu wang yan* 豈復望顏]), and they chose to prevent the boy from "turning back from time to time" (*dang shi fu qian* 當時複遷). This mix of seemingly inconsistent feelings makes it hard to describe people's attitude toward the deceased. Although the topic of remembering and recalling often appears in the depiction of death events, there are many circumstances in which people could not bear to hold in their mind an image or memory of a deceased person, whether for reasons that are articulated or just hinted at obliquely. Oblivion is presented in many such cases as not only an unavoidable but also a necessary reaction to pain, sorrow, and expected suffering. It was practiced by ordinary people in their daily routines, recorded by them in various ways, and came to be intertwined with the effort of keeping memories, which made oblivion not a vacuum space but rather one filled by different psychological processes.

This mixture also makes it difficult to define the nature of entombed writings, in which the intentions of remembering and forgetting are often juxtaposed with one another. The very large number and the various forms of such materials have made these artifacts one of the most important subjects in recent studies of traditional China. In the existing scholarship, these findings have long been considered evidence of the survivor's intention to commemorate. Entombed bronzes, for instance, are among the earliest evidence of people's remembrance of their deceased ancestors. Although some of them were not specifically for funerary use, the bronzes that were found in tombs from the Western and Eastern Zhou periods share phrases that commemorated former rulers of kingdoms, such as "to promote their glory and accomplishments" (*yang jue guang lie* 揚乎光剌) and "to inherit [the accomplishments] of ancestors and predecessors" (*si nai zu kao* 嗣乃祖考). They serve to appreciate and honor the tomb occupants and other deceased ones related to them. The expression of memorialization is also seen in entombed manuscripts, especially those dating back to the Warring States period (ca. 453–221 BCE). In the bamboo slip texts found in tomb no. 1 at Wangshan 望山, Hubei Province (excavated in 1965), the dead ancestors of the tomb occupant are referred to as deities; they received both sacrificial products and respect from survivors.[2] For more than eight centuries, the centrality of remembrance had been kept as a basic principle when producing entombed writings.

The situation changed in the early imperial period, as the practice of removing the deceased from memory became much more explicit during the first two centuries of that era. Evidence of intentional forgetting (or obliviating) can be observed in popular entombed documents, including "tomb-informing texts" (*gaodice* 告地策), "tomb inventory lists" (*qiance* 遣冊), "plot-purchasing writs" (*maidiquan* 買地券), and so forth. Some basic information about the dead is left unmentioned in these materials, such as their social status, their moral achievements, or their position in the lineage. Producers of these artifacts appear to be more concerned with the feelings of the survivors, for they make efforts to reveal the multiple or even contradictory psychologies of those who remained living, where the silence about certain individuals or affairs is especially pronounced. This silence—which causes a blank space in the written work—places impediments in the path of recollection, thereby making oblivion the immediate result.

This newer tendency provides the context for the present study. This chapter is concerned with how the conception of oblivion is represented through a particular genre of entombed documents, "tomb-quelling texts" (*zhenmuwen* 鎮墓文), the largest number of which date to the Eastern Han dynasty (25–220 CE).[3] The texts are often found on the outside of small unglazed pottery jars excavated from a few late Han and Jin dynasty (ca. 130–400 CE) tombs.[4] They are among the most representative indicators of how people forgot a dead person. Most of these texts and objects were produced out of pragmatic consideration, which means that the producers or their sponsors followed not only the official ideology of the society but also their own personal preferences. They did not hide their individual attitude toward the dead but chose to announce it, though it might be an unusual or even a maverick choice. Given the relatively large number of tomb-quelling texts that have been excavated, they can also be employed to understand the typical psychology and practices during a certain time period. Used widely among different areas and groups, these artifacts add to our knowledge of how the majority of the society thought about their lives and how they would express that. To what extent did people treat their deceased relatives or friends as part of the past, which had already been exiled from their day-to-day experience? In what sense was oblivion an active construct in ancient China—one that implied people attempted to keep or build certain kinds of order—both for individuals and society? These are the questions that will be addressed in my discussion below.

Oblivion Materialized, Oblivion Textualized: Sources for Understanding Chinese Death Events

Scholars of ancient history often face difficulties when deciding which materials to use. Many have argued that since oblivion was a common phenomenon in the premodern world, almost all types of historical remains can add to our knowledge about it.[5] This is not to say that our present research should have so wide a scope. Instead, to reach each layer of *oblivion*, it is necessary to make sure that the evidence "can reflect the earlier implication of such a notion, before it is synthesized into a single chronicle, fictional or scholarly."[6] Because oblivion is a specific activity that becomes visible through the *missing part* of the past, it is unjustifiable to take detailedness as the criteria for selecting materials: the more details they provide, the fewer "blanks"—the objects we are looking into—they could leave. Blankness comes at the cost of exhaustive descriptions, which makes it possible to identify the unknown part of human experience.

It is also unreasonable to take authoritativeness as the basic standard for choosing primary sources. Even though the makers of the material might have a reputation in historical writing (e.g., Sima Qian and Ban Gu, who have long been admired for their documentation of history), this does not mean that they can provide what we need. These producers and writers were not the ones who experienced the process of *oblivion* in real circumstances. They introduced logic and order into events, wherein the respect for certain social norms and established rules was unavoidable. The narrative of a real participant may reveal the disordered or even self-contradictory elements in a particular event, which is usually more reflective of the real situation. What has shaped people's memory is not necessarily their intention to obey the unified principle of a larger community. In many cases, the real context of oblivion is the mixture of multiple voices that all reside in a single mind and are expressed by only one person.

This requires us to turn to excavated materials for help. Such sources, including entombed vessels, images, and documents, as well as other archaeological finds, provide new perspectives for interpreting the human psychology and practices in early China. What deserves more attention among these artifacts are the entombed epigraphs of pragmatic forms. Such materials, according to Timothy M. Davis, include three major categories: burial plot-purchasing contracts, grave inventory lists, and tomb-quelling texts.[7] The majority of them have been discovered in the real tomb space (i.e., within chambers of the tomb proper or an underground passageway of the tomb), while some appear to have been used as ritual tools in mortuary ceremonies.

One feature of these epigraphs is that they contain both material and textual elements that are equally important. If we have a look at the material carrier of these documents, it is easy to notice that the raw material can be either expensive or cheap: wood, clay, lead, iron, brick, or tile. In some circumstances, the raw material was made into a vessel to bear the written work. In other situations, texts were written on the material directly. The textual elements of such epigraphs are also informative, as they cannot be regarded as sharing the same tradition as received texts—the works of "learned men." Since many of the epigraphs have been found in the tombs of commoners, it can be argued that they were not made to serve the elite class who controlled the production of most classics. Also, because the language of many entombed epigraphs is colloquial and unmodified, it is a reasonable assumption that they were made and used by commoners and ritual specialists who were not sufficiently trained in writing. These entombed objects, therefore, could be useful in understanding the mortuary activity of nonelites in ancient China.

Eastern Han China witnessed the flourishing of many types of entombed epigraphs. Tomb-quelling texts, with the largest number appearing in the late first century and the entire second century CE, are particularly unique in reflecting how people forgot, remembered, and commemorated the deceased.[8] Though they are called "tomb-quelling texts" nowadays and have been considered to bear the function of quelling underground evils, the role played by such artifacts in real funerals was not limited to the physical force of quelling. These materials are significant in reflecting what commoners were most likely to say when confronted with the death of someone they knew. Since they indicate the real situation of "forgetting the dead" on various levels, tomb-quelling texts are among the most honest indicators of a particular form of oblivion.

Because most tomb-quelling texts do not reflect the social role of a dead person, there are limited political connotations attached to them. This is why I believe that they were used by individual people or families to express their true feelings about death, dying, and the dead. Both the material carrier and textual content of the quelling documents show that they served for relatively private uses, which made them short on expressing lofty ideologies. Since many tomb-quelling texts have been discovered on poorly made vessels (usually clay or pottery bottles), they are very different from writings that were produced to preserve collective memories, such as stone or bronze inscriptions. One example is the tomb-quelling jars found in the tomb M5 of the Tongguan-Diaoqiao 潼關-吊橋 cemetery, Shaanxi Province. All of the jars with tomb-quelling texts on their surfaces are made of unpolished gray pottery rather than precious material. However, according to the scale of the entire tomb and the quality of the other entombed products, the grave belongs to the grand lieutenant (the official of *Taiwei* 太尉) of Eastern Han, Yang Zhen 楊震 (54–124 CE).[9] The quality of the tomb-quelling vessels does not necessarily indicate the social significance of the tomb occupants, and it cannot perfectly reflect the requirement of social hierarchies, political obligations, or moral principles. Made of cheap and plain material, the vessels reveal the fragile side of the relationship between the living and the dead—that the deceased are to be trivialized, ignored, and forgotten.

Meanwhile, "oblivion" is explicitly expressed in tomb-quelling texts as an integral part of them. Although many other entombed documents only hint at the idea of oblivion, tomb-quelling texts mention it directly in their language. Producers of tomb-quelling texts often used formulaic expressions to convey oblivion, such as "longtime forgetting" (*chang xiang wang* 長相亡/忘) and "do not remember/miss each other" (*wu xiang nian/wu xiang si* 無相念/無相思).[10] These phrases mostly appear in the documents as part of a conversation. In a fragmented text written in 166 CE, the phrase "longtime forgetting" appears as one person's exhortation to another:

> The longtime forgetting . . . Leave [some places] and remove the calamity. Do not let *fuchong* . . . Move to another place . . . and let the posterity transfer . . .
> 長相亡 . . . 兄去□□除央, 復重不 . . . 移他鄉 . . . 使子孫轉 . . . ¹¹

It is very possible that the subject and object of that "longtime forgetting" are mentioned in the missing text, which makes the quoted paragraph a logical whole. Another example specifies who the two sides are.

> The living belong to the West Chang'an, the dead belong to the East Taishan. Do not remember each other during happiness. Do not miss each other during bitterness.
> 生人屬西長安, 死人屬東大山, 樂無相念, 苦無相思。¹²

The conversation takes place between the dead and the survivors. Both of them are required to avoid "remembering/missing each other," which separates the two and prevents them from the feeling of closeness. This psychological estrangement is strengthened by geographical segregation. The dead and survivors are arranged in different areas: the "West Chang'an" 西長安 signifies an affluent society in the earthly world, while the "East Taishan" 東大山 is the location of the underworld courts and offices.¹³ The concept of oblivion is therefore presented as not only the mental separation between two groups of people but also their physical distancing. This is usually the necessary condition for forgetting someone or something, even based on modern people's understanding.

In addition, tomb-quelling texts reflect the multiple sides of oblivion that make the concept even more ambiguous. Although tomb-quelling texts directly employ terms and phrases with the meaning of oblivion, this does not mean that the producers of the artifacts were suggesting that the deceased should be forgotten perpetually. Instead, they acknowledged the temporariness of oblivion, redefining the phenomenon of forgetting as conditional and circumstantial: as the living and the dead are urged to forget each other when they are arranged in different dwelling places, the disremembrance is partly based on the loss of physical contact. It seems that people in the Eastern Han period sometimes reversed their own decisions, summoning a dead person for a reunion after they had "forgotten" them. A text excavated in 1972 ends with a sentence looking forward to the reuniting of the dead and their living acquaintances.

> The *hun* soul of the dead should return to the coffin chambers. They should not fly recklessly about, nor cause disturbance [to the living]. [We will] reunite after ten thousand years. 死者魂歸棺槨，無妄飛揚而無憂(擾)，萬歲之後乃復會。[14]

Although it is difficult to tell whether or not the survivors were willing to have a reunion with the deceased, they acknowledged its likelihood and delineated it in the entombed documents they produced. How could people complete this seemingly self-contradictory task, the combination of forgetting and recalling? How could forgetfulness turn to its opposite when it had already happened? Were there any conditions needed to make this possible? These questions are not clearly answered in the text, but they remind us that "oblivion" may have multiple implications in tomb-quelling texts. It appears to be a dual-faceted concept, signifying both the disappearing and reappearing of memories. It is also possible that this way of conceptualizing oblivion reflects the real situation in practice, in which people left room for the "disappeared" memory to become reincorporated into their experiences after they had erased it. The two processes were intertwined with each other.

Writings of Oblivion: From Erasing to Recalling

As mentioned earlier, tomb-quelling texts provide a new interpretation of "forgetting the deceased," such that the dead may still have chances to be recalled after they are unremembered. This aspect can be seen from the textual elements of tomb-quelling texts. The content of the text represents a whole story that contains the beginning, deepening, and the end of oblivion, wherein the erasure and revival of memories intertwine with each other throughout the entire process.

In her study of the practice of oblivion in the Roman political culture, Harriet Flower argues that the editing and erasure of memories took place within the context of each community's culture of writing in most ancient civilizations.[15] The written form has provided an expression of oblivion with the particular grammar that helps construct people's discourse and cognition; by expressing oblivion as words, phrases, and sentences, people not only convey the complicated relationship underlying this notion but also persuade themselves about it. Tomb-quelling texts are good examples to illustrate this point. Their language, using particular rhetorical and logical devices, reflects the changing relationship between the living and the dead. Survivors explicitly claim that they have good reason to erase the deceased from memory, though they also leave room for those erased memories to revive.

In terms of the cause of oblivion, producers of tomb-quelling texts argued that the dreadfulness of death makes forgetting a method of release. The texts depict oblivion as growing from the unbalanced relationship between the living and the dead that evokes fear among survivors, as the panic brought by this relationship might lead to living people's avoidance of proximity to the deceased. The dead and the living are involved in a victimizer-victim relationship—the deceased are usually troublemakers, and the living passively tolerate what they bring about. In a text produced in 170 CE, the deceased person is portrayed as a malevolent force that causes instability to the earthly world.

> The Emperor of Heaven issues an order to move [the residency documents of] Liu Boping, [who formerly resided in] Dongjun Village of Luodong Township. [He] had a poor destiny and [died] at a young age. . . . Neither physicians nor medications could cure [his illness]. There will be a few months of *chongfu*; it is during this time that evil ghosts may bring diseases [to living people].
> 天帝下令移前雒東鄉東郡裏劉伯平，薄命早（死）。. . . 醫藥不能治，幾月重複，適與同時，魅鬼屍注。[16]

Chongfu 重複 ("entanglement") is considered to be one of the critical factors that contributes to the living's intense aversion to the deceased.[17] It brings evils and illnesses, and is usually difficult to prevent because no one can precisely predict when and how the *chongfu* will happen.[18] This uncertainty, with its potential to provoke anxiety, challenges people's willingness to preserve all memories about a deceased person: if the deceased always triggers frightening thoughts about an unforeseeable menace, calamity, or trauma, it is hard for that person to be venerated and memorialized by others. No one could bear such an individual in their mind without any reluctance or revulsion.

On the other hand, the dead appear to be more powerful and aggressive, while the living are often weak and vulnerable. Once a calamity is brought by the dead to the human world, the survivors have to acknowledge their inability to control the disaster. In some depictions in tomb-quelling texts, when a punishment is imposed on the deceased in the underworld, people above the ground may also encounter health problems but may have nothing to do with their misfortune.

> The offices of the government report to the Eastern Direction with respect: since the punishment and sentence [for the dead] happen in the East, when the regular review and examination [in the underground court] come, [the living] will suffer intense illnesses on feet and knees, cry all day long, and cannot go to sleep during the night. . . . [The offices of the government] report to the Western Direction with respect: since the punishment and sentence [for the dead] happen in the West, when the regular review and examination [in the underground court] come, [the living] will suffer intense illnesses in their stomach.
> 縣官敢告東方, 吏事生於甲乙, 謀議欲來, 暴病足膝, 旦且哭啼, 夜不得臥, . . . 敢告西方, 吏事生於庚申, 謀議欲來, 暴病腹□。[19]

Similar patterns of sentences recur within the passage. The consequence of punishing the deceased, that is, the "intense illnesses" of the living, is repeated to intensify the speech, to emphasize the inevitability of the disaster, and to present the malignant deceased as an overwhelming force. Since the underworld punishment could happen almost anywhere—no matter whether from "the Eastern Direction" 東方 or "the Western Direction" 西方—the threat to living people could also occur anywhere. Helplessness therefore becomes a common situation faced by survivors. Deeper trepidation arises, and people's intimacy with the deceased gradually dissolves.

This fear is followed by the farewell between the living and the dead, which is a metaphoric expression of oblivion. In a text written in 172 CE, the living and the dead are described as heading to different domains.

> Living people travel above to the sunny (yang) realm, while the dead travel below to the shady (yin) realm. Living people ascend to the high terrace; dead people descend deep [into the earth] and conceal themselves.
> 生人上就陽, 死人下歸陰, 生人上就高臺, 死人深自藏。[20]

From the Warring States to Han periods, *yin* 陰 and *yang* 陽 were often used in daily language to refer to two types of energy essential to both the human body and the cosmos.[21] When used to mark different locations, *yang* was usually associated with the realm above the ground where people extend their earthly life, and *yin* with the underworld that remains unchangeable.[22] Therefore, it can be argued that the quoted text describes not only the valediction between the two parties but also the removal of one's trace from the domain of the other: the remnants of the dead people are wiped off from the *yang* world, leaving this realm entirely to the living. By granting the two groups different domains, the text asserts that the dead are no longer a part of the *yang* realm, that they make no contributions to the running of the earthly world, and that they have nothing to do with the lives of survivors. The living are considered to construct their own lives without the help of the deceased. The dead, with their accomplishments and vestiges denied by survivors, are supposed to be forgotten.

However, neither fear nor farewell necessarily gives rise to the permanent loss of memories. If we take oblivion as a long-term undertaking, it is easy to notice some unresolved questions hidden in tomb-quelling texts: What will happen as the current survivors die? Will they take the same journey as the previously deceased? Is it likely for the newly and previously deceased to meet each other in the *yin* realm? It seems that survivors hesitate to entirely erase the dead from memories when dispelling them from the earthly domain. A text excavated from Jiangsu Province partly illustrates this process.

> The name of the ghost of the dead man is Tianguang. The Emperor of Heaven and the Spiritual Instructor have already known your name. [You] must immediately leave [the current place] to the area three thousand *li* miles away. If you do not leave immediately, the [. . .] Officer in Nanshan will come and eat you. Proceed with haste, according to the statutes and ordinances.
> 死者鬼名為天光，天帝神師已知汝名，疾去三千里。汝不即去，南山□□令來食汝，急如律令。[23]

This paragraph is an order filled with deterrents. It deters not only the ghost of the deceased but also the living, declaring that no one can protect the deceased from being banished. Survivors keep silent over their previous connections with the dead and follow the ordinances to expel them away. This silence, probably unnoticed by the survivors themselves, removes warmth and friendliness from the relationship between the living and the dead, and thus leads to the consequence of oblivion. The deceased are absent from the living's view, and the living find it unnecessary to recall their dead acquaintances.

But there remains the possibility that living people may also suffer banishment once they die. It appears that three underground rulers, "Emperor of Heaven" (*Tiandi* 天帝), "Spiritual Instructor" (*Shenshi* 神師), and the unnamed official from Nanshan (南山□□令), are specifically in charge of dispelling ghosts, and they repeat their job once the ghost of a dead person appears. When a living person dies and transforms into a ghost, the ghost is to be expelled by these rulers just as was done with those who had died earlier. Since everyone is bound to die someday and will be expelled to another world, the realm of the dead continues to accept new members, giving the newly and previously deceased a chance to meet each other. "Forgetting the dead," therefore, seems to be a paradox. If survivors still expect to become reacquainted with the previously deceased, how can we say that they have already forgotten them?

One possible explanation is that oblivion is an intentional act that can be controlled by individuals themselves. When people find it necessary to forget somebody, they are able to "forget" that person by silencing or destroying everything that reminds them of the person's goodness or even presence. On the other hand, once they find oblivion unnecessary, they can stop erasing the person from their memories and begin to recall them. In this sense, tomb-quelling texts describe individuals as not only able to recognize oblivion but also having the capability to manipulate it. Both oblivion and remembrance can be utilized by survivors to alleviate their anxiety about the terrible nature of death, dying, and the dead, and they therefore can be regarded as deliberate choices of individual persons.

The Spatial Layer of Oblivion: Marginalizing, Partitioning, and Revitalizing

Spatial representations of death can be found in both the inner and outer design of tombs. There are already very rich discussions on the relationship between space and remembrance, and many of them focus on the aleatory nature of remembering, its fragility and fragmentation, and the utter futility of the effort to perpetuate memory by producing materials that might restore it.[24] Oblivion, however, as another side of human memory, has not been fully discussed. Although many ancient artifacts have been understood as having the function of erasing one's memories, the mechanism of their usage remains unclear in many aspects.

This requires us to turn back to tomb-quelling texts, the visible materials located at certain places in the tomb space. Bearing the thought of their producers, these documents should be read and interpreted from not only the textual layer but also other nontextual aspects. For example, the material carrier of the documents—vessels or raw material—had taken up a certain space in the tomb, and the placement of these objects is a specific indicator of people's attempts to commemorate or to forget. As Andreas Schönle argues in his study of Russian architecture, the original location of an artifact should be seen as a metaphorical element of its existence.[25] When something occupies a large or an important area, the most direct impression we get is that the thing is of critical significance to someone and that people have made efforts to restore it. If an entity is found in a peripheral place that it is even unnoticeable to most audiences, we may conclude that those people who put it here probably wanted to leave it unremembered.

But the real situation is often more complicated. According to Robert Weyeneth, at least three spatial strategies have been used in the human history to materialize memories: to control (1) the absolute and relevant location of an artifact, (2) the size or scale of the artifact, and (3) the number of the artifact.[26] All of these three methods are noticeable in the arrangement of objects in the tomb space, and the first one, which is related to the location of those materials, is specifically conspicuous when it comes to the Chinese tomb-quelling texts. As discussed earlier, the textual elements of these archaeological finds provide a dynamic landscape such that survivors often forget the dead to different extents. The spatial layer of the findings suggests a similar process. Since tomb-quelling texts have been discovered scattered in different locations of the grave space, it is very possible that such ways of placement also signify different stages of forgetting. Three typical strategies were used to arrange these materials to present the dead as a group that is to be forgotten.

Marginalizing

Marginalization is probably one of the most frequently used forms of design to show the relative insignificance of something or somebody to the external environment. In many cases, it also serves as a spatial strategy that prevents someone or something from being recalled. In ancient China, the significance of entombed products is marked by their spatial placement that indicates which product is more likely to be preserved and to invite certain memories. The tomb space is divided into several zones according to their distance from the corpse.

- The location where the tomb occupant (or the coffin) was placed is considered to be the most "sacred" because it is usually the most inaccessible and secluded part of a tomb, which bears the function of containing and hiding the body of the deceased.[27] It is often occupied by the most precious goods and products (e.g., bronzes) and those objects that are most associated with the personal or social identity of the tomb occupant.

- The other parts of the room are less important in terms of their sacredness, such as the corners or locations near the walls. They are typically occupied by cheaper vessels, such as those made of clay.

- The most peripheral zones of the tomb space, like side chambers or passageways, are the least sacred. Most remains are found fragmented in these places, not only because there were no effective ways to protect them but also due to the poor quality of these objects.

Many vessels with tomb-quelling texts are placed in these marginal areas. Some of them are found in corners of the main chamber, and others in side chambers. Among them, many vessels near the walls are broken. As the walls fell down, both the vessel and the text on it were bound to be damaged. One such case is the tomb of the Litun 李屯 site, near Luoyang (excavated in 1974). A clay bottle with tomb-quelling texts was placed in the northwest corner of the main chamber, which is relatively far from the corpse. Due to the fallen wall on the northwest corner, this bottle is partly broken and the text has become blurred to some extent (see fig. 11.1). Other products near the central part of the chamber have remained intact.[28] The marginal location of the vessel determined that its textual content would be erased or even destroyed. This, in a certain sense, was out of people's intention to lessen the importance of certain memories: although such vessels were used to express people's mourning of the deceased, they stopped bearing their memorializing function as they were broken.

Another example comes from the Zhangwan 張灣 cemetery in Lingbao 靈寶, Henan Province. In the tomb M3 (excavated in 1972), a bottle with tomb-quelling texts was placed in the northeast corner of the ear chamber of the tomb, though more luxurious products (e.g., bronze and lacquer vessels) were found in the main and front chambers of the tomb (see fig. 11.2). The bottle itself was found mixed with the pieces of other clay vessels when it was excavated.[29] Because of its distance from the corpse, it is very possible that the vessel was considered less sacred—or, less significant—than many other entombed objects to both the

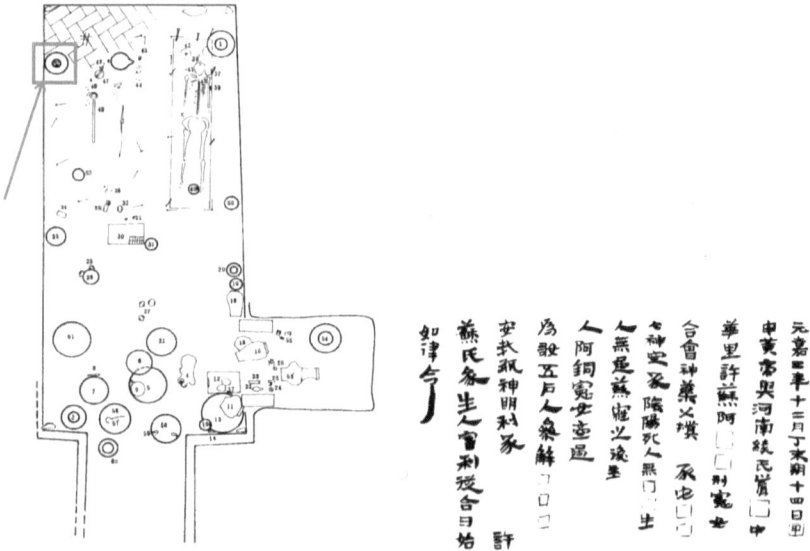

Figure 11.1. The layout of the Litun tomb and the text on the tomb-quelling bottle. The square marks the location of the bottle in the tomb space. Source: Luoyang shi wenwu gongzuodui 洛陽市文物工作隊, "Luoyang Dong Han Litun Yuanjia er'nian mu fajue jianbao" 洛陽東漢李屯元嘉二年墓發掘簡報, *Kaogu yu wenwu* 2 (1997). Fair use.

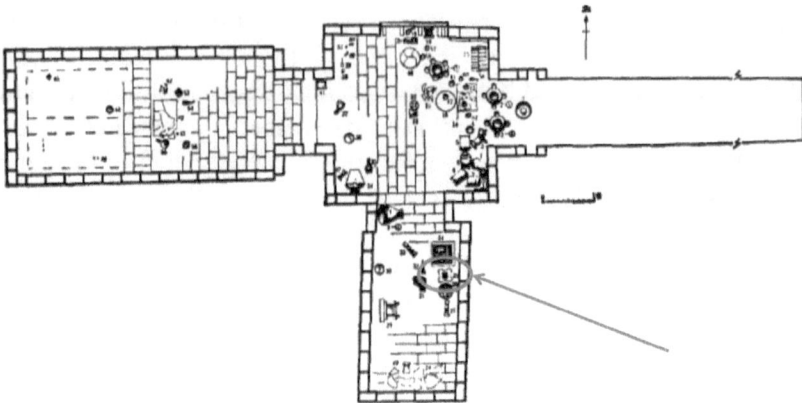

Figure 11.2. The layout of tomb M3 of the Lingbao cemetery, Zhangwan. The circle marks the location of the tomb-quelling bottle in the original tomb space. Henan sheng bowuguan 河南省博物館, "Lingbao Zhangwan Han mu" 靈寶張灣漢墓, *Wenwu* 11 (1975). Fair use.

deceased and the burial participants. First, there was no specific location in the ear chamber (e.g., tables or platforms) to place entombed goods. This means that some products, including the tomb-quelling bottle, were just scattered on the floor of the room without any physical protection. Second, since the ear chamber itself is built with earth and clay rather than stronger material such as stone or bricks, it is more likely to collapse, which makes goods in the ear chamber more likely to be destroyed. Therefore it seems that the vessel and its textual content were probably ruined on purpose. Since people did not view the information contained by the bottle as so significant in influencing either the afterlife of the dead or the everyday life of survivors, it was bound to be marginalized, neglected, and forgotten.

PARTITIONING

Different from marginalizing, the strategy of partitioning not only locates some objects at a certain place but also makes them separated from other facilities. This strategy was applied to a large number of material constructions in the Xin (9–23 CE) and Eastern Han periods. As the chamber tomb became more popular, the design of partitioning was often used in a tomb space so that different zones of a tomb could be clearly divided. The dividers included gates and walls, which physically encompassed the corpse and locked it in a particular area of the tomb. In the tomb of a Fengjun Ruren 馮君孺人 (18 CE), the corpse is placed in the central chamber and surrounded by seven gates and nine walls (see fig. 11.3). This makes the whole tomb space similar to a multilayered prison that locks the dead in the innermost, closed cell. Dividers in the tomb space function as thresholds and locks, imprisoning the dead in the tomb, partitioning them from the earthly world, and preventing them from troubling survivors.

Many carriers of tomb-quelling texts bear the function of dividers. They are placed near the gates or passageways of a tomb, probably representing the builder's intention of partitioning one realm from another. A tomb-quelling bottle excavated from Baoji 寶雞 (Shaanxi Province) in 1979 provides illustrative evidence. The tomb consists of a long entryway, a main chamber, and two side chambers, all of which are interconnected but separated from each other by brick gates. The bottle with the tomb-quelling text is located on the southeast side of

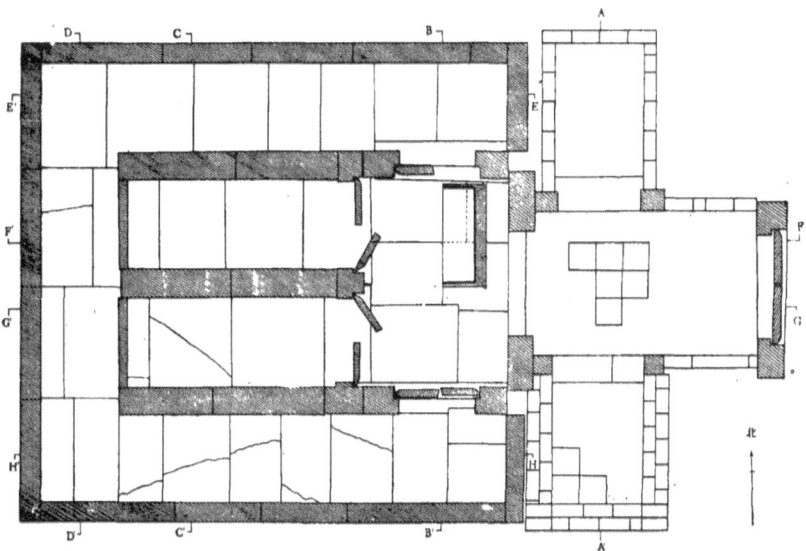

Figure 11.3. The layout of the tomb of Fengjun Ruren. Nanyang diqu wenwudui 南陽地區文物隊 and Nanyang bowuguan 南陽博物館, "Tanghe Han Yuping taiyin Fenjun Ruren Han huaxiangshi mu" 唐河漢鬱平大尹馮君孺人漢畫象石墓, *Kaogu xuebao* 2 (1980). Fair use.

the entryway, the transitional part between the inner and outer space of the tomb. During the excavating process, the text was discovered buried together with other pottery vessels and miniaturized daily equipment, such as a model wellhead and a cooking stove. They were found randomly scattered when being unearthed (see fig. 11.4).[30] Placed inside the chamber, the vessel was probably used to indicate that this specific place was exclusively for the deceased, and to partition this "dead-only" area from the outer space, the "survivor-only" zone.

This isolation of spaces resulted in the erasure of memories. Because the inner space of the tomb was separated from the outer area by such material signs, people in the living world were expected to have no connection with the world beyond. The corpse and entombed products would no longer be seen by survivors; they were therefore expected to be

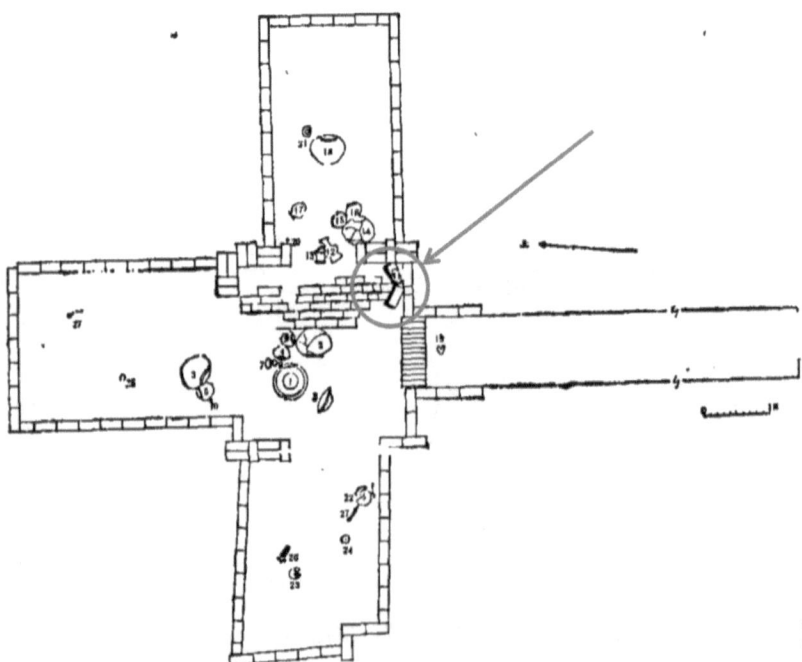

Figure 11.4. The layout of the tomb in Baoji. The circle marks the original location of the tomb-quelling text in the tomb space. Source: Baoji shi bowuguan 寶雞市博物館, "Baoji shi Chanchechang Han mu" 寶雞市鏟車廠漢墓, Wenwu 3 (1981). Fair use.

unremembered. The knowledge about the dead, carried by the products but buried deep in the grave, thus became unknown to people above the ground. In other words, tomb-quelling texts, along with the walls and gates, facilitated the process of "forgetting the dead" by spatially partitioning the world of the dead from that of survivors. They marked the gap between the underworld and the earthly life and created obstacles that prevented survivors from encroaching on the domain of the deceased to understand their life beyond. As living people were prevented from being close to the dead, their connection to the nonliving entities became loosened. As time went by, the image of the dead became vague in their minds.

Revitalizing

If both marginalizing and partitioning are for erasing the dead from the earthly world, another spatial implication of tomb-quelling texts—the revitalization of memories—attests that the deceased are only partly or temporarily removed from living people's memories: they still have the chance to be recalled. This is seen in the placement of many tomb-quelling texts in the transitional area between the tomb space and the ground above. As mentioned earlier, such a particular location suggests that some tomb-quelling texts were used to separate the dead from the living. This placement is also open to another explanation, which verifies the role played by tomb-quelling texts in the transformation of a newly deceased person into a member of the world beyond. These materials, in the minds of many burial participants, could give the dead a new identity to keep them existing somewhere else in perpetuity. In other words, they were considered to revitalize the dead and therefore might reflect the effort of the living to guarantee the happy afterlife of the dead. The deceased were carefully treated and arranged; they were not entirely forgotten.

One specific example of an area in which revitalizing took place is the tomb's entryway. It appears to be an installation separating two domains, the underground and the earthly space. This makes it a dual-facing liminal space that faces not only the dead but also the living. The entryway was also related to the rite of sacrificing (*ji* 祭), which made the place a significant component of death ritual. According to Zheng Zhong's 鄭眾 (d. 83 CE) commentary on the *Zhouli* 周禮, it was often employed as the space for the ritual of *yanji* 衍祭/延祭: "The rite of *yanji* is held in the entryway of a tomb" 衍祭, 羨之道中.[31] And this rite, albeit subscribing to the basic principle of mortuary ritual, was frequently used to deal with the relationship between two groups of living people, the host and the guests of the ceremony.

> With regard to the rite of *yan*, the text *Quli* says that the guest may visit, offer food products, and [chant] sacrificial speeches. The host delivers speeches to [respond to] the guest. Then the guest sits down. [So *yan* means] the host invites the guest to offer sacrifice.
> 延祭者,《曲禮》曰客若降等執食興辭, 主人興辭於客, 然後客坐, 主人延客祭是也。[32]

Although the quoted passage only depicts the interplay between survivors, these people are practicing in the rite of *yanji* to show respect to the deceased. Both food and chanting are offered and expected to be "eaten" and "heard" by the tomb occupant, and an ordered and harmonious interpersonal relationship is displayed before the deceased: the host treats the guest with politeness and the rules of etiquette, while the guest's behavior also shows certain degree of amiability and courtesy. The deceased are portrayed as re-obtaining their eyesight, hearing, and the ability to make judgments. They are considered as being there, "supervising"—and probably even "evaluating"—the action of the living, which makes it necessary for these survivors to behave properly in front of them.

Some might argue that these polite behaviors were part of the ritual to please the ghost rather than the deceased. This opinion seems to be reasonable, but it neglects the fact that the one to be pleased in the ritual of *yanji* was considered to understand and respect the basic behavioral code of the human world, which enabled them to become qualified "supervisors" and "judges" of the living. In this sense, the entryway of the tomb provided a space for survivors to revitalize the deceased: with the help of the *yanji* ritual, the tomb occupant regained the bodily function and knowledge that had belonged to them when they were still alive. They were, therefore, actively engaged in the activity of the living and became part of their memories.

Oblivion in Ritual Practices: Emptying and Refilling

Generally speaking, the term *ritual practice* is often interpreted as a formal behavioral system comprising four main elements: actor-participants, audiences, scripted episodic behaviors, and ritual artifacts.[34] The four components are fully identifiable in the extant record of Eastern Han mortuary rituals. Tomb-quelling texts, usually regarded as the fourth component—ritual artifacts—but also reflecting the function of the other three elements, were frequently utilized to facilitate the ritual process. In many cases, they were used as a tool for ritual participants to display the ideal relationship between the dead and the living.

As we have already mentioned, the living, at least when participating in a death event, attempted to partly forget the dead to avoid fear and anxiety. This can be illustrated by many tomb-quelling texts, which represent the process of oblivion as including two important stages, *emptying* and *refilling*. These two concepts were first used by Theodor Gaster in the *Thespis: Ritual, Myth, and Drama in the Ancient Near East* (1950). In his discussion, *emptying* signifies the attempt to remove something from the real world through ritual practices, such as in purgation (to purify a community from offense and contagion) and mortification (to suspend animation by fasts, mourning, and so forth). *Filling/refilling*, on the other hand, indicates the process of adding to/maintaining certain existing elements, such as invigoration (to secure the replenishment of life) and jubilation (to exult at the revival of a person/entity).[35] They function from two opposite directions that are supplementary to one another.

The two concepts are useful in our analysis of oblivion in the context of early imperial China, especially in terms of those circumstances related to death and dying. Oblivion, when it comes to a mortuary ritual in the Han period, can be observed in two different kinds of practices: to empty the traces of the deceased from the living world and to refill the earthly realm with these traces. Throughout a death ritual in Han times that includes three primary stages, that is, "mourning" (*sang* 喪), "burying" (*zang* 葬), and "sacrificing" (*ji* 祭),[36] emptying and refilling are most often observed in the second stage, the burying step. The action of oblivion, therefore, reflects these two different notions in the same set of ritual behavior.

Burying rituals in the Han period are widely viewed as contributing to the improvement of the afterlife of the deceased, but a bettered afterlife does not necessarily mean that the dead must be remembered and worshiped by survivors. On the contrary, a number of ritual activities served to facilitate oblivion by limiting further interaction between the living and the dead: they helped to ensure that the dead could continue their afterlife in the absence of survivors and that survivors would not need to be overly concerned with what was going on in the underworld. Tomb-quelling texts were thus used to cut off the link between the two groups. By utilizing these texts as tools to empty and refill certain ritual elements, the living participants of mortuary rites erased their remaining memories of the deceased while leaving room for these memories to revive. In this seemingly self-contradictory process, ritual participants redefined the deceased and gave them a new identity.

Among the series of activities in the burying stage, there are two smaller steps in which tomb-quelling texts were most likely to play a significant role. One was the step of "displaying products" (*chenqi* 陳器), which happened before the tomb was enclosed.[37] According to the *Yili* 儀禮, as the chariot sending the dead to the graveyard had been prepared, all of the spirit objects (or, *mingqi* 明器), that is, goods that were only for the use of the deceased, should have been displayed beside the chariot.

> Display spirit objects at the west of the stationing position of the chariot. The wooden shelf, *zhe*, is placed upon it horizontally. The wood to support the grave structure, *hengmu*, is horizontally placed by three and vertically placed by two. Three straw mats, or *kangxi*, are added upon them. . . . Then the spirit objects are provided from the southwestern side [of the tomb]. All done.
> 陳明器於乘車之西。折，橫覆之。抗木，橫三，縮二。加抗席三。 . . . 器西南上，綪。[38]

Since the vessels with tomb-quelling texts were only for the use of burials, they should be regarded as a specific type of spirit objects that were among the displayed products. Both the vessels and texts were therefore exhibited in front of funeral participants for them to look at. But this step was not solely for the aim of exhibiting entombed products. Rather, during the process of exhibition, another ritual happened just beside the display. The activity of "dispelling ghosts" (*qugui* 驅鬼) followed a conventionalized pattern of emptying, aiming at expelling evils from both the living and the dead.

> The *fangxiangshi* wears fur of bear. He has four golden eyes, black top and red skirts. He has a dagger axe in his hands and waves shields. . . . When people arrive at the graveyard,

before the coffin is buried, [*fangxiangshi*] uses his dagger axe to strike four directions to dispel the ghost *fangliang*.
方相氏掌蒙熊皮，黃金四目，玄衣朱裳，執戈揚盾，... 及墓，入壙，以戈擊四隅，驅方良。[39]

Although many scholars tend to treat "displaying products" and "dispelling ghosts" as two different procedures, I would argue that the former should be seen as an important part of the latter because of the involvement of tomb-quelling texts in both of them. Many tomb-quelling texts contain exorcistic content in both their textual and nontextual elements. As they were displayed beside the tomb, the textual content was visible to the funeral audience and could make them understand the importance of exorcism in the ritual. The pigment of the texts, made of cinnabar granules (*zhusha* 朱砂), was also believed to have the force of quelling evils. It was considered to represent the positive power of the cosmos, *yang* 陽, which belongs to the earthly world and has the potential to suppress the negative power, *yin* 陰, the basic component of the underworld and the deceased. Here, the emptying function of tomb-quelling texts was represented as the combination of dispelling and repressing. Its mechanism imitated the work of an exorcist, which cleansed the ritual space and prevented evil components from appearing before ritual participants.

It was in these circumstances that oblivion came to appear. As tomb-quelling texts helped to remove evil elements from death ritual, they also helped to erase some negative aspects of the deceased from living people's memories. In the Han period, it was widely believed that harmfulness was an essential feature of the dead. People often said that after a person dies, they become ghosts, keep their consciousness, and come to harm other people ("*shiwei rensi weigui, youzhi, neng hairen*" 世謂人死為鬼，有知，能害人).[40] However, no matter how vicious a dead person could be, there remained the possibility that they might be forgiven in certain ways. Tomb-quelling texts, facilitating the exorcism practice that dispelled those ghosts away, helped people to pardon the deceased: although the death of somebody may bring about disasters, such calamities can be removed by using these objects. Once the chaos disappears from the earthly world, there is no need to mention it or recall it. The image of the dead therefore appears harmless to survivors. Their dangerous qualities are pardoned and dismissed, while their innocuous characteristics remain there.

Oblivion as a way of refilling is also seen in the ritual of burying. Although tomb-quelling texts could only be read and viewed by survivors before they were buried, once they were placed deep in the tomb space, the artifacts instead began to impact the members of the underworld. The texts were often expected to help the dead revive in a metaphorical sense, bearing words of celebrations about the deceased being able to obtain a new way of living in their current dwelling place. For instance, a sentence was discovered on five bottles from the tomb M2 of the Tongguan-Diaoqiao cemetery in Shaanxi (excavated in 1959).

> The *xionghuang* in the bottle is beneficial to sons and grandsons [because it makes the dead] peaceful under the earth
> 中央雄黃利子孫安土.[41]

According to the existing scholarship, the material *xionghuang* 雄黃 was considered a medicine with magical power in the Han period.[42] Many practitioners of early Taoism viewed it as an essential material in alchemy, which was used for prolonging the lives of ordinary people. In the *Baopuzi* (fourth century CE), *xionghuang* is described as one of the five most important minerals that were used to revitalize the dead.

> The "five minerals" are *dansha*, *xionghuang*, *baifan*, *zengqing*, and *cishi*. . . . Take one *liang* pile of each of them, and carry them by different vessels. If you want to make the dead alive and the deceased person has been dead for less than three days, you should take one *daogui* pile of the compound to mix with water, and use it to wash the dead body. Then you should pour another one *daogui* pile of the mixture into his/her mouth, then the dead one will immediately revive.
> 五石者, 丹砂、雄黃、白礬、曾青、慈石也。 . . . 色各一兩, 而異器盛之。欲起死人, 未滿三日者, 取青丹一刀圭和水, 以浴死人, 又以一刀圭發其口內之, 死人立生也。[43]

It appears that *xionghuang* helps to revive the dead by filling them with new energy. Since the dead body is required to be washed thoroughly, the significance of this practice can be understood as giving a new identity to the deceased. The old personality becomes diluted in the *xionghuang* water, through which a new person comes into the earthly world.

This further substantiates the power of tomb-quelling texts in adding to new memories about the deceased. Although the dead, with the danger and chaos they bring, are bound to be partly removed from the world of the living, they are able to return to people's memories because they can obtain a new, harmless identity with the help of tomb-quelling texts. Used as significant tools in the ritual of revival, the texts played an important part in the process of redefining the deceased person. They had their power displayed through both textual and nontextual components, and were utilized by funeral participants to refill the dead with the energy and characteristics of a living entity. In this process, the old identity of the dead was erased, which closed a chapter of one's life but also pushed the seemingly "dead" person into a new phase, a phase where the deceased reobtained the opportunity to create new experiences for those still alive.

Conclusion

It is observable that oblivion had its specific practical history in ancient China. In the context of death events, the idea of forgetting penetrated the real practice of ordinary people. While it could be expressed either consciously or unconsciously, the intentional aspect of oblivion came to be more explicitly articulated during the Eastern Han period. People appeared to have reached a consensus about oblivion, which could be noticed from a wide range of activities they promoted. Tomb-quelling texts, as both a ritual tool and an entombed product, provide evidence that people forgot the deceased through a process: once oblivion was provoked by certain circumstances, it came to be facilitated by human intervention, and then became intertwined with remembrance. As a result, the Eastern Han conception of oblivion was presented as not only a compound of various feelings but also an intersection in the road toward more than one direction: living people could determine their way to go—to keep the dead *remembered*, or to have them *forgotten*, or *partly remembered and partly forgotten*. Once they stepped on their road and found the direction disappointing, they could return to the intersection and make the choice again, as the object of forgetting and remembering—the dead—were supposed to be always waiting there.

    This is how, through the reversal of an event that seemed to have elapsed, people could release themselves from death anxiety. People found themselves victorious over death when making efforts to redefine the dead. Those who already passed away, whether they experienced a natural death or a violent one, were thought to be "suspended" somewhere, waiting to be exiled to another realm or to return to the side of their loved ones. Death was, therefore, considered as an indefinite state, where the living retained the ability to determine where the deceased would go. In that sense, the relationship between the living and the dead appears to be, at least to some extent, reconciled: the dead do not always leave living ones depressed, and the living help to keep the deceased ones undisturbed.

This reconciliation partly explains why people in the Eastern Han were so expressive on the topic of dying and vanishing. Modern readers have already observed the passion of writers of that period when touching on these sorrowful themes, and many recent scholars have attributed it to the specific socioreligious environment, which is often described as the intermixture of various religions that persuaded people to pursue happiness in their afterlife. But I would like to offer another explanation that is based on my analysis of entombed products, especially tomb-quelling texts. It is perhaps the subtle connection between death and other social phenomena that made those Eastern Han authors courageous enough to talk about the end of one's life, the perishing of a precious object, or the ultimate failure of a splendid event. In his famous piece, "The Poem of Seven Sorrows" ("Qi'ai shi" 七哀詩), Wang Can 王粲 (177–217 CE) bemoaned:

> Again I have to abandon my Central Empire
> Heading to the area of barbarians.
> My loved ones mourned, my friends followed.
> And I saw nothing as I left
> Despite the white bones strewn all over the land.
> 複棄中國去，委身適荊蠻。
> 親戚對我悲，朋友相追攀。
> 出門無所見，白骨蔽平原。

The poet portrays various kinds of loss—the loss of his motherland, his friends and loved ones, and the lives of his people. It is difficult to see such a dense description of vanishment in literary works from earlier periods, though the three aspects of loss were also part of ordinary people's lives in those eras. Considering the specific importance of forgetting in the daily practice of individuals in his time period, it is probably the improved relationship between the living and the dead that prepared the poet to frankly approach his subject.

Notes

1. The original text is from Nanyang shi bowuguan 南陽市博物館, "Nanyang faxian Dong Han Xu Aqu muzhi huaxiangshi" 南陽發現許阿瞿墓誌畫像石, *Wenwu* 文物 8 (1974): 73–75, 41. My English translation is partly based on Wu Hung's English version in the *Monumentality in Early Chinese Art and Architecture* (Stanford, CA: Stanford University Press, 1995), 201–2. Some revisions are made according to my personal understanding. Other English translations of the Chinese original texts in this study are finished by me. Throughout the article, the majority of the Chinese versions of tomb-quelling texts are copied from Huang Jingchun 黃景春, "Zaoqi maidiquan zhenmuwen zhengli yu yanjiu" 早期買地券鎮墓文整理與研究 (East China Normal University, PhD diss.: 2004) and excavation reports in the last five decades.

2. See Hu Pingsheng 胡平生 and Li Tianhong 李天虹, *Changjiang liuyu chutu jiandu yu yanjiu* 長江流域出土簡牘與研究 (Wuhan: Hubei jiaoyu chubanshe, 2004), 60.

3. In Chinese scholarship, these entombed artifacts are usually named "*zhenmuwen*" 鎮墓文, "*jiechuwen*" 解除文, "*jiezhewen*" 解謫文, and so forth. In English, they are called "tomb-stabilizing texts," "celestial ordinances for the dead," "grave-securing writs," and other names. In this study, I use "tomb-quelling text" to name this particular type of archaeological find, because it indicates two major functions of those artifacts: (1) to lock the dead in the underworld to prevent them from returning and (2) to repress the underground evils to prevent them from vexing both the deceased and the living.

4. Timothy M. Davis, "The Religious Functions of Entombed Epigraphy," in *Entombed Epigraphy and Commemorative Culture in Early Medieval China* (Leiden: Brill, 2015), 92–151.

5. Gordon S. Shrimpton, *History and Memory in Ancient Greece* (Buffalo, NY: McGill-Queen's University Press, 1997), 86.

6. Norman M. Klein, *The History of Forgetting: Los Angeles and the Erasure of Memory* (New York: Verso, 1997), 7.

7. Timothy M. Davis, "Potent Stone: Entombed Epigraphy and Memorial Culture in Early Medieval China" (Columbia University, PhD diss., 2008), 15–16.

8. According to Lü Zhifeng 呂志峰, the majority of the recent excavated tomb-quelling texts are dated to the time period from 128 to 179 CE. See Lü, "Dong Han zhenmuwen kaoshu" 東漢鎮墓文考述, *Dongnan wenhua* 東南文化 6 (2006): 73–77.

9. See Shaanxi sheng wenwu guanli weiyuanhui 陝西省文物管理委員會, "Tongguan Diaoqiao Handai Yangshi muqun fajue jianji" 潼關吊橋漢代楊氏墓群發掘簡記, *Wenwu* 1 (1961): 56–66.

10. In classical Chinese literature, the character *wang* 亡 is often interchangeable with another character, *wang* 忘. Both of them can be utilized to

signify the status or practice of oblivion. For example, in the *Lunheng* 論衡, 亡 is used to indicate the temporary status of forgetting: "There were three thousand people who guzzled [liquor], drank throughout the long night, and forgot the period and time" 牛飲者三千人, 為長夜之飲, 亡其甲子 ("Yuzeng" 語增). In the *Liezi* 列子, the character 忘 is frequently used to present the common status of amnesia in daily life: "Huazi who lived in Yangli of the Song region suffered amnesia in his middle age. [If he] took something in the morning, [he might] forget it in the evening. [If he] arranged something in the evening, [he might] forget it in the [next] morning. [If he] was on the road, [he might] forget to walk. [If he] was [resting] in the room, [he might] forget to be seated" 宋陽裏華子中年病忘, 朝取而夕忘, 夕與而朝忘; 在塗則忘行, 在室則忘坐 ("Zhou Muwang" 周穆王). For a detailed analysis of this anecdote, see Albert Galvany's contribution in this volume.

11. For transcriptions and images, see Wang Yulong 王育龍, "Xi'an Kunlunchang Dong Han mu qingli ji" 西安昆侖廠東漢墓清理記, *Kaogu yu wenwu* 考古與文物 2 (1989): 45–59.

12. For transcriptions, see Ikeda On 池田溫, "Chûgoku rekidai boken ryakko" 中國歷代墓券略考, *Tôyô-bunka kenkyûjo kiyô* 東洋文化研究紀要 86 (1981): 193–278. This text is titled as "Xiping si'nian Xushi zhenmuwen" 熹平四年胥氏鎮墓文 in Huang, "Zaoqi maidiquan zhenmuwen zhengli yu yanjiu," 127.

13. See Lian Shaoming 連劭名, "Han-Jin jiechuwen yu daojia fangshu" 漢晉解除文與道家方術, *Huaxia kaogu* 華夏考古 4 (1998): 75–86.

14. For transcriptions and images, see Xu Yulin 許玉林, "Liaoning Gexian Dong Han mu" 遼寧蓋縣東漢墓, *Wenwu* 4 (1993): 54–70.

15. Harriet I. Flower, *The Art of Forgetting: Disgrace and Oblivion in Roman Political Culture* (Chapel Hill, NC: University of North Carolina Press, 2006), 7.

16. For the transcription and images, see Luo Zhenyu 羅振玉, *Zhensongtang ji guyiwen* 貞松堂集古遺文, vol. 15 (Hong Kong: Chung Chi Bookstore, 1968), 142.

17. See Anna Seidel, "Cong muzang de zangyi wenshu kan handai zongjiao de guiji" 從墓葬的葬儀文書看漢代宗教的軌跡, trans. Zhao Hongbo 趙宏博, in *Faguo hanxue* 法國漢學 vol. 7 (Beijing: Zhonghua shuju, 2002), 118–48.

18. Huang Jingchun defines *chongfu* as a situation wherein the death of one person causes the demise of another individual: if the time of birth of a living person coincides with that of a dead one, or the two persons are familiar with each other, or the age of a living person is the same as that of a deceased individual, the ghost of the dead may return and attack the survivor. See Huang, "Zaoqi maidiquan zhenmuwen zhengli yu yanjiu," 15–16.

19. The original text is usually titled as "Dong Han Huandi Yongshou er'nian Liu Mengling zhenmuwen" 東漢桓帝永壽二年(156)劉孟陵鎮墓文 in modern scholarship. See Jiang Shou-Cheng 姜守誠, "Hong Kong Collection of 'Songren' Releasing Bamboo Tablets and Taboos Custom of Burial Rituals during Hanjin

Dynasties" 香港所藏 "松人"解除木牘與漢晉墓葬之禁忌風俗, *Cheng Kung Journal of Historical Studies* 成大歷史學報 12 (2006): 1–64.

20. For the transcription, see Wu Rongzeng 吳榮曾, "Zhenmuwen zhong suojiandao de Dong Han daowu guanxi" 鎮墓文中所見到的東漢道巫關係, *Wenwu* 3 (1981): 56–63.

21. Constance A. Cook, *Death in Ancient China: The Tale of One Man's Journey* (Leiden: Brill, 2006), 24–25.

22. See Wu, "Zhenmuwen zhong suojiandao de Dong Han daowu guanxi," 58.

23. For the original transcription and images, see Jiangsu sheng wenwu guanli weiyuanhui 江蘇省文物管理委員會, "Jiangsu Gaoyou Shaojiagou Handai yizhi qingli" 江蘇高郵邵家溝漢代遺址清理, *Kaogu* 考古 10 (1960): 18–44.

24. Adrian Forty, *Concrete and Culture: A Material History* (London: Reaktion Books, 2012), 198.

25. Andreas Schönle, *Architecture of Oblivion: Ruins and Historical Consciousness in Modern Russia* (DeKalb, IL: Northern Illinois University Press, 2011), 5.

26. Robert R. Weyeneth, "The Architecture of Racial Segregation: The Challenges of Preserving the Problematical Past," *Public Historian* 27, no. 4 (Fall 2005): 11–44.

27. According to Jan Assmann, when it comes to the tombs of ancient Egyptians, the conception of "sacred" is closely related to the idea of "secret." Both indicate the inaccessibility, seclusion, and hiddenness of a certain object in the tomb space. See "The Ramesside Tomb and the Construction of Sacred Space" in *The Theban Necropolis: Past, Present and Future*, eds. Nigel Strudwick and John H. Taylor (London: British Museum Press, 2003), 46–52. From my personal perspective, Assmann's explanation can also be applied to the entombed products in early China. Although other noncentral zones of the tomb also played important roles as they were probably used for specific rituals, circumambulation, or preventing evil influences from coming in, it does not mean that their degree of sacredness could be compared with that of the space where the dead body was placed.

28. Luoyang shi wenwu gongzuodui 洛陽市文物工作隊, "Luoyang Dong Han Litun Yuanjia er'nian mu fajue jianbao" 洛陽東漢李屯元嘉二年墓發掘簡報, *Kaogu yu wenwu* 2 (1997): 1–7.

29. Henan sheng bowuguan 河南省博物館, "Lingbao Zhangwan Han mu" 靈寶張灣漢墓, *Wenwu* 11 (1975): 75–93.

30. Baoji shi bowuguan 寶雞市博物館, "Baoji shi Chanchechang Han mu" 寶雞市鏟車廠漢墓, *Wenwu* 3 (1981): 46–52.

31. "Chunguan: Taizhu" 春官・大祝. The original text is from Li Xueqin 李學勤, *Zhouli zhushu* 周禮註疏 (Beijing: Beijing daxue chubanshe, 1999), 659.

32. Li Xueqin, "Chunguan: Taizhu," 665.

33. Yang Hua 楊華, "Sui, feng, qian‐jiandu suojian Chudi zhusang lizhi yanjiu" 襚、賵、遣—簡牘所見楚地助喪禮制研究, *Jianghan kaogu* 江漢考古 2 (1999): 33–42; Lai Guolong, "The Baoshan Tomb: Religious Transitions in Art, Ritual, and Text during the Warring States Period (480–221 BCE)" (University of California, PhD diss.: 2002), 56–60.

34. For related discussions, see Michael Suk-Young Chwe, *Rational Ritual: Culture, Coordination, and Common Knowledge* (Princeton, NJ: Princeton University Press, 2001), 25–29; Albertina Nugteren, "Introduction to the Special Issue 'Religion, Ritual, and Ritualistic Objects,'" *Religious* 10 (2019): 1–13.

35. Theodor Herzl Gaster, *Thespis: Ritual, Myth, and Drama in the Ancient Near East* (New York: Gordian Press, 1975), 76–77.

36. Shen Wenzhuo 沈文倬, *Dong Zhou liyue wenming kaolun* 東周禮樂文明考論 (Hangzhou: Zhejiang daxue chubanshe, 1999), 18.

37. Li Rusen 李如森, *Handai sangzang lisu* 漢代喪葬禮俗 (Shenyang: Dongbei daxue chubanshe, 2003), 71.

38. "Jixi li" 既夕禮. The original text is from Zheng Xuan 鄭玄 and Jia Gongyan 賈公彥, *Yili zhushu* 儀禮注疏, ed. Peng Lin 彭林 (Beijing: Beijing daxue chubanshe, 1999), 735–36.

39. "Xiaguan sima" 夏官司馬. The original text is from Zheng Xuan and Jia Gongyan, *Zhouli zhushu* 周禮注疏, vol. 28, ed. Peng Lin (Shanghai: Shanghai guji chubanshe, 2010).

40. "Lunsi" 論死. The original text is from *Qinding Siku quanshu huiyao: Zibu Lunheng pian* (*Qianlong yulan ben*) 欽定四庫全書薈要・子部・論衡篇 (乾隆禦覽本), vol. 20, 11.

41. See Shaanxi sheng wenwu guanli weiyuanhui, "Tongguan Diaoqiao Handai Yangshi muqun fajue jianji," 59.

42. For related scholarship, see Liu Weipeng 劉衛鵬, "Handai zhengmuping suojian shenyao kao" 漢代鎮墓瓶所見"神藥"考, *Zongjiaoxue yanjiu* 宗教學研究 3 (2009): 1–7; Lei Zhihua 雷志華, "Handai wushi yanjiu" 漢代五石研究 (PhD diss.: Shanxi University, 2013): 47–48.

43. Wang Ming 王明, *Baopuzi neipian jiaoshi* 抱樸子內篇校釋 (Beijing: Zhonghua shuju, 1985), 78.

Chapter 12

Lost in Where We Are
Tao Yuanming on the Joys of Forgetting and the Worries of Being Forgotten

MICHAEL D. K. ING

The fifth century poet and intellectual, Tao Yuanming 陶淵明, was keenly aware of the limitations entailed in being an embodied creature with a finite life span. He found joy in activities that enabled him to temporarily forget these limitations. On the fifth day of the fifth month in 421, Tao and a few of his neighbors made a trip to Xie Brook 斜川.[1] In a poem bearing that name ("An Outing to Xie Brook" 游斜川), Tao describes the event. In the preface to the poem he explains that while taking in the scenery, a series of terraced hills jutting out from the marshland caught their attention.[2] These hills reminded them of Mt. Kunlun 崑崙山—a mythical mountain thought to be inhabited by immortals. The imposing spectacle of permanence stood in contrast to the brevity of their lives—reminding Tao that human life is transient. Tao explains, "We sorrowed over the swift passing of days and months, and grieved that our years would not remain" (悲日月之遂往, 悼吾年之不留).[3] These hills trigger reflections on finitude. As a response, "Each of them recorded their age and birthplace in order to remember the day" (各疏年紀鄉里, 以記其時日). Thus, in response to the ephemeral nature of life, Tao and his companions engage in an act of permanence—they

327

mark their existence by recording time, place, and name. The poem itself reads,

	The year begins, and suddenly I'm 50;	開歲倏五十
2	My life ebbs toward its return to rest.	吾生行歸休
	Thinking about it stirs my soul;	念之動中懷
4	And so this morning I take a trip.	及辰為茲游
	The air is mild and the sky is clear;	氣和天惟澄
6	We arrange our seats next to the far-flowing stream.	班坐依遠流
	In the weak rapids, silver bream race;	弱湍馳文魴
8	In the deep valley, chattering seagulls fly.	閑谷矯鳴鷗
	Over broad marshland we cast our wandering eyes;	迥澤散游目
10	And reflectively gaze at the terraced hills.	緬然睇曾丘
	Although it pales in comparison to Ninefold Peak,[4]	雖微九重秀
12	In looking around, it cannot be matched.	顧瞻無匹儔
	Tilting the bottle I welcome my companions;	提壺接賓侶
14	Cups are filled and toasts are made.	引滿更獻酬
	I don't know if after today	未知從今去
16	There will be another moment like this.	當復如此不
	In the midst of drinking we set free our roaming wishes,	中觴縱遙情
18	Forgetting this thousand years of worry.	忘彼千載憂
	And so we prolong today's pleasures;	且極今朝樂
20	For tomorrow they are not to be found.	明日非所求[5]

This poem highlights Tao's experience with finitude—time can feel pressing and life can feel brief, given the human capacity to reflect on things that outlast ourselves. Line 18 likely draws from the *Nineteen Old Poems* 古詩十九首—a collection of poetry Tao frequently alluded to; originally composed in the second half of the Han dynasty (25–220 CE).[6] The fifteenth poem, which takes up the theme of seeking pleasure in the brevity of life, begins with the lines, "We live for but a hundred years, yet bear the burdens of a thousand" (生年不滿百, 常懷千歲憂).[7] The idea here is that we recognize that the time we have to live is disproportionate to the concerns we often bear. Human beings are able to worry about far more things than we can actually address. We worry about the uncertainty of the future, and sorrow over the frustrations of the past. We fret over periods long before we were born and long after we die; and, building on this, we worry about things in the present that go beyond our power to control.

In "An Outing to Xie Brook," we find that the frivolity of the moment allows Tao and his friends to (at least momentarily) forget their thousand years of worry. This chapter explores the joys of forgetting finitude. It begins with a discussion of how Tao understands these limitations, and then explores Tao's attempts to forget these limitations through the enjoyment of ale, good company, and an unperturbed home. We discover the world through Tao's poetry as a place characterized by constraint, which he often discusses in terms of time. Part of this constraint is tied to being human—intellectually, we are acutely aware of our limitations; and physiologically, we are limited by a body that constrains us to a particular place. Tao believed that it is not possible to transcend these limitations, but that it is possible to forget them; and for him, forgetting them is a source of great joy. Yet he also realized that these constraints cannot permanently be forgotten or overcome; while moments of delight may be prolonged, there is no way to forever transcend time. Furthermore, while Tao's "craft of oblivion" is, in part, about constructing spaces where he can forget and be forgotten, he only wants to be forgotten by those who seek to unsettle his forgetting; in the end he can never give up the seriousness of himself in wanting to be remembered by later generations of like-minded people.

The Tyranny of Time

A recurring theme in Tao's poetry is the pressing nature of time, understood as the unrelenting change of the world we inhabit and the relative brevity of human life.[8] For Tao, time is pressing because, as human beings, we are distinct from other natural objects in the world such as mountains and rivers that seem to endure forever. Furthermore, unlike plants, we do not go through cycles of birth in the spring, death in the fall, and rebirth the following spring. And unlike other animals, we are keenly aware of the brevity of our lives. In Tao's collection of "Miscellaneous Poems" 雜詩, he explains that "the sun and moon have their revolving cycles; but when I die, I will not rise again" (日月有環周, 我去不再陽).[9] Time is pressing because human beings have one, quite limited chance to live. Yet time is also pressing in a more general sense for Tao. Time is not hospitable to human hopes. In the same collection of poems Tao states, "If you meet the right moment, you must work hard; months and years do not wait on humanity" (及時當勉勵, 歲月不待人).[10] This neglect of humanity verges on hostility in other poems. The second poem of the series reads, "Days and months toss people aside; and our ambitions do not reach their aim" (日月擲人去, 有志不獲騁).[11] The seventh poem, describing the cycle of time says, "The days and months are unwilling to slow down; the four seasons press upon and compel each other" (日月不肯遲, 四時相催迫).[12] "Days and months" in these poems is more literally translated as "the sun and moon." The picture Tao paints is one where natural aspects of the world are antagonistic in particular ways. They compete with each other and with human beings to the point that we can be at odds with these forces in the world. Time, manifest in the physical forms of the sun and moon, pushes us aside as they move on their way. Time, here, is best understood as representing not just the past, present, and future, but also a pervasive and persistent condition of the world; and in this light, as Tao says in another poem, "Human life is like a sojourn" (人生若寄).[13]

Borrowing a phrase from Alexander Huang, there is a kind of tyranny of time in Tao's poems.[14] Time passes, is uncaring, and even crushing; and as human beings we are ever conscious of our place in time. As Huang explains in discussing the notion of tragedy in premodern Chinese literature, "The Classical Chinese tragic character is ostracized by Time with an acute awareness of this exile, a reality he cannot avoid."[15] Something similar seems to be happening for Tao. As in "An Outing to Xie Brook," the world presents numerous reminders of longevity, yet human beings remain incapable of achieving longevity. This is despite the claims made by contemporaries of Tao about the possibility of not only longevity, but of immortality.[16]

The term *nine* (*jiu* 九) is a homophone for the term *long lasting* (*jiu* 久); and in Tao's day, the ninth day of the ninth month was commonly associated with longevity.[17] This double-nine day was a time where many people focused on practices they believed could extend their lives. Some of these practices involved ingesting elixirs, including elixirs made with minerals and herbs.[18] Tao often expressed a subtle skepticism about immortality, as he does in two poems written on double-nine days.[19] The first is titled "Residing in Leisure on the Ninth Day" 九日閑居.

	Life is short, yet our hopes are long and many,	世短意常多
2	Which is why people delight in long life.	斯人樂久生
	This day and month have arrived in accordance with the seasons;	日月依辰至

4	And all people love its name.	舉俗愛其名
	The dew is brisk, the warm winds have ceased;	露淒暄風息
6	The air is clean, and the sky is clear.	氣澈天象明
	The shadows of departing swallows no longer remain;	往燕無遺影
8	The sound of arriving geese echoes.	來雁有餘聲
	Ale will push out all concerns;	酒能祛百慮
10	And chrysanthemums will halt the waning years.	菊為制頹齡
	But what of the man in the rustic hut?	如何蓬廬士
12	Empty, he watches the turns of time.	空視時運傾
	The dusty cup disgraces the bare bottle;	塵爵恥虛罍
14	In vain these cold flowers bloom.	寒華徒自榮
	Fixing my robe I leisurely sing to myself;	斂襟獨閑謠
16	Distant reflections stir deep feelings.	緬焉起深情
	Settling into this perch certainly brings many joys;	棲遲固多娛
18	Why would just hanging on not count as success?	淹留豈無成[20]

The second poem is titled "The Ninth Day of the Ninth Month in the Year 409" 己酉歲九月九日.

	Gradually, the fall season wanes;	靡靡秋已夕
2	Cool wind mixes with the morning dew.	淒淒風露交
	Creeping vines will not bloom again;	蔓草不復榮
4	And trees in the courtyard are bare and withered.	園木空自凋
	Fresh air cleanses any lingering haze;	清氣澄餘滓
6	So deep, the bounds of the heavens stretch high.	杳然天界高
	The plaintive cry of the cicadas echoes no more;	哀蟬無留響
8	While flocks of geese call from cloudy mists.	叢雁鳴雲霄
	The transformations of the world seek after and follow upon each other;	萬化相尋繹
10	How could human life not be hard?	人生豈不勞
	From antiquity all have had to die;	從古皆有沒
12	But thinking of it worries my heart.	念之中心焦
	What can I use to calm my feelings?	何以稱我情
14	With cloudy ale I'll please myself.	濁酒且自陶
	I do not know about 1,000 years,	千載非所知
16	So for the moment I'll use this to lengthen today.	聊以永今朝[21]

The first poem concludes with Tao finding joy in "just hanging on," while the second concludes with Tao "lengthening the day." In both cases, immortality or longevity lays beyond his reach (although for different reasons). These poems tie together a number of the themes already mentioned, including the way that our hopes extend beyond our ability to realize them, the ways in which the changes of the world make life hard, and the possibility of at least prolonging a meaningful moment. These poems also suggest that there is no way to transcend the limitations of life. Building on Lonnie Aarssen (who is borrowing from Albert Camus), Tao cannot escape the nagging worry of self-impermanence.[22] Nonetheless, these poems reveal that this nagging worry can be coped with, and even forgotten. They offer at least one strategy for coping with the limitations of life; namely, the enjoyment of good ale.

The Ecstasy of Ale and the Intoxication of Friendship

Ale appears in various forms throughout Tao's poetry. If not *the* dominant image in Tao's work, it is certainly one of the most dominant images—showing up in approximately one-third of his poems. By Tao's time, there was a robust culture of consuming alcoholic beverages, particularly among the elite. These beverages were made from fermenting grains including millet and wheat (in the north), and most often in Tao's case, rice (in the south).[23] Tao usually drank what would be referred to today as rice wine (similar to *sake* in Japanese culture).[24] I have chosen to translate the term Tao often uses for this drink (*jiu* 酒) as "ale" since the term *wine* might import ideas and images from Western wine culture that are not appropriate in Tao's case. Additionally, grain fermentation in Tao's time often took place at warmer temperatures, as does modern-day ale production.[25]

Ale is discussed throughout Chinese literature long before Tao and is well-attested in material artifacts predating Tao by over 1,500 years. By Tao's time there were agricultural manuals, which are now lost, that likely detailed the production of ale. A century after Tao, Jia Sixie's 賈思勰 manual, the *Qimin Yaoshu* 齊民要術, outlined over thirty ways of making alcoholic beverages.[26] As Charles Kwong explains, ale came to be associated with a wide, and often divergent, array of ideas long before Tao, including "social catalyst and moral corruptor, emotional anesthetic and intensifier, later as psychological liberator, artistic inspiration and spiritual transporter." Kwong continues, "Exciting and numbing the rational mind chemically, [ale] can be an aid to merriment and an agent of social-emotive bonding if imbibed in moderation, a disruptor of moral consciousness and temporary exorcist of grief if consumed to excess. In later times it also became an intensifier of emotions, a stupefying drug facilitating political and psychological escapism, and a philosophical transporter sending one's spirit to a transcendent plane, including a proven elevation of the creative impulse."[27]

Tao believed that ale enabled him to enjoy life by allowing him to temporarily forget the limitations entailed in being an embodied creature with a finite life span. This joy often came from drinking ale in the company of like-minded people, which fostered a communion of sorts as the boundary between self and other became more porous. This is captured quite well in the fourteenth poem of the "Drinking Ale" 飲酒 series that Tao writes.

	Old friends appreciate my tastes;	故人賞我趣
2	So they arrive carrying a jug of ale to share.	挈壺相與至
	We spread our mats and sit under a pine tree;	班荊坐松下
4	And after several cups, get tipsy.	數斟已復醉
	A group of venerable men jumbled about in random conversation,	父老雜亂言
6	Losing track of whose cup should be filled next.	觴酌失行次
	No longer aware of ourselves,	不覺知有我
8	How would we know the order of things?	安知物為貴
	So far off and distant, lost in where we are;	悠悠迷所留
10	In ale there is such flavor!	酒中有深味[28]

In this poem we find Tao drinking with a group of old friends. As they drink, their conversation and formalities of drinking become jumbled. Eventually they are "no longer aware of themselves," and things beyond themselves seem to blend together. Tao states that they felt "far off and distant, lost in where they are." In his notes on this poem, James Hightower elucidates this line quite nicely, explaining that "in this state we are really uncertain about where we are, but not about where we should be."[29] Indeed, for Tao, ale serves to loosen the boundaries between things—destabilizing a sense of self rooted in a particular time and place. This is perhaps why in another poem—drawing from the *Zhuangzi* 莊子—Tao states that ale allows him to "forget the world" (*wang tian* 忘天).[30] While ale causes a kind of forgetting, however, it also generates a greater awareness of one's interconnectedness with the world. This is a common theme in the *Zhuangzi* where, for instance, in the "Heaven and Earth" 天地 chapter readers find Laozi telling Confucius, "One who forgets [all] things, forgets the world; and can be properly named one who has forgotten himself. A person who has forgotten himself can be termed 'one who enters into [unity] with the world'" (忘乎物, 忘乎天, 其名為忘己。忘己之人, 是之謂入於天).[31] These vignettes highlight the possibility of a communal self where the individual is liberated from the limited form of one thing and merges with all things, thereby allowing what the *Zhuangzi* might call "a free and easy wandering" (逍遙遊).[32] Zhuangzi is less clear about ale's power to realize these interconnections; but for Tao, ale facilitates this forgetting of the self and world, and enables a merging with other people and things.

In the same poem where Tao writes about forgetting the world, he also mentions an old friend who gave him the ale. When presenting Tao with the ale his friend "said drink it and you'll become an immortal" (乃言飲得仙).[33] Tao does not attain immortality, but ale does seem to enable him to temporarily transcend life's normal boundaries, specifically with regard to time. While Tao is often skeptical about the possibility of immortality, ale seems to allow for a glimpse into immortal life—a temporary forgetting of time's restraints. The loss of an end point to one's life is tied to the loss of a firm conception of one's self—our identities at least partially predicated on an awareness of an end; and this, for Tao, I suspect, induces a realization of a new self, a communal self that seems to endure like the heavens and the earth.[34] In this regard, ale is a sacred drink—immortalizing and sanctifying those who consume it. But the sanctification in this context is not an ablution of wrongdoing through entering into a divine covenant, as with many Christian traditions that involve wine; rather, the sanctification that occurs is a trimming away of fetters of the self that often limit the individual from communing with other things that are separated by time and space. As such, ale for Tao is a kind of holy communion; in light of this, it makes sense that Tao concludes the poem in the "Drinking Ale" series by stating that "In ale there is such flavor."

The themes of ale and companionship are central to Tao's work. Not only does Tao repeatedly state his desire to find friends to drink with, or his enjoyment when he finds such friends, but in his poetry he parallels the effects of ale with the effects of good company. In the first poem that Tao writes in a series "imitating old poems" 擬古, he describes his interaction with a now distant friend. In previous meetings, he says,

"Without saying a word, our hearts were drunk; and not from sharing a cup of ale" (未言心相醉, 不在接杯酒).[35] For Tao, friendship is intoxicating, and true friends understand each other without having to say a word. Much like ale, companionship interrupts the tyranny of time; good conversation facilitates enjoyable forgetting. This is nicely illustrated in a lengthy poem Tao writes about "Returning to Live on the Farmstead" 歸園田居. In 405 CE, Tao Yuanming left the last government post he held and spent the rest of his life as a farmer. This poem appears to have been written early in this period. The last few lines are relevant to the point about companionship and time; however, I quote the poem in its entirety, as it raises issues addressed later in this chapter (as well as highlighting issues examined previously).

	When young I did not fit in with the common tune,	少無適俗韻
2	My nature was rooted in a love of hills and mountains.	性本愛丘山
	By mistake I fell into a dusty net,	誤落塵網中
4	And all of a sudden 30 years had passed.	一去三十年
	The trapped bird longs for his former woods,	羈鳥戀舊林
6	The fish in the pond dreams of his old lake.	池魚思故淵
	I break up the uncultivated land on the border of the southern wilds,	開荒南野際
8	And keep to my awkwardness in returning to the farm.	守拙歸園田
	My homestead is a couple of acres,	方宅十餘畝
10	My thatched roof covers several rooms.	草屋八九間
	Elms and willows shade the back eaves,	榆柳蔭後簷
12	Peach and plum trees unfold in front of the hall.	桃李羅堂前
	The distant village is hazy and indistinct,	曖曖遠人村
14	Smoke from households floats gentle and soft.	依依墟里煙
	A dog barks far down some lane,	狗吠深巷中
16	A cock crows from atop a mulberry tree.	雞鳴桑樹巔
	In my home there is no dust or disorder;	戶庭無塵雜
18	A bare room allows for plenty of repose.	虛室有餘閑
	Trapped in a cage for so long,	久在樊籠裡
20	I can finally go back to being myself.	復得返自然
	Out here in the countryside there are few worldly affairs;	野外罕人事
22	In my narrow lane carriages rarely appear.	窮巷寡輪鞅
	The bright sun is blocked out by my bramble gate;	白日掩荊扉
24	The bare room keeps out dusty thoughts.	虛室絕塵想

	Sometimes I go into the village,	時復墟曲中
26	Bending the grass the villagers come and go.	披草共來往
	When we see each other there is no convoluted talk;	相見無雜言
28	We only discuss the growth of our hemp and mulberry trees.	但道桑麻長
	Day after day my hemp and mulberry trees grow taller,	桑麻日已長
30	And day after day my fields grow wider.	我土日已廣
	I often fear the arrival of frost and hail,	常恐霜霰至
32	When my crops will wither and fall like the grass and weeds.	零落同草莽
	I plant beans beneath the southern mountain;	種豆南山下
34	The grass flourishes, but bean sprouts are few.	草盛豆苗稀
	I wake up early to clear out the wild brush,	晨興理荒穢
36	And return home with the moon and hoe on my shoulder.	帶月荷鋤歸
	The path is narrow as the grass and trees grow thick,	道狹草木長
38	The evening dew wets my clothes.	夕露沾我衣
	Wet clothes are not worth begrudging,	衣沾不足惜
40	Just let my hope not be in vain.	但使願無違
	It's been long since I've enjoyed the mountains and marshes;	久去山澤游
42	And given release to the pleasure of the forests and wilds.	浪莽林野娛
	So I take my children and their cousins by the hand,	試携子姪輩
44	And part the brush, walking to a desolate village.	披榛步荒墟
	We pace and wander among tombs and graves,	徘徊丘壟間
46	Lingering where the previous inhabitants once lived.	依依昔人居
	The spots for wells and fireplaces are still there;	井竈有遺處
48	The decayed stumps of bamboo and mulberry trees remain.	桑竹殘朽株
	I ask someone gathering firewood,	借問採薪者
50	"What happened to all these people?"	此人皆焉如
	He responded to me, saying,	薪者向我言
52	"They are dead and gone; none are left."	死沒無復餘
	In one generation the court and market change;	一世異朝市
54	These are truly not empty words.	此語真不虛
	Life is a dream-like transformation;	人生似幻化
56	In the end we return to bare nothingness.	終當歸虛無
	With deep sorrow I come back with only my walking stick,	恨恨獨策邊

58	Winding through a rugged path covered with bushes.	崎嶇歷榛曲
	The mountain brook is clear and shallow,	山澗清且淺
60	And so I use it to wash my feet.	遇以濯吾足
	I strain my recently brewed ale,	漉我新熟酒
62	And prepare a chicken to gather the neighbors.	隻雞招近局
	As the sun sets, the room darkens;	日入室中闇
64	A small fire replaces the candle's light.	荊薪代明燭
	We delight in getting together, and grieve that night is so short;	歡來苦夕短
66	Another dawn has already arrived.	已復至天旭[36]

Tao desires liberation from the constraints of official life; and seeks a "return" to the hills and mountains of his homeland. The poem transitions from the contentment Tao finds in his home and in farming to a worry he discovers about his success as a farmer. His first outing to the mountains actually ends in a visit to a deserted village, which triggers reflection on time—much like this village, very little of us will remain once time has moved on. Tao's response is to gather his neighbors to eat, drink, and converse—taking such delight that the party, which started before sunset, lasts until sunrise. While the poem does not explicitly mention forgetting, the idea that "night is so short" and that "another dawn has already arrived" suggests that in their revelry they have lost track of time. This deceptively simple phrase (i.e., losing track of time) is full of complex connotations in Tao's case. As he demonstrates throughout his poetry, the effects of time can be temporarily halted when good company is present. Friendship can preserve the moment. This kind of living in the moment for Tao means a trimming away of the past and future (the "thousand years of worry" 千歲憂), where the moment in front of him is the only moment that matters. In poems such as these, Tao gets caught up and carried away with friends, seeming to transcend the problem of time, but the world itself calls him back to remind him that the tyrant of time can be forgotten, but never conquered. Another dawn will always arrive.

A Place to Forget

In "Returning to Live on the Farmstead" Tao describes his home as removed from the troubles of the world—his bramble gate blocks out the sun, his simple thatched-roof house is surrounded by trees, and the interior of his home is largely bare (especially from the "dusty" affairs of officialdom). Tao works to construct a place to forget—a space where he can be forgotten by those who seek to snare him in the "dusty nets" of the world, and space where he can forget the limitations of time. A good home is an empty space to be occupied by camaraderie and revelry.

Tao's craft of oblivion is building these spaces of forgetting. In his writing, he constructs these spaces in descriptions of outings he takes with friends and family (as seen previously) and in descriptions of his home. We find both of these spaces in "A Reply to Mr. Liu of Chaisang" 酬劉柴桑—a poem written to an official turned recluse.[37]

	Living in rustic circumstances, few people seek my attention;	窮居寡人用
2	And at times I forget the cycle of the seasons.	時忘四運周
	The gate and courtyard are covered in fallen leaves;	門庭多落葉
4	With a pang I see that it's already Fall.	慨然已知秋
	New mallows thrive along the north wall;	新葵鬱北牖
6	And good grain grows in the southern fields.	嘉穟養南疇
	If I do not make merry now,	今我不為樂
8	How do I know another year will come?	知有來歲不
	I tell my wife to bring the children;	命室攜童弱
10	Today is a great day to embark on a far-off journey.	良日登遠游[38]

In his home, Tao can forget and be forgotten. He does not lament when people of the dusty world do not seek him out. In his home he forgets the turns of time. Yet Tao's forgetting of time in this poem is bittersweet as he comes to see that a new season has already arrived. This poem suggests that not all forgetting of time is good. While it is good to forget the constraints of time so that we lengthen enjoyable moments, it is somehow not good to lose track of the seasons. There may be a practical significance for this inasmuch as Tao was a farmer; but the more central point appears to be about the impossibility of lengthening more than a moment. In other words, a festive outing might lengthen the day, but it cannot lengthen a month or year. In short, we should not forget that when it comes to the totality of our lives, our time is inevitably limited. If a season slips by, we may have missed many moments that deserved to be lengthened. Parts of this are predicated on Tao's skepticism of immortality—since immortality is not possible, the moment cannot be paused indefinitely; and since we cannot live forever, losing track of our years means losing the vigor we could have used to enjoy previous moments. Time, in this regard, can go by so fast that a moment has passed before you know it; and not forgetting the brevity of life actually serves as an impetus for enjoying the moment. More practically speaking, feelings like sadness, here evoked in reaction to the speed of time, can also function to slow things down.[39] In contrast to feelings like anger, which serve as a kind of hurried feeling to push things forward, sadness works to encourage distance and deliberation. In other words, sadness, like ale, can be a temporary remedy to the quickness of time; it prolongs the moment, which is especially useful if sadness is provoked in realizing a joyful moment must come to an end.

The last line of the poem is an allusion to the journeys immortals (or those seeking immortals) make to far-off worlds.[40] Yet Tao and his family do not have the means for such a journey. They are not equipped with the right food and drink or accompanied by the right guides. Indeed, the most they can hope for is an outing to Xie Brook.

The themes of forgetting, journeying, and constructing secluded space are bound together in what is perhaps Tao's most famous piece of writing—"A Record of the Peach Blossom Spring" 桃花源記.[41] While lengthy, the essay and accompanying poem are largely a meditation on forgetting.

> In the Taiyuan era (376–396 CE) of the Jin dynasty there was a man from Wuling 武陵 who worked as a fisherman. [One day] he traveled along a stream; and, forgetting how far he had gone, all of a sudden came upon a grove of peach trees that lined the banks for several hundred paces. There were no other trees in their midst. Their fragrant blossoms were beautiful and fresh; and their fallen petals completely covered [the ground]. The fisherman marveled at the scene; and he pressed forward, curious to find the end of the grove. At the grove's end, there was a spring, which was up against a mountain; and the mountain had a small opening that appeared to hold a glimmer of light. The fisherman left his boat, and entered into the opening. At first, the passageway was very narrow—only wide enough for one person to pass through, but after dozens of paces it opened up into a wide and bright scene. The land was flat and broad, with homes orderly arranged. There was verdant farmland, lovely ponds,

and various trees including mulberry and bamboo. Paths in the fields crisscrossed, and roosters and dogs called to each other. In the midst of this, people came and went in the work of farming, and the clothes the men and women wore were just like those worn by people from the outside world. The young and the old enjoyed themselves, finding delight together.

When they saw the fisherman, they were quite startled. They asked him where he was from; and once he had answered all their questions, they invited him to return with them to their homes where they set out ale, killed a chicken, and prepared a meal. When the other villagers heard about the fisherman, they all came asking for news, and explained that the first generation fled there to avoid the chaos of the Qin dynasty (221–206 BCE), bringing their wives, children, and neighbors to the remote area and never going out again; and because of this they were separated from people from the outside world. They asked what era it was, but knew nothing of the Han dynasty (206 BCE–220 CE), let alone the Wei or the Jin (220–420). The fisherman spoke about one thing at a time, telling them everything he knew; at which they all sighed. The people again invited him to their homes, where they set out food and drink. He stayed for several days, after which he announced his departure. The people told him, "There is no reason to tell those from the outside world about this." He left, found his boat, and followed the same route home, carefully marking his path along the way. When he reached the prefecture headquarters, he gained an audience with the prefect and told him about his experience. The prefect immediately sent men to follow his trail. They searched for the markings the fisherman left along the way, but got lost and could not find the path.

In Nanyang 南陽 there was Liu Ziji 劉子驥, a gentleman of lofty ideals who, hearing about this, made plans to go.[42] This was never realized though, as not long after, he got sick and died. After that, there was no one who asked about the ford.[43]

晉太元中，武陵人捕魚為業。緣溪行，忘路之遠近，忽逢桃花林，夾岸數百步，中無雜樹，芳華鮮美，落英繽紛。漁人甚異之。復前行，欲窮其林。林盡水源，便得一山。山有小口，髣髴若有光。便捨船，從口入。初極狹，纔通人；復行數十步，豁然開朗。土地平曠，屋舍儼然。有良田、美池、桑竹之屬。阡陌交通，雞犬相聞。其中往來種作，男女衣著悉如外人。黃髮垂髫，並怡然自樂。見漁人，乃大驚。問所從來，具答之，便要還家，為設酒殺雞作食。村中聞有此人，咸來問訊；自云先世避秦時亂，率妻子邑人，來此絕境，不復出焉，遂與外人間隔。問今是何世，乃不知有漢，無論魏晉。此人一一為具言所聞，皆嘆惋。餘人各復延至其家，皆出酒食。停數日，辭去。此中人語云：「不足為外人道也。」既出，得其船，便扶向路，處處誌之。及郡下，詣太守說如此。太守即遣人隨其往，尋向所誌，遂迷不復得路。南陽劉子驥，高尚士也。聞之，欣然規往，未果，尋病終。後遂無問津者。

	When the Ying clan[44] wrecked havoc on the heavenly order,	嬴氏亂天紀
2	Worthies fled the era.	賢者避其世
	Huang and Qi went to Mt. Shang,[45]	黃綺之商山
4	And these people likewise left.	伊人亦云逝
	Their traces gradually vanished;	往跡浸復湮
6	The trail they followed fell into disuse.	來逕遂蕪廢
	They commended each other to work hard while farming;	相命肆農耕
8	And at sunset they followed each other back to rest.	日入從所憩
	Their mulberry and bamboo trees provided plenty of shade;	桑竹垂餘蔭
10	And their beans and grains were planted according to the seasons.	菽稷隨時藝
	From spring silkworms they collected long threads;	春蠶收長絲
12	And from the fall harvest they paid no king a tax.	秋熟靡王稅
	Rugged paths crisscrossed in the distance;	荒路曖交通
14	Roosters crowed and dogs barked.	雞犬互鳴吠
	Their ritual vessels followed the models of antiquity;	俎豆猶古法
16	And their clothing had no new style.	衣裳無新製
	The young roamed free, singing;	童孺縱行歌
18	And the old found delight in making visits.	班白歡游詣
	Lush grass let them know the season was mild;	草榮識節和
20	Bare trees informed them the wind was harsh.	木衰知風厲
	Even though they kept no records of a calendar,	雖無紀曆志
22	The four seasons still naturally completed the year.	四時自成歲
	Happily overjoyed;	怡然有餘樂

24	Why would they toil for "knowledge" and "wisdom"?	于何勞智慧
	Their remarkable tracks were hidden for five hundred years;	奇蹤隱五百
26	Then one morning this divine realm was uncovered.	一朝敞神界
	But the pure and the shallow have different sources;	淳薄既異源
28	And so after a while they returned to obscurity.	旋復還幽蔽
	Let's ask those gentlemen who roam throughout the world,	借問游方士
30	How they reach a land beyond the dust.	焉測塵外地
	I want to tread on light wind,	願言躡輕風
32	Rising up high to seek my match.	高舉尋吾契[46]

In this piece, we see the fisherman forget how far he had traveled, which is key to his discovering a forgotten place; the people from this forgotten place have not only forgotten the era of the ruling dynasty, but have forgotten time beyond the most basic measurements; fearing that he would forget the way back, the fisherman marks his path; and after the death of Liu Ziji, it seems that the world has again forgotten this unnamed village. Much could be said about this essay and poem, however, the main point for our purposes is that this group of people appears to have forgotten the tyranny of time—they go about delighting in their work and in each other's company, and the only worry they express is when news arrive from the outside world. They are "happily overjoyed" in forgetting what Tao might call their "thousand years of worry." Notably, however, these people do not completely transcend time. They are not immortals; despite the peach tree imagery at the outset of the essay and the description of their village as a "divine realm."[47] Instead, they work hard at farming to produce food to eat and clothes to wear; and their life span does not appear to be beyond what is normal—while 500 years have passed since they left, it was their ancestors who fled, not them. Indeed, the lifestyle of these people is actually quite mundane. What makes them so divine, however, is their capacity to forget and be forgotten, even if each of them still only has their so-called one hundred years of life.

What is remarkable about this people and their land, other than their divinely unremarkable daily life, is how similar their place of forgetting is to Tao's home.[48] Like "Returning to Live on the Farmstead," we discover peach and mulberry trees, beans, chickens, dogs, farm fields, daytime labor, evening respite, visits from neighbors, ale, and perhaps most importantly, a dust-free environment. Where the people behind the Peach Blossom Spring seem to differ from Tao's home, however, is in their ability to persist in this state for an extended period of time. Tao might be able to bring about a day of hard work followed by an evening of enjoyment, but they were able to live this way for several generations; and even after someone from the dusty world broke through to their land, they were able to be forgotten again. This is quite unlike Tao in "Returning to Live on the Farmstead," who even though living in a dust free home, continuously worries about his crops, and is constantly made to remember that time will eventually cover all our remains.

The last four lines of the "Peach Blossom" poem express Tao's wish to find a community similar to the one behind the Peach Blossom Spring. The reference in line 29 to "gentlemen who roam throughout the world" is likely a reference to a vignette in the Zhuangzi. The "Great Ancestral Teacher" 大宗師 chapter describes three figures, Zisanghu 子桑戶, Mengzifan 孟子反, and Ziqinzhang 子琴張, who delight in conversation and "share in friendship with each other" (相與友).[49] They playfully ask, "Who is able to ascend to the heavens and roam in its mists; twisting and turning with the infinite; living life so as forget each other; on and on without end" (孰能登天遊霧, 撓挑無極, 相忘以生, 無所終窮?). Their friendship appears to be rooted in a mutual desire to be precisely this kind of person. When Zisanghu dies, Confucius's disciple finds the other two singing and carrying on in celebration.

    Hey ho, Sanghu! 嗟來桑戶乎
    Hey ho, Sanghu! 嗟來桑戶乎
    He's indeed gone back to what is true; 而已反其真
    While we are still human, oh well! 而我猶為人猗[50]

When Confucius hears about this, he explains that these men are "those who roam beyond the world" 遊方之外者.[51] He describes them as able to "forget" 忘 and "leave behind" 遺 their bodies at death, "returning again and again to the end and the beginning" 反覆終始, "idly roving beyond dust and dirt" 芒然彷徨乎塵垢之外.[52] There are a number of parallels in this vignette with Tao's essay and poem, culminating in Tao's wish to rise up and meet his match. Indeed, the last line of the poem, when read in light of this passage from the Zhuangzi, is a call for community—Tao wants to share in similar friendship, to create a village of like-minded people; a village hidden away from the dusty world.

Interestingly, this fellowship from the *Zhuangzi*, like the people described in "The Peach Blossom Spring," does experience death. Yet their attitude is an authentic levity predicated on their ability to forget. This is a recurring theme in Tao's work, as we have already seen. Yet Tao's attitude remains in tension with the *Zhuangzi* in a number of ways. Unlike Mengzifan, Ziqinzhang, and Zisanghu, Tao is unable, or perhaps unwilling, to forget the seriousness of his own existence. While these men are able to completely let go of themselves—joining with the natural transformations of the world to be forgotten, Tao worries that the transformations of the world will actually leave him forgotten.

In "An Outing to Xie Brook," Tao and his friends "recorded their age and birthplace in order to remember the day," yet they go on to "forget their thousand years of worry." This highlights the tension between desiring to forget and desiring not to be forgotten. Tao seeks to forget the limitations imposed by the world, but he does not want the world to forget him. Forgetting the constraints of time brings joy, but being completely forgotten is worthy of apprehension. Tao's poetry reveals a person who does not want to be forgotten, even if he wants to forget himself.

Conclusion

Notions of memory, time, companionship, and ale are mixed together in a poem Tao writes called "Returning to My Old Home" 還舊居.[53]

	In the past, my home was in the capital;	疇昔家上京
2	And after six years I left it, to return.	六載去還歸
	Today is my first time back;	今日始復來
4	I'm stricken with sadness, so much to lament.	惻愴多所悲
	Crisscrossing paths have not moved from their old places,	阡陌不移舊
6	But some of the village's homes are gone with time.	邑屋或時非
	I walk about my old residence,	履歷周故居
8	Yet few of my old neighbors remain.	鄰老罕復遺
	Step by step I search for traces of the past,	步步尋往迹
10	These are places I am quite reluctant to part with.	有處特依依
	In the midst of this flowing illusion of 100 years,	流幻百年中
12	Hot and cold push against each other daily.	寒暑日相推

	I often fear that the end of this great transformation	常恐大化盡
14	Will come before my vigor begins to decline.	氣力不及衰
	Tossing this thought aside, I do not dwell on it;	撥置且莫念
16	And instead, for the moment I raise my cup.	一觴聊可揮[54]

As Tao wanders through his old town, he is reminded of how swiftly time moves on. In "Returning to Live on the Farmstead," Tao describes a similar scene, saying, "In one generation the court and market change." Over a period of twenty or thirty years the people involved in a particular sphere of activity will be slowly replaced, such that a completely new group of people eventually occupy the same space. Thus, what was once familiar becomes largely foreign; despite one's reluctance to hang on to the past. The best Tao can do in a world where "hot and cold push against each other daily" is to celebrate the time he has with the vigor that remains.

In *The Importance of Living*, the author, Lin Yutang, contrasts the "Dreamer" with the "Realist." He states, "The Dreamer says 'Life is but a dream,' and the Realist replies, 'Quite correct. And let us live this dream as beautifully as we can.'"[55] Tao is a realist. Life is dreamlike in that it is ephemeral and controls us much more than we control it; yet a few things like a space to forget that is filled with family, friends, and ale can render life not only worth living, but worth enjoying. Indeed, these places of forgetting leave us lost in where we are.

Notes

1. On dating issues for this poem see A. R. Davis, trans., *T'ao Yüan-ming* (Cambridge: Cambridge University Press), vol. II, 41–43.

2. On the geography of these hills see Davis, *T'ao Yüan-ming*, vol. I, 50–52.

3. Xingpei Yuan 袁行霈, ed., *Tao Yuanming ji jianzhu* 陶淵明集箋注 (Beijing: Zhonghua shuju, 2003), 91. Hereafter, *TYMJ*. At times I modify a poem in accordance with character variants listed in Yuan's text. All translations are my own, although I remain indebted to (influenced by) the translations of James Robert Hightower in *The Poetry of T'ao Ch'ien* (Oxford: Clarendon Press, 1970) and A. R. Davis (*T'ao Yüan-ming*).

4. Part of Mt. Kunlun.

5. Yuan, *TYMJ*, 91.

6. On the *Nineteen Old Poems* see Maoyuan Ma 馬茂元, *Gushi shijiushou chutan* 古詩十九首初探 (Shanxi: Shanxi renmin chubanshe, 1981); Zong-qi Cai,

The Matrix of Lyric Transformation: Poetic Modes and Self-Presentation in Early Chinese Pentasyllabic Poetry (Ann Arbor: University of Michigan, Center for Chinese Studies, 1996), 61–94; and Yu-Kung Kao, "The Nineteen Old Poems and the Aesthetics of Self-Reflection," in *The Power of Culture: Studies in Chinese Cultural History*, ed. Willard J. Peterson, Andrew H. Plaks, and Ying-shih Yü (Hong Kong: The Chinese University Press, 1994), 80–102.

7. Qingzhong Zhang 張清鐘, *Gushi Shijiushou huishuo shangxi yu janjiu* 古詩十九首會說賞析與研究 (Taipei: Taibei Shangwu Yinshuguan 1988), 96.

8. I explore this more fully in "Things Endure While We Fade Away: Tao Yuanming on Being Himself," *Philosophy East & West* 69, no. 2 (2019): 395–418.

9. Yuan, *TYMJ*, 344. On the genre *za* 雜 ("miscellaneous") see Davis, *T'ao Yüan-ming*, vol. II, 125–29.

10. Yuan, *TYMJ*, 338.

11. Yuan, *TYMJ*, 342. See also Hightower's comment on this poem (*The Poetry of T'ao Ch'ien*, 188): "It is time that leaves a man in the lurch."

12. Yuan, *TYMJ*, 352. See also the fifteenth poem in "Drinking Ale" 飲酒.

13. Yuan, *TYMJ*, 13 榮木.

14. Alexander Huang, "The Tragic and the Chinese Subject," *Stanford Journal of East Asian Affairs* 3, no. 1 (2003): 55–68.

15. Huang, "The Tragic and the Chinese Subject," 61.

16. For more on the notion of immortality during this period, see Robert Ford Campany, *Making Transcendents: Ascetics and Social Memory in Early Medieval China* (Honolulu: The University of Hawai'i Press, 2009).

17. For more on this day see A. R. Davis, "The Double Ninth Festival in Chinese Poetry: A Study of Variations upon a Theme" in *Wen-lin: Studies in the Chinese Humanities*, ed. Chow Tse-tsung (Madison: University of Wisconsin Press, 1968), 45–64.

18. It is worth noting that the character for *ale* is a rhyme word for "nine" and "long-lasting."

19. See also "Drinking Alone in Continuous Rain" 連雨獨飲 (Yuan, *TYMJ*, 125) and "An Elegy for My Cousin, Jingyuan" 祭從弟敬遠文 (Yuan, *TYMJ*, 547–48).

20. Yuan, *TYMJ*, 72.

21. Yuan, *TYMJ*, 224.

22. Lonnie Aarssen, "Leisure Drive," Musings One, 10/4/2014, http://www.musingsone.com/2014/10/leisure-drive.html.

23. For more on the history of alcoholic beverages in China see Hsing-Tsung Huang, *Science and Civilization in China*, vol. 6, part 5 (Cambridge: Cambridge University Press, 2000), 149–291; and Peter Kupfer, "Amber Shine and Black Dragon Pearls: The History of Chinese Wine Culture," *Sino-Platonic Papers* 278 (June 2018).

24. Michael Nylan, *The Chinese Pleasure Book* (New York: Zone Books, 2018), 136n40.

25. Nonetheless, there are many differences, which is why many scholars translate *jiu* 酒 as wine.

26. Huang, *Science and Civilization*, 169.

27. Charles Kwong, "Making Poetry with Alcohol: Wine Consumption in Tao Qian, Li Bai and Su Shi," in *Scribes of Gastronomy: Representations of Food and Drink in Imperial Chinese Literature*, ed. Isaac Yue and Siufu Tang (Hong Kong: Hong Kong University Press, 2013), 45.

28. Yuan, *TYMJ*, 268.

29. Hightower, *The Poetry of T'ao Ch'ien*, 146.

30. Yuan, *TYMJ*, 125, "Drinking Alone in Continuous Rain" 連雨獨飲.

31. Guo Qingfan 郭慶藩, *Zhuangzi jishi* 莊子集釋 (Beijing: Zhonghua shuju, 1989), 12.428 ("Tian di" 天地). See also 6.242 ("Da zong shi" 大宗師) and 15.537 ("Ke yi" 刻意).

32. This is the title of the opening chapter.

33. Yuan, *TYMJ*, 125.

34. On the relationship between the end of life and identity see Jeff Malpas, "Death and the Unity of Life," in *Death and Philosophy*, ed. Jeff Malpas and Robert C. Solomon (New York: Routledge, 1998), 120–34.

35. Yuan, *TYMJ*, 315.

36. Yuan, *TYMJ*, 76–89.

37. Liu Chengzhi 劉程之, also known as Li Yimin 劉遺民, was an official in charge of Chaisang who left to Mt. Lu in 402 to join what would become Huiyuan's White Lotus Society.

38. Yuan, *TYMJ*, 142.

39. George A. Bonanno, *The Other Side of Sadness: What the New Science of Bereavement Tells Us about Life After Loss* (New York: Basic Books, 2009), 32.

40. For more on the notion of immortals in poetry before and after Tao's time see Fengmao Li 李豐楙, *You yu you: Liuchao Sui-Tang youxianshi lunwenji* 憂與遊: 六朝隋唐遊仙詩論文集 (Taipei: Xuesheng shuju, 1996).

41. For background on the piece see Davis, *T'ao Yüan-ming*, vol. I, 197–201 and vol. II, 140–43.

42. A famous recluse of the time.

43. This is a reference to *Lunyu* 18/6. See Yang Bojun 楊伯峻, ed., *Lunyu yi zhu* 論語譯注 (Beijing: Zhonghua shuju, 1980), 193–95.

44. The family name of the emperor of the Qin dynasty.

45. Two of "the Four Whiteheads" 四皓, who became a famous recluse and lived during the Qin dynasty.

46. Yuan, *TYMJ*, 479–80.

47. Stephen R. Bokenkamp notes that the peach trees are on the outside of the world, not the inside. See "The Peach Flower Font and the Grotto Passage," *Journal of the American Oriental Society* 106, no. 1 (1986): 65–77, 69.

48. I thank Wang Yu for pointing out how similar the village behind the Peach Blossom Spring was to Tao's home life.

49. The entire vignette appears in Guo Qingfan, *Zhuangzi jishi*, 6.264–71.
50. Guo Qingfan, *Zhuangzi jishi*, 6.266.
51. Guo Qingfan, *Zhuangzi jishi*, 6.267.
52. Guo Qingfan, *Zhuangzi jishi*, 6.268.
53. For background on this poem see Davis, *T'ao Yüan-ming*, vol. I, 88–90 and vol. II, 79–80.
54. Yuan, *TYMJ*, 215–16.
55. Yutang Lin, *The Importance of Living* (New York: Harper, 1998), 10.

Contributors

K. E. Brashier received his BA from University of Oxford as a Rhodes Scholar, his MA from Harvard University, and his PhD from University of Cambridge, after which he taught Chinese religions (eventually as the Thomas Lamb Eliot Professor of Religion and Humanities) at Reed College from 1998 until his retirement in 2021. Author of *Ancestral Memory in Early China* (Harvard University Asia Center, 2011) and *Public Memory in Early China* (Harvard University Asia Center, 2014), he is currently studying the idea of hell in late imperial China. In 2006, he was recognized as the national Outstanding Baccalaureate Colleges Professor of the Year by the CASE/Carnegie Foundation, but his chief goal in life remains a futile attempt to get his two cats to respect him.

Albert Galvany worked as a postdoctoral researcher at the École Pratique des Hautes Études (Paris), the Internationales Kolleg für Geisteswissenschaftliche Forschung (Erlangen), the University of Cambridge, and the Pompeu Fabra University (Barcelona) before joining the University of the Basque Country UPV/EHU, where he currently is an associate professor in the Department of Philosophy. His research articles on early Chinese intellectual history and classical Chinese philosophy have been published in some of the most important journals in those fields.

Michael D. K. Ing received his PhD from Harvard University in 2011, and is an associate professor in the Department of Religious Studies at Indiana University. He is the author of *The Dysfunction of Ritual in Early Confucianism* (Oxford University Press, 2012) and *The Vulnerability of Integrity in Early Confucian Thought* (Oxford University Press, 2017).

Esther Sunkyung Klein works at the Australian National University and researches premodern Chinese historiography, philosophy, and literature. She is the author of *Reading Sima Qian from Han to Song: The Father of History in Pre-modern China* (Brill, 2019). She has also published on the authorship of the *Zhuangzi*, Wang Chong's epistemology, and other issues relating to the history and transmission of ideas. Her current project focuses on approaches to truth and evidence in premodern China, including both the philosophical and historiographical traditions.

Rens Krijgsman is an associate professor at the Research and Conservation Center for Unearthed Texts, Tsinghua University (Beijing). Krijgsman's work focuses on the materiality and literary form of unearthed manuscripts from the Warring States period to the early empires. He has written on rhyme, reading, multitext manuscripts, historical perceptions of text and manuscripts, cultural memory, and intertextuality. He is the author of the book *Early Chinese Manuscript Collections: Sayings, Memory, Verse, and Knowledge* (Brill, 2023), where he analyzes how multiple, originally distinct philosophical, historical, poetic, and technical texts were brought together within the space of individual manuscripts. And he is currently completing work on a second book, tentatively titled *Studies and Translations of the Tsinghua Manuscripts: Narrating Springs and Autumns of Zheng, Qin, Jin, and Chu* (Tsinghua University Press, forthcoming), a study and translation of Warring States narrative accounts of the Springs and Autumns period from volumes 6 and 7 of the Tsinghua University manuscripts.

Xiang Li is a PhD Candidate in the Department of History, University of California, Santa Barbara. She obtained her MA from the Department of East Asian Languages and Cultures, Columbia University (2018). As a comparative historian, she focuses on both ancient China and Mediterranean civilizations, especially on how the regional forms of Late Antiquity became globalized or came to be attested by "foreign" contexts. Her PhD dissertation, as a fruit of her interest in the production of non-knowledge and disinformation in both Han China and imperial Rome, is titled "Words Disenchanted, Words Reenchanted: Local Elite Propaganda and the Internal Collapse of Ancient Imperium, the Qing-Xu-Yan 青-徐-兗 Area and the Region of Gaul."

Olivia Milburn is currently professor at the School of Chinese, University of Hong Kong. Her research focuses on the history and culture of the

Jiangsu-Zhejiang region of China, in particular the ancient kingdoms of Wu and Yue. Her publications in this field include *The Glory of Yue: An Annotated Translation of the Yuejue shu* (Brill, 2010); *Cherishing Antiquity: The Cultural Construction of an Ancient Chinese Kingdom* (Harvard University Press, 2013); she has also completed a translation of the *Wu Yue chunqiu*. Olivia Milburn's recent research has been on the early development of historical fiction, with publications including *The Empress in the Pepper Chamber: Zhao Feiyan in History and Fiction* (University of Washington Press, 2021).

Franklin Perkins is professor of philosophy at the University of Hawai'i at Mānoa and is editor of the journal *Philosophy East and West*. Perkins is the author of *Leibniz and China: A Commerce of Light* (Cambridge University Press, 2007), *Leibniz: A Guide for the Perplexed* (Continuum, 2007), *Heaven and Earth Are Not Humane: The Problem of Evil in Classical Chinese Philosophy* (Indiana University Press, 2014), and most recently, *Doing What You Really Want: An Introduction to the Philosophy of Mengzi* (Oxford University Press, 2021).

Mercedes Valmisa obtained her PhD from Princeton University in 2017, and her MA from National Taiwan University in 2011. She currently is assistant professor of philosophy at Gettysburg College. Her first book, *Adapting: A Chinese Philosophy of Action* (Oxford University Press, 2021) examines how Classical Chinese relational ontology and epistemology inform an open-ended model of efficacious action (adapting), particularly well-suited to deal with the unfinished, entangled, and unpredictable character of life.

Newell Ann Van Auken is the author of *Spring and Autumn Historiography: Form and Hierarchy in Ancient Chinese Annals* (Columbia University Press, 2023) and *The Commentarial Transformation of the Spring and Autumn* (State University of New York Press, 2016), and coeditor of *Studies in Chinese and Sino-Tibetan Linguistics: Dialect, Phonology, Transcription and Text* (Academia Sinica, 2014). Her articles have been published in *Asia Major*, *Early China*, *JAOS*, *Monumenta Serica*, and *NAN NÜ*. She teaches at the University of Iowa.

Paul Nicholas Vogt is assistant professor of Early Chinese History in the Department of East Asian Languages and Cultures, Hamilton Lugar School of Global and International Studies, Indiana University, Bloomington. His work explores the Western Zhou era (ca. eleventh to eighth century BCE) as both historical milieu and cultural construct. His book, *Kingship, Ritual, and Royal Ideology in Western Zhou China* (Cambridge University Press, 2023), explores the royal ritual of that period based on contemporary bronze inscriptions. He is currently working on a second monograph on the ideological, literary, and aesthetic concerns behind tales of Western Zhou history in both transmitted texts and ancient manuscripts.

Tobias Benedikt Zürn is an assistant professor of premodern Chinese literature at Hong Kong University of Science and Technology. In his first book project, provisionally titled "Text/Bodies: The Huainanzi's Construction as a Powerful Scripture of the Way," he asks what are texts and what did people historically do with them? By drawing on book history, material culture, and religious studies, he argues that the *Huainanzi*, one of the most important texts from the early Han dynasty (206 BCE–220 CE), was created to serve as a powerful, textual embodiment of the Way that could actualize cosmic order by its mere presence. Tobias Zürn's research has been published in the *Journal of Asian Studies* and *Early China*, as well as in various edited volumes. He is also the cofounder of the international research project "Global Reception of the Classic *Zhuangzi*" and the "Global Daoist Studies Forum," a virtual venue that seeks to promote the study of Daoism and foster the global community of scholars in Daoist studies.

Index

Aarssen, Lonnie, 332, 346n22
abdication, 51, 52, 54–55, 56, 67n8, 68n16, 68n24, 75
actualization, 248–50, 261–62, 263
ale, 119, 124, 139, 329, 331, 332–37, 339, 340, 342, 344–45, 346n12, 346n18
amnesia, 224, 225, 227, 228, 230, 231, 233, 234, 235, 239n15, 243n55, 324n10
  childhood, 229, 243n43
  cultural, 7, 25, 28, 30, 31, 41, 42, 43n1
  structured, 124, 144n12
  See also forgetting
ancestors, 5, 18n23, 59, 73, 74, 91n6, 124, 125–27, 128, 134, 135, 136–37, 140, 143n9, 144n19, 145n22, 217, 227, 283, 293n47, 297, 298, 299, 342
  ancestor cult, 5
  ancestral sacrifice, 19n23, 139, 288
  ancestral spirits, 121, 135, 136, 139
  ancestral temple, 73, 224, 280
aphorism, 80, 81
argumentative, 53, 63, 64, 183, 184
Aristotle, 272, 291n18
Assmann, Aleida, 3, 17n12, 20n32, 50, 66n5, 244n59

Assmann, Jan, 66n2, 294n54, 325n27
attention 12, 77, 78, 79, 80, 82, 92n20, 93n28, 153, 155–60, 161, 162, 164, 166, 168, 169, 172, 173, 174n7, 175n12, 176n19, 177n29, 222, 225
Augé, Marc, 3, 18n13
Augustine, 244n59, 272
austerity, 277
authorship
  of the Liezi, 216–17

Baihutong 白虎通, 127, 145n30, 145n34, 147n44, 185, 186, 187, 197, 205n35, 205n36, 206n41, 206n45, 265n9
bamboo slips, 51, 56, 66n6, 67n8, 189, 299
Ban Gu 班固, 90n1, 300
  See also Hanshu
baobian 褒貶 (praise and blame), 27
Baopuzi 抱朴子, 320, 326n43
Bao Si 褒姒, 57, 58
Barthes, Roland, 247, 264n8
battle 31, 47n31, 74, 98, 100, 103, 106, 107, 114n23, 294n52
bi 蔽 (block, blinker), 161–62, 166, 177n31
bian 貶 (blame, criticize), 27, 198

353

biji 筆跡 (brush traces), 207n47
Bo Yi 伯夷, 84, 85, 87, 90, 95n55, 185
Boileau, Giles, 140, 148n63
Borges, Jorge Luis, 1, 2, 17n1
Brashier, K. E., 6, 20n28, 143n6, 144n13, 145n21, 145n25, 145n29, 148n48, 148n52, 148n60, 148n63, 294n54
Brockmeier, Jens, 50, 66n1, 66n4
bronze inscriptions, 19n23, 73, 302
building, 32, 33

Cai Yong 蔡邕, 121
Cai zhonglang ji 蔡中郎集, 143n5, 207n52
Candau, Joël, 8, 21n34
Cang Jie 倉頡, 183, 187, 202n13, 207n49
cangji 藏跡 (hide traces), 183, 196, 211n91
canon, 26, 44n3, 49, 50, 66n5, 89, 242n38
  orthodox canon, 26
Carruthers, Mary, 4, 18n15
causal, 51, 54, 55, 56, 62
cemetery, 302, 311, 312, 320
chaos, 52, 126, 130, 131, 281, 319, 321, 340
Chen She 陳涉, 74
cheng 成 (completed), 164, 165, 172, 173
  cheng xing 成形 (fixed forms), 158
  cheng ren 成人 (complete person), 217
Chu 楚, state of, 31, 56, 57, 58, 59, 63, 65, 69n29, 74, 76, 77, 86, 87, 159, 168, 206n46, 220, 223
chuan 傳 (transmission, tradition), 28, 72, 89, 189, 191, 227
Chuci 楚辭, 93n39, 143n3, 185, 187, 190, 199, 204n29, 207n48, 208n53

Chunqiu 春秋, 19n27, 27–34, 35, 36, 37–41, 42, 43, 44n8, 45n13, 45n16, 46n22, 46nn25–26, 63, 89, 91n5, 138, 148n59, 193, 212n103, 241nn30–32, 241n35
Cicero, 80, 93n34
cinnabar granules, 319
codependency, 258, 261, 262
commemoration, 74, 109, 110, 126, 190, 191, 192, 198, 199, 200, 209n63, 276, 280, 298, 301, 309
Confucian 94n43, 131, 190, 202n12, 218, 219, 226, 229, 230, 231, 233, 234, 243n44
  classics or texts, 85, 122, 144n16, 274
  school (*ru jia* 儒家), 5, 13, 217, 221, 229, 235
  tradition, 146n41
  way, 170, 231, 236, 291n17
Confucianism, 130, 145n35, 150n74, 265n13
  Han Confucianism, 87
Confucius (Kongzi 孔子), 28, 29, 77, 78, 127, 139, 145n26, 164, 170, 187, 193, 194, 202n12, 203n25, 208n53, 209n60, 211n91, 212n103, 218, 219, 226, 239n13, 240n24, 244n61, 276, 282, 283, 334, 343
  as editor or composer, 27, 28, 29, 44n7, 89, 91n5
  and forgetting, 78, 169, 218, 236, 240n23, 291n22
  and memory, 220, 235, 236, 239n15, 291n22
conjunction, 31, 33–34, 43
Connerton, Paul, 7, 20n32

Da Dai liji 大戴禮記, 145n33, 240n21, 272, 293n42
Dai De 戴德, 272
Dai Sheng 戴聖, 272

Index | 355

dao 道 (the Way), 122, 123, 128, 130–32, 134–38, 139, 140–41, 142, 146nn40–41, 147n45, 148n62, 149n67, 150n70, 150n73, 182, 183, 190–95, 198, 199, 200, 210n82, 213n106, 274
  ti dao 體道 (embodied way), 183, 196, 198, 199, 200nn1–2, 211n88, 211n91, 213n105
Daode jing 道德經, 93n30, 122, 123, 129, 130, 131, 132, 133–35, 136, 138, 140, 141, 142, 143n8, 145n35, 146nn40–41, 147n46, 147n48, 148nn62–63, 149n68, 150n72
  See also *Laozi*
Davis, Timothy M., 301, 323n4, 323n7
de 德 (transformative power/force/virtue), 30, 94n46, 125, 128, 130, 131, 132, 135, 136–38, 139, 140, 141–42, 144n16, 148n57, 149n67, 167, 210n76
death, 5, 16, 36, 47n31, 54, 74, 76, 95n55, 98, 100, 101, 102–105, 107, 108, 109, 113n20, 113n22, 119, 121–22, 124, 133–34, 142, 145n25, 147nn47–48, 159, 167–68, 185, 192, 194, 195, 199, 211n84, 219, 225, 232–33, 263, 278, 279, 293n47, 298, 299, 302–304, 305–308, 309, 312, 313, 315, 317, 318–21, 321–22, 323n23, 324n18, 325n27, 329, 336, 342, 343, 344, 347n34
  of the author, 247, 248, 264n8
De Reu, Wim, 251, 252, 266nn19–21
Di Ku 帝嚳, 205
discursive/dualistic thinking, 122, 123, 131, 132, 142, 146nn40–41, 147nn45–46
Du of Song 宋督, 32

emotions, 36, 76, 78, 79, 158–59, 160, 164, 176n21, 208n53, 225, 231–32, 234, 240n24, 241n36, 243n48, 244n58, 274, 276, 278–80, 283, 285, 286–88, 295n61, 332, 333
epigraphs, 297, 301
Erya 爾雅, 184, 203nn19–20
event(s), 27, 28, 33, 35, 46n22, 49, 50, 51, 56, 57, 59, 62, 63, 64–65, 71, 72, 73, 80, 81, 82, 84, 89, 98, 99, 100, 101, 106, 108, 109, 110, 113n20, 186, 192, 221, 223, 235, 236, 247, 271, 300, 321, 327
excavated materials, 51, 56, 66n6, 105, 110n1, 127, 140, 156, 216, 238n8, 297, 299, 301, 303, 307, 310, 311, 313, 320, 323n8

Fan Li 范蠡, 107, 108
Fei Yi 肥義, 78
Fengjun Ruren 馮君孺人, 313
finitude, 327, 328, 329
fire, 33, 34, 35, 36, 45n18, 46n22, 103–104, 105, 193, 228, 337
  Qin Shihuang 秦始皇 (or First Emperor of the Qin), 83, 84, 186, 187
fishnet allegory, 250–52, 254, 255, 258, 259, 261, 262
Flower, Harriet I., 4, 18n19, 304, 324n15
forgetting, 1–8, 25, 29, 56, 62, 64, 71, 72, 73, 74, 75, 76, 77, 78, 79, 80, 81, 82, 87, 90, 91n6, 92n11, 92n14, 98, 99, 100, 101, 102, 105, 108, 122, 124, 128, 133, 141, 147n48, 153, 154, 155, 161, 162, 163, 165, 166, 167, 168, 169, 170, 171, 172, 173, 174n3, 174n7, 178n55, 178n56, 183, 217, 218, 219,

356 | Index

forgetting (continued)
220, 222, 223, 224, 226, 227, 234, 235, 236, 237, 239n11, 247, 250, 252, 254, 258, 259, 260–62, 267n31, 271, 272, 273, 274–76, 277, 278, 283, 284–85, 286–88, 299, 302, 303, 306, 309, 321, 322, 328, 333, 334, 337, 338, 339, 342, 344, 345
  and attention, 155, 156, 157–60, 164, 169, 177n29, 179n72
  and elision, 56
  and erasure, 182, 198, 199, 200, 298, 304–305, 307, 308, 309, 314, 318, 319, 321
  and forgiving, 98, 100, 224
  and happiness/joy, 76, 77–78, 88, 220, 232–34, 303, 329, 335, 342
  and memory, 1, 17n10, 20n30, 41, 49, 50, 56, 74, 215, 227, 236, 250, 262, 263, 271, 285, 298, 304, 321
  as absentmindedness, 7, 73, 221, 222, 224
  as disease/defection, 75, 227
  as neglect/obliteration, 7, 72, 73, 75, 76, 79, 82, 89, 90, 147n48, 155, 312
  cognitive, 17n7, 122, 123, 126, 145n22
  danger of, 26, 88, 109, 156, 165, 279, 285, 287, 291n21, 294n52
  longtime, 302–303
  parental, 278–80
  partial, 157, 234, 244n59
  phenomenology of, 274, 286, 289n2
  positive value of, 79, 160, 235, 236, 291n22, 305
  ritualized, 122, 123, 126, 142
  selective, 7, 164–66, 169, 288
  silent, 72, 87, 88
  total, 163, 167, 234, 244n59
  See also amnesia; oblivion; wang 忘; zuowang 坐忘
formula, 51, 55, 73, 87, 302
friends, 74, 91n6, 170, 300, 308, 322, 329, 332–37, 338, 343, 344, 345
fu 父 (suffix to male names), 32, 35, 38, 46n24
Fuchai, King of Wu 吳王夫差, 98, 99, 100, 100–105, 106, 107, 108, 109, 110, 113n21, 113n23, 114n26, 206n39, 224
Fuxi 伏羲, 249

gaodice 告地策 (tomb-informing texts), 299
Gaozu 高祖, 81, 95n57
  See also Liu Bang
Gaster, Theodor, 317, 326n35
ghosts, 123, 125, 127, 135–36, 139, 148n54, 156, 160, 176n29, 213n106, 305, 307, 308, 316, 318, 319, 324n18
  See also shen 神
Gongsun Long 公孫龍, 202n14
Gongsun Sheng 公孫聲, 100, 102, 103, 104, 113n22
Gongyang 公羊, 27, 28, 30, 31, 32, 33–34, 35, 36, 38, 42, 43, 44n9, 45n17, 45n20, 46n27, 47n32
Graham, Angus C., 204n26, 216, 238n4, 238n6, 241n25, 241n27, 241n29, 242n38, 291n17
Grandee Zhong 大夫種, 107, 108
Graziani, Romain, 20n31, 172, 174n9, 179n73, 239n11, 242n37
grief, 43, 231, 278, 281, 333
Guanzi 管子, 136, 148n55, 175n10, 203n18, 229, 243n45, 266n26
Guhua pinlu 古畫品錄, 207n47
Guliang 穀梁, 27, 28, 30, 32, 33–34, 35–36, 38–39, 40–41, 42, 43,

Index | 357

44n9, 45nn17–18, 46nn23–24,
  46nn28–29, 138, 148n58,
  212n103
Guodian 郭店 (tomb and
  manuscripts), 127, 145n28,
  148n62, 175n11, 231, 239n14,
  243nn49–51
Guoyu 國語, 19n27, 65, 93n38,
  110n1, 115n31, 115n38, 223
Guo Xiang 郭象, 251

Han 漢 dynasty, 80, 97, 107, 109,
  156, 181, 184, 185, 186,
  202n16, 203n18, 207n52,
  211n91, 242n38, 246, 272, 299,
  328, 340
  Eastern (Later), 97, 107, 109, 119,
    120, 121, 124, 127, 143n7, 186,
    205n34, 207n52, 298, 299, 301,
    302, 303, 312, 317, 321, 322
Han Feizi 韓非子, 114n26, 177n31,
  191, 192, 209n65, 211n88,
  212n98, 224, 241n33, 244n64,
  265n13
Hanshu 漢書, 44n12, 45n13, 90n1,
  90n4, 91n5, 95n67, 111n2,
  144n18, 145n22–23, 145n25,
  248, 265n9
  See also Ban Gu
Hartley, L. P., 43, 43n1, 47n35
Heidegger, Martin, 154, 174n3,
  178n61
hermeneutics, 247, 248–49, 260
hierarchy, 27, 32, 34, 35, 36, 37, 38,
  39, 40, 41, 217, 228, 232, 275,
  282, 283, 302
Hightower, James, 333, 345n3,
  346n11, 347n29
history, 5, 29, 50, 57, 60, 61, 65, 75,
  80, 87, 88, 93n34, 95n66, 99,
  110, 285, 300, 309, 321
  and calendrics, 81

  excess of, 88
  making of, 80, 90
  informative, 56
  narrative, 27, 63
  of ideas (intellectual history), 6,
    30, 215, 216
  recorded, 98
  textual, 200n2, 237n1, 272, 290n8
historiography, 49, 51, 56, 65, 72, 77,
  78, 79, 81, 84, 88, 206n40
Hou Ji 后稷, 86, 205n32
Huai, King of Chu 楚懷王, 76
Huainanzi 淮南子, 114nn26–27,
  115n31, 125, 143n4, 150n73,
  154, 156, 161, 165, 166, 172,
  174n5, 175nn12–14, 176nn16–
  17, 176n20, 176nn19–24,
  176nn26–29, 177n41, 179n72,
  181, 182, 183, 184, 193, 196,
  199, 200, 201nn6–8, 202n13,
  202n16, 207n49, 211nn85–87,
  211nn89–90, 211nn92–95,
  212nn96–98, 212nn100–102,
  213n106, 213n108, 222, 224,
  241nn27–28, 241n33, 243n42,
  290n11
  and *Xunzi*, 161, 163, 164, 165,
    167, 171
  and sages, 182, 183, 196–98,
    201n3, 201n5
  attention in, 156–60
  forgetting in, 156–60
  shen (spirits) in, 156
Huan, Duke of Qi 齊桓公, 61, 191
Huang, Alexander, 330, 346n14
Huangdi 黃帝, 183, 186
Huazi 華子, 213n105, 225–26, 227,
  228, 229–236, 243n55, 324n10
hui 悔 (regrets), 279
Huizi 惠子, 162, 167
hun 魂 (soul, essence), 121, 134, 304
Hundun 渾沌, 232–33, 243n55

hunger, 88, 277, 278, 287

image, 100, 108, 122, 128, 132, 139, 151n74, 182, 189, 197, 201n10, 209n57, 218, 246–49, 250, 251, 252–53, 254–57, 257–59, 260, 261–62, 263, 264, 264n1, 264n4, 264n6, 265n10, 266n25, 290n6, 298, 301, 315, 319, 332, 342
imagination, 271
  and memory, 289n3
immortality, 76, 147n47, 211n95, 330, 332, 334, 338, 346n16
impermanence, 332
Ing, Michael D. K., 273, 290n8, 290nn10–12, 290n14, 294n55, 295nn62–63

James, William, 2, 17n3
ji 記 (remembrance, record), 81, 82, 83, 86, 174n7, 182, 183, 189, 227, 236, 327
Jia Yi 賈誼, 19n26, 71, 80, 81, 88
jian ai 兼愛 (inclusive care), 164
jian/xian 見 (see, appear, manifest), 28, 104, 121, 139, 142, 154, 155, 157, 159, 160, 161, 163, 165, 168, 172, 187, 197, 218, 221, 222, 262, 286, 297, 322, 336, 341
Jiang 姜, Lady, 40
Jiang Yuan 姜嫄, 205
Jiao shi yilin 焦氏易林, 125, 144n17
judgments, 27, 28, 29, 42, 72, 154, 155, 161, 164, 165, 168, 252, 316
junzi 君子 (nobleman, gentleman), 28, 155, 218, 274

Kern, Martin, 19n23, 92n14, 206n42, 290n13

Kohn, Livia, 20n31, 178n55, 239n11, 260, 267n30
Kongfu of Song 宋孔父, 32, 35, 36, 42, 46n22
Kuaiji mountain 會稽山, 98, 105, 109, 114n31
Kuang Heng 匡衡, 126, 127, 145n24
Kwong, Charles, 332, 347n27

Laozi 老子, 93n30, 143n8, 146n36, 146n39, 146n43, 147n46, 148nn49–51, 148n53, 146n56, 146n61, 149nn65–66, 193, 194, 201n9, 210nn77–78, 224, 228, 241n34, 264n3, 334
  See also *Daode jing*
legend, 51, 52, 53, 55, 56, 63, 65, 67n10, 81, 100, 107, 115n37
Legge, James, 46n25, 251, 291n14
Levi, Jean, 19n24, 209n65, 210n73, 210n75, 233, 237n3, 238n5, 239n10, 239n13, 243n54
Lewis, Mark Edward, 18n22, 19n24, 83, 94n45, 203
li 理 (patterns, coherence), 71, 80, 81, 88, 161, 163, 281
  tianli 天理 (natural coherence), 158, 171
li 禮 (rituals), 83, 84, 125, 127, 129, 131, 132, 140, 142, 183, 186, 210n76, 217, 218, 227–28, 272, 273, 278, 279, 283, 285, 286, 287, 288, 291n17, 294n56, 295n59, 301, 315, 316, 317, 318, 341
  and ancestral spirits, 128, 135, 282, 284, 285, 316, 319
  and forgetting, 122, 126, 128, 129, 169–70, 272–76, 285, 286, 289, 294n52, 294n54, 320, 321

and memory, 126, 128, 191, 263, 272–76, 285, 288, 289, 294n54, 321
  mourning and death, 279, 283, 287, 301, 315, 317
  ritual theory, 272, 288
Li Ling 李零, 57, 69n27, 143n7, 238n8
Li Yiji 酈食其, 81
Liang Cai, 87, 95n59
Liezi 列子, 143n4, 149n68, 176n23, 176n25, 215–17, 221, 222, 223, 224, 225, 227, 229, 232, 233–36, 237nn1–3, 238nn4–6, 238n9, 239n10, 240n25, 241n27, 241n29, 242n38, 244n61, 324
Liji 禮記, 47n33, 124, 143n10, 144n15, 144nn19–20, 145n27, 145n31, 147n44, 148n54, 148n62, 227, 240n23, 242n41, 272–73, 275–78, 279, 281, 282, 283, 285, 286, 287, 288, 290n14, 291n16, 291nn19–22, 292n25, 292nn27–28, 292n30, 292n32, 292nn34–38, 293nn40–42, 293nn44–46, 293nn48–51, 294n53, 294nn55–58, 295nn59–60, 295nn62–63
Lin Yutang, 345, 348n55
listing order, 34, 36
Liu An 劉安, 181, 196, 211n85
Liu Bang 劉邦, 81
  See also Gaozu
Liu Che 劉徹, 79, 181
  See also Wu, Emperor (Han)
Liu Heng 劉恆, 73
  See also Wen, Emperor (Han)
Liu Xiang 劉向, 92n27, 185
Liu Xin 劉歆, 91n5, 127
Locke, John, 154, 174n2
Loraux, Nicole, 4, 18n18

Lord Huan of Lu 魯桓公, 40
Lord Huan of Qi 齊桓公, 61
Lord Wen of Jin 晉文公, 60, 61
Lord Xiang of Qi 齊襄公, 40, 58, 59
Lord Zhuang of Lu 魯莊公, 40
Lu 魯, state of, 27, 29, 38, 40, 203n25, 226, 229, 230, 235
Lüshi chunqiu 呂氏春秋, 112n8, 142, 150n71, 206n46, 240n20, 241n25, 241n27, 244n64, 290n11
Lunheng 論衡, 98, 111n3, 145n32, 186, 187, 205n37, 207n50, 208n53, 208nn55–56, 324n10, 326n40
Lunyu 論語 (also *Analects*), 77, 78, 88, 89, 92n24, 95n69, 145n26, 209n58, 217, 219, 220, 221, 225, 239n12, 239n14, 239n15, 240nn16–20, 240nn22–24, 244n56, 244n62, 263, 264n2, 280, 291n17, 292n22, 347n43

maidiquan 買地券 (plot-purchasing writs), 299, 323n1
mangran 芒然 (oblivion), 170
Mattice, Sarah, 253, 266n22
Mawangdui 馬王堆 (tomb and manuscripts), 133, 143n8, 147n47, 148n56, 149n65
memory, 1–8, 29, 41, 42, 50, 53, 61, 63, 64, 65, 71, 99, 100, 104, 105, 106, 107, 108, 110, 122, 126, 128, 129, 134, 144n16, 153, 154, 178n55, 190, 191, 217, 218, 219, 220, 221, 222, 224, 225, 228, 229, 231, 233–35, 236, 239n15, 260, 264, 271, 272, 276, 277, 279, 280, 281, 283, 284, 287, 288, 289n5,

memory (continued)
  291n15, 294n54, 295nn60–61,
  298, 299, 301, 304, 309, 344
 aesthetics of, 19n23
 attention and, 153, 222, 223
 auxiliary, 209n63, 276, 283
 cultural, 3, 7, 50, 64
 danger of, 3, 281, 283, 285, 288
 embodied, 124, 272, 286
 fading, 122, 126, 128, 129, 143n9
 forgetting and, 1, 17n10, 20n30, 41,
  49, 50, 56, 74, 215, 227, 236,
  250, 262, 263, 271, 285, 298,
  304, 321
 historical, 8, 71, 79
 harmful, 223, 225, 236
  obdurate, 221, 225
  of the deceased, 281, 287, 288,
   298, 299, 301, 318, 320
  parental, 217, 276, 277, 278, 279,
   293n41
  phenomenology of, 271, 288,
   289n3
  recovery of, 234, 243n55, 250
  sense-memory, 271, 287, 292n24
  textual, 210n77
  traumatic, 106, 107
  See also commemoration; recall;
   remembrance; *ji* 記
Mengzi 孟子, 19n27, 189, 201n3,
 205n38, 207n53, 208n57
Mengzifan 孟子反, 343, 344
metaphor, 82, 91n4, 140, 147n48,
 151, 159, 182, 183, 200,
 202n17, 211n91, 232, 294n53,
 306, 309, 320
Michalowski, Piotr, 43n1
mie 滅 (loss, obliteration, erasure),
 72, 82, 84, 85, 86–87, 89, 158,
 160, 182, 183, 196, 198
Milburn, Olivia, 57, 62, 69n26,
 69n28, 69n32, 69n34, 111n3

ming 名 (name/fame), 35, 36, 68n24,
 84, 85, 109, 130, 132, 137, 140,
 147n45, 171–72, 182, 185, 196,
 197, 205n34, 230, 307, 331,
 334
mingqi 明器 (spirit objects), 318
mirror, 158, 160, 163, 171
Möller, Hans-Georg, 251, 253,
 266n15, 266n17, 266n21
Mohists, 95n70, 164
mo ji 墨跡 (ink traces), 189
mortuary, 273, 301, 315, 317, 318
 See also death
Mozi 墨子, 162
Mozi 墨子, 114n26, 202n18, 243n44
Mu of Zhou, King 周穆王, 76
Mu Tianzi zhuan 穆天子傳, 76, 99
murder, 32, 35, 40, 46n22, 47n31,
 98, 113n23, 223, 224, 225,
 241n30
music, 109, 139, 140, 148n63, 169,
 170, 193, 218, 253, 267n35,
 274, 279, 294n53

narrative, 27, 28, 29, 49, 50–51, 52,
 53–56, 57, 59, 60–62, 63–65,
 68n24, 83, 84, 92n20, 97, 98,
 99–100, 102, 107, 110, 112n12,
 113n13, 113n16, 186, 206n46,
 229, 235, 236, 249, 273,
 300
niaoji 鳥跡 (bird track), 183
niaoshu 鳥書 (bird writings), 187
Nietzsche, Friedrich, 88, 95nn61–62,
 95nn65–66
nostalgia, 235

oblivion, 4, 6, 20n30, 29, 41, 43, 72,
 82, 84, 85, 153, 155, 156, 157,
 160, 162, 165, 166, 167, 169,
 171, 173, 216, 219, 220, 224,
 225, 230, 233, 234, 236, 260,

298, 299, 300, 301, 302, 303, 304, 305, 306, 307, 308, 317, 319, 321, 324n10, 329, 338
  intransitive, 172
  partial, 157, 234, 244n59
  paradoxical, 235, 236, 242n37
  total, 170, 173, 227, 233, 235
  See also forgetting; *mangran* 芒然; *wang* 忘
offspring, 184, 195, 203
origin, 54, 55, 57, 59, 60, 61, 62, 68n24, 123, 128, 138, 248, 265n9, 283, 285, 288

pace, 53, 56, 64, 336, 339
paraphrasing, 33, 42
parents, 75, 147n48, 227, 277, 281, 282, 283, 285, 287, 292n24, 292n31, 298
  deceased, 144n19, 276–77, 279, 281, 283, 287, 292n38
See also memory (parental); forgetting (parental)
Pei Yin 裴駰, 76, 92n17
perception, 154, 160, 161, 163, 164, 172, 173, 175n12, 221, 225, 271, 277, 278, 289n3
  distort, 160, 163, 176n21, 221, 222
  unbiased, 156, 160, 161, 163, 164, 165, 167, 171
Pines, Yuri, 56, 57, 62, 65, 67n8, 68n25, 69n26, 69n32, 69n37, 92n14, 294n52
procreation, 194, 210n75, 211n84
Puett, Michael, 95n70, 175n10, 176n18, 179n72, 198, 202n11, 213n107, 243n52

qi 氣 (vital energy, ethereal essence), 119, 120, 121, 156, 157, 160, 176n21, 231, 328, 331, 345

Qi 齊, state of, 31, 37, 39, 40, 45n13, 61, 68nn23–24, 86, 87, 159, 222, 294n53
qiance 遣冊 (tomb inventory lists), 299
Qian Han ji 前漢記, 205n34
Qin 秦 dynasty, 19n26, 74, 85, 340, 347nn44–45
  bibliocaust, 82, 85
Qin 秦, state of, 31, 57, 59, 60, 86, 87
qing 情 (emotional dispositions, natural tendencies), 208n53, 231, 243nn48–49, 266n25, 284, 331
Qu Yuan 屈原, 76, 77, 211n95
qugui 驅鬼, 318

rank, 32, 34, 36, 37, 38, 39, 40, 43, 53, 124, 135, 154
recall, 73, 190, 208n53, 219, 222, 225, 227, 228, 229, 234, 263, 271–72, 283, 285, 298, 304, 308, 310, 315, 319
See also remembrance
reciprocity, 227, 228, 233
Red Di 赤狄, 60, 61
regression, 229, 233
remembrance, 28, 41, 98, 110, 113n21, 124, 126, 128, 134, 135, 144n16, 144n19, 147n48, 182, 183, 186, 196, 250, 271, 289, 298, 299, 308, 309, 321
See also memory; recall
ren 仁 (benevolence, moral quality), 30, 130, 131, 132, 138, 146n40, 146n41, 169, 170, 185, 209n60, 218, 247, 282
Ricoeur, Paul, 149n70, 272, 274, 276, 289n1, 289n3, 290nn6–7, 291n18, 292n23
Ribot, Théodule-Armand, 2, 17n2

362 | Index

Riegel, Jeffrey K., 205n32, 206n46, 272, 290nn8–10
rong 戎 (tribe), 58, 59, 61
Rongchenshi 容成氏, 50, 51, 52, 53, 55, 56, 62, 63, 64, 65
Ruists, 183, 190, 193, 195, 196
  See also Confucian

sacrifices, 82, 83, 122, 123, 126, 127, 128, 134, 135, 137, 138, 140, 142, 145n25, 147, 155, 294n52
  feng 封 and shan 禪, 82, 83, 84, 186
sacrificial altars, 91n6, 135
sages, 6, 78, 81, 86, 89, 123, 124, 132, 135, 160, 164, 168, 181, 182, 183, 190, 191, 192, 194, 197, 198, 200, 201n3, 201n5, 207n49, 211n86, 213n106, 244n62, 246, 247, 248, 249, 250, 251, 255, 262, 263, 265n13, 266n25, 284, 285
  as traceless, 198, 202n16
  sage rulers, 122, 136, 138, 183, 187, 190, 192, 193, 196, 198, 199–200, 202n15, 211n91, 217
  See also shengren 聖人
Sanli 三禮, 273
Schönle, Andreas, 309, 325n25
selection, 49, 50, 52, 53, 57, 61, 62, 64–65, 68n24, 89, 90, 94n54
self-cultivation, 5, 155, 189, 217, 219, 221, 260, 262
Shaanxi 陝西, 114n25, 120, 302, 313, 320
Shang 商 dynasty, 60, 185, 193
shen 神 (spirits/spiritual agency), 103, 121, 123, 124, 125, 127, 134–36, 139, 140, 156–58, 160, 179n72, 194, 196, 283, 297, 307, 342
sheng 生 (life/growth), 57, 83, 103, 104, 121, 137, 157, 158, 159, 163, 167, 189, 194, 218, 230, 231, 254, 257, 284, 294n53, 303, 306, 320, 328, 330, 331, 336, 343
shengren 聖人 (sage), 181, 191, 201n5
Shennong 神農, 52, 53
Shentu Di 申徒狄, 185
shi 謚 (posthumous titles/names), 35, 36, 43, 185, 186, 190, 197, 200
shi 尸 (stand-in, corpse), 171–72, 182, 197, 275, 280
Shi 詩 (also Shijing 詩經 and Odes), 19n27, 73, 84, 85, 89, 91n6, 124, 148n62, 174n7, 193, 263, 267n35
Shiji 史記, 28, 29, 40, 44n11, 49, 53, 68nn23–24, 71–79, 82–89, 90n2, 91n4, 91n6, 92nn10–14, 92nn16–25, 92n27, 93n29, 93nn31–33, 93nn36–37, 93n39, 94nn41–42, 94n44, 94n46, 94n48, 94nn50–51, 94nn53–54, 95nn55–57, 95n68, 95n71, 96n72, 96nn75–76, 110n1, 112n12, 113nn14–15, 113n20, 114n26, 114n30, 115n37, 115n40, 143n4, 145n29, 147n48, 174n7, 206n44, 213n108, 240n20, 240n23, 241n35, 265n9, 293n41
  See also Sima Qian
shrines, 106, 123, 124, 125, 126, 134, 135–36, 145n24, 297
Shu 書 (also Shangshu 尚書 and Documents), 19n27, 73, 84, 85, 91n6, 92n14, 193
shu 述 (transmission), 72, 89
Shu Qi 叔齊, 84, 185
Shu Xi 束皙, 263, 267n35
Shuihu zhuan 水滸傳, 85
Shun 舜, 51, 53, 54, 55, 63, 68n18, 68n24, 86, 138, 209n60

Index | 363

Shuoyuan 說苑, 113n15, 185, 205n33, 241n35, 244n64
Shuowen jiezi 說文解字, 75, 92n15, 93n40, 184, 203nn22–23, 204n26, 265n9
si 思 (think, attend), 91n6, 125, 139–40, 155, 186, 190, 218, 219, 263, 302, 303, 335
  siji 思跡 (contemplation on traces), 190
Sima Qian 司馬遷, 71, 76, 77, 79, 81, 82, 83, 84, 86, 88–90, 92n26, 94n42, 94n54, 95n57, 95n66, 300
  See also *Shiji*
Simin yueling 四民月令, 124, 144n14
Six Classics, 193, 194
skill, 77, 99, 169–71, 173, 178n62, 191, 194, 207n53, 226, 229, 279, 298
Song 宋, state of, 31, 32, 37, 61, 86, 225, 226, 227
space, 33, 34, 85, 90, 122, 124, 142n1, 196, 286, 287, 288, 298, 299, 309, 314, 316, 329, 338, 339, 345
  and time, 33, 34, 182, 287, 334
  interpretative, 36
  ritual space, 125, 319
  symbolic, 50
  tomb space, 301, 309–10, 311, 312, 313, 314, 315, 320, 325n27
spokes, 191
Spring and Autumn period, 27, 28, 29, 40, 57, 64, 115n40
storytelling, 50
(Sui) Wuzi 隨武子, 275
Sunshu Ao 孫叔敖, 206n46

Taiyi 太一, 181
Tang 湯, 51
Tang Jungyi 唐君毅, 262

Tao Yuanming 陶淵明, 209n58, 327, 335
teleology, 285
ti 體 (embodiment), 128, 139, 170, 182, 198
tidao 體道 (embody the Way), 183, 196, 211n88
tian 天 (heaven), 72, 101, 103, 124, 125, 126, 128–29, 132, 134, 136, 137, 138, 145n24, 146n41, 162, 168, 171, 177n41, 196, 243n48, 331, 341, 343
  all under heaven (*tianxia* 天下), 185, 186, 196, 199, 212n96
  and earth, 121, 156, 186, 189, 198, 226, 334
  mandate of, 126, 127, 187
  son of, 54, 55, 76, 79, 91n6, 95n57, 102, 123, 126, 284
  tiandi 天帝 (Emperor of heaven), 305, 307, 308
  Way of heaven (*tiandao* 天道), 285
  will of, 101
time
  absolute, 51, 55
  narrative, 55
  legendary, 52, 53, 55
Todorov, Tzvetan, 3, 18n13
traces, 182, 183–84, 185–88, 189, 190–98, 199–200, 202n12, 202n14, 203n18, 205n38, 206nn39–40, 207n47, 207n53, 209n65, 211nn90–91, 233, 249, 265n13, 276, 298, 317, 341, 344
transience, 222
translation, 25–26, 41–42, 45n14
transmission, 8, 28, 29, 72, 84, 87, 89, 90, 95n71, 236, 249, 255, 263

Venuti, Lawrence, 26, 41–42, 44n3, 47n34

wan wu 萬物 (myriad beings/things), 161, 163, 181, 183, 184, 190, 192, 194, 195, 196, 198, 199, 200

wang 忘 (oblivion, forgetting), 71, 72, 73, 74, 75, 76, 77, 78, 79, 80, 81, 88, 91n6, 92n14, 100, 101, 102, 103, 106, 114n30, 128, 133, 147n48, 153, 155, 157, 159, 165, 166, 167, 168, 170, 171, 174n7, 217, 218, 219, 220, 222, 223, 224, 227, 240n23, 247, 250, 251, 255, 258, 260, 262, 274, 275, 277, 278, 281, 282, 284, 286, 287, 292n22, 302, 323n10, 328, 333, 334, 338, 340, 343

wang 亡 (destroy, ruin, loss), 58, 60, 75, 127, 133, 147n48, 154, 178n55, 219, 221, 227, 263, 267n35, 302, 303, 323n10

Wang Bi 王弼, 133, 143n8, 148n62, 246–48, 250, 252–57, 258, 259, 260, 261, 262, 263, 264n3, 264n8, 265n10, 265nn12–13, 266n23, 266n26, 267n31

Wang Can 王粲, 322

Wang Chong 王充, 128, 187, 189, 208n53, 212n103

Wei 衛, state of, 37, 60–61, 62, 211n91

weiyan 微言 (subtle words), 27, 91n5

Wen, Emperor (Han) 漢文帝, 73, 88

Wen of Zhou, King 周文王, 125, 144n16, 276

wen 文 (writings, cultural patterns), 28, 84, 85, 162, 183, 189, 218, 263, 265n12, 281

Western Zhou period, 19n23, 20n30, 51, 285, 293n52

Weyeneth, Richard, 309, 325n26

Wheelwright Bian 輪扁, 191, 192, 210n67

White, Hayden, 63, 69n35

Wu, Emperor (Han) 漢武帝, 79, 94n45, 181

Wu of Zhou, King 周武王, 51, 59, 86, 87, 185

wu 無 (nonbeing), 182, 198, 199

wuji 無跡 (traceless), 182, 183, 194, 195, 212n104

wuwei 無為 (nonaction; not doing; effortless), 133, 135, 136, 137, 170, 172, 196, 197, 198, 212n96, 212n98

Wu Yue chunqiu 吳越春秋, 97, 98, 99, 99–105, 106, 107, 109, 110, 111nn3–4, 113n22

Wu Zixu 伍子胥, 77, 92n20, 100, 101, 102, 103, 104, 113nn20–22

Wu 吳, state of, 61, 77, 105, 106, 108, 224

xiang 相 (physiognomy), 207n47, 207n53, 209n57, 265n12

Xiang Yu 項羽, 81, 87

xiao 孝 (filiality, filial piety), 126, 130, 131, 150n74, 217, 247, 276, 277, 280, 282, 285

Xiaojing 孝經, 123, 293n43

Xici zhuan 繫辭傳, 249, 255, 264n4, 265n9

Xie He 謝赫, 207

xin 心 (heart/mind), 76, 105–106, 125, 154, 158, 160, 161, 162, 163, 165, 168, 171, 172, 174n7, 176n19, 178n55, 191, 227, 229, 230, 231, 251, 277, 286, 331, 335

xin 信 (credibility, trustworthy), 79, 89, 90, 137, 219, 240n15, 279

xing 形 (physical form, shape), 104, 137, 157, 158, 163, 165, 166, 167, 169, 181, 194, 195
  cheng xing 成形 (fixed forms), 158
  wu xing 無形 (shapeless), 182, 194, 197, 210n82
xing 性 (natural dispositions), 157, 158, 171, 189, 198, 230, 231, 243nn48–49, 335
Xinian 系年, 50, 56–57, 59–62, 63–65, 110n1, 294n52
xionghuang 雄黃, 320
xue 學 (study, learning), 219, 228
Xu Gan 徐幹, 207n49
Xu Shen 許慎, 184
  See also Shuowen jiezi
xu 虛 (emptiness), 85, 137, 157, 160, 162, 163, 172, 182, 336
Xuanyuan 軒轅, 52, 53
Xun Kuang 荀況, 190
Xunzi 荀子, 19n24, 19n27, 94n46, 115n35, 115n40, 143n10, 155, 156, 161–64, 165–67, 171, 173, 176n29, 177n41, 190–91, 192, 193, 195, 202n15, 209n60, 209n63, 211n88, 230, 231, 243n47

Yan Hui 顏回, 169, 170, 172, 226, 236
Yang Bojun 楊伯君, 45n16, 216, 238n4
Yang Xiong 揚雄, 123, 240n24, 262, 263, 267n34
Yang Zhen 楊震, 302
Yao 堯, 51, 52, 54–55, 63, 81, 82, 93n38, 95n55
yi 義 (propriety, principle, rightness), 30, 35, 71, 77, 85, 89, 91n5, 125, 130, 131, 189, 197, 209n60, 218, 239n14, 262, 263

yi 意 (intentions), 28, 74–75, 125, 160, 166, 250, 251, 252, 254–55, 256–58, 259, 260, 261, 262, 265n12, 266nn25–26
Yili 儀禮, 318, 326n38
yin 淫 (licentiousness), 281
youxia 遊俠 (unconstrained heroes), 84
Yu 禹, 51, 54, 55, 86, 138, 209n60
yuan 怨 (resentment), 77, 88, 282, 283
Yue 越, state of, 61, 92n20, 97–98, 99, 100, 101, 102, 104, 105, 106, 107, 108, 109, 110, 110n1, 165, 168
Yuejue shu 越絕書, 98, 102, 110n1, 111n3

Zengzi 曾子, 282, 293n43
Zhang Tang 張湯, 79
Zhao of Chu 楚昭王, King, 74
Zhao of Qin 秦昭王, King, 86
Zhao Wenzi 趙文子, 275
Zheng 鄭, state of, 37, 57, 58, 59, 223
zhenmuwen 鎮墓文 (tomb-quelling texts), 299, 323n3
zhenren 真人 (true person, genuine), 168, 181, 201n5
zhi 志 (intention, will, purpose), 77, 106, 125, 133, 155, 157, 159, 162–63, 175n14, 222, 231, 277, 330
zhi 知 (know, understand, awareness), 35, 92n14, 103, 104, 121, 133, 137, 147n45, 155, 157, 158, 162, 163, 165, 168, 169, 170, 171, 172, 187, 189, 218, 219, 220, 223, 227, 228, 244n61, 262, 278, 307, 319, 328, 331, 333, 338, 341

Zhonglun 中論, 207n49
Zhongyong 中庸, 124
Zhou 周, state of, 61
Zhou 周公, Duke of, 60, 75, 147n48
Zhouli 周禮, 290n11, 315
Zhouyi 周易, 246, 247, 248, 249, 253, 254, 255, 259, 263, 264n4, 265n12
Zhuang of Chu 楚莊王, King, 206n46
Zhuang Zhou 莊周, 165, 191
Zhuangzi 莊子, 6, 20n30, 68n16, 71, 88, 94n46, 150n73, 156, 160, 161, 164, 165, 166, 167, 168, 169–73, 177n41, 178n55, 178n62, 179n72, 183, 191, 192, 193, 194, 195, 197, 199, 200, 201n10, 210n82, 211n88, 215, 217, 228, 232, 233, 235, 236, 239n11, 242n38, 250, 251, 252, 253, 255, 256, 258, 265n13, 333, 334, 343, 344
Zhuanxu 顓頊, 81
Zhushu jinian 竹書紀年, 76
Zigong 子貢, 209n60, 226, 235, 236, 244n61
Zilu 子路, 77, 218, 220
Ziqinzhang 子琴張, 343, 344
ziran 自然 (spontaneous, self-so), 198, 230, 335
Zisanghu 子桑戶, 343, 344
Zisi 子思, 279
Zixia 子夏, 219, 293n41
Zizhang 子張, 293n41
Zuo Qiuming 左丘明, 28, 29
zuowang 坐忘 (sitting and forgetting, sitting in oblivion), 169, 236, 260
Zuozhuan 左傳, 28, 29, 38, 64, 65, 101, 110n1, 223, 224

www.ingramcontent.com/pod-product-compliance
Lightning Source LLC
Chambersburg PA
CBHW031703230426
43668CB00006B/90